旅游让世界和生活更美好
BETTER TOURISM, BETTER LIFE, BETTER WORLD

旅游减贫案例故事

（中英文双语版）

BEST PRACTICES OF POVERTY ALLEVIATION THROUGH TOURISM

(CHINESE-ENGLISH BILINGUAL EDITION)

世界旅游联盟 ◎编著

中国·武汉

内 容 简 介

世界旅游联盟自成立以来，一直践行"旅游促进减贫"使命，积极推动旅游减贫和旅游助力乡村振兴。七年来，世界旅游联盟联合中国国际减贫中心、世界银行等单位，根据可持续性、可复制性、可量化、创新性等评比标准，遴选发布了300个旅游减贫和旅游助力乡村振兴优秀案例，形成具有借鉴意义的乡村发展理念，为全球减贫事业贡献中国方案。

2025年是中国巩固拓展脱贫攻坚成果同乡村振兴有效衔接五年过渡期的最后一年，世界旅游联盟与中国国际减贫中心、华中科技大学出版社合作，从往期案例中选取部分典型案例，编撰《旅游减贫案例故事（中英文双语版）》，进一步宣传乡村旅游创新、协调、绿色、开放、共享的发展理念，继续落实联合国2030年可持续发展议程，为实现"旅游让世界和生活更美好"而持续努力。

Content Summary

Since its inception, the World Tourism Alliance (WTA) has been steadfastly committed to its mission of "poverty reduction through tourism", actively leveraging tourism as a catalyst for poverty alleviation and rural revitalization. Over the past seven years, the WTA has collaborated with the International Poverty Alleviation Center in China and the World Bank to identify and published 300 exemplary practices of poverty reduction and rural revitalization through tourism, which were evaluated based on sustainability, replicability, quantifiability and originality, shaping a valuable rural development philosophy and contributing China's proposal to the global fight against poverty.

As 2025 marks the final year of China's five-year transitional period to consolidate and build on the achievements made in poverty alleviation so as to promote rural revitalization, the WTA, in partnership with International Poverty Reduction Center in China and Huazhong University of Science and Technology Press, has compiled the selected cases from the 300 exemplary practices to further advocate the innovative, coordinated, green, open and shared development of rural tourism. Moving forward, the WTA will continue to implement the United Nations 2030 Agenda for Sustainable Development and champion its vision of "Better Tourism, Better Life, Better World".

图书在版编目（CIP）数据

旅游减贫案例故事：汉英对照 / 世界旅游联盟编著. —— 武汉：华中科技大学出版社，2025.3.
ISBN 978-7-5772-1693-5

Ⅰ．F592.3

中国国家版本馆CIP数据核字第202576XD46号

旅游减贫案例故事（中英文双语版） 世界旅游联盟 编著
Lüyou Jianpin Anli Gushi（Zhong-yingwen Shuangyu Ban）

策划编辑：李 欢		
执行编辑：魏雨楠		
责任编辑：鲁梦璇 阮晓琼		责任校对：李 弋
封面设计：普曦乐 廖亚萍		责任监印：周治超

出版发行：华中科技大学出版社（中国·武汉）　　电话：（027）81321913
地　　址：武汉市东湖新技术开发区华工科技园　　邮编：430223
录　　排：华中科技大学惠友文印中心
印　　刷：湖北新华印务有限公司
开　　本：787 mm×1092 mm　1/16
印　　张：21.5
字　　数：604千字
版　　次：2025年3月第1版第1次印刷
定　　价：168.00元

投稿邮箱：283018479@qq.com
本书若有印装质量问题，请向出版社营销中心调换
全国免费服务热线：400-6679-118　　竭诚为您服务
版权所有　侵权必究

目录 /Contents

北京市怀柔区渤海镇四渡河村：乡村"文化·文旅·文人"发展道路 001
Siduhe Village, Bohai Town, Huairou District, Beijing City:
　The Rural Development Path of "Culture, Tourism and People" 004

河北省张家口市张北县小二台镇德胜村：德胜模式实现从脱贫到振兴的跨越 008
Desheng Village, Xiaoertai Town, Zhangbei County, Zhangjiakou City, Hebei Province:
　Desheng Model Drives the Leap from Poverty Alleviation to Revitalization 012

山西省临汾市乡宁县关王庙乡云丘山村：云丘山景区农旅融合带村脱贫模式 017
Mount Yun Village, Guanwangmiao Township, Xiangning County, Linfen City, Shanxi Province:
　Integration of Agriculture and Tourism in Mount Yun Scenic Area Drives Rural Poverty Alleviation 020

内蒙古自治区兴安盟阿尔山市林俗村：大兴安岭特色乡村旅游目的地 024
Linsu Village, Arxan City, Xing'an League, Inner Mongolia Autonomous Region:
　A Characteristic Rural Tourism Destination in the Greater Khingan Mountains 027

辽宁省盘锦市大洼区：农旅融合助力乡村振兴 031
Dawa District, Panjin City, Liaoning Province:
　Agriculture-Tourism Integration to Boost Rural Revitalization 035

吉林省白山市靖宇县花园村：松花江畔景区化村庄振兴样板 040
Huayuan Village, Jingyu County, Baishan City, Jilin Province:
　A Rural Revitalization Model on the Banks of the Songhua River 043

黑龙江省伊春市铁力市：特色民宿驱动农旅融合 048
Tieli City, Yichun City, Heilongjiang Province:
　B&B Service with Local Characteristics Driving Agriculture-Tourism Integration 051

上海市金山区朱泾镇待泾村：芳香经济助力乡村振兴 055
Daijing Village, Zhujing Town, Jinshan District, Shanghai City:
　The Flower Economy Promoting Rural Revitalization 058

江苏省南京市江宁区黄龙岘茶文化村：茶旅融合蝶变美丽乡村 062
Huanglongxian Tea Village, Jiangning District, Nanjing City, Jiangsu Province:
　Shaping A Beautiful Countryside through Tea-Tourism Integration 065

江苏省苏州市吴江区谢家路村：农文旅深度融合助力蚕丝之乡化茧成蝶 070
Xiejialu Village, Wujiang District, Suzhou City, Jiangsu Province:
　In-depth Integration of Agriculture, Culture and Tourism Rejuvenating the Home of Mulberry Silk 073

浙江省丽水市景宁畲族自治县大均乡：文旅融合绽放"五朵畲花" 078
Dajun Township, Jingning She Autonomous County, Lishui City, Zhejiang Province:
　Integration of Culture and Tourism for Development of Five Villages with the She Nationality Characteristics 082

旅游减贫案例故事（中英文双语版）
Best Practices of Poverty Alleviation through Tourism (Chinese-English Bilingual Edition)

浙江省杭州市淳安县下姜村：打好脱贫攻坚战，旅游减贫成效明显 **088**
Xiajiang Village, Chun'an County, Hangzhou City, Zhejiang Province:
 Winning the Battle Against Poverty , and Achieving Remarkable Progress in Poverty Alleviation through Tourism 092

安徽省黄山市歙县卖花渔村："盆景+"产业融合新模式赋能乡村振兴 **097**
Maihuayu Village, Shexian County, Huangshan City, Anhui Province:
 "Potted Landscape +," A New Model of Industry Integration to Empower Rural Revitalization 101

福建省龙岩市上杭县古田红色旅游区：红色旅游高质量可持续发展 **106**
Gutian Red Tourist Area, Shanghang County, Longyan City, Fujian Province:
 High-Quality Sustainable Development of Red Tourism 110

江西省婺源县篁岭村：共享经济领航与复兴"篁岭晒秋" **116**
Huangling Village, Wuyuan County, Jiangxi Province:
 Revitalizing the Scenery of "Autumn Harvest" through Sharing Economy 120

山东省日照市岚山区官草汪村：渔文旅融合助力乡村振兴 **125**
Guancaowang Village, Lanshan District, Rizhao City, Shandong Province:
 Promoting Rural Revitalization through Fishery-Tourism Integration 128

山东省济宁市泗水县龙湾湖乡村振兴示范区：新型合伙人机制激活乡村文旅新业态 **133**
Longwan Lake Demonstration Zone for Rural Revitalization, Sishui County, Jining City, Shandong Province:
 The New Partnership Mechanism Activates the New Type of Business in Rural Cultural Tourism 137

河南省洛阳市洛宁县罗岭乡：爱和小镇助力乡村振兴 **142**
Luoling Township, Luoning County, Luoyang City, Henan Province:
 The Aihe Town for Rural Revitalization 145

湖北省恩施土家族苗族自治州宣恩县：紧扣"融合"，全域旅游发展助力脱贫致富 **150**
Xuan'en County, Enshi Tujia and Miao Autonomous Prefecture, Hubei Province:
 Alleviating Poverty through Integration and All-For-One Tourism Development 153

湖南省张家界市武陵源区："世界自然遗产旅游+"的脱贫之路 **158**
Wulingyuan District, Zhangjiajie City, Hunan Province:
 Road to Poverty Alleviation through "World Natural Heritage Tourism + " Model 162

广东省肇庆市封开县：贺江碧道画廊景区建设粤桂省际廊道美丽乡村示范带 **167**
Fengkai County, Zhaoqing City, Guangdong Province:Developing the Hejiang River Green Corridor into the Beautiful
 Countryside Demonstrantion Belt of the Guangdong-Guangxi Inter-Provincial Corridor Demonstration 170

广西壮族自治区河池巴马瑶族自治县：充分发挥生态优势，打造特色旅游扶贫 **175**
Bama Yao Autonomous County, Hechi City, Guangxi Zhuang Autonomous Region:
 Give Full Play to Ecological Dominance and Create Featured Tours for Poverty Alleviation 179

海南省琼中黎族苗族自治县红毛镇什寒村：构建多方共建、融合发展的什寒模式 **184**
Zahan Village, Hongmao Town, Qiongzhong Li and Miao Autonomous County, Hainan Province:
 Form a Zahan Model with Co-Construction and Integrated Development 188

重庆市武隆区仙女山街道荆竹村：一二三产"+旅游"助推乡村蝶变 **194**
Jingzhu Village, Xiannushan Sub-district, Wulong District, Chongqing City:
 The Primary, Secondary and Tertiary Sectors "+ Tourism" Driving the Transformation of the Countryside 197

四川省眉山市丹棱县幸福村：农文旅融合"古村模式"赋能乡村振兴 201
Xingfu Village, Danling County, Meishan City, Sichuan Province:
　　The "Ancient Village Model" Integrating Agriculture, Culture, and Tourism to Empower Rural Revitalization 205

四川省阿坝藏族羌族自治州九寨沟县：全域旅游促进乡村脱贫奔小康 210
Jiuzhaigou County, Aba Tibetan and Qiang Autonomous Prefecture, Sichuan Province:
　　All-Area-Advancing Tourism Drives Rural Poverty Alleviation and Prosperity 214

贵州省黔南布依族苗族自治州荔波县朝阳镇洪江村：艺旅融合探索乡村扶贫新路径 220
Hongjiang Village, Chaoyang Town, Libo County, Qiannan Buyi and Miao Autonomous Prefecture, Guizhou Province:
　　Integration of Art and Tourism Explores a New Model of Rural Poverty Alleviation 223

云南省丽江市玉龙纳西族自治县白沙镇玉湖村：生态立村、旅游富村、文化兴村 228
Yuhu Village, Baisha Town, Yulong Naxi Autonomous County, Lijiang City, Yunnan Province:
　　Village Development through Ecology, Tourism and Culture 231

西藏自治区拉萨市尼木县卡如乡卡如村："核乡寻忆"沟域休闲项目模式 236
Karru Village, Karru Township, Nyêmo County, Lhasa City, Tibet Autonomous Region:
　　"Memory in Walnut Town" Leisure Valley Project Model 239

陕西省延安市黄龙县白马滩镇：研学旅游激活乡村经济 244
Baimatan Town, Huanglong County, Yan'an City, Shaanxi Province:
　　Stimulating the Rural Economy with Study Tours 247

甘肃省临夏回族自治州临夏市妥家村：全域全季旅游助力乡村振兴 252
Tuojia Village, Linxia City, Linxia Hui Autonomous Prefecture, Gansu Province:
　　Promoting Rural Revitalization through the Development of All-Area-Advancing and All-Season Tourism 255

宁夏贺兰山东麓葡萄酒产业园区管理委员会：葡萄酒文旅融合模式 259
Ningxia Helan Mountain East Foothill Wine Industry Park Management Committee:
　　"Integration of Wine and Cultural Tourism" Model 262

新疆维吾尔自治区喀什地区塔什库尔干塔吉克自治县瓦尔希迭村：塔吉克高原山村化茧成蝶 266
Warxidi Village, Taxkorgan Tajik Autonomous County, Kashgar Prefecture, Xinjiang Uygur Autonomous Region:
　　The cocoon-to-butterfly transformation of a Tajik village on the Pamir Plateau 269

中国旅游集团：对口帮扶香格里拉，打造标杆项目 273
China Tourism Group: Provide Counterpart Support to Shangri-La and Build a Benchmarking Project 277

中山大学：旅游脱贫的"阿者科计划" 282
Sun Yat-sen University: Tourism-based Poverty Alleviation Project "Azheke Plan" 286

携程集团：携程度假农庄助力乡村振兴 292
Trip.com Group: Country Retreats Launched to Boost Rural Revitalization 296

途牛旅游网：天津桐画精品民宿助力乡村振兴 301
Tuniu.com: Tianjin Tonghua Boutique Homestay Contributes to Rural Revitalization 305

飞猪：数字攻略文旅服务平台助力乡村振兴 310
Fliggy: Digital Strategy Cultural Tourism Service Platform Boosts Rural Revitalization 313

抖音集团："山里DOU是好风光"，以数字能力助力乡村文旅高质量发展 317
Douyin Group: "Visit Great Scenery in Mountains on Douyin" Project: Leveraging Digital Capabilities for High-Quality Development in Rural Culture and Tourism 321

穷游网：甘肃省甘南藏族自治州夏河县非遗节日"香浪节"助力乡村振兴 327
Qyer.com: Boosting rural revitalization by hosting the Xianglang Festival in Xiahe County, Gannan Tibetan Autonomous Prefecture, Gansu province 330

北京市怀柔区渤海镇四渡河村：
乡村"文化·文旅·文人"发展道路

收录于《2023世界旅游联盟：旅游助力乡村振兴案例》

摘要

　　北京市怀柔区渤海镇四渡河村地处北京北部山区，村集体经济薄弱，面临人口结构、产业要素、市场营收等发展难题。四渡河村以党建引领为抓手，以青年力量为基石，通过打造文化空间、盘活文旅产业和引领青年参与，形成四渡河"文化·文旅·文人"的特色发展路径，打造乡村振兴的北京样板。

挑战与问题

北京市怀柔区渤海镇四渡河村，地处燕山山脉，村辖2个自然村164户305人，主产为板栗和民宿旅游，板栗年产量20万—25万公斤，特色民宿32家。2016年四渡河村被认定为低收入村，经济发展面临产业结构单一、无产业带头人、农产品认可度低、销路渠道有限等挑战，同时还面临着人口老龄化严重和青年人才匮乏等困境。

措施

1. 打造全民参与的文化空间

一是打造童心港湾基地，涉及色彩绘画、户外写生、机器人编程、手工制作、工作坊、植物认知、非遗传统文化等内容，共计开展课程59次，参与人数达600多人次。二是打造青年施展空间，设置青年社会实践场地，积极联动清华、北大等20余所高校的2000多名青年大学生到村开展社会实践和"红色1+1"支部共建活动，鼓励青年学子到乡村锻炼本领、施展才干。三是打造幸福晚年驿站，为村里老人提供午晚餐饮食补助、节日慰问与福利，还邀请北京中医药大学的30多名青年医师来到幸福晚年驿站为村民开展中医义诊和健康讲座活动。

2. 盘活文旅融合在地产业

一是构建京郊板栗品牌，四渡河村主动与海底捞集团的餐桌零食部门、抖音集团员工零食供应以及滴滴出行的下午茶零食服务等分销渠道建立合作关系，在扩大板栗影响力的同时，促进村民和村集体增收。二是构建京郊团建品牌，四渡河村推出露营、烧烤、餐饮、登山、徒步、座谈会议与场景教学等团建项目，为客户定制专属团建活动，吸引"城里人"走进乡村看小康。三是构建京郊研学品牌，将板栗文化、民宿体验、组装天文设备以及夜间观星等活动串点成线，使用乡村场景优势创新开发研学项目。

3. 构建青年参与的实践平台

一是开创青年志愿品牌，发起四渡河村全球青年计划，招募青年志愿者、创业团队、规划师以及合作支持方等，为村集体发展提供青年力量。二是开启竞赛比拼擂台，作为2022年、2023年首都"挑战杯"系列竞赛发榜单位，四渡河村以"揭榜挂帅"赛制欢迎在京高校学生投榜、竞榜、揭榜。三是开设人才实践舞台，如联合北京京北职业技术学院制作200余条短视频，打造村级宣传矩阵；联合北京林业大学园林学院策划、设计、制作四渡河村民宿文化导航图等。

血式的内生动力畅通城乡要素流动。

3. 用好青年创新才智

四渡河村积极靠拢青年、汇聚青年才智，主动走向高校，开办学科竞赛、志愿服务、社会实践等青年想参与、能融入、有收获的活动，鼓励高校青年深入乡村、调研乡村、治理乡村、回馈乡村，与青年才俊一起让创意才思在乡村落地生根。

成效

四渡河村黏合多方利益需求，多维度打造四渡河村消费场景，开创出团建、研学、培训、实践、民宿管理以及板栗助农等合作项目，带动整村创收持续增长，破解村集体增收难题。目前累计接待政府、高校、企业等组织的团建项目20余项，营业收入5万余元；举办8期亲子游活动，吸引了130余组家庭参与，创收10余万元；吸引50余名志愿者参与童心港湾、团建品牌、研学品牌等文旅宣传志愿活动，共帮扶村内创收4万余元。四渡河村入选国家乡村振兴局发起的"乡村振兴在行动"2022年度创新典型，制作的文旅短视频《古往今来四渡河》获得第十三届北京国际电影节三等奖，四渡河村的旅游吸引力持续增强。

经验与启示

1. 用好乡村场景优势

四渡河村因地制宜，靠山吃山、靠水吃水，将"步步高升"石阶、宠物盲盒、景观盲盒、瞭望观星点等乡村"小资源"与童心港湾、幸福晚年驿站、青创空间、特色民宿等村域空间设施一起融入乡村场景中，打造出别具一格的京郊品牌。

2. 用好外部社会资源

四渡河村主动链接政、企、社、民等外部资源，与多方建立合作共赢的长效机制，助推四渡河集研学、团建、民宿、农特为一体的文旅融合品牌发展，以造

下一步计划

四渡河村将持续吸引青年力量，助力四渡河"文化·文旅·文人"的发展路径，用文旅融合路径打造乡村振兴中国式现代化样板。一是联动滴滴出行团委、美团民宿、海底捞集团党群中心等新型经济组织和新型社会组织的力量，发挥各自优势向四渡河村注入高质量发展动力。二是使用好已经搭建的乡村振兴青年社、中外青年融合基地、筑梦空间等20余个平台资源，通过各类乡村实践项目全面助力乡村振兴。三是继续用好"青振京郊"专项赛等比赛机制，吸引青年人到村创新创业，立足四渡河村发展实际，助力村镇振兴。

旅游减贫案例故事（中英文双语版）
Best Practices of Poverty Alleviation through Tourism (Chinese-English Bilingual Edition)

Siduhe Village, Bohai Town, Huairou District, Beijing City:

The Rural Development Path of "Culture, Tourism and People"

Included in *WTA Best Practices of Rural Revitalization through Tourism 2023*

Abstract

Siduhe Village is located in the mountainous area of northern Beijing. Its collective economy is weak and faces development challenges such as population structure, industrial factors, and market revenue. While advancing the Party building work, Siduhe Village relies on the strength of the youth, and has created cultural spaces, revitalized the culture and tourism industries, and guided the participation of the youth. It has formed a characteristic development path featuring "culture, tourism and people", and a model for rural revitalization in Beijing.

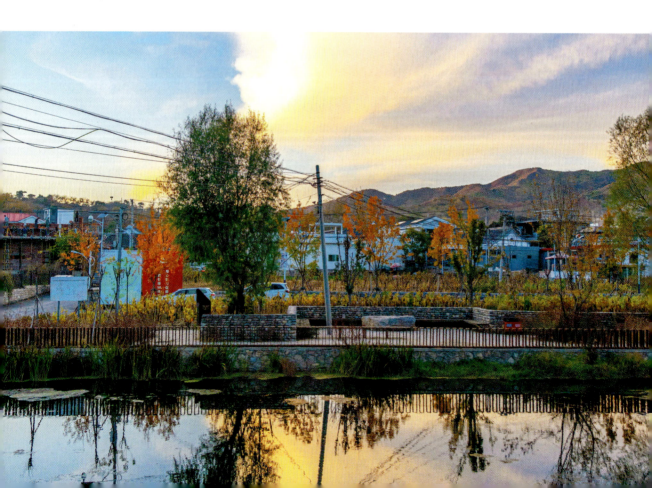

Challenges and Problems

Siduhe Village, Bohai Town, Huairou District, Beijing City, is located in the Yanshan Mountains, with jurisdiction over two natural villages with 164 households of 305 people. Its main sources of income are chestnuts and homestay tourism. It produces 200,000-250,000 kilograms of chestnuts a year, and has 32 characteristic homestays. In 2016, Siduhe Village was identified as a low-income village. Its economy faces difficulties such as the lack of diversity and leaders, low recognition for its agricultural products, and limited sales channels. At the same time, it also faces severe population aging and a shortage of young talents.

Measures

1. Create cultural spaces for all to participate

Firstly, the Children's Harbor is built and has offered 50 sessions on such content as color painting, outdoor sketching, robot programming, handicrafts, workshops, plants, and intangible cultural heritage, attracting more than 600 participants. Secondly, spaces are created for young people to exert themselves. Specifically, the youth social practice site was set up, and Siduhe Village actively contacted more than 20 colleges and universities such as Tsinghua University and Peking University, which organized more than 2,000 college students to carry out social practice and "1+1" Party branch joint building activities in the village, encouraging young students to hone their skills and contribute to the countryside. Thirdly, a senior care station is established to provide lunch and dinner subsidies, holiday visits and benefits for the elderly in the village. Siduhe Village also invited more than 30 young doctors from the Beijing University of Chinese Medicine to the station to provide free diagnosis services and give health lectures to the villagers.

2. Revitalize the culture and tourism industries and integrate them with other local industries

Firstly, building the brand of chestnuts produced in the suburbs of Beijing. Siduhe Village supplies chestnuts to Haidilao Group as complementary snacks for customers, to Douyin Group as complimentary snacks for employees, and to Didi Chuxing as afternoon snacks, to expand its sales channels and the influence of chestnuts, and increase the income of villagers and village collectives. Secondly, building the brand as a team-building destination in the suburbs of Beijing. Siduhe Village has launched team-building projects such as camping, barbecue, catering, mountaineering, hiking, symposiums and scenario-based teaching, and customized team-building activities for customers to attract urbanites to the countryside. Thirdly, building the brand of study tour destination in the suburbs of Beijing. It has strung together activities such as chestnut picking, homestay experience, assembling astronomical equipment and stargazing at night, and developed innovative study tour projects by leveraging its advantages in rural scenes.

3. Build a practice platform for the youth

Firstly, building a youth volunteer brand. Siduhe Village has launched the Global Youth Program to recruit young volunteers, startup teams, planners and partners to empower the development of the village collective. Secondly, organizing competitions. It solicited proposals from the 2022 and 2023 "Challenge Cup" series of competitions, and welcomed college students in Beijing to share their ideas. Thirdly, setting up a social practice stage. For example, it co-produced with Beijing Jingbei Vocational College more than 200 short videos to form a village-level publicity matrix, and worked with the School of Landscape Architecture of Beijing Forestry University to plan, design and produce the map of Siduhe Village's homestay culture.

Results

Siduhe Village converges multiple interest groups, and has created consumption scenarios in multiple dimensions, and launched cooperative projects such as team-building, study tours, training, practice, homestay management, and chestnut consumption to drive the continuous growth of village income and solve the problem of income increase facing the village collective. So far, it has received more than 20 batches of participants from the government, colleges and universities, and enterprises for team-building activities, with a revenue of more than 50,000 yuan. It has organized eight parent-child tours, involving more than 130 groups of participants, generating more than 100,000 yuan. It has attracted more than 50 volunteers to participate in the publicity activities for the Children's Harbor, the team-building brand, and the study tour brand, generating more than 40,000 yuan. Siduhe Village was acknowledged as the 2022 Innovation Model of "Rural Revitalization in Action" initiated by the National Rural Revitalization Administration, and the short video *Sidu River from Ancient to Present* it produced won the third prize of the 13th Beijing International Film Festival. Siduhe Village's appeal to tourists has been enhanced.

Experience and Inspirations

1. Make good use of rural scenes

Siduhe Village adapts measures to local conditions, makes good use of mountains and waters, and incorporates the "Step by Step" stone steps, blind boxes of pets and landscapes, and stargazing points, as well as facilities such as the Children's Harbor, the senior care station, the Youth Innovation Space, and characteristic homestays into rural scenes, to build a

unique suburban destination brand.

2. Make good use of external resources

Siduhe Village took the initiative to establish contacts with governments, enterprises, social organizations, and individuals, and has established a long-term win-win cooperation mechanism with multiple parties to help build up Siduhe's brand as a destination for study tourism, team-building, with homestays and characteristic agricultural products, and to unblock the flow of urban and rural factors with the endogenous growth drive.

3. Make good use of innovative young people

Siduhe Village actively approaches young people and gathers young talents. It took the initiative to work with colleges and universities, and organized subject-specific competitions, volunteer services, social practices and other rewarding activities that young people want to participate in and can fit into. It encourages college students to go deep into the countryside, conduct field surveys, participate in rural governance, and give back to the countryside. It works with young people to turn their creative ideas into reality in the countryside.

Next Steps

Siduhe Village will continue to attract young people, develop the path of "culture, tourism and people," and promote culture-tourism integration to create a model of rural revitalization and Chinese modernization. Firstly, it will work with the organizational forces of new-type economic organizations and new-type social organizations including the Communist Youth League Committee of Didi Chuxing, Meituan Homestay, and the Party and Mass Relations Center of Haidilao Group, and give full play to their respective advantages to inject high-quality development impetus into the village. Secondly, it will make good use of existing 20-plus platforms such as the Rural Revitalization Youth Club, the Sino-Foreign Youth Cooperation Base, and the Dream Building Space, and comprehensively facilitate rural revitalization in all respects through various rural practice projects. Thirdly, it will continue to organize competitions, including the "Youth for the Revitalization of Suburb Beijing" competition, to attract young people to seek innovations and start their own businesses in the village, and contribute to rural revitalization based on the reality of the village.

旅游减贫案例故事（中英文双语版）
Best Practices of Poverty Alleviation through Tourism (Chinese-English Bilingual Edition)

河北省张家口市张北县小二台镇德胜村：
德胜模式实现从脱贫到振兴的跨越

收录于《2020 世界旅游联盟：旅游减贫案例》

摘要

　　河北省张北县德胜村构建了以乡村旅游为主线的融合性产业，开发农业的多功能性，建设了农业观光采摘园、平安福农业科技园、光伏经济示范园、民宿餐饮一体化体验园、绿色乡居建筑博览园等乡村旅游设施。通过企业主导、带动农民、村企共创、延长产业链、提升价值链，用资本整合资源，以市场引领发展，产业要素深度融合，构建了参与性的增收保障体系，形成了可持续发展的机制。德胜村为可持续发展提供持久动力，农民生活质量不断提升，其获得感、幸福感、安全感不断增强。凭借脱贫攻坚与乡村振兴的有效衔接，全村实现了从脱贫到小康的历史性跨越。

挑战与问题

河北省张北县德胜村属于典型的农耕村，下辖6个自然村，总面积20205亩，其中耕地面积5085亩。全村549户1176人，其中建档立卡贫困户145户290人，贫困发生率1.5%，是张北县典型的贫困村。该村长期处于自然发展状态，建设无规划、农民无产业、产品无品牌、致富无门路、发展无人才、集体无经济。农民收入长期在低位徘徊，人居环境较差，村庄破败、道路泥泞，村庄空心化严重。多数农民外出打工谋生，留守人员多为老弱病残，缺少可持续发展的产业、机制和动力，发展缺活力、脱贫少支撑、振兴没路径。

措施

1. 坚持规划先行

将建设乡村旅游与精准扶贫相结合，以打造张北全域旅游的"体验窗口名片"为愿景目标，构建"一环串联、两轴引领、五区联动"的规划格局。其中，五大功能分区包括德胜乡社文化服务区、星光迷境有机康养区、林田艺园景观体验区、润马公社生活体验区以及润马牧场互动旅游区。打造三大特色游憩线路和四大客群旅游路线，构建慢行游憩道路闭环。德胜文化广场、德胜印象展馆、德胜农业示范园及"德胜源"餐厅等基础建设项目均已完成，德胜乡村旅游体系初步形成。

2. 坚持产业带动

按照"培育主体，开发主业，形成主导"的思路，进行整体规划；产业增强引领性，实现增值增收；发展落脚持续性，提供长久动力。发展现代生态农业示范园区，开发农业的多种功能，使产业链由单纯的农田种植的生产端向综合产业的体验端转变，效益由产品销售的经济效益向经济、社会、生态、资源效益的全面性转变，产业定位由过去的一产向一、二、三产融合发展转变，对农民形成综合带动。马铃薯产业增加经营性收入，光伏产业增加流转性收入，民宿产业增加财产性收入，企业就业增加劳务性收入。目前德胜以旅游为核心的综合产业已覆盖全体村民，为村民提供各类就业岗位300多个，已有30多位农村青年成为企业员工。

3. 坚持品牌先导

德胜村已建成民宿180套，形成兼具多种风格的京西北民宿群，即"德胜宿集"；已组建村民文艺队2支，设计了公司logo，实施了《德胜尊老助学办法》，制定了《德胜村民守则》，李勇艺术小院落成，策划了《德胜村—揽胜楼联合运营方案》，筹建德胜艺术社；成立德胜平安福生态农业科技发展有限公司，并在中医农业、生态农业微生物种养殖方面取得成效。德胜马铃薯在第十九届中国绿色食品博览会上获得金奖，德胜村获评全国"一村一品示范村"、全国"绿色无公害示范基地"。德胜平安福生态农业科技发展有限公司获评"河北省科技型中小企业""张家口市市级农业科技园区"。

4. 坚持平台集聚

河北农业大学乡村振兴研究院在德胜村落户，同时，国家住房和城乡建设部、中国八所知名院校以及中国建筑材料工业协会等机构携手合作，在德胜村共同创建了"绿色乡居建筑博览园"。此外，还成立了"中国德胜绿色乡居发展联盟"，并成功举办了绿色乡居文化旅游大会。为了促进当地发展，教育部"农校通"平台被引进，并着手规划德胜食品安全小镇的建设。

同时,"游帮学"团队也被引入,致力于德胜青少年研学基地的规划与发展。

5. 坚持人才引进

在德胜村成立了"乡村振兴研究院",实施文化品牌人才建设。邀请北京崇贤馆世纪文化传媒有限公司董事长、北京崇贤馆创始人李克及张德欣、左宁等知名人士出任德胜(张北)实业集团有限公司的智库专家顾问委员会成员。德胜村已成为各类人才创新创业的热土,高端人才的不断加入,为乡村振兴注入了蓬勃活力。

6. 坚持模式引领

"企业带动,农民参与;平台合作,品牌助力;文化引领,同创共享"的模式,使企业回归农村、资本回归农业、农民回归家乡,共创美好生活,建设幸福德胜。通过土地流转、民宿出租和实施田园综合体建设,资源变资产、资金变股金、农民变股东,农民成为真正意义上的资产权益人,成为德胜模式的践行者和受益者。

成效

德胜村构建了以乡村旅游为主线的融合性产业,开发农业的多功能性,建成农业观光采摘园、平安福农业科技园、光伏经济示范园、民宿餐饮一体化体验园、绿色乡居建筑博览园等乡村旅游设施。2019年接待游客6000余人次,2020年接待游客5万多人次。通过资源聚集、要素融合、合作发展,生态资源和农业多元化功能得到开发利用,为可持续发展提供了持久动力。农民生活质量不断提升,2020年,农民年人均收入达到16400元,比2017年增加了90.7%;集体经济收入逾150万元。脱贫攻坚与乡村振兴的有效衔接,使德胜村实现了从脱贫到小康的历史性跨越。

经验与启示

1. 脱贫攻坚必须形成推动发展的新动能

受自然及人文条件的限制,德胜村很难有内生动力。德胜(张北)实业集团有限公司入驻,首要是促进产业发展,不仅带来投资,更带来市场化的理念方法和运行机制,用企业化的方式管理农业,用现代化的理念引导农民,用工程化的思路实施项目,用科学化的方法参与管理。如此一来,既能提升效率又可对接市场,既能增加收入又可规避风险,找到了城乡融合发展实现乡村振兴的路径之一。

2. 脱贫攻坚必须有价值理念和情怀

德胜(张北)实业集团有限公司以"企业带领农民共同致富,建设幸福美丽德胜新村"为价值理念,第一取向不是开发赢利,而是担当责任。目前,该企业已投入1.3亿元,全部用于德胜村的公共基础设施和产业先期培育,虽然眼下自身收入不多,却为当地建起了以乡村旅游为核心的新型业态,为农民持续就

业增收打下了基础,也为企业未来发展铺平了道路,真正实现了深度融合、合作共赢、同创共享,甘当一支永不撤离的帮扶"工作队"。

3. 脱贫攻坚必须有可复制的模式

德胜模式的核心在于带动与共享。带动是将利益留给农民,按照市场的方式引领产业,参与治理,规避风险,保障增收;共享是将长远利益与农民共享,在于未来产业和服务收益,在于今后市场和预期,在于模式的有效复制。只有不断地复制并在新的实践中提升完善模式,才会有新的机遇和市场,才能获得品牌信誉,才能持续获得收益。

4. 扶贫攻坚的落脚点必须在于带动农民

只有激发农民积极参与、自我"造血"、持续增收、生活幸福,才能真正体现企业的价值所在,这也符合党的政策和农民的意愿,且更符合发展的价值理念和长远利益。没有农民的主体参与,农村就不可能得到深耕与发展,更不具备生命活力。目前,德胜村以乡村旅游为主线的各产业链条上的就业岗位和产业终端的收入主体,都是德胜村及其周边的村民。

下一步计划

"十四五"期间,德胜村继续按照企业带动、农民主体、市场运作、科技支撑、村企协同的原则,实现"六个新"的发展目标:构建生态种植养殖、农产品加工供应链、民宿康养旅游、绿色装配式建筑和文化产业的"4+1"产业新格局;搭建企业创业、员工创新、农民致富、集聚要素、合作共享的新平台;培育具有市场传播力、诚信守德、绿色生态、健康安全的德胜系列新品牌;提升可复制推广的"企业+农村,平台+品牌,同创+共享"的德胜发展新模式水平;建设乡村振兴研学、农民科技培训、产业发展实践、先进文化传播的多业态教育新基地;构建要素整合、村企共建、创业就业、创新发展的参与性保障新体系。

旅游减贫案例故事（中英文双语版）
Best Practices of Poverty Alleviation through Tourism (Chinese-English Bilingual Edition)

Desheng Village, Xiaoertai Town, Zhangbei County, Zhangjiakou City, Hebei Province:

Desheng Model Drives the Leap from Poverty Alleviation to Revitalization

Included in *WTA Best Practices in Poverty Alleviation through Tourism 2020*

Abstract

Desheng Village, Zhangbei County, Hebei Province, has built an integrated industry with rural tourism as the focal point. They have developed a multi-functional agricultural system and has built tourism facilities around this such as agricultural sightseeing picking parks, Ping'anfu agricultural science and technology parks. They have also built B&Bs, catering integration experience parks and green rural residential architecture expo parks.

Leadership enterprises have driven farmers to co-create the village based on mutual efforts for extended industrial chains, enhanced value chains, integrated resources through capital, and market-leading development. This helps with achieving in-depth integration of industrial elements, building a participatory income increase guarantee system, and developing a sustainable development mechanism. The Desheng Model has provided a lasting impetus for the sustainable development of the village and has improved the living quality of farmers. It has also enhanced their sense of accomplishment, happiness, and safety. They have also effectively linked poverty alleviation and rural revitalization which has led to an impoverished standard of living to a more prosperous one.

Challenges and Problems

Desheng Village, Zhangbei County, Hebei Province, is a typical farming village with six natural villages under its governance. It has a total area of 20,205 *mu*, 5,085 *mu* of which is arable land. There are 1,176 people of 549 households in the village, 290 people and 145 archived impoverished households of which have a poverty incidence of 1.5%. This statistics make it a typical poverty-stricken village in Zhangbei County. For a long time, the village has had no natural development. Nor is there any construction plan. There were no plans for industry for farmers, brand for products, or ways to improve their lives. It also lacks talent for development, economy for collectives, or a way to reduce a dilapidated and hollow village. Most farmers go out to work for a living and leave the elderly, weak, sick, and disabled behind. As a result, there is a lack of industries, mechanisms and motivations for sustainable development, growth vitality, poverty alleviation support and no revitalization path.

Measures

1. Planning-pioneering

The construction of rural tourism has been combined with targeted poverty alleviation to create an "experience window card" of the all-for-one tourism in Zhangbei County. They have also built a planning pattern of "one loop in series, two axes leading, and five areas connected". In other words, five functional areas have been set up. They are: Desheng Community Cultural Service Area, Xingguang Mijing Organic Healthcare Area, Lintian Yiyuan Landscape Experience Area, Runma Commune Life Experience Area, and

Runma Ranch Interactive Tourist Area. Also, three characteristic recreational routes and four tourist routes catering to different visitor segments have been built so that tourist groups can enjoy a closed-loop slow recreational path system. The infrastructure projects such as Desheng Cultural Plaza, Desheng Impression Exhibition Hall, Desheng Agricultural Demonstration Park and "Deshengyuan" Restaurant have all been completed and the Desheng rural tourism system has been initially developed.

2. Industry-driven

The plan has been carried out in accordance with the idea of "fostering the main body, developing the main business and forming the leadership". In addition, the role of industries in leading has been enhanced for both value and income increase. The sustainable developmental goal has been promoted to provide long-term momentums. The village has developed modern eco-agricultural demonstration parks and explored multiple functions of agriculture to realize the transformation of the industrial chain from the production of single farmland planting to the comprehensive industries. This is an all-round transformation of benefits from the economic benefits of product sales to the economic, social, ecological, and resource benefits. The high-end transformation of the industrial positioning from the primary industry to the integrated development of the primary, secondary and tertiary industries motivates the farmers to advance village development. The village has also developed the potato industry for more operating income, the photovoltaic industry for more circulating income and the B&B industry for more property income. Also, it has promoted corporate employment for more labor income. Presently, the comprehensive industries with tourism as its core cover all villagers, which generate more than 300 job opportunities and help more than 30 rural youth find jobs at enterprises.

3. Brand-leading

Desheng Village has built 180 sets of B&Bs and developed a group of B&Bs with multiple styles of Northwest Beijing called the "Desheng B&B Clusters". The village has formed two art teams of villagers for their cultural heritage. They designed company logos and implemented *Methods to Respect the Elderly and Assist Students in Education in Desheng Village*. They formulated *Desheng Villagers' Code* and completed Li Yong Art Academy. Also, the *Joint Operation Plan between Desheng Village and Lansheng Building* has been organized to prepare for the establishment of Desheng Art Club. The agricultural brand is Desheng Ping'anfu Ecological Agriculture and Technology Development Co., Ltd. and it has been established.

They made remarkable achievements in microbial breeding of traditional Chinese medicine agriculture and ecological agriculture. Desheng Potato has won the gold medal at the 19th China Green Food Expo which make the village a national "One Product for One Village Demonstration Village" and a national "Green Pollution-Free Demonstration Base." Desheng Ping'anfu Agriculture Company was approved as "Hebei Province Science and Technology Based Small and Medium-sized Enterprise" and "Zhangjiakou Municipal Agricultural Science and Technology Park".

4. Platform-integrating

The Rural Revitalization Research Institute of Hebei Agricultural University has landed in Desheng County. Many platforms, including the Ministry of Housing and Urban-Rural Development, Eight Universities in China, have jointly created the "Green Rural Residence Architecture Expo Park". The "China Desheng Green Rural Residence Development Alliance" was established to hold the Green Rural Residence Cultural Tourism Conference. Also, the "Agri-School Connect" platform of the Ministry of Education has been introduced for the planning and construction of Desheng Food Safety Town and the "You Bang Xue" (means that tourism drives study) team has been also introduced for the planning and construction of Desheng Youth Research Study Base.

5. Talent-introducing

The Rural Revitalization Research Institute has been established in the village to implement the recruitment and cultivation of talents for cultural brands. Li Ke, Chairman of Beijing Chongxianguan Century Culture Media Co., Ltd. and founder of Beijing Chongxianguan, Zhang Dexin, Zuo Ning and other celebrities have been introduced as members of the Think Tank Expert Advisory Committee of

Desheng(Zhangbei) Industrial Group Co.,Ltd. As a result, the village has attracted all kinds of talents for innovation, entrepreneurship, resulting in an energized and revitalized rural revitalization program.

6. Model-guiding

Through the model of "enterprise driving, farmers' participation, platform cooperation, brand assistance, cultural guidance, co-creation and sharing", and enterprises that develop well in rural areas, the farmers have a higher standard living. The land transfer, B&B leasing, and rural pastoral complex construction have transformed resources into assets. They have also converted capital into equity and turned farmers into shareholders. This means that farmers have become real asset owners and also practitioners and beneficiaries of the Desheng Model.

importantly, the quality of life of farmers has been improved. In 2020, the per capita income of farmers reached RMB 16,400, an increase of 90.7% over 2017. The collective economic income reached more than RMB 1.5 million. The complementary linkage between poverty alleviation and rural revitalization has achieved a historic leap from poverty alleviation to a higher standard of living.

Results

The village has built an integrated industry with rural tourism as the main driver. It has also developed multi-function agricultural products and has built tourism facilities such as an agricultural sightseeing park. The Ping'anfu agricultural science and technology parks, photovoltaic economic demonstration parks, B&B and catering integration experience parks and green rural residence architecture expo parks have all been constructed. The village welcome more than 6,000 tourists in 2019, and more than 50,000 tourists in 2020. Through resource aggregation, element integration and cooperative development the village is on a path of sustainability. Other ecological resources and agricultural diversified functions have been developed and utilized, thus providing a lasting impetus for sustainable development. More

Experience and Inspirations

1. New driving force for poverty alleviation

Natural and cultural limitations restrict the endogenous potential of the village. The introduction of Desheng(Zhangbei) Industrial Group Co.,Ltd. can promote industrial development, attract investments and create viable marketing structures. They can also lead to operating mechanisms that include modern agricultural management systems guided by advanced scientific concepts and engineering ideas to improve market efficiency. This will increase income and limit risk exposure. The integrated development of urban and rural areas is another rural revitalization model.

2. Values and feelings for poverty alleviation

The Desheng(Zhangbei) Industrial Group Co.,Ltd. has prioritized responsibility instead of profit.

It has done so by applying the concept that "enterprises should lead farmers to become prosperous and build a happy and beautiful new Desheng Village". The enterprise has invested 130 million yuan in public infrastructure and industrial pre-cultivation. Despite its current low profits, it has built a new business model with rural tourism as the core for local areas. It has laid a foundation for continuous employment and income increase for farmers. Also, it has paved the way for the future development of the enterprise. The enterprise is voluntary to provide continuous support for village development to achieve in-depth integration, win-win cooperation, co-creation and sharing.

3. Replicable models for poverty alleviation

The core of the Desheng Model places the role of driving and sharing at the center. Driving means that benefits belong to farmers and that market-based management ensures the involvement of farmers in governance. This is expected to limit risk exposure and achieve income growth. Sharing signifies that long-term benefits are shared with farmers, in whom lies the future of the industry. Constant iteration also spur improvements and replicability.

4. Driving farmers as a poverty alleviation goal

The motivation, active participation and farmers' self-improvement reflect the value of enterprises, which are in line with the Party's policy and farmers' wishes and long-term interests of development. In-depth exploration and agricultural development cannot be achieved without the participation of farmers. Today local villagers and those from surrounding villages are the primary source of employment at industrial chains for rural revitalization.

Next Steps

During the "14th Five-Year Plan" period, the Desheng Village will work to achieve new developments based on the following. Firstly, application of the principles of enterprise driving, with farmers as the main body; market operation, technological support and village-enterprise collaboration, that is, building a new "4 + 1" industrial pattern of ecological planting and breeding, agricultural product processing supply chain, B&B healthcare tourism, green prefabricated construction and cultural industry. Secondly, developing a new platform for business entrepreneurship, employee innovation, farmers' enrichment, element aggregation, cooperation and sharing. Thirdly, fostering Desheng's new brands infused with cultural integrity, green ecology, health and safety. Fourthly, enhancing a replicable and promotable new Desheng development model of "enterprise + countryside, platform + brand, co-creation + sharing". Fifthly, establishing new education bases for multi-format businesses for research study on rural revitalization, technology training for farmers and industrial development practice. Sixly, dissemination of advanced culture, creating a new guaranteed participatory system characterized by element integration, village-enterprise co-creation, entrepreneurship and employment and innovative development.

山西省临汾市乡宁县关王庙乡云丘山村：

云丘山景区农旅融合带村脱贫模式

收录于《2021世界旅游联盟：旅游助力乡村振兴案例》

摘要

　　云丘山景区以"企业有利润、村民有利益、村委有效益"的三有定位，成功孕育出了"农旅融合、村企共建"的"云丘模式"，使云丘山村基础设施建设、村容村貌发生了翻天覆地的变化。云丘山景区现已发展成为全国"景区带村"旅游扶贫示范项目，成为山西转型的"排头兵"、世界级旅游目的地。

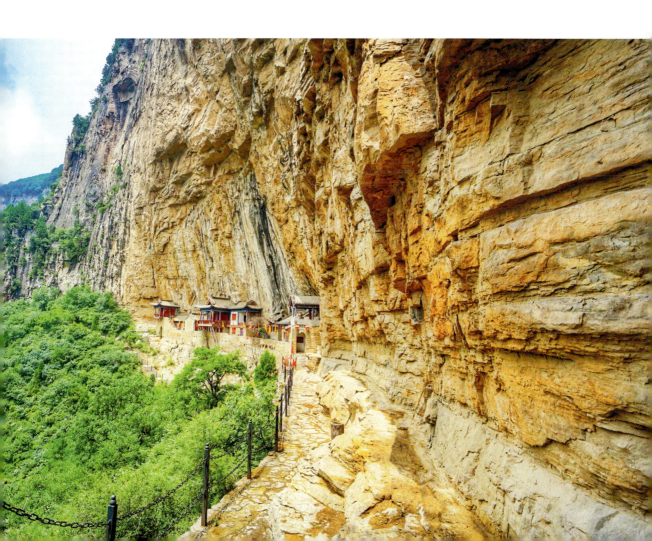

挑战与问题

山西省临汾市乡宁县云丘山村是典型的旅游乡村，因地处云丘山旅游景区而得名。云丘山景区所在的乡镇农村地域封闭，农民思想较为保守，农业生产落后。旅游产业发展与美丽乡村发展"两张皮"，无法实现深入融合，两者之间不但起不到相互促进的作用，反而相互削弱，阻碍整体发展。特别是景区规划建设中有需要整村搬迁安置的农民，不仅存在搬迁难问题，而且整体存在搬迁后农业生产难、土地流转农民就业难、增收难的问题。云丘山旅游开发公司是由当地煤炭企业转型而来，面对全新的产业建设，也面临人才短缺等难题。

措施

1. 围绕"规划先行"，充分利用各项政策

自 2005 年起，乡宁县委、县政府出台了一系列政策文件，明确支持云丘山景区的开发工作，乡政府也积极响应，并努力争取中央、省、市政策的支持，为景区的开发提供了坚实的后盾。专业的设计团队和专家队伍受邀参与到景区的规划与建设中，服务、规范、质量、品牌、宾客第一、员工第一等意识由此在云丘山村逐步确立起来，并持续得到强化。

2. 围绕"文旅融合"，不断壮大旅游产业

云丘山景区围绕非物质遗产文化民俗等丰富的文化遗存，引入科技手段来强化保护，并创新展示方式，展现儒、释、道三教合一的独特魅力；围绕 9 座国家级传统村落，紧密结合其民俗背景，致力于恢复这些村落的历史原貌与格局，以此为基础培育古村落文旅新业态；选准主题定位，在康家坪古村打造国内一流的民宿；保护每一处生态，封山禁牧，植树造林，开发世界罕见冰洞奇景——云丘山冰洞群。

3. 围绕"农旅融合"，实现村企共赢

云丘山景区建设移民新村 105687 平方米，整村搬迁 16 个自然村共 561 户居民，人居环境大大改善。引导村民自主创业，开办乡村旅馆、农家乐；积极吸纳村民参与景区建设和运营，增加其收入，安排当地 269 名建档立卡贫困户在云丘山景区就业，月人均收入达 2950 元。景区建设方面，优先吸收当地村民承包工程，帮助他们组建工程队。当地农民还组建了上河优质粮食种植专业合作社，进行土地流转，并返聘村民种植有机粮食和有机菜、药、茶等，保护开发翅果油树等农业产业。对于建档立卡的贫困户，景区为他们提供担保贷款，支持他们进行畜禽养殖。这些举措真正实现了农民收入与农业、旅游产业的有机结合。

成效

历经 20 年潜心打造，云丘山景区先后开发自然景源 42 处、人文景源 77 处，如今已成为国家 5A 级旅游景区。截至 2021 年，景区累计投资 23.95 亿元，年接待游客量超过 120 万人次，实现了 1.6 亿余元的旅游综合收入。云丘山景区全方位带动乡宁县 8 个乡镇、80

多个村庄的发展，助力 2573 户建档立卡贫困户、共计 8793 人脱贫致富，户均增收超过 22000 元。当地农民彻底转变为产业工人，实现了"人人有班上、家家有轿车，老有所养、老有所依"的美好生活。云丘山景区现已发展成为全国"景区带村"旅游扶贫示范项目，景区已成为山西转型的"排头兵"、世界旅游目的地。

经验与启示

1. 科学规划

景区发展规划与乡村发展规划必须相互融合。为实现"打造国内一流目的地景区"的目标，周边乡村的发展实质上与景区的发展息息相关、相辅相成。只有当双方目标一致、规划相互融合、共同努力时，才能形成双向驱动机制，促进彼此的共同发展。

2. 保护生态

在开发过程中，景区内的文化遗产得到了很好的保护和挖掘；杜绝了乱砍滥伐，景区生态面貌焕然一新；人居环境大大改善，云丘山村成了名副其实的美丽乡村。

3. 农旅融合

旅游产业作为朝阳绿色产业，其带动乡村发展、促进农民致富、辐射周边发展的作用极为明显。只有农旅深度融合，彼此才能实现深层次促进和发展。景区发展了，农民收入增加了，生产生活条件改善了，农民得到的实惠越多，景区发展就越会得到更为普遍的支持和拥护，从而形成发展的源泉活力，实现景区

发展和乡村振兴的一举两得。

4. 回馈社会

2017 年，云丘山景区投资 1900 余万元与专家合作建成"元谷希望农场"，为身心障碍者提供职业技能教育培训。截至 2021 年，该农场先后招收 19 名身心障碍者，其中 7 人已具备正常生活和工作的能力，顺利融入社会从业。如今，他们不仅能自食其力，还能赚取收入以支持家庭生活。

下一步计划

围绕建设国内一流景区和乡村振兴的双向发展目标，在景区发展方面，进一步完善云丘山国家 5A 级景区品牌，重点对环境卫生整治、智慧景区建设、研学旅行等方面进行新改善、大提升，实现景区带动促进和辐射作用的全新飞跃。在乡村振兴方面，坚持将农村人居环境整治与旅游产业发展有机结合起来，重点展示民俗文化挖掘和传承、古村古道古井等古文化、民宿文化；加快推进 22 万头现代化生猪养殖基地、8000 亩有机旱作小麦基地的建设，同时依托特有的自然生态资源，全面建成药茶、腌菜、糕点、文创产品、面粉等观光加工生产线和高标准设施蔬菜标准化示范基地，力争早日把云丘村建设成为全国一流的生态文明建设示范村。云丘山景区重点发展乡村旅游、休闲、度假、康养产业，还要把当地有机旱作农业的"云丘山"品牌发展成特色农业品牌，真正实现景区发展与乡村振兴的深度融合。

旅游减贫案例故事（中英文双语版）
Best Practices of Poverty Alleviation through Tourism (Chinese-English Bilingual Edition)

Mount Yun Village, Guanwangmiao Township, Xiangning County, Linfen City, Shanxi Province:

Integration of Agriculture and Tourism in Mount Yun Scenic Area Drives Rural Poverty Alleviation

Included in *WTA Best Practices of Rural Revitalization through Tourism 2021*

Abstract

The Mount Yun Scenic Area has successfully bred the "Yunqiu Model" which features "agriculture and tourism integration, village-enterprise co-construction". It is based on the positioning of "earnings for enterprises, benefits for villagers, and profits for village committees". Also, it helps promote massive changes in infrastructure construction and the appearance of the village. The scenic area has developed into a national poverty alleviation demonstration project through tourism characterized by "scenic area development driving village development" and has become a pioneer in the transformation of Shanxi Province into a global tourist destination.

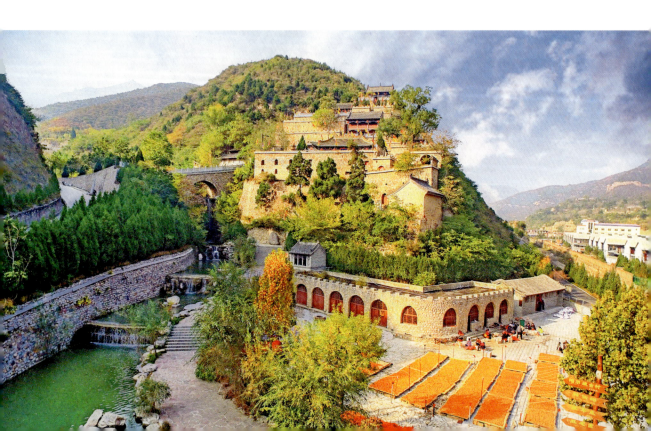

Challenges and Problems

The Mount Yun Village in Xiangning County, Linfen City, Shanxi Province, is a typical tourist village. It takes its name from its location in the Mount Yun Scenic Area. The village and town where the scenic area is located are geographically confined. Farmers here are conservative in their ways and thinking while agricultural production is backward. Thus, it is difficult to achieve full integration of tourism industry development and the development of beautiful village. Farmers who need to be relocated and resettled in another village during the planning and construction of the scenic area cannot support themselves. Their relocation present many challenges. Another difficulty is in agricultural production and employment. Farmers who have transferred their land have seen their income increase. As it transitions from being a local coal company, the Mount Yun Development Company faces talent and labor shortage for the brand-new industrial construction.

Measures

1. Utilize policies with planning at the center

Since 2005, the Xiangning County Party Committee and the county government have cooperated in issuing policy documents to support the development of the Mount Yun Scenic Area. The township government has also actively responded and strived to obtain support from the central, provincial, and municipal agencies for policies that drive the development of the scenic area. Professional design and expert teams were invited to participate in the planning and construction of the scenic area. The awareness of service, standardization, quality, brand, guest first, and employee first was gradually established and continuously strengthened in Mount Yun Village.

2. Develop the tourism industry through cultural and tourism integration

The Mount Yun Scenic Area has captured and displayed the integration of Confucianism, Buddhism and Taoism. They have done this by focusing on rich cultural relics such as intangible cultural folk customs, the introduction of technologies with emphasis on protection, innovative methods and an outstanding image. Moreover, based on the surrounding nine national traditional villages and their folk customs, it has restored the original pattern to cultivate new business systems of cultural tourism in the ancient village. Additionally, the correct theme positioning has been selected to develop a national first-class B&Bs in the Kangjiaping Ancient Village. More importantly, great efforts have been made to protect ecology, close mountains to ban grazing, plant trees and develop the Mount Yun Ice Cave Group.

3. Achieve a win-win situation between villages and enterprises through agriculture and tourism integration

A new resettlement village of 105,687 square

meters has been built in the scenic area. Meanwhile, the relocation of 561 residents from 16 natural villages has improved the settlement. Villagers have been guided to start their own businesses to operate rural hotels and agritainment. They have been encouraged to get involved in the construction and operation of the scenic area to increase their income. As a result, 269 people from archived impoverished households found jobs at the scenic area, with an average monthly income of 2,950 yuan. Contract projects of local villagers have been prioritized in the construction of the scenic area to form an engineering team. Furthermore, local farmers have organized the Shanghe Quality Food Growing Professional Cooperative to transfer villagers' land and recruited them to grow organic food, organic vegetables, herbal teas, etc., thus protecting and developing agricultural industries such as Elaeagnus mollis. Also, guaranteed loans have been provided to archived impoverished households for livestock and poultry breeding to achieve the organic integration of farmers' agricultural income and tourism industries.

Results

After a 20-year effort, 42 natural scenic and 77 humanistic sites have been successively developed which helped transform the scenic area into a national 5A-level scenic spot. Currently, the scenic area has registered an accumulated investment of 2.395 billion yuan. Its annual tourists' reception has exceeded 1.2 million, with a comprehensive tourism income of more than 160 million yuan. It has helped 8,793 people from 2,573 archived impoverished households in more than 80 villages from eight towns in Xiangning County move out of poverty and elevate their standard of living. The average household income has increased by more than 22,000 yuan. Local farmers have also fully shifted and have become industrial workers, ensuring "jobs for each person, cars for each household, care and support for the elderly". As a result, the scenic area has now developed into a national poverty alleviation demonstration project through tourism characterized by "scenic area development driving village development". It has become a pioneer in the transformation of Shanxi Province into a global tourist destination.

Experience and Inspiration

1. Scientific planning

The scenic area planning development must be integrated with rural development planning. With the goal of building a domestic first-class scenic spot, the surrounding villages on the scenic area development are closely intertwined and interdependent. Only through the same goal can integrated planning and joint efforts drive each other for common development.

2. Ecological protection

Concrete measures have been made to protect and optimize the cultural heritage in the scenic area, eliminate deforestation for a renewed ecological environment and improve human settlements for transformation into a beautiful village.

3. Agricultural and tourism integration

Tourism is a rising green industry that radiates peripheral development. Through the years, it has played a prominent role in driving rural development by helping farmers improve their household income. Only through the in-depth integration of agriculture and tourism can the mutual in-depth promotion and development be achieved. With the development of the scenic area, farmers can receive more benefits such as income increase and better conditions for production and living. In turn, they will be in a position to offer more support for the scenic spot development, thereby forming a driving force for rural revitalization.

4. Contribution to society

A total of more than 19 million yuan has been invested into the scenic area for the building of the "Yuangu Hope Farm" in cooperation with professors. The goal is to provide educational services for the physically and mentally handicapped. Over the past three years, 19 people with physical and mental disabilities have been recruited. Currently, seven of them lead normal lives and work to support themselves and their families.

Next Steps

With the dual goals of building a domestic first-class scenic area and achieving rural revitalization, the national 5A-level scenic spot brand of the Mount Yun will be further enhanced. The improvement and upgrade of environmental sanitation is a priority. Also, the focus will be on the establishment of a smart scenic area and research tour that are expected to drive the radiating effects of development. The improvement of rural human settlements and the development of the tourism industry will be organically integrated. Also, the display of folk culture and its legacy, ancient culture and the construction of B&Bs in ancient villages, roads and wells will be highlighted. Construction of modern pig breeding bases of 220,000 heads and organic dry-land wheat bases of 8,000 *mu* will be accelerated. Sightseeing processing production lines such as medicinal tea, pickles, pastries, cultural and creative and artisanal products, flour and high-standard facilities for vegetable standardization bases will be built based on unique natural biological resources. Efforts will be made to get an early start in transforming the Mount Yun Village into a national first-class demonstration village for ecological construction. Overall, the Mount Yun Scenic Area will showcase rural tourism development, leisure, vacation and healthcare industries. It will advance organic dry-land farming as Mount Yun's characteristic agricultural brand. All these will achieve the full integration of scenic area development and rural revitalization.

旅游减贫案例故事（中英文双语版）
Best Practices of Poverty Alleviation through Tourism（Chinese-English Bilingual Edition）

内蒙古自治区兴安盟阿尔山市林俗村：
大兴安岭特色乡村旅游目的地

收录于《2023 世界旅游联盟：旅游助力乡村振兴案例》

摘要

内蒙古自治区兴安盟阿尔山市白狼镇林俗村结合本地区独特的林俗文化、冰雪资源与矿泉资源，以打造全域旅游、四季旅游为引擎，通过"旅游+"模式，将林俗村打造成为独具特色、富有活力的美丽乡村，成为大兴安岭地区最具地域特色的文化体验地、冰雪观赏和运动目的地，以及矿泉养生休闲度假地。

挑战与问题

林俗村地处大兴安岭中段岭脊南侧,西与蒙古国毗邻,边境线长40千米。林俗村距离阿尔山市中心34千米,国铁白阿线和省道S203线从村东面穿过。1952年开始,数以万计来自全国各地、各个民族的建设者来到白狼镇从事林业生产,伐木收入是他们的主要经济来源。在林业限伐和禁伐以后,大部分林业从业人员只能够靠打零工和采山货勉强维持生活,多数处于低收入温饱阶段。2011年,林俗村被列为自治区重点贫困村。

措施

1. 发展民宿产业

2018年,政府通过棚户区改造收回房屋50间用于开发白狼镇林俗村民宿。民宿以打造"一座乡土博物馆,一座时光穿梭机"为设计理念,房屋外貌包括20世纪60年代的茅草房、70年代的毛石勾缝房、80年代的红砖房、90年代的松木和白桦木木刻楞饰面房,以及21世纪新型碳化木饰面房等多种房屋形态。民宿客房内部还原了20世纪60年代至90年代,不同时期林业工人的居住环境,展现完整的林俗文化,使游客能够体验不同年代白狼林区的生产生活特色。

2. 展现林俗文化

一是修建阿尔山林俗博物馆。阿尔山市委、市政府加大林俗文化保护力度,在博物馆原来500多平方米建筑面积的基础上扩建到现在的1200余平方米,馆内陈列展示了早期林业发展的史料、林业工人生产生活工具,以及当地动植物标本等极具历史价值的展品,是一座独具特色的林区全景式博物馆。二是修建民族团结彩绘墙、中华民族文化长廊、大舞台、文创园等设施,不定期举办非遗展示、传统婚礼、文艺演出等宣传展演林俗文化。

3. 创新产业发展模式

林俗村在运作模式上采取公司化运营,成立旅游合作社，居民将个人资源、资产等入股到经营主体参与分红，实现旅游开发公司、村集体与居民的共赢。林俗村利用林下资源发展林下产品加工项目，深度开发山野特产，培育自主品牌；组织滚冰节、林俗文化节等节庆活动，不断延伸和拓展产业链条，带动村民致富增收。

成效

白狼镇林俗村大力发展生态旅游，带动47户贫困户脱贫增收，为林业家属500余人提供就业岗位。目前白狼镇直接和间接从事旅游的人数达800余人，家家户户搞旅游，人人变成旅游从业者，每年人均增收2300元。

经验与启示

1. 多方帮扶

一是政策帮扶，在各类规划、资金和项目中，向贫困村倾斜，使旅游和扶贫同规划、同推进、同显效。二是企业帮扶，将一部分扶贫资金入股当地旅游企业，由贫困户持股分红，同时支持鼓励企业和商铺吸纳贫困户就业，采购贫困户土特产。三是智力帮扶，鼓励村干部、致富带头人、经营户参加各类培训，提高创新创业能力。

2. 全面保护

从保护的意义来说，林俗村改造规划是为了保护优秀的林俗文化遗产，保护传统地区居住建筑群、街巷格局和居住生活形态，保护地方习俗及非物质文化遗产，保留典型的历史发展痕迹和浓郁的历史文化风貌。

下一步计划

下一步白狼镇将继续坚持在政策协调、资金投入、人员培训、产业培育等方面积极支持和推动林俗村发展。林俗村将在旅游品牌打造、旅游项目建设、产业优势互补等方面迈出更坚实的步伐，进而推动阿尔山区域经济全面发展，走出一条欠发达地区利用后发优势助推发展的新道路。

Linsu Village, Arxan City, Xing'an League, Inner Mongolia Autonomous Region:

A Characteristic Rural Tourism Destination in the Greater Khingan Mountains

Included in *WTA Best Practices of Rural Revitalization through Tourism 2023*

Abstract

Linsu Village of Bailang Town, Arxan City, Inner Mongolia Autonomous Region, combines the unique forest custom culture, ice and snow resources and mineral spring resources to develop all-for-one tourism and four-season tourism. On top of this, it adopts the "tourism +" model and tries to build itself into a unique and dynamic beautiful village, and the most distinct destination to experience local culture, appreciate the snow scenery, do sports and relax and enjoy the mineral springs in the Greater Xing'an Mountains area.

Challenges and Problems

Linsu Village is located on the south side of the ridge in the middle section of the Greater Xing'an Mountains, adjacent to Mongolia to the west, with a borderline of 40 kilometers long. Linsu Village is 34 kilometers from the city center of Arxan, and runs through the Baicheng Arxan Railway Line and Provincial Highway S203 in the east. From 1952, tens of thousands of builders of various ethnic groups from all over the country flocked to Bailang Town to engage in forestry and make their living on logging. After the government restricted and banned the practice of logging, most forestry workers had to make a living by doing odd jobs and picking forest goods, and could only meet their subsistence needs with low income. In 2011, Linsu Village was identified as a key poor village in the autonomous region.

Measures

1. Develop the homestay industry

In 2018, the government recovered 50 houses through the renovation of shanty towns for the development of homestays in Linsu Village. With the vision to build "a local museum, a time shuttle", the appearance of the homestays varies from the thatched house commonly seen in the 1960s, the rubber grouting house in the 1970s, the red brick house in the 1980s, to the house with pine and birch woodcut veneer in the 1990s, and the house with new-type carbonized wood veneer in the 21st century. The interior of the guest rooms restores the living environment of forestry workers in different periods from the 1960s to the 1990s, showing the forest culture in its full, and allowing tourists to experience the different lifestyles of Bailang's forest area in different eras.

2. Show the forest culture

Firstly, the Arxan Forest Customs Museum is built. Arxan Municipal Party Committee and Municipal Government have intensified the conservation of forest customs and culture. The museum is expanded from the original 500-plus square meters to more than 1,200 square meters in the construction area, and displays historical materials about forestry in its early days, tools used by forestry workers for production and domestic purposes, and local animal and plant specimens, among other exhibits of great historical value. It is a unique museum giving

a panoramic view of the forest area. Secondly, a colored painting wall is created dedicated to the solidarity of different ethnic groups, so is a corridor designed to show China's ethnic cultures, a big stage, and a cultural and creative park. Intangible cultural heritage displays, traditional weddings, and theatrical performances are held from time to time to promote and showcase forest customs and culture.

3. Reform the industrial development model

Linsu Village adopts the corporatization model. A tourism cooperative was established, and the villagers invested their resources and assets in business entities to become shareholders and receive dividends, so as to achieve a win-win situation for the tourism development company, the village collective and the villagers. Linsu Village has also developed the under forest product processing industry, deeply developed mountain specialties, and cultivated local brands. It has organized festivals such as the Ice Rolling Festival and the forest customs and culture festival, and continuously extended the industrial chain, to increase the income of the villagers.

Results

By vigorously developing eco-tourism, Linsu Village has lifted 47 households out of poverty, and provided jobs for more than 500 family members of the forest workers. At present, the tourism industry in Bailang directly and indirectly hires more than 800 people, involving nearly every household and every individual, boosting the increase in per capita income by 2,300 yuan per year.

Experience and Inspirations

1. Assistance from multiple sources

The plans, funds and projects of various

kinds all tilt toward the poor village, and tourism development and poverty alleviation are planned, and advanced simultaneously to ensure that they take effect at the same time. Secondly, enterprise assistance. Part of the poverty alleviation funds was invested in local tourism enterprises where poor households hold shares for receiving dividends. Meanwhile enterprises and shops are encouraged to hire poor people and purchase local products from poor households. Thirdly, intellectual support. Village cadres, poverty relief leaders, and business operators are encouraged to participate in various types of training programs to improve their ability to innovate and start a business.

2. Comprehensive protection

In terms of the significance of protection, the renovation plan of Linsu Village is to protect the heritage of excellent forest customs and culture, protect the residential buildings, street patterns and lifestyles in traditional areas, protect local customs and intangible cultural heritage, and retain typical historical development traces and distinct historical and cultural styles.

Next Steps

In the next step, Bailang Town will continue to actively support and promote the development of Linsu Village in terms of policy coordination, capital investment, personnel training, and industrial cultivation. Linsu Village will take more solid steps in tourism branding, tourism project development, and leveraging complementary industrial advantages, so as to promote the comprehensive economic development of the Arxan region and embark on a new path for underdeveloped areas to use the latecomer's advantage to promote development.

辽宁省盘锦市大洼区：
农旅融合助力乡村振兴

收录于《2022世界旅游联盟：旅游助力乡村振兴案例》

摘要

辽宁省盘锦市大洼区立足于推进乡村振兴发展，通过提升乡村环境、丰富村民生活，传承非遗文化、发扬辽河口文化，深挖稻蟹种养、实现农旅融合，在全省率先培育和扶持认养农业、休闲农业、民宿经济等，推动产业融合，形成了乡村旅游产业链，不断助力乡村振兴发展。全区乡村旅游经济呈现蓬勃发展态势，现已跻身"全国休闲农业与乡村旅游示范县""全国民宿产业发展示范区""中国最具特色旅游目的地"和"全国百佳旅游目的地"行列。

挑战与问题

大洼区在全面开展美丽乡村建设之前，乡村旅游发展存在诸多问题。农村基础设施落后、居住环境脏乱差、产业基础薄弱、村民生活习惯落后等问题尤为突出。村民们对乱扔乱倒、乱堆乱放等陋习司空见惯，没有养成讲文明、树新风、爱清洁、会生活的良好习惯。村民们的主要收入来源依靠传统的农业种植和养殖业。乡村旅游开发项目缺少规划，不少项目存在着较大盲目性和同质性，依葫芦画瓢，盲目上马。项目开发只重规模，不讲质量，粗制滥造，建了拆、拆了改，既浪费了项目资金，又造成了项目的低质量，导致旅游市场认可度不高。

措施

1. 提升乡村环境，丰富村民生活

将农村人居环境整治作为美丽乡村建设的突破口，聚焦"脏乱差"等陋习，农村环境卫生治理率、生活垃圾无害化处理率等指标达到100%。连续开展"水乡之韵"文化广场、"美丽大洼"书画摄影、"情满水乡"诗歌朗诵、"民俗乡韵"文化遗产等文化活动，群众性文化活动实现经常化、体系化。

2. 传承非遗文化，发扬辽河口文化

高度重视非物质文化遗产保护工作，积极探索创新思路举措，建立健全名录体系，一大批珍贵、濒危的非物质文化遗产得到有效抢救和有力保护。辽河口文化是大洼区的特色地域文化，融合了诸多文化元素。提升建设农垦荣兴博物馆、红海滩湿地科技馆等各种辽河口文化展示窗口与体验途径。

3. 深挖稻蟹种养，实现农旅融合

大洼区依托全省首个国家现代农业产业园、"中国好粮油"行动示范区和乡村振兴产业园建设，深挖稻蟹种养基因，通过红海滩湿地科技馆、蟹蟹王国等景区传播稻蟹文化，促进稻蟹种苗繁育、生产加工、市场销售产业链协同发展，盘锦大米和盘锦河蟹产业已成为大洼区文化产业的代言符号。此外，大洼区还打造了以"农"字为特色的农耕文化游、农业科普游、

农庄休闲游、农家体验游和农村生态游,构建了集休闲观光、农耕体验于一体的乡村旅游产业链。

成效

大洼区已有二界沟古渔雁文化、西安镇上口子高跷秧歌、田庄台小吃等国家、省、市、区各级非遗保护项目106个。特别是对田庄台小吃文化的挖掘、保护和利用,推进了非遗项目化、产业化发展,还带动了食材、包装、文化旅游等整个产业链条的发展。盘锦大米和盘锦河蟹两个品牌的估值分别达到525.7亿元和295.5亿元。全区共有A级景区14家,其中5A级景区1个,4A级景区2个,3A级景区11个,催生了各具特色的乡村休闲度假游的快速发展,形成了"北旅田园""七彩庄园""芦湖小镇""辽河绿水湾""金球1948生态农场"等多个以田园风光为特色的旅游景区,打造了特色民宿村20个、床位超过2000张,促进村民增收致富。2021年,乡村旅游年接待游客58.25万人次,乡村旅游年平均收入超2.56亿元。

经验与启示

1. 改善环境要先行

乡村要发展旅游产业,需要好的环境吸引人、留住人。近年来大洼区的美丽乡村建设可谓是全国闻名。大洼区不断提升美丽乡村建设和管理水平,全力打造宜居、宜游的全域美丽乡村,为发展乡村旅游提供了前提条件并打下了坚实基础。

2. 民宿经济做引领

通过建设一村一品、一村一景、一村一韵的美丽乡村示范村,全力推进民宿产业发展。例如荣兴街道荣兴村以民宿为载体,盘活闲置老宅资源,建设了集旅游度假、休闲农业、民俗特色为一体的荣兴稻作人家民俗村,年接待观光游客超10万人,住宿过夜游客超3万人。

3. 融合发展是关键

大洼区以旅游带动农业、农业促进旅游的发展思路,将现有的采摘农业、认养农业与科普研学等元素融合发展，结合"互联网+"的创新形式，着力发展智慧农业、观光农业和休闲农业。连续多年开展开海节、插秧节、丰收节、冬捕节、乡村美食节、稻草艺术节等系列乡村旅游文化品牌活动，涵盖了稻作文化、渔雁文化、湿地文化等不同时期大洼区辽河口文化的精髓。2021年9月21日，首届中国乡村文化产业创新发展大会在大洼区成功举办，对宣传盘锦旅游资源、展示盘锦乡村振兴丰硕成果、推介盘锦乡村文化旅游融合发展起到了极大的推动作用。

下一步计划

为了进一步促进大洼区的可持续发展，促进乡村振兴发展，让农民共建共享发展成果，未来将注重以下几个方面。一是组建民宿协会推进乡村民宿品牌化发展，盘锦市将组建以大洼区为核心和试点的"盘锦民宿"品牌，建立多层次立体化的品牌体系，带动民宿集约发展、农家乐特色发展，通过生态优先、文旅融合、扶优扶特、改造提升，全面规范提升民宿发展水平。二是组建旅游产业联盟促进乡村旅游大发展，大洼区将成立大洼旅游产业联盟，围绕"旅游品牌打造、项目推介营销、知识产权保护、专业技能培训、成果转化孵化"等重点内容，凝聚全区涉旅企业力量，构建全方位、全业态、全链条、全要素的旅游产业生态圈。三是坚持产业融合促进生态旅游大发展，在乡村旅游的规划设计、建筑开发、经营管理、旅游产品设计等诸多方面，要注重凝练乡土特色、弘扬乡土文化、挖掘乡村记忆、保护乡村原生态环境。将旅游产品与农业的产业环节进行有效衔接，以此形成一个较为完整的乡村旅游生态产业链，深度推进产业融合和乡村振兴。

Dawa District, Panjin City, Liaoning Province:

Agriculture-Tourism Integration to Boost Rural Revitalization

Included in *WTA Best Practices of Rural Revitalization through Tourism 2022*

Abstract

  Aimed to promoting rural revitalization and development, Dawa District in the city of Panjin City, Liaoning Province, has improved its rural environment, enriched villagers' lives, inherited intangible cultural heritage, promoted the culture of Liaohe Estuary, developed the rice-crab co-culture system, and integrated agriculture and tourism. It is the first in the province to cultivate and promote community-supported agriculture, leisure agriculture and homestay economy. Through the integration of industries, it has formed a rural tourism industry chain, and continuously boosted rural revitalization and development. Its rural tourism economy is developing vigorously, winning it such honors as the National Demonstration County for Leisure Agriculture and Rural Tourism, National Demonstration Area for the Development of Homestay Industry, the Most Characteristic Tourism Destination in China and Top 100 Tourist Destinations in China.

Challenges and Problems

Before the Beautiful Countryside initiative was fully launched, Dawa District faced many problems in the development of rural tourism. The most prominent problem had to do with the backward rural infrastructure, dirty and messy living environment, weak industrial foundation and bad habits of villagers, including littering, and bad sanitation habits. A more civilized, healthier lifestyle was to be advocated. The villagers mainly lived on traditional farming and aquaculture. Rural tourism development projects were not well planned, resulting in many cases of blind and repetitive construction. Many projects were rushed copycats. The preference of size over quality produced sub-standard buildings only to be dismantled years later to make room for new construction projects. This was a waste of money, and the projects thus developed were of poor quality, hard to win the heart of tourists.

Measures

1. Improve rural environment and enrich the life of villagers

Dawa District started the Beautiful Countryside initiative by improving the rural living environment. Focus was placed on changing the dirty and messy environment. So far the environmental sanitation service and harmless treatment of domestic waste have covered all rural areas in the district. It has organized many major cultural events: "The Charm of Water Towns" Cultural Square, the "Beautiful Dawa" Painting, Calligraphy and Photography Exhibition, the "Love for Water Towns" Poetry Recitation Event, and the "Rural Folk Customs" Cultural Heritage. Mass cultural

activities have become regular and systematic.

2. Inherit the intangible cultural heritage and carry forward the Liaohe Estuary culture

Dawa District attaches great importance to the protection of intangible cultural heritage, actively explored innovative ideas and measures, and established a sound list system. A large number of precious and endangered intangible cultural heritage items are effectively rescued and protected. Liaohe Estuary culture is a distinct local culture of Dawa District, a mix of many cultural elements. Dawa District has also upgraded the farming-themed folk customs museum, Honghaitan Wetland Science Museum and other windows and channels to display and experience Liaohe Estuary Culture.

3. Develop the rice-crab co-culture system to realize agriculture-tourism integration

While striving to build Liaoning's first national modern agricultural industrial park, a demonstration area for the "Good Grain and Oil in China" action, and an industrial park for rural revitalization, Dawa

District vigorously advocates its tradition of rice-crab farming, mainly through the Honghaitan Wetland Science Museum and the Crab Kingdom. It promotes the coordinated development of the whole industrial chain covering rice and crab seedling breeding, production, processing and marketing. The Panjin rice and Panjin river-crab industry has become a symbol of Dawa District's cultural industry. In addition, Dawa District has developed farming tours, agricultural science popularization tours, leisure farm tours, farm-stays and rural ecological tours, and constructed the rural tourism industry chain integrating leisure, sightseeing and farming experience.

Results

Dawa District boasts 106 national, provincial, municipal and district-level intangible cultural heritage items under protection, including the migratory fishing men in Erjiegou, Yangge on stilts in Xi'an Town, and Tianzhuangtai snacks. In particular, the identification, conservation and utilization of the "Tianzhuangtai Snacks" have promoted the development and industrialization of intangible cultural heritage projects, as well as the development of the whole industrial chain of food materials, packaging, and foodie tours. The Panjin Rice and Panjin River Crab brands are valued at 52.57 billion yuan and 29.55 billion yuan respectively. The district is home to 14 rated tourist attractions, including one 5A-level scenic spot, two 4A-level ones and eleven 3A-level ones, giving rise to the rapid development of rural leisure and vacation tourism with different characteristics. There are a number of scenic spots featuring idyllic scenery, such as Beilv Garden, Colorful Manor, Luhu Town, Liaohe Green River Bay and Golden Ball 1948 Ecological Farm. There are also 20 homestays with more than 2,000 beds. The villagers have seen their income increase. In 2021, the rural areas received 582,500 tourists, and the income from tourism exceeded 256 million yuan.

Experience and Inspirations

1. Prioritize environmental improvement

To develop rural tourism, we need a good environment to attract and retain people. In recent years, Dawa Distric has established a nationwide

reputation for its progress in building a beautiful countryside. It has continuously improved the environment and governance level of villages, made every effort to build a livable and tourist-friendly countryside, and laid a solid foundation for the development of rural tourism.

2. Develop the homestay economy

While building demonstration villages for the building of a beautiful countryside with emphasis on differentiated scenery and development, Dawa Distric has gone all out to develop the homestay industry. For example, Rongxing Village in Rongxing Sub-district, has repurposed abandoned residential houses into homestays, and built a Rongxing rice-farming folk-customs village integrating tourism, holidaymaking, leisure agriculture and folk customs. It receives more than 100,000 tourists a year, including over 30,000 overnight visitors.

3. Integrated development is the key

To allow agriculture and tourism support and reinforce each other, Dawa Distric promotes the integrated development of the existing U-pick farms, community-supported agriculture and science popularization-themed study tours, and combine them with the Internet, to strive to develop intelligent agriculture, sightseeing agriculture and leisure agriculture. For years running, it has launched several rural tourism events, such as the Festival of the Launch of the Fishing Season, the Rice Transplanting Festival, the Harvest Festival, the Winter Fishing Festival, the Rural Food Festival and the Rice Straw Art Festival, capturing the essence of local Liaohe Estuary culture in different periods, such as rice-farming, migratory fishing operations and the wetland. On September 21, 2021, it hosted the First Rural Cultural Industry Innovation and Development Conference, which played an important role in raising public awareness of Panjin's tourism resources, showing Panjin's achievements in rural revitalization and promoting Panjin's rural culture-tourism integration.

Next Steps

In order to promote the sustainable development

and revitalization of rural Dawa, and engage and share the development fruits with farmers, more efforts will be made in the following aspects.

Firstly, establish a homestay industry association and build up local homestay brands. Panjin City will launch the "Panjin Homestay" pilot project with Dawa District at the core, and establish a multi-level three-dimensional brand system, to drive the intensive development of homestays and the differentiated development of farm-stays. By prioritizing ecological conservation, integrating culture and tourism, supporting leading and unique operators, and improving the overall quality, it will tighten regulation over the homestay industry on the whole.

Secondly, establish a tourism industry alliance to promote the development of rural tourism. The Dawa Tourism Industry Alliance will be set up, tasked with tourism branding, project promotion and marketing, intellectual property protection, professional skills training, and commercialization and incubation of innovations. It will pool the strength of tourism-related enterprises in Dawa District to construct a comprehensive tourism ecosystem that covers all business forms, the whole industrial chain and all factors.

Thirdly, adhere to integration across industries to promote the development of ecotourism. In the planning and design of rural tourism, construction, business operations, tourism product design and other aspects, Dawa District should pay particular attention to identifying and capturing local characteristics, promoting local culture, awakening rural nostalgia, and protecting the rural ecological environment. It will effectively link up tourism products with the industrial links of agriculture, thus forming a relatively complete industrial chain of rural tourism, and deeply promote industry integration and rural revitalization.

旅游减贫案例故事（中英文双语版）
Best Practices of Poverty Alleviation through Tourism（Chinese-English Bilingual Edition）

吉林省白山市靖宇县花园村：
松花江畔景区化村庄振兴样板

收录于《2023世界旅游联盟：旅游助力乡村振兴案例》

摘要

吉林省白山市靖宇县花园口镇花园村以乡村生态保护和开发为着眼点，以农文旅融合为主抓手，以花园村山清水秀的原生态资源为乡村活化的主线，对村落进行原味改造，打造"望得见山、看得见水、记得住乡愁"的文旅产业，使花园村从名不见经传的小村庄逐渐成为网红热门打卡地，实现社会效益和经济效益双丰收。

挑战与问题

吉林省白山市靖宇县花园口镇花园村地处长白山西坡，靠近头道松花江和抚长高速公路，虽然在持续推进美丽乡村建设工作中取得了显著成效，但与深入实施乡村振兴战略目标相比，仍存在一定差距。一是乡村公共服务薄弱。乡村交通道路与停车场、公共厕所、垃圾箱、人居环境，以及乡村公共休闲空间的配套建设水平不高，严重影响了乡村整体形象，影响了游客的乡村旅游体验。二是乡村旅游资源没有有效盘活，居民缺乏依靠旅游去辅助农业转型升级、促进农村经济社会协调发展的意识。三是乡村传统文化保护传承不足，散落在乡间的非物质文化遗产缺乏传承、展示与产业化发展的平台。

措施

1. 提升村容村貌

花园村充分借助松花江生态旅游风景区创建国家4A级旅游景区的有利契机，新建生态停车场、太阳能路灯、充电桩、雨水井、监控设备及管理用房，加大村庄绿化、美化力度。同时，用文字、绘画、情景展现等方式，将中国传统哲学、乡村哲学、民俗哲学、百姓生活哲学等内容植入花园村整个村庄建设中，使花园村基础设施、村容村貌日趋完善。

2. 完善旅游设施

花园村以景区打造为抓手，修建了游船码头、游客服务中心、景区步道、旅游厕所等设施，开发了松花江水上航线、人文哲学小村、星空共享农场、映山红广场等景观，购进画舫船、电瓶船、景区观光车等，极大完善了旅游设施。

3. 丰富旅游业态

花园村围绕"心往长白山·松花江上游"的主题，借助"长白山之夏""长白山之冬"节庆品牌，不断丰富游船节、蓝莓节、露营节等沉浸式体验，大力开

展森林康养游、水上赛事游、运动休闲游、民宿度假游、乡村体验游等项目，积极承办"长白山之夏"开幕式、"松花江冬捕节"等活动，彻底打响花园村品牌。同时全面启动"吃住行游购娱"一船通（一票通）旅游新业态，让游客尽享白山松水美景，更好兑现良好生态价值。

成效

目前花园村有专门从事旅游餐饮服务的餐馆6家，能够开展旅游接待的庭院民宿32家，集餐饮、住宿、娱乐于一体的高端民宿1家。村内民宿单日可接纳游客100余人，民宿的发展带动村民年均增收近万元。2021年花园村接待游客1.2万人次，带动村民人均增收500元，回引返乡创业和务工人员5人；2022年接待游客7.5万人次，带动村民人均增收1200余元，回引返乡创业和务工人员18人；2023

年接待游客 15.4 万人次，带动村民人均增收 1500 余元，回引返乡创业和务工人员 32 人。

经验与启示

1. 因地制宜

遵循乡村自身发展规律，充分体现农村特点，顺应乡村文化肌理，保留乡风、乡味、乡情、乡貌和乡愁，发展有历史记忆、地域特色、品质业态的景区化村庄，避免一窝蜂式的照搬照抄和大拆大建。

2. 生态优先

注重生态环境和人居环境的提升，坚守生态保护底线，把真山真水真空气、原汁原味原风情作为景区村庄建设最大的优势、最好的品牌，把"绿色惠民、富民强村"的理念贯穿于景区和村庄建设的全过程。

3. 创新发展

始终坚持创新理念、创新思路、创新举措，积极有效突破土地、资金等瓶颈制约和制度障碍，推行"公司+专业合作社+农户"的新型发展模式，带动村民增收致富，提升将乡村旅游资源转化为美丽经济的创新能力。

4. 主客共享

一方面对于村民而言，村庄是享受美好生活、品质生活的生态空间；另一方面从游客的体验角度来看，村庄需要充分满足游客日益增长且不断更新的旅

游新需求。因此，需要持续推动乡村旅游供给侧结构性改革，促进乡村旅游提档升级。在追求乡村振兴的过程中，村庄致力于发展成为让村民和游客共享利益、共享美好生活的旅游目的地。

下一步计划

下一步靖宇县将把握时机，不断突破。一是围绕市场需求，首先要完善配套服务设施，加快完善导览标识、旅游厕所等设施，为域内外游客提供更加便捷舒适的游览环境；其次要鼓励支持景区周边农户因地制宜开展本土餐饮、风情民宿等特色化服务，在松花江生态旅游景区及周边扩充高质量餐饮、住宿等服务项目，满足游客多样化需求。二是围绕旅游供给，丰富产品体系。一方面将松花江优质水产品与渔猎文化、冰雪旅游深度融合，变资源优势为经济效益，打造好水域、好鱼种、好品牌、好效益，探索一条具有靖宇特色的渔业可持续发展道路；另一方面深度开发松花江 80 千米游船线路，丰富水上航运功能，完善沿江景点打造，全力打造"松花江三峡"文旅 IP，加快松花江旅游带建设，切实打造长白山北部生态经济区发展新引擎。

Huayuan Village, Jingyu County, Baishan City, Jilin Province:

A Rural Revitalization Model on the Banks of the Songhua River

Included in *WTA Best Practices of Rural Revitalization through Tourism 2023*

Abstract

Huayuan Village of Jilin Province focuses on rural ecological conservation and development, the integration of agriculture and tourism, and its original ecological resources while promoting rural revitalization. It has transformed the village look while keeping original flavor, and developed a tourism industry that makes it "see the mountains, see the water, and feel homesick". Huayuan Village has gradually gained popularity on the Internet, become a must-visit for many, and generated both social and economic benefits.

Challenges and Problems

Huayuan Village sits on the western slope of Changbai Mountains, close to the first branch of Songhua River and the Fusong-Changchun Expressway. Although it has achieved remarkable results in building a beautiful village, it is still considerably behind the goals of fully implementing the strategy of rural revitalization. Firstly, rural public services were weak. The supporting infrastructure, including rural roads and parking lots, public toilets, garbage bins, living environment and rural public leisure space was poor in quality, which seriously affected the overall image of the village and the rural tourist experience. Secondly, rural tourism resources were not effectively utilized, and residents lacked the awareness of promoting agricultural transformation and upgrading and the coordinated economic and social development through tourism development. Thirdly, the protection and inheritance of rural traditional culture was insufficient, and it lacked a platform for inheriting, displaying and industrializing the intangible cultural heritage scattered in the village.

Measures

1. Improve the village appearance

Seizing the opportunity brought by Songhuajiang Scenic Area's applying for the status of a national 4A-level scenic spot, Huayuan Village has added

eco-parking lots, solar street lights, charging piles, rainwater wells, monitoring equipment and management rooms, and stepped up in greening and beautifying the village. At the same time, the contents of traditional Chinese philosophy, rural philosophy, folklore philosophy, and the life philosophy of the common people are embedded in the village design and development by means of text, painting, scene representation, etc. The village infrastructure and appearance are becoming better and better.

2. Improve tourist facilities

While developing scenic spots, Huayuan Village has built the cruise ship terminal, the tourist service center, scenic trails, and tourist toilets, among other facilities, developed Songhua River cruise routes, the Village of Humanities and Philosophy, the Starry Sky shared farm, the Azalea Square and other attractions, and purchased traditional-style tourist boats, battery boats, battery carts, etc., greatly improving tourist facilities.

3. Enrich the operational types of tourism

Making full use of its proximity to Changbai Mountains and Songhua River, and the festival brands of "Summer in Changbai Mountains" and "Winter in Changbai Mountain", the village has enriched immersive experiences by hosting the cruise festival, the blueberry festival, and the camping festival, and vigorously promoted forest tours for health preservation, water event tours, sports and leisure tours, homestay and vacation tours, and other rural life experience tours. It has also undertaken the opening ceremony of "Summer in Changbai Mountains" and the "Winter Fishing Festival on Songhua River", building up its visibility as a destination. Meanwhile, it has launched an all-access pass covering food, accommodation, travel, sightseeing, shopping and entertainment services, allowing tourists to fully enjoy the beautiful scenery of Changbai Mountains and Songhua River, while it can better capitalize on the sound ecological environment.

Results

Huayuan Village has six restaurants specializing in providing catering services to tourists, 32 courtyard homestays that can accommodate tourists, and 1 high-end homestay that offers catering, accommodation and entertainment services. The village's homestays can receive more than 100 tourists in a single day, and have increased the annual income of villagers by nearly 10,000 yuan. In 2021, Huayuan Village received 12,000 tourists, increased the per capita income for villagers by 500 yuan and attracted five migrant workers to come back and start their own business or work in the village; in 2022, it received 75,000 tourists, increased the per capita income of villagers by more than 1,200 yuan, and attracting 18 migrant workers back; and in 2023, it received 154,000 tourists, the per capita income of villagers increased by more than 1,500 yuan, and 32 migrant workers returned.

Experience and Inspirations

1. Adapt to local conditions

Huayuan Village follows the law of rural development, fully reflects the characteristics of the countryside, preserves the texture of rural culture, and retains rural customs, flavors, feelings and appearance, and people's love of nature. It strives to develop into a scenic village with historical memory, regional characteristics, and high-quality businesses, and avoid blind copying and large-scale demolition and construction.

2. Prioritize ecological conservation

Particular effort is made to improve the ecological and living environment. The village safeguards the priority of ecological conservation, and considers the beautiful landscape, fresh air, and authentic countryside life as its biggest asset and best brand. Throughout the whole process of attraction and village construction and development, it has always acted on the belief that "green development will benefit and enrich the people and the village".

3. Promote innovation-driven development

Huayuan Village always embrace innovative ideas, approaches and measures, and has actively

and effectively broken bottlenecks and institutional obstacles regarding land and capital, and introduced the new development model that brings together companies, specialized cooperatives and farmers. It has increased the income of villagers, and improved the innovation ability to generate economic benefits from rural tourism resources.

4. Create shared benefits for villagers and visitors

On the one hand, for the villagers, the village is an ecological space to enjoy a better life. On the other hand, from the perspective of tourists, it needs to fully meet the growing and ever-evolving needs of tourists. Therefore, it needs to continue with the supply-side structural reform of and promotes the upgrading of rural tourism. In the pursuit of rural revitalization, it works to grow into a tourist destination with shared benefits and a better life for both villagers and visitors.

Next Steps

In the next step, Jingyu County will continue to seize opportunities and make breakthroughs. Firstly, to meet the market demand, it shall improve supporting service facilities. Specifically, it needs to move faster to improve the way-finding signs for tourists and the tourist toilets, to provide a more convenient and comfortable environment for tourists from inside and outside the region. It is also necessary to encourage and support farmers around scenic spots to provide specialty catering and accommodation services based on local conditions, and expand high-quality catering, accommodation facilities in and around the Songhuajiang eco-tourism scenic area to meet the diversified needs of tourists. Secondly, it shall enrich the product portfolio and increase the supply of tourism products. It is necessary to deeply integrate the high-quality aquatic products of Songhua River with fishing and hunting culture and winter tourism, generate economic benefits from advantageous resources, create a good water environment for high-quality fish species, establish good brands with sound profitability, and explore a path for the sustainable development of fishery with Jingyu's characteristics. Meanwhile, it plans to develop the 80-kilometer cruise route on the Songhua River, enrich the functions of water navigation, improve the scenic spots along the river, make every effort to build the "Three Gorges on Songhua River" brand, accelerate the development of the Songhua River Tourism Belt, and effectively foster a new engine for the development of the eco-economic zone in the north of Changbai Mountains.

旅游减贫案例故事（中英文双语版）
Best Practices of Poverty Alleviation through Tourism（Chinese-English Bilingual Edition）

黑龙江省伊春市铁力市：
特色民宿驱动农旅融合

收录于《2022 世界旅游联盟：旅游助力乡村振兴案例》

摘要

　　黑龙江省伊春市铁力市深入践行"绿水青山就是金山银山"的理念，牢牢把握"生态立市、旅游强市、产业兴市"发展定位，坚持生态优先、绿色发展、产业融合，将发展全域旅游作为推动乡村振兴的有效载体，大力发展休闲农业和乡村旅游，通过休闲度假、旅游观光、休闲垂钓、农家风味餐饮、特色民宿等旅游休闲集群驱动农旅融合发展。

挑战与问题

伊春市铁力市位于黑龙江省中心部位，行政区划面积为3776.3平方千米，市辖5镇、3乡，有行政村71个，总人口278291万人，其中农业人口84691人，占总人口的30.43%。铁力市生态环境良好，自然资源富集，旅游要素丰富，发展旅游优势明显。然而乡村旅游基础设施条件相对薄弱、旅游产品亟待创新、乡村旅游融合度不高、具有人文特色和山水优势的乡村资源未得到有效挖掘和深度开发仍是制约铁力市旅游发展的主要问题。

措施

1. 科学规划促发展

立足资源禀赋和比较优势，把旅游产业作为经济增长的重要引擎和转型发展的重要动能。综合考虑全市乡村旅游资源禀赋，因地制宜编制了《铁力市全域旅游发展总体规划》，从顶端长远谋划旅游发展，确定开发以铁力乡村为原乡生活载体的乡村旅游业态，充分考虑相关旅游项目的布局规划及交通、通信、供水、供电、环保等公共服务设施的建设，确保旅游资源得到高品质开发和可持续利用，为旅游助力乡村振兴打下坚实基础。

2. 环境整治抓创建

高品位改造村庄绿化，按照"一环两带三通道、点状穿插建绿地、花果飘香进万家"的思路积极推进乡村绿化工程，村庄绿化覆盖率由7.9%提升至36.5%，乡村开启"美颜模式"；高水平推进"五项革命"，农村生活垃圾收集率、处理率以及常住户卫生厕所普及率分别达到90%、100%和86.1%，农村生活垃圾"四分法"成为全省典范；持续完善乡村健身路径、体育设施和文化信息共享活动室等设备设施，硬化、美化、亮化基本实现全覆盖。

3. 丰富业态谋振兴

建成一批有影响力、品牌化的特色民俗，如北星田园生态民宿、成子民宿、途远萌宠部落等；引入酒章文创这一特色旅游景区项目；开展区域旅游文化节、举办冬季森林冰雪欢乐季；积极探索"旅游+电商"模式，通过电商平台销售特色产品，大力推动"铁力森鲜"这一区域公用品牌建设，提升铁力市农林产品的附加值和品牌影响力，促进全市农业产业转型升级。

成效

北星村以集体运营方式，投资240万元打造"北星田园生态民宿"，建成民宿15处。年丰朝鲜族乡成子渔村以自营方式，投资420万元打造成子民宿，建成民宿26处；投资945万元实施"途远萌宠部落"特色主题民宿项目，建成民宿14处。年丰朝鲜族乡长山村成子民宿，年接待游客近1.5万人次，旅游收益可达到160万元；萌宠部落民宿每年可接待游客3万人次左右，收益可以达到90万元左右。同时，通过餐饮配套、特产服务配套带动乡内其他旅游景点、民宿、渔村的客流量，额外增收约70万元。民宿经济有效促进了农旅融合，实现了农业增效、农民增收和农村增美。

另外，通过"途礼—乡村伴手礼"服务平台，对外销售本地特色农产品，可实现增收25万元；为本地百姓提供就业、创业的机会可助民增收15万元。每年全乡由乡村旅游及其衍生项目所带来的经济收益

可达到 360 万元，年接待游客约 5 万人次，为当地 70 余人提供就业机会。

销售流通环节，形成生态旅游与生态农产品产业相互促进的良好势头，整体提升铁力市农林产品的附加值和品牌影响力。

经验与启示

1. 积极发展民宿经济

尊重乡村特质，依托良好的乡村旅游资源、人文底蕴、农副产品，通过建设成子民宿、萌宠部落、北星田园生态民宿等一批精品民宿项目，因地制宜发展乡村特色经济，将好山好水好空气变为铁力旅游的最大名片。

2. 大力依托电商平台

积极利用电商平台销售特色产品，借助网红直播对外推介铁力产品，"铁力森鲜"品牌知名度和美誉度持续提升。通过打通旅游产品及农产品的生产加工、

下一步计划

铁力市将继续依托良好生态，按照多点开花、错位发展原则，突出打造市场化、规模化、专业化、精品化、个性化的旅游项目，大力发展亲子互动、运动营地、文化体验等特色项目；推进途远萌宠部落民宿二期和酒章文创特色旅游景区等精品旅游项目建设；举办一系列乡村特色文化旅游节庆活动。结合美丽宜居村庄创建行动，进一步挖掘乡村发展潜力，持续推动旅游与文化、生态、产业融合发展，形成示范引领效应，打造乡村振兴的"铁力样板"。

Tieli City, Yichun City, Heilongjiang Province:

B&B Service with Local Characteristics Driving Agriculture-Tourism Integration

Included in *WTA Best Practices of Rural Revitalization through Tourism 2022*

Abstract

Tieli is a county-level city in the prefecture-level city of Yichun, Heilongjiang province. It remains committed to the concept that "lucid waters and lush mountains are invaluable assets", and firmly positions itself as an "eco-city with a strong tourism industry and other booming industries". It has prioritized ecological conservation, promoted green development and industrial integration, and considered all-area-advancing tourism as an effective vehicle for rural revitalization. It vigorously develops leisure agriculture and rural tourism, and drives the integrated development of agriculture and tourism through cluster zones of leisure and vacationing, sightseeing, angling, catering, and B&B services.

Challenges and Problems

Tieli City is located at the center of Heilongjiang Province, with an administrative area of 3,776.3 square kilometers. Under its jurisdiction are five towns, three townships and 71 administrative villages, with a total population of 278,291, including 84,691 agricultural population, accounting for 30.43% of the total. The ecological environment is good, and natural resources and tourism elements are abundant, giving it obvious advantages to develop tourism. But its rural tourism infrastructure was weak, tourism products were outdated, rural tourism resources lacked integration, and rural resources with cultural heritage and natural scenery were yet to be identified and developed. These were the main problems restricting the development of tourism in Tieli City.

Measures

1. Promote development through science-based planning

Based on resource endowments and comparative advantages, Tieli City makes the tourism industry an important drive for economic growth, transformation and development. Taking into account its rural tourism resources, it prepared the Master Plan for Tourism Development according to local conditions, a top-level design for long-term tourism development. It determined to develop rural tourism in the Tieli countryside, and gave full consideration to the distribution of tourism projects and public service facilities such as transportation, communications, water supply, power supply and environmental protection, to ensure high-quality development and sustainable utilization of tourism resources, and lay a solid foundation for rural revitalization through tourism.

2. Improve the environment

Tieli City greened the villages according to high standards, by building one green ring, two green belts and three green corridors, with small green spaces scattered in between, and flowers and fruit trees growing everywhere, and increased the greening rate from 7.9% to 36.5%. The countryside is getting more and more beautiful. It also transformed waste collection and treatment, toilets, sewage treatment, energy mix and vegetable gardens in villages according to high standards. The collection and treatment rates of household garbage and the penetration rate of sanitary toilets

in permanent households have reached 90%, 100% and 86.1%, respectively. It has continued to improve rural fitness roads, sports facilities, culture and exchanges rooms and other equipment and facilities. Basically all the roads are hardened, all the facilities and signs beautified and entire villages are lit at night.

3. Diversify business forms

It has built a number of influential brands, such as Beixing Rural Ecological B&B, Chengzi B&B and Tuyuan Pets' Club; introduced the Jiuzhang Cultural and Creative Project; organized regional tourism and culture festivals and the winter forest season; integrated tourism with e-commerce, developed special e-commerce products, and built up the regional public brand of "Tieli Sen Xian" (forest produce in Tieli) to enhance the added value and brand influence of agricultural and forestry products, and promote the transformation and upgrading of agriculture in the city.

Results

Beixing Village invested 2.4 million yuan in the Beixing Rural Ecological B&B which is operated by the village collective and has 15 facilities. Chengzi Fishing Village in Nianfeng, a Korean-ethnicity township, invested 4.2 million yuan to build and operated Chengzi B&B, with 26 facilities. There is also the Tuyuan Pets' Club, with an investment of 9.45 million yuan and 14 facilities. In particular, Chengzi B&B in Changshan Village receives nearly 15,000 tourists annually, with an annual income of 1.6 million yuan. The Tuyuan Pets' Club receives about 30,000 tourists every year, and with an annual income of about 900,000 yuan. At the same time, catering and specialty services can boost the flow of tourists to other tourist attractions, home-stay facilities and fishing villages in the township, which can increase the income by 700,000 yuan. Thus the B&B economy has effectively promoted the integration of agriculture and tourism: agriculture is more efficient, farmers are richer and villages more beautiful.

In addition, an e-commerce platform was launched to sell local specialty agricultural products, which can generate an income of 250,000 yuan. Through employment and entrepreneurship opportunities, local people can increase their income by 150,000 yuan. Every year, rural tourism and its derivative projects can generate an income of 3.6 million yuan, and bring in about 50,000 tourists, and provide more than 70 employment opportunities for local people.

Experience and Inspirations

1. Actively develop the B&B economy

Respecting the characteristics of the countryside, making good use of rural tourism resources, cultural heritage, agricultural and sideline products, Tieli City has built a number of boutique B&B projects such as Chengzi B&B, Pets' Club, and Beixing Rural Ecological B&B, developed specialty industries based on local conditions, and turned the beautiful natural environment and scenery into the biggest asset to lure tourists.

2. Vigorously develop e-commerce

Tieli City actively develops e-commerce to sell specialty products and hires famous live-streamers to promote and sell local products. The brand awareness and reputation of "Tieli Sen Xian" continues to improve. By linking up the production, processing, sales and distribution links of tourism products and agricultural products, Tieli City has produced a good momentum for mutual reinforcement between ecotourism and organic agricultural products, and boosted the added value and brand influence of its agricultural and forestry products as a whole.

Next Steps

Tieli City will continue to make good use of its good ecological environment, and follow the principle of multiple growth points and differentiated development. It will highlight market-oriented, large-scale, specialized, boutique and customized tourism projects, especially parent-child tours, sport-themed camping tours and cultural tours. It will advance the second phase of Tuyuan Pets' Club and Jiuzhang Cultural & Creative Project, and hold a series of festivals and celebrations with rural characteristics to attract tourists. In the drive to make villages more beautiful and livable, it will further tap the development potential of villages, continuously promote the integration of tourism with culture, ecological conservation and other industries, and set an exemplar of rural revitalization for the rest of the country.

上海市金山区朱泾镇待泾村：

芳香经济助力乡村振兴

收录于《2022 世界旅游联盟：旅游助力乡村振兴案例》

摘要

  上海市金山区朱泾镇待泾村围绕乡村振兴战略，大力推动乡村旅游，积极引进社会资本，主动探索未来之路。2017 年 2 月，600 亩（1 亩约为 666.67 平方米）"花开海上"生态园正式开园，凭借超高"颜值"一炮而红，截至 2021 年已累计接待游客约 130 万人次。2020 年 10 月，待泾村围绕 113 亩点状供地，率先探索农村集体经营性建设用地使用权作价入股新模式，启动了"上海南郊·花海芳香小镇"的建设项目，这一举措成功激活了 3800 亩的土地资源，使得产业特色鲜明突出，村容村貌日新月异。农民家庭人均年收入也由 2017 年的 2.3 万元增长到 2021 年的 3 万余元，村民的生活福祉不断提升，人均可支配收入不断提高。

挑战与问题

待泾村面积 6.25 平方千米，一直贴着"穷村"的标签，存在着许多问题。一是产业单一，经济薄弱。整个村子以农业为主，是几乎没有产业的"纯农村"，村民主要依靠种田维持生计，经济收入有限，困难时期一天三顿只能喝粥。二是发展质量低。20 世纪 80 年代，为了改善生活条件，村民们纷纷开始养猪养鸭，虽然收入有所增长，但不规范的养殖方式却给村庄环境带来了严重破坏。河道被垃圾填满，夏日里臭气弥漫，蚊蝇滋生，严重影响了村民生活，破坏了生态环境。三是土地利用效率低。2001 年以前村内部分区域地势低洼，每逢防汛季节便容易遭受水淹，导致庄稼收成不好，严重影响村民收入。

措施

1. 推进村庄改造，改善村容村貌

精心编制《上海市金山区朱泾镇待泾村村庄规划（2018—2035）》。拆除 100 余个养殖大棚，面积超过 4.5 万平方米；对人居环境实现全覆盖整治，共计 1200 余户；整治全村 14 条村级河道共计 14.2 千米，开展截污纳管、二次自来水改造、"四好农村路"建设等重点项目，极大改善农村人居环境，提升村民的生活质量和健康水平。

2. 引进社会资本，抢抓重大机遇

引进杭州蓝天园林生态科技股份有限公司，通过对 600 亩低洼地进行整体开发，将低洼地打造成以赏花为特色的"花开海上"生态园。这个生态园逐步成为市民观光游览、参与文体娱乐和徒步健身等各类活动的网红"打卡点"。2020 年，待泾村与衡山集团签订精品民宿项目，将村民闲置农宅打造成为特色民宿。根据规划，首批将改造 20 户农宅作为民宿，其中 6 户作为试点先行改造，目前已有 4 户率先完成了改造并投入试运营，且在试运营阶段保持了较高的入住率与满意度。

3. 探索作价入股，打造芳香小镇

以"花开海上"生态园项目为基础，待泾村持续推进"上海南郊·花海芳香小镇"建设，实现收益共享。待泾村以集体建设用地作价入股的方式与蓝城花开海上建设管理有限公司共同开发建设芳香小镇 2 期共 3800 亩，其中 113 亩转性为经营性集体建设用地，用于小镇中心、精品酒店、度假民宿群等开发建设，将花海旅游与文化教育、花艺民宿、健康养生等产业相结合。

成效

待泾村产业发展不断壮大，产业布局不断优化，第一产业、第二产业和第三产业持续融合发展。"花开海上"生态园流转费比同类土地高 5%；生态园每

年门票收入的 10% 作为分红收益返还给待泾村经济合作社；生态园招工优先面向待泾村村民，全年解决当地农民就业 120 人，旺季还可以增加临时工 80 余人。村民们的收入来源也变得多元化，他们以"保底+分红"的模式每年至少可以获得近 200 万元的股金收入，加上土地流转费及房屋租赁费（租金）、村民在园区打工的工资收入（薪金）、自家种植农产品销售收入，再加上养老保障金，每户农户都至少拥有了"1+4"的保障体系，成了名副其实的"五金"农民。

经验与启示

1. 善于找准自身优势

待泾村一是生态资源丰富，全村共有农户耕地面积 6335 亩。二是区位优势便利，与枫泾镇兴塔隔河相望，亭枫公路（320 国道）横贯村域中部，交通便利。三是土地分布集中，村域范围内的土地呈块状分布，便于整合土地资源，盘活闲置土地，破除发展瓶颈，促进产业发展。正是在各方面优势的叠加下，"花开海上"生态园才有建设的基础。

2. 敢于探索发展新路

"上海南郊·花海芳香小镇"项目点状供地的 99 宗土地，在办理"农转用"后，区别于常规"农地入股"的转包、出租、互换、转让等模式，没有通过国家征收，而是由待泾村村集体将 40 年使用权直接作价入股。根据协议这 99 宗集体土地入股时限为 40 年，与国有土地同权同价。土地入股后获得的股权收益，按照保底加收益分配模式，持续为壮大镇、村集体经济赋能。一方面有利于激活沉睡资源、助力产业发展，另一方面通过村集体经济的壮大让失地农民有了长效的增收渠道，村民可以长期分享土地所承载的产业项目发展带来的多重红利。

3. 勇于加强村企合作

村企双方建立市场化合作平台，大力发展苗木花卉、家庭园艺产业和农业观光旅游，并配套建设农业与旅游服务设施。随着蓝城集团接盘生态园，"花开海上"生态园踏上了向花海小镇的升级转型之路，其规模也从原来的 600 亩扩大到 3800 亩。"花开海上"和待泾村的共识是，企业只有做好对乡村的反哺才能获得长远发展，乡村要做好环境、服务等配套。双方需携手合作，才能真正依靠乡村游推动第一、二、三产业融合发展。与此同时，木守、明月松间和衡山等民宿企业也不断加盟，在村企间建立起日益深厚的信任基础上，乡村旅游产业才能不断发展，乡村振兴亦能不断深入。

下一步计划

一是待泾村将根据市场需求，继续利用村民闲置宅基地打造民宿集群，扩大民宿规模，依托民宿集群为村庄带来显著的经济和社会效益，带动游客辐射效应，使旅游功能最大化，让待泾村成为浦南地区乡村旅游新地标。二是在自身产业不断发展兴旺的同时，以 320 国道文旅连廊建设为契机，加强与西部乐高乐园的联动，形成东西呼应、优势互补，大力带动待泾村乡村旅游、民宿产业的发展。三是"上海南郊·花海芳香小镇"将以"优势互补、时间错位"为策略，探索夜间旅游新模式，开挖"花文化+夜间旅游"项目，并通过亲子科普营、闺蜜乐享团等主题活动，不断丰富全年不同时段的旅游活动和产品，带动景区"芳香经济"新引擎。

旅游减贫案例故事（中英文双语版）
Best Practices of Poverty Alleviation through Tourism (Chinese-English Bilingual Edition)

Daijing Village, Zhujing Town, Jinshan District, Shanghai City:
The Flower Economy Promoting Rural Revitalization

Included in *WTA Best Practices of Rural Revitalization through Tourism 2022*

Abstract

While implementing the strategy of rural revitalization, Daijing, a village in the town of Zhujing, Jinshan District of Shanghai City, has vigorously promoted rural tourism, actively introduced social capital, and actively blazed a new path. In February 2017, the 600 *mu* (1 *mu* is approximately 666.67 square meters) "Blooming Sea" Ecological Park was officially opened, and became an instant hit with its beautiful landscape. So far, it has received about 1.3 million tourists cumulatively. In October 2020, Daijing Village introduced the new model of investing with the right to the use of 113 *mu* of scattered rural collective land for operational and construction purposes, and started the development of the Fragrant Flower Sea Town project in the southern suburb of Shanghai. The project puts into good use 3,800 *mu* of land, and stimulates distinctive industries. It has completely changed the village look and increased the per capita annual income of farmers from 23,000 yuan in 2017 to more than 30,000 yuan. The wellbeing of villagers has been constantly improved, and the per capita disposable income has also been on the rise.

Challenges and Problems

Daijing Village covers an area of 6.25 square kilometers, and has long been labeled as poor, faced with many problems. Firstly, the economy was undiversified and weak. The village lived almost entirely on agriculture, with virtually no industrial economy. Locals lived on farming, and the income was meagre. Sometimes they had to tighten their belt and had nothing but porridge for food. Secondly, the quality of development was low. In the 1980s, in order to make some money, many farmers raised pigs and ducks, which did generate some income, but at the expense of the environment due to pollution. The river was full of garbage, and smelt badly in summer. The swarming mosquitoes and flies became a serious headache for the villagers. The ecological environment was damaged. Thirdly, land use efficiency was low. Before 2001, some of the low-lying areas were often flooded during the flood period, resulting in poor harvest and a big drop in the income of villagers.

Measures

1. Improve the village environment and look

The Plan for Daijing Village, Zhujing Town, Jinshan District, Shanghai City(2018-2035) was prepared. According to this plan, more than 100 breeding sheds were dismantled, covering an area of more than 45,000 square meters; the living environment was improved, benefiting more than 1,200 households; and 14 village-level river courses were cleared, stretching for a total of 14.2 kilometers. Major projects such as sewage interception and pipeline laying projects, secondary tap water renovation projects and the construction of "Four Good" rural roads have been carried out, and have greatly improved the living environment and the health of villagers.

2. Introduce social capital and seize major opportunities

Hangzhou Bluesky Landscape Ecological Technology Co., Ltd. was introduced to develop 600 *mu* of low-lying land into the "Blooming Sea" Ecological Park, featuring flower appreciation. The park has come to be a popular destination for sightseeing, recreation and sports, hiking and fitness activities. In 2020, Daijing Village signed a boutique homestay project with Hengshan Group to build the idle dwellings into characteristic homestays. The first batch involves 20 households, including 6 pilot households, four of which have been put into trial operation, and seen a high occupancy rate and satisfaction rate since.

3. Developing the Fragrant Flower Sea Town by investing with the land use right

Based on the "Blooming Sea" Ecological Park project, Daijing Village continues to develop the Fragrant Flower Sea Town in south suburb of Shanghai and share the benefits with all stakeholders. Daijing Village jointly develops the second phase of the Fragrant Flower Sea Town of 3,800 *mu* by investing with the use right to collective land for construction with Blue Town Huakai Haishang Company, of which 113 *mu* is converted into collective construction land for operations, and will be used for the construction and development of the town center, boutique hotels, and homestay cluster, etc. It's hoped to combine flower-themed tours with culture, education, floriculture-themed homestays, health preservation and other industries.

Results

The industries in Daijing Village have been growing, the industrial layout is being improved, and the integrated development of the primary, secondary and tertiary sectors continues. The "Blooming Sea" Ecological Park pays 5% higher than the market value for land circulation fees, and allocates 10% of its annual ticket income to the village economy co-operatives as dividends. It prefers local villagers in recruitment and has offered 120 local jobs throughout the year, with additional more than 80 temporary jobs during the peak season. The villagers can earn at least nearly 2 million yuan from the guaranteed returns and dividends for their shares, in addition to the land circulation fee and house rental fee (rent), the wage income from working in the park (salary), the sales income of farm produce and the pension. In this way, each rural household has at least five sources of income.

Experience and Inspirations

1. Identify own advantages

Firstly, Daijing Village is rich in ecological resources, with a total arable land area of 6,335 *mu*. Secondly, the village is conveniently located, facing Xingta of Fengjing Town across the river, with Tingfeng Road (320 National Highway) running across the middle of the village. Thirdly, the land is mostly concentrated in blocks, making it easier to consolidate and put idle land into good use, thus to remove development bottlenecks and promote industrial development. All these advantages combine to lay the foundation for the "Blooming Sea" project.

2. Dare to explore new paths for development

While converting the 99 plots of agricultural land into non-agricultural land for the Fragrant Flower Sea Town project, the village did not adopt the conventional conversion mode, including contracting, lease, swap or transfer of the land use right, or have them requisitioned by the state; instead, the village collective directly invested in the project with the right to the use of these plots for the upcoming 40 years, with the same rights and at the same price as state-owned land. The equity income thus obtained is distributed in the form of guaranteed returns plus profit distribution, to continue to empower the collective economy of the town and the village. This is conducive to putting dormant resources into good

use and boosting industrial development. Meanwhile, it can strengthen the village collective economy, provide a sustainable source of income for farmers who have transferred their land use right, and allow them to share the multiple dividends brought by the development of industrial projects built on the land for a long time to come.

3. Strengthen village-enterprise cooperation

A market-oriented platform is built for the cooperation between the village and enterprises to vigorously develop the seedling and flower industry, home gardening industry and agricultural sightseeing tours, and build supporting agricultural and tourist service facilities. After taken over by Blue Town Group, the "Blooming Sea" ecological park started to upgrade into the Fragrant Flower Sea Town, and expanded its scale from 600 *mu* to 3,800 *mu*. Both the project team and the village agree that enterprises can achieve long-term development only if they do a good job in nurturing the countryside, and the village should do a good job in supporting the environment and services, so that they can form synergy and truly drive the integration of the primary, secondary and tertiary sectors through tourism development. At the same time, Muh Shoou, YAKAMOZ, and Hengshan homestay enterprises have also partnered up with the village. Only based on enhanced cooperation and mutual trust between the village and enterprises can the rural tourism industry continue to develop, and rural revitalization continue to deepen.

and expand the scale of homestays, to bring remarkable economic and social benefits to the village, attract more tourists, maximize the tourism function, and become a new rural tourism landmark in Punan area.

Secondly, while continuing to drive the development of rural industries, it will take the opportunity of building the 320 National Highway Cultural and Tourism Corridor to strengthen the linkage with the Legoland in the west, reinforce each other, and vigorously promote the development of rural tourism and homestay industry in the village.

Thirdly, the Fragrant Flower Sea Town project will tap into complementary strengths, stagger the visit hours, and develop night tours themed on the flower culture. It will organize parent-child popular science camps and female-only tours, and continuously diversify tourism activities and products at different time periods throughout the year, and develop new drivers for the flower industry in scenic spots.

Next Steps

Firstly, Daijing Village, according to the market demand, will continue to build homestay clusters based on the abandoned residential land

旅游减贫案例故事（中英文双语版）
Best Practices of Poverty Alleviation through Tourism（Chinese-English Bilingual Edition）

江苏省南京市江宁区黄龙岘茶文化村：
茶旅融合蝶变美丽乡村

收录于《2023 世界旅游联盟：旅游助力乡村振兴案例》

摘要

江苏省南京市江宁区黄龙岘茶文化村坚持以绿色发展为引领、农业产业为支撑、美丽乡村为依托，科学规划茶乡产业与乡村旅游发展模式，通过村企共建、农民主体的运营模式，按照"完善配套、提升供给、产业融合"的原则，以文旅产业为抓手，探索"茶产业＋可持续发展"道路，打通绿水青山和金山银山的转化通道，打造宜居、宜业、宜游的美丽黄龙岘。

挑战与问题

江苏省南京市江宁区黄龙岘茶文化村占地0.91平方千米，茶园2000多亩，总人口2155人。村庄东邻战备水库，西接牌坊水库，四周茶山、竹林环绕，环境优美，生态资源丰富。然而村庄地处偏僻的丘陵地带，地域封闭、交通落后、基础薄弱、信息闭塞，长期处于自然发展状态。当地气候、土地适合种植茶树，农作物单一、产品附加值低，村民经济收入水平低，多数村民外出打工谋生，村庄空心化严重，缺少可持续发展的产业、机制和动力。

措施

1. 创新发展模式

黄龙岘茶文化村运用村企共建方式，创新合作模式，在党支部统一领导下，联合企业、茶叶合作社、农家乐行业协会、茶叶品质研究所、景区管理办公室、景区物业管理公司6部门，搭建"1+6"管理平台，强化村庄环境卫生、生态治理、文化传承、旅游服务等功能，助推乡村旅游品质提升。

2. 完善基础设施

黄龙岘茶文化村尊重村庄原有的生态肌理、环境优势和农业特色，开展厕所革命、房屋出新、雨污分流及杆管线下地等环境整治工程；坚持"经济发展交通先行"思路，实施生态旅游绿道工程，建成100千米美丽乡村循环线、45千米自行车专用线和22千米最美夜跑道；建成涵盖千亩茶园观光道、千年古官道、仙林竹荫道、诗画黄龙潭的生态观光区；建成涵盖茶文化博物馆、茶缘阁、黄龙大茶馆、乡村民宿的黄龙岘茶文化慢生活旅游区，同时完善餐饮、住宿、停车场等旅游配套设施，打造黄龙岘特色乡村旅游体系。

3. 促进茶旅融合

黄龙岘茶文化村以120亩集体茶园为试点，与南京农业大学茶业研究所合作，建立种、管、养、采、

炒标准化茶叶体系，并成功推出了"龙针""龙毫"这两个具有黄龙岘特色的茶叶品牌；运用"互联网+"模式，开展茶叶、茶干、笋干等特色农产品网络销售，带动农民增收；发挥节庆、假日效应，举办黄龙岘茶文化旅游节、茶乡音乐节、国风艺术节、自行车赛事、夜跑、江宁周末露营等活动，促进农旅深度融合。黄龙岘充分挖掘文旅资源，对山林、茶园、水库等生态资源进行创意设计，打造了"住茶园、赏茶景、购茶产、品茶饮、玩茶俗"的茶文化旅游产品精品线路。

成效

黄龙岘茶文化村生态环境持续优化。现有生态茶园2600多亩、竹林2000亩、松林1000亩，绿化覆盖率达到85%。村内道路已由泥泞路升级为符合二、三级公路标准的道路，并配备了5200平方米露营地和10194平方米的生态停车场等旅游配套设施，使得黄龙岘成了一个设施完备、景致宜人、生态友好、美丽宜居的美丽乡村。村民收入稳步增加，黄龙岘茶文化村创新土地流转机制，累计流转土地6425亩用于旅游项目开发。全村已有43户开设了茶楼、餐厅、客栈等特色经营项目，自主创业比例超过了80%，创业户年收入突破30万元。茶叶的年销售总额平均每年增长近20%，村民的人均年收入从原来1.8万元增加到了现在的4.3万元。此外，黄龙岘的发展还辐射带动了周边200多名大学生和1500多名村民实现了就业创业和致富增收。

经验与启示

1. 坚持产业导向

黄龙岘茶文化村通过总体规划布局，以"生态产业化、产业生态化"为导向，茶产业为支撑，打造集观光休闲、乡村民宿、科普研学、红色教育、自驾露营、康养体育等功能于一体的旅游度假胜地。坚持深化"旅游+""+旅游"的产业融合模式，打造新产品、开发新线路、培育新业态，以旅游建设带动乡村人文、环境、经济的可持续发展。

2. 坚持思路创新

黄龙岘茶文化村面临资金紧张、资源要素缺乏等困难。一是积极统筹形成乡村振兴建设合力，政协、统战、宣传、文化（含诗社、作协、文学馆等）、供销及交通等部门纷纷"下乡"，为乡村振兴出谋划策，各展其长。二是丰富旅游经营业态，引入社会资金、

电商平台、专业团队、创客队伍等社会投资和运营主体，共同参与村庄的投资、建设和运营，丰富景区旅游业态、提升乡村旅游内涵。

3. 坚持以人为本

黄龙岘茶文化村在建设过程中，重视村民主体地位，鼓励村民积极参与旅游建设，共享乡村旅游资源和成果。对收益快、村民可自主经营的农家乐项目，村集体主动退出；对投资大、标准高的民宿、文化类新业态，村集体率先进入，做好示范引导。

下一步计划

一是加强旅游宣传力度，黄龙岘以独特的自然人文景观、民俗风情以及传统手工艺品等旅游资源为依托，与旅游电商、现代物流企业建立紧密合作关系，加大线上线下宣传力度，加强品牌营销，推动乡村旅游与现代信息技术结合，促进"旅游+农业+互联网"的模式融合发展。二是推进综合配套建设，延伸拓展旅游辐射范围，建设岘下精品民宿村，提档升级茶文化博物馆、童趣园等项目。三是提升旅游服务水平，紧贴游客需求，建立基层服务人员管理和培训机制，提高经营管理和服务水平，推动乡村旅游提质升级，打造精品旅游目的地，为乡村振兴、旅游富民持续提供动力。

Huanglongxian Tea Village, Jiangning District, Nanjing City, Jiangsu Province:

Shaping A Beautiful Countryside through Tea-Tourism Integration

Included in *WTA Best Practices of Rural Revitalization through Tourism 2023*

Abstract

Huanglongxian Tea Village of Jiangsu Province scientifically plans the development of the tea industry and rural tourism industry while promoting green development, with the agricultural industry as the support, and based on the beautiful countryside environment. Under the operation model featuring cooperation between the village and enterprises and with farmers as the mainstay, it works to improve supporting facilities, increase the supply and promote the integrated development of industries. Starting with the tourism industry, it has explored the path of tea industry plus sustainable development, opening up the channel of turning lucid waters and lush mountains into economic benefits, and making Huanglongxian Tea Village a beautiful place suitable for living, working and traveling.

Challenges and Problems

Huanglongxian Tea Village covers an area of 0.91 square kilometers, with more than 2,000 *mu* of tea gardens and a total population of 2,155. On the one hand, the village is adjacent to the Zhanbei Reservoir in the east and the Paifang Reservoir in the west, surrounded by tea hills and bamboo forests, with a beautiful environment and rich ecological resources. On the other hand, it is located in a remote hilly area, with backward transportation conditions and poor infrastructure. It is uninformed and has long been in a state of natural development. The local climate and soil conditions are suitable for planting tea trees. Local crops lack diversity, and the added value of agricultural products is low. Hence before developing the tea and tourism industries, the villager had meager income, and most had to migrant to cities to make a living. The village was hollowed out seriously, and lacked necessary industries, mechanisms and motivation for sustainable development.

Measures

1. Introduce a new development model

Under the unified leadership of the Party branch, Huanglongxian Tea Village worked with enterprises and introduced a new cooperation model. It has jointly established a "1+6" management platform with six groups of stakeholders, namely enterprises, tea cooperatives, the farmhouse industry's association, the tea quality research institute, the scenic area administrative office, and the scenic property management company, to improve the village's environmental sanitation, ecological governance, cultural inheritance, and tourist services, and thus improve the rural tourist experience.

2. Improve infrastructure

Respecting the village's original ecological texture, environmental advantages and agricultural characteristics, Huanglongxian Tea Village launched projects to improve its environment, including the toilet revolution, house renovation, rainwater and sewage separation, and moving poles and pipelines underground. Believing that "transportation infrastructure shall come first for economic development", it implemented the Eco-tourism Greenway Project, and built a 100-kilometer rural circulation line, a 45-kilometer bicycle line and a 22-kilometer night-time running track. An eco-tourism area is in place, covering a sightseeing path through the thousand *mu* tea garden, the thousand-year-old official road, the Xianlin bamboo-shaded path, and the picturesque Huanglong Pond. There is also a slow-life tourist area consisting of the tea culture museum, the Chayuan Pavilion, Huanglong Tea House and rural homestays. Meanwhile, tourist facilities such as catering, accommodation facilities and parking lots were improved, to create a rural tourist service system with Huanglongxian's own characteristics.

3. Promote the tea-tourism integration

At the 120 *mu* collective tea garden, Huanglongxian Tea Village cooperated with the Tea Industry Research Institute of Nanjing Agricultural University and the two jointly piloted a standardized tea production system covering planting, management, cultivation, picking and frying, and launched local tea brands such as "Long Zhen" and "Long Hao". Adopting the "Internet +" approach, Huanglongxian Tea Village organized online sales of tea, dried tea, dried bamboo shoots and other specialty agricultural products to increase farmers' income. On festivals and holidays, it organized the Tea Culture and Tourism Festival, the Music Festival, the Chinese-Style Art Festival, biking events, night jogging events, and Jiangning weekend camping events, to promote the deep integration of agriculture and tourism. Huanglongxian Tea Village has dug deep into its cultural and tourism resources, creatively designed ecological resources such as mountains and forests, tea gardens, reservoirs, etc., and developed a boutique route allowing tourists to live in the tea garden, appreciate the tea garden scenery, buy tea products, and enjoy tea and the tea ceremony.

Results

The ecological environment of Huanglongxian Tea Village continues to improve. At present, there are more than 2,600 *mu* of eco-tea gardens, 2,000 *mu* of bamboo forest, 1,000 *mu* of pine forest, and the green coverage rate reaches 85%. The roads in

the village have been upgraded from muddy roads to second- and third-level highway standards, and 5,200 square meters of campsites and 10,194 square meters of eco-parking lots and other tourist facilities have been built. The village now boasts sound and complete facilities and pleasant scenery, and is eco-friendly, beautiful and livable. The income of the villagers has increased steadily. Huanglongxian Tea Village introduced a new mechanism for land use right transfer, and a total of 6,425 *mu* of land transferred for tourism development. There are 43 households that have opened tea houses, restaurants, and inns, more than 80% of the villagers have started their own business, and the annual income of the self-employed households has exceeded 300,000 yuan per household. The average annual growth rate of tea sales is nearly 20%, and the per capita annual income of villagers has increased from 18,000 yuan to 43,000 yuan. The tea industry has driven more than 200 college students and more than 1,500 villagers to increase income through employment and entrepreneurship.

Experience and Inspirations

1. Stay industry-oriented

Huanglongxian Tea Village has prepared a master plan, with focus on "industrial ecology and eco-friendly industries". With the tea industry as the support, it works to develop a tourist resort that offers a wide range of services including sightseeing, leisure, rural homestays, popular science education, study tours, education on the CPC history, self-driving tours, camping, health preservation and sports. It continues to improve the "tourism +" and

"+ tourism" industrial integration models, develop new products, new routes, and new business forms, and promote rural cultural, environmental and economic sustainability through tourism development.

2. Continue to introduce innovative ideas

In response to such difficulties as lack of funds and resources, Huanglongxian Tea Village actively coordinated stakeholders to produce synergy for rural revitalization. Departments of the CPPCC, the United Front, Publicity, Culture (including poetry clubs, writers' associations, literature museums, etc.), Supply and Marketing Cooperatives, and Transportation have all sent officials to the countryside to contribute their wisdom and expertise to rural revitalization. Meanwhile, it has introduced social investment and operation entities such as social funds, e-commerce platforms, professional teams, and maker teams to jointly participate in the investment, construction and operation of the village to enrich the operational types of tourism in the scenic spots and the connotation of rural tourism.

3. Stay people-centered

In the development of Huanglongxian Tea Village, the villagers' main role is highlighted and they are encouraged to actively participate in tourism development, and share rural tourism resources and achievements. The village collective has taken the initiative to exit from farmhouse projects which have quick returns and can be operated by villagers independently, while investing in high-standard homestays and cultural projects that require a large investment, to set an example and develop demonstration projects.

Next Steps

Firstly, step up efforts to promote Huanglongxian Tea Village as a tourist destination. Relying on unique natural and cultural landscapes, folk customs, traditional handicrafts and other tourist resources, the village will work closely with tourism e-commerce platforms and modern logistics enterprises, strengthen online and offline publicity and brand marketing, apply more information technology to the rural tourism industry, and promote the integrated development of tourism, agriculture and Internet. Secondly, advance infrastructure construction. Huanglongxian Tea Village will extend and expand the influence of its tourism industry, build the Xianxia boutique homestay village, and upgrade projects such as the tea culture museum and the children's amusement park. Thirdly, improve tourist services. It will keep the needs of tourists in mind, establish a management and training mechanism for frontline service personnel, improve the level of operation and management, improve the rural tourist experience, build itself into a boutique destination, and continue to inject impetus into income increase through tourism development and rural revitalization.

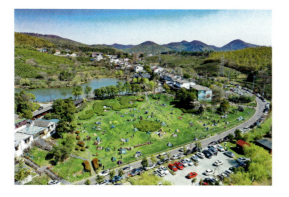

旅游减贫案例故事（中英文双语版）
Best Practices of Poverty Alleviation through Tourism (Chinese-English Bilingual Edition)

江苏省苏州市吴江区谢家路村：
农文旅深度融合助力蚕丝之乡化茧成蝶

收录于《2022世界旅游联盟：旅游助力乡村振兴案例》

摘要

江苏省苏州市吴江区震泽镇谢家路村坚持农文旅深度融合发展，定位低密度、亲情式、高品质的旅居度假，强化共同富裕发展导向，通过与浙江大学周玲强教授领导的旅游团队进行长达八年的陪伴式合作，谢家路村不仅让悠久的蚕桑文化在农村生根，还让多元的发展机遇惠及农民生活，同时让蓬勃的文旅产业推动农业发展，走出了一条"村美业特农民富，水韵桑田稻花香"的内生式乡村振兴发展新路，走出了一条"产业与文化共荣，居民与游客共享，人与自然和谐共生"的乡村旅游高质量发展之路，成为"中国·江村"乡村振兴示范样板。

挑战与问题

谢家路村位于长三角生态绿色一体化发展示范区，是中国历史文化名镇和全国著名蚕丝之乡，全村面积3.949平方千米，户籍人口接近1700人。2016年之前，谢家路仍存在集体经济发展滞后、基础设施落后、"散乱污"现象突出、产业基础薄弱等问题，村民大多外出打工，村里留守的村民基本都在60岁以上。传统蚕桑产业后继无人，亟须转型升级。

措施

1. 坚持生态文明理念，打造绿色低碳环境

近年来，谢家路村已累计腾退了落后工业企业7家，整理出了土地35亩，在尽力保留厂房等设施的基础上，将宝贵的空间资源用于关键项目的建设。横跨周生荡的500千伏高压线有碍观瞻，极大阻碍了美丽乡村建设，为此村里投入高达2700万元将其整体迁移。搬迁高压线的同时，还对周生荡及入湖河道逐步进行生态修复及清淤，科学规划基础设施建设，实现生活污水接管全覆盖，逐步展现出"村舍相望、水天相接、蚕桑人家"的江南湿地水乡风光。

2. 坚持产业融合理念，精雕甜蜜假日产品

谢家路村以"水韵谢家"为乡村旅游品牌，着力构建第一、二、三产融合发展的资源生长型产业体系，创新打造甜蜜假日特色主题产品，以蚕式慢生活吸引长三角中高端客群。通过盘活利用近50亩厂房土地、300亩林地和80户民居，开展乡村主题招商，先后签约了莫干山民宿会长单位西坡酒店管理公司、大理网红农场柴米多团队等国内行业翘楚，投资运营民宿、餐饮、文旅项目，将旧农舍、厂房、仓库、改建成网红餐厅与精品民宿。

3. 坚持数字赋能理念，形成多元化销售链

一是从"客人"到"主人"，谢家路生态农业合作社推出"预定承包"的新型订单销售方式，通过把消费者转变成农产品的"主人"，实现真正的"私人定制"，让消费者获得更多的乡村体验。二是从"线下"到"线上"，农产品、太湖雪蚕丝制品等都已通过抖音等平台进行网络直播销售。本地企业太湖雪在疫情期间实现电商销售额超1.5亿元。三是从"田间"到"舌尖"，震泽镇湿地片区设立了多个采摘、垂钓等活动体验点，从亲自采摘到现场制作，再到品尝美味，丰富多彩的农业体验活动，让震泽的乡村旅游更具特色、更有滋味。

成效

谢家路村，一个以蚕桑为主题的村落，通过丝绸创意的巧妙融合，成功推动了乡村度假产业的升级，实现了"一颗茧的升华"的奇迹。借助农文旅融合和文创赋能，一朵小小的"蚕茧花"将一颗蚕茧的价值从原先的0.1元提升到10元，效益放大近100倍。近年来，谢家路村共接待游客超50万人次，成为远近闻名的网红度假村。2020年以来，受新冠疫情影响，震泽镇湿地片区紧紧抓住了本地游客，谢家路村的人均到访率、逗留时间、人均消费客单价较2019年明显上升，2020年游客量20万人次以上，旅游收入935万元。截至2021年，谢家路村共吸纳本村312人就业，还吸引了32人返乡创业。2021年谢家路村村级收入790万元，村级可支配收入522万元，

村民人均收入达3.9万元，成为内生式发展促乡村振兴标杆村。

经验与启示

1. 高位度创新乡村经营管理模式

树立系统运营观，建立政府、村集体、村民与工商资本等多方协作联动机制。震泽镇湿地片区的四个村委会共同出资1000万元，设立了苏州震泽湿地资源管理有限公司，以统一的标准对区域内村民的闲置房屋、林地等资源进行有计划地收储、修缮、改造、出租及合作经营，为每户村民带来了平均3万元的年租金收入。震泽湿地文化旅游发展有限公司承担相关政府性投入的工程项目建设，同时开展湿地片区运营招商工作。谢家路村依托太湖雪蚕桑文化园等现代农业基地，深度推进"公司+基地+农户"的发展模式，引导农民由传统的田间劳动者向农业工人转变。

2. 高质量形成开放兼收的利益链接机制

居民成为谢家路乡村旅游发展的建设者、文明生活的传递者和丝绸文化的带入者，实现"居民与乡村共成长"是谢家路村可持续发展的核心要义。太湖雪采用"公司+基地+农户"的模式，带动谢家路村在内的近500名60岁以上的蚕农转型为新农人，打造出震泽镇独具特色的"蚕娘经济"新气象。高质量的乡村发展除了生产、生活、生态，还有生意，要看老百姓有没有在做生意。在震泽镇本地，百丽餐饮创始人谭桂芳的餐吧、孙晓东的摄影工作室和张文轩的民宿都成为谢家路村的网红打卡地，居民的深度参与让疫情之下的谢家路村展示出内生式发展的独特韧性。

3. 高能级打造"陪伴式"智库平台

震泽镇以开放合作的姿态和久久为功的精神与浙江大学共建"最强大脑"智库平台。该平台采用"教授工作室+民宿"的创新运营模式，并结合"工作室+博士硕士课堂"的产学研模式，成功打造了"浙大旅游研究所震泽基地"，成为乡村振兴的示范项目。震泽镇与浙大团队以陪伴式的合作模式编制完成了《震泽中国特色小镇申报方案》《江苏·震泽丝绸文化风情小镇总体规划》《震泽省级湿地公园总体规划》《谢家路特色田园乡村旅游规划》等规划，为谢家路村项目的顺利实施提供了坚实的保障。

下一步计划

谢家路村将持续深入推进内生式发展模式，打造全国乡村旅游重点村、低碳旅游示范村，成为长三角蚕桑主题微度假目的地。一是做好提升规划，编制环谢家路乡村旅游提升规划，聚焦本地与周边游市场，突出绿色、低碳，联合震泽省级湿地公园及周边乡村，形成联动发展模式，进一步完善谢家路旅游产品与配套设施，建立低碳旅游服务体系。二是推动文旅融合，进一步盘活村庄闲置资源，加大新业态招商力度，保护传承村落蚕桑文化，精雕"甜蜜度假"品牌，用好本地人力资源，吸纳更多原住村民员工，助其实现家门口致富，成为全国乡村旅游重点村。三是推动数字赋能，借助数字科学技术，助力村庄智慧智能化。采用"互联网+旅游+乡村"的模式，推出具有交互性、沉浸式的体验型旅游产品，打造数字型文旅乡村。

Xiejialu Village, Wujiang District, Suzhou City, Jiangsu Province:

In-depth Integration of Agriculture, Culture and Tourism Rejuvenating the Home of Mulberry Silk

Included in *WTA Best Practices of Rural Revitalization through Tourism 2022*

Abstract

Xiejialu, a village in the town of Zhenze Town, Wujiang District of Suzhou City, Jiangsu Province, adheres to the in-depth integrated development of agriculture, culture and tourism, and positions itself as a low-density, friendly and high-quality staycation and holiday-making destination. It strengthens the development orientation toward common prosperity. After eight years of close cooperation with the tourism development group led by Prof. Zhou Lingqiang of Zhejiang University, it has allowed the long-standing sericulture industry to take root, benefited farmers with diverse development opportunities, and boosted agricultural development with the flourishing cultural and tourism industry. Thus it has explored a new path of endogenous rural revitalization that features "beautiful, prosperous villages with specialty industries including mulberry-tree and paddy-rice growing". It has blazed a path of high-quality development of rural tourism that features "industrial and cultural prosperity, development fruits shared by villagers and tourists, and harmonious coexistence between man and nature". It has become a model of rural revitalization in Wujiang District.

Challenges and Problems

Xiejialu Village, located in the Demonstration Zone for Integrating Ecological Conservation and Green Development in the Yangtze River Delta, is a famous historical and cultural town in China and a famous silk production base in China, with an area of 3.949 square kilometers and a registered population of nearly 1,700. Before 2016, Xiejialu Village suffered from such problems as lagging development of the collective economy, backward infrastructure, a messy, dirty living environment and a weak industrial foundation. Most of the villagers had left for work, and those who remained were basically over 60 years old. In particular, the traditional sericulture industry was in severe shortage of workers and needed to be transformed and upgraded.

Measures

1. Adhere to the concept of ecological conservation and create a green and low-carbon environment

In recent years, seven backward industrial enterprises have been vacated in Xiejialu Village, and 35 *mu* of land cleared and leveled. While preserving existing facilities including plants, the village has reserved valuable space for the construction of key infrastructure. The 500 kV high-voltage line across Zhousheng Lake blocked the view, and greatly damaged the image of a beautiful countryside. So the village spent 27 million yuan moving the line. At the same time, it conducted ecological restoration and desilting at Zhousheng Lake and the rivers entering the lake, and scientifically planned infrastructure construction to realize full coverage of domestic sewage pipelines, and gradually create a beautiful water town landscape typical in the south of the Yangtze River.

2. Adhere to the concept of industry integration and develop boutique holiday-making products

While building the "Shuiyun Xiejia" tourism brand, Xiejialu Village strives to build a resource-growing industrial system that integrates the development of the primary, secondary and tertiary sectors, develop holiday-themed products, and attract medium and high-end customers in the Yangtze River Delta with slow life. It has put nearly 50 *mu* of factory land, 300 *mu* of forest land into good use and engaged 80 households, and organized investment promotion activities. It has signed contracts with Xipo Hotel Management Co., Ltd., the president unit of Mogan

Mountain Homestay Association, and Chimido, an Internet-famous farm in Dali, among other domestic market leaders, to invest in and operate homestays, restaurants and cultural and tourism projects. Old farmhouses, factories, warehouses are turned into Internet-famous restaurants and boutique homestays.

3. Adhere to the concept of digital empowerment and diversify the sales channels

Firstly, turn consumers from guests into hosts. Xiejialu Eco-agricultural Cooperative has introduced the order-based sale method which gives consumers the say over what to grow and how to grow in the fields, to get the truly customized products and have a real rural experience. Secondly, the sale of products is expanded from offline to online. Xiejialu Village has organized live-streaming sale sessions for its agricultural products and Taihu Snow silk products. At the height of the Covid-19 epidemic, Taihu Snow, a local enterprise, registered e-commerce sales revenue of over 150 million yuan. Thirdly, develop the farm-to-table tour. Visitors can try picking and angling in many places in the wetland area of Zhenze Town, and then prepare themselves a delicious meal with what they harvested from fields or ponds. The colorful farming experience activities have made Zhenze Town's rural tours more distinctive and enjoyable.

Results

The incorporation of mulberry silk elements has upgraded the rural tourism industry, creating a miracle in the sericulture-themed Xiejialu Village. Through the integration of agriculture, culture and tourism, and empowerment by culture and creativity, the price of tiny silkworm cocoons has soared from 0.1 yuan each to 10 yuan each, an increase of nearly 100 times. In the past three years, Xiejialu Village has received more than 500,000 tourists, becoming an Internet-famous resort. Since 2020, due to the Covid-19 impact, Zhenze Town has mainly relied on local tourists. In 2020, the per capita visit rate, length of stay and per capita consumer spending of Xiejialu Village increased significantly compared with 2019, it received more than 200,000 tourists, and earned 9.35 million yuan from tourism. By 2021, Xiejialu Village had hired 312 local villagers, and attracted 32 migrant workers to return and start business. In 2021, the income of Xiejialu Village was 7.9 million yuan at the village level, the disposable income 5.22 million yuan, and the per capita income of villagers reached 39,000 yuan, making it a model village for endogenous development and rural revitalization.

Experience and Inspirations

1. Reform the rural operation and management model

Xiejialu Village has established the concept of systematic operation, and a multi-party cooperation mechanism that involves the government, village collectives, villagers and industrial and commercial capital. The four village committees in the wetland area of Zhenze Town have jointly invested 10 million yuan to establish Suzhou Zhenze Wetland Resources Management Co., Ltd. It has developed uniform standards, and taken over, repaired, transformed, leased and operated the idle houses, forest land and other resources in the area in a planned way, bringing an average annual rental income of 30,000 yuan to each villager. Zhenze Wetland Culture & Tourism Development Co., Ltd. is responsible for engineering construction of projects invested by the government, and attracting investment. Based on modern agricultural bases such as Taihu Snow Silkworm Culture Park, Xiejialu Village has advanced the development model that brings together the company, bases and farmers, and guided farmers to change from traditional field workers to "agricultural workers".

2. Establish an open and inclusive interest linkage mechanism of high quality

The key to the sustainable development of Xiejialu Village is to engage the residents in rural tourism development, the spread of social and civility and the silk culture. By working with agricultural bases and farmers, Taihu Snow has engaged and trained nearly 500 sericulturists over the age of 60 from Xiejialu Village and nearby villages, creating a unique sericulture economy in Zhenze Town. To promote high-quality rural development, we need not only to improve the ways of production and life, and ecological environment, but also create a thriving business scene. Tan Guifang's dining bar, Sun Xiaodong's photography studio, and Zhang Wenxuan's homestay have all become Internet-famous sites. The in-depth participation of residents has demonstrated the unique resilience of endogenous development in Xiejialu Village during the epidemic.

3. Build a high-level cooperative think tank platform

With the attitude of open cooperation and the eye on long-term benefits, Zhenze Town jointly built

the think tank platform with Zhejiang University, and adopted the innovative operation model that combines professor studios and homestays, and the cooperation model that involves studios, doctoral and postgraduate programs. The Zhenze Base of Academy of Tourism and Leisure, Zhejiang University has become a demonstration project of rural revitalization. Through close cooperation, Zhenze Town and the team of Zhejiang University co-prepared Zhenze's Application Plan for the Status of Town with Chinese Characteristics, Master Plan for Developing Zhenze Silk Culture Town in Jiangsu, the Master Plan for Zhenze Provincial Wetland Park, and Xiejialu Plan for Developing Rural Tourism with Characteristics, to guide and support the implementation of the Xiejialu project.

Next Steps

Xiejialu Village will continue to push forward the endogenous development model, build national key villages for rural tourism and demonstration villages for low-carbon tourism, and become mini-vacation destinations with the theme of sericulture in the Yangtze River Delta.

Firstly, it will make the improvement plan. It will plan for improving rural tourism around Xiejialu Village, with focus on the local and surrounding tourism markets, highlight green and low-carbon elements, and form a coordinated development model that involves the Zhenze Provincial Wetland Park and surrounding villages. It will further improve tourism products and supporting facilities, and establish a low-carbon tourist service system.

Secondly, it will promote the integration of culture and tourism. It will put idle resources in villages into better use, double down on attracting investment to new business forms, protect and inherit the sericultural culture of villages, build up the brand of "Sweet Holiday," make good use of local human resources, and create more jobs for local villagers so that they can work and earn money in their hometown. The purpose is to build Xiejialu Village into a state-level key village for rural tourism.

Thirdly, it will promote digital empowerment. Digital technology will be used to make rural tours more intelligent. By bringing Internet, tourism and the countryside together, it will launch interactive, immersive and experiential tourism products and build a digital village with a booming cultural and tourism industry.

旅游减贫案例故事（中英文双语版）
Best Practices of Poverty Alleviation through Tourism（Chinese-English Bilingual Edition）

浙江省丽水市景宁畲族自治县大均乡：
文旅融合绽放"五朵畲花"

收录于《2021世界旅游联盟：旅游助力乡村振兴案例》

摘要

　　浙江省景宁畲族自治县大均乡始终坚定"绿水青山就是金山银山"的发展理念，优化空间布局和环境协调融合，着力构建全域旅游发展新格局，逐步形成三杆大均、水韵泉坑、田园伏叶、畲寨李宝、古驿新庄"五朵畲花"齐绽放的局面，有效促进了民族区域社会经济又好又快发展，让乡村旅游成为乡村振兴新引擎，为旅游助力乡村振兴提供了生动的畲乡样本。

挑战与问题

浙江省景宁畲族自治县大均乡面积86平方千米，森林覆盖率89%，下辖5个行政村60个自然村，户籍人口4479人，全乡畲族人口占总人口的35.4%。大均乡民族风情浓郁，自然景观秀丽，历史文化悠久，但是由于地处浙西南山区，交通等基础设施滞后，旅游资源开发程度较低，年轻劳动力大量外出务工，一些农户人走屋空，甚至一度出现"空心村"现象。如何壮大农村产业基础、吸引年轻群体回流、激活乡村振兴，成为大均乡发展所面临的难题。

措施

1. 传承古风古韵

大均乡5个行政村中，现有省级历史文化古村落重点村1个、一般村2个。为加强对自然景观和文物古迹的保护，大均乡坚持修旧如旧，投资1900余万元开展历史文化古村落建设，目前已完成大均、伏叶、李宝等3个村的保护和提升工程。充分利用古村、古宅、古道、古树等资源打造有品质的景观，如将大均村村口有着1100余年历史的古樟打造成"迎客唐樟"景观；充分开发利用大均古街，将其打造成为"中国畲乡之窗"景区的核心景点，让古风古韵成为大均乡的金字招牌。

2. 坚持村景融合

依托各村资源优势，按照"一村一品"进行村庄规划，还原农村"望得见山，看得见水，记得住乡愁"的本色，成功打造三杆大均、水韵泉坑、田园伏叶、畲寨李宝、古驿新庄"五朵畲花"齐绽放的局面。目前，全乡5个行政村中，已建成大均村、李宝村、伏叶村三个3A级景区村。

3. 联动串联景点

大均乡距县城13千米，为进一步完善交通圈，特地开通了专班公交，每日在县城和大均乡之间往返

28趟，以满足游客和当地居民的出行需要。此外，还有畲乡绿道从县城延伸至大均泉坑村，有效串联起了景宁县城、凤凰古镇、畲乡之窗景区等区块，形成美丽小环线，游客可利用公共自行车、观光游览车等绿色交通工具沿绿道骑行游玩。畲乡绿道不仅提升了大均乡的知名度和美誉度，也串联起了沿线大量的优质民宿，有效带动民宿经济的发展，成为助推村民致富和乡村振兴的"致富绿道"。

4. 引导民宿迭代升级

大均乡创新民宿发展模式，全面提升民宿产业的核心竞争力，打造大均乡"品质旅游，民宿担当"这一金名片，走出了一条从无到有、从弱到强、从俗到精的嬗变之路。伏叶村民宿农家乐产业完成了从"食在农家的1.0版本"到"兼具旅游六要素的2.0版本"，再到"有文化有内涵的3.0版本"的三次升级，形成了高、中、低农家乐民宿发展层次，可同时满足不同消费层次、不同文化背景游客的需求。

5. 开发畲族特色业态

大均乡以国家级非物质文化遗产代表性项目畲族

婚俗体验为核心，定期举办农民畲歌赛、梅山西瓜节、伏叶民族乡村百花大会、畲族渡亲节、洗井泼水节、彩虹跑、花园跑、中国畲乡国际铁人三项赛等畲族传统民俗活动；为游客增设民族书屋、畲画馆、畲药馆、畲族服饰体验馆、畲绣馆、畲茗工坊等文化场馆和工艺品游购馆。

6. 发展特色水域经济

大均乡立足优越水环境，积极打造浮伞漂流、天然沙滩烧烤、游泳池、露营目的地等休闲游基地，推出泼水节、冬泳联赛等品牌亲水活动，深度开发水上瑜伽康养、桨划游船体验等项目。以涉水救援业务培训为载体，大均乡成功吸引了 IRIA 国际搜救教练联盟急流救生训练基地和省消防应急救援基地入驻，以此成为全国四个水域救援培训基地之一。

成效

1. 民生保障、百姓安居

大均乡强力推进危旧房改造工作，共拆改十余栋幢危房；完成畲乡之窗国家 4A 级景区的提升工作；5 个行政村均全面完成饮用水达标提标建设工程，实现村村饮用水安全；大力推进垃圾分类，推进垃圾分类试点乡镇建设，新建四分类垃圾收集房 8 个、户内外二分桶 2498 套，建立垃圾兑换回收便民服务站 1 个；全面完成厕所革命，完成全乡 15 个公厕的修缮工作；配齐各类设施 168 个，粉刷墙面 500 多平方米。大均乡实现了乡村的美丽蜕变，人居环境不断改善，群众和游客的幸福感倍增，满意度不断提升。

2. 集体增收，百姓致富

2020 年大均乡 5 个行政村全年实现村集体经济总收入 182.33 万元，较 2014 年增长 169%。农村人均可支配收入 25377 元，较 2014 年增长 132%。2020 年全乡接待游客 148.12 万人次，实现营业收入 2379.74 万元，其中农家乐民宿营业收入 1650 万元。

3. 文旅支撑，产业兴旺

大均乡现已形成以文旅产业为支柱，以水域救援产业、精品研学产业为补充的生态产业集群。全乡共有民宿 33 家，农家乐 58 家，餐位数 3000 余个，床位数 557 张，其中金宿 2 家、银宿 2 家。水域救援

产业规模不断扩大，2018年至今，水域救援培训基地已完成各类培训120余班次，培训学员3500余人，创收培训费用2100余万元。

大均乡产业振兴和畲乡之窗效应已经初步显现，先后入选"省级旅游风情小镇""浙江省4A级景区镇"等。

公路边、铁路边、水边、山边、城边、村边等六个区域进行洁化、绿化、美化，旨在实现城美、村美、房美的目标）""厕所革命""美丽乡村建设"等重点工作，开展环境整治，进一步改善景区周边乡村的基础设施、公共服务和人居环境，夯实乡村旅游发展基础。开展美丽庭院、花样农家评比等活动，最大限度地调动村民的积极性，激发村民的"爱美之心"。深入开展"五水共治（治污水、防洪水、排涝水、保供水、抓节水）"，清理河道逾15千米，清理出垃圾逾45吨，治理黑臭河1条、小微水体5条。通过4A级景区乡镇的建设，让大均乡的广大群众和外地游客共享发展成果，主客之间真正实现了"美人之美、美美与共"。

3. 融合数字技术

作为全市首个开通5G网络的乡镇，大均乡创新推出智慧旅游导览系统，在为游客提供智能化自助服务的同时，也为农家乐民宿提供了宣传推广的平台。例如，伏叶村根据田园定位，发展数字农业休闲体验园，打造鱼菜共生的现代化农业实践体验、数字共享菜园；泉坑村引入采用以色列MABR技术进行污水处理的系统，不仅可在旅游旺季满足全村污水处理的需求，还将污水处理点打造成乡村景观，供村民和游客休憩游览，此乃全市首例。诸多相关举措全面提升了旅游服务品质，实现"数字+旅游"，使数字赋能乡村振兴。

经验与启示

1. 深挖文化底蕴

大均乡畲族文化底蕴深厚，文化传统悠远，人文优势鲜明，是畲族文化的重要聚集地。如李宝村以"魅力畲寨"的理念指导规划，紧抓"风情畲寨"的定位，助推洞宫畲王寨项目开工建设，带动村庄整体发展。

2. 改善人居环境

大均乡依托"小城镇综合整治""六边三化三美（在

下一步计划

旅游助力乡村振兴之路，任重而道远。在新时代的新起点上，大均乡将继续集水域救援、山林经济和文旅融合的产业发展于一体，以"5G通信+智慧生态治理平台"和"两山金融服务+乡村生态信用评定体系"为技术与金融的"两翼"，推动"两山"理论在大均乡域的创新实践，加速融合发展，拓宽致富之路，进一步彰显民族文化特色，全力打造乡村振兴畲乡新样板。

Dajun Township, Jingning She Autonomous County, Lishui City, Zhejiang Province:

Integration of Culture and Tourism for Development of Five Villages with the She Nationality Characteristics

Included in *WTA Best Practices of Rural Revitalization through Tourism 2021*

Abstract

In adherence to the concept of "lucid waters and lush mountains are invaluable assets", the Dajun Township, Jingning She Autonomous County, Lishui City, Zhejiang Province, has optimized the layout and coordinated integration of its environment. It hopes to build a new all-for-one tourism template by gradually advancing the common development of the five villages with the cultural and traditional elements of the She ethnic group. Emphasis on education, business and punting in Dajun Village, charming Quankeng Village, idyllic Fuye Village, the She minority village — Libao Village, and the ancient courier station — Xinzhuang Village are among those covered in a comprehensive plan which has advanced the sound and rapid social and economic development of ethnic regions. It has effectively developed rural tourism into an efficient engine for rural revitalization and facilitated rural revitalization through the development of the elements of the culture, tradition, heritage and history of the She minority group.

Challenges and Problems

With an area of 86 square kilometers and a forest coverage rate of 89%, Dajun Township includes 60 natural villages with five administrative villages. With a registered population of 4,479 people, 35.4% of which consists of the She ethnic minority. Despite rich native customs, picturesque natural landscapes and long history and culture in the township, it has limited infrastructure, including transportation and tourism resources due to its mountainous location in the southwest Zhejiang Province. A large number of young laborers have opted to work outside. Some peasant households left their hometowns and a number of "hollow villages" have appeared. Strengthening the rural industrial base has been a problem in the township, along with attracting the young to return to their hometowns so they can become proud participants in the development and vitalization of the rural lifestyle.

Measures

1. Ancient styles and charm

Among the five administrative villages in the township, one is a provincial-level historical and cultural ancient village and two are general villages. To enhance the protection of natural landscapes, cultural relics and historical sites, the township has invested more than 19 million yuan in the construction of historical and cultural ancient villages and restored them to their original form. Dajun Village, Fuye Village and Libao Village have been successfully protected and upgraded. Resources like ancient villages, ancient residences, ancient roads, and ancient trees have been fully utilized to create

quality landscapes. For example, the 1,100-year-old ancient camphor tree at the entrance of Dajun Township has been developed into a guest-greeting venue. What's more, the ancient streets of Dajun Township have been thoroughly explored as a core scenic spot of the "Window of the She Township in China", making antique styles and charm into the township's "golden brand".

2. Emphasize the village-scenery integration

In reliance upon the advantages in resources of each village, in accordance with concept of "one product for one village" in village planning, and to restore rural nature as a "wonderland bearing lucid waters, lush mountains and nostalgia", remarkable achievements have been achieved in the five villages with the She Nationality characteristics that emphasizes education, business and punting in Dajun Village, charming Quankeng Village, idyllic Fuye Village, the She minority village — Libao Village, and the ancient courier station — Xinzhuang Village. Currently, among the five administrative villages in the township, three are 3A-level scenic villages — Dajun, Libao and Fuye.

3. Improve the connectivity of scenic spots

As Dajun Township is 13 kilometers away from the county, 28 shuttle buses from the county to the

township are opened daily for residents and travelers alike. In addition, the She Township greenways extend from the county to Quankeng Village of Dajun Township, and connect such blocks as Jingning County, Phoenix Town, and the scenic spot of the "Window of the She Township". This forms a beautiful loop line, allowing tourists to ride along the greenways through green transport such as public bicycles and sightseeing buses. The greenways have boosted the popularity and reputation of the township and increased the interconnectivity of quality B&Bs along the route. This has substantially improved the economic development of the B&Bs and created a "rich greenway" for rural revitalization and the prosperity of the villagers.

4. Guide the iterative upgrading of B&Bs

Through the innovative development of B&Bs and enhancement of the industry's core competitiveness, the township has created its golden brand of "Quality Tourism, B&Bs Responsibility" which has evolved from scratch, from weakness to might and from basic to refined. The agritainment industry of Fuye Village has been upgraded from its basic version 1.0 in food supply to version 2.0 which integrates the six elements of tourism. From there, it has been elevated to version 3 which signifies a wealth of cultural products and offers. The gradual elevation of scale has stratified B&Bs at high, middle and low levels, allowing it to the varying demands of tourists at different consumption levels and with different cultural backgrounds.

5. Develop the She nationality native businesses

Dajun Township takes the She Nationality wedding experience as the core of the national intangible cultural respresentative heritage and regularly holds traditional customs such as singing contests of farmers, Watermelon Festival of Meishan Village, Hundred Flowers Conference of Fuye Village, Bride Escorting Festival of the She Nationality, Well-Washing and Water-Sprinkling Festival, Color Run, Garden Run, and the International Triathlon Race of Chinese She Township are regularly staged. Moreover, cultural venues and craft shopping halls, ethnic bookstores, She Nationality galleries, She Nationality medicine halls, She Nationality costume experience halls, She Nationality embroidery halls, and She Nationality tea workshops are also set up for tourists.

6. Develop the local water economy

Leisure activities such as rafting, natural beach barbecues, swimming pools and camps are created based on the superior water environment. Similarly, it can be optimized to launch the Water-Sprinkling Festival, Winter Swimming League and

other branded activities and projects such as water yoga rehabilitation and boat paddling. The IRIA rapids life-saving training base and the provincial fire emergency rescue base are also successfully launched in the township with water rescue training as a carrier, making the township one of the four such training bases in China.

Results

1. Improve people's livelihood for peaceful life

The township has demolished and renovated more than ten dilapidated houses through vigorous renovation; upgraded the national 4A-level scenic spot of the "Window of the She Township"; five administrative villages have been covered by up-to-standard safe drinking water; promoted the construction of pilot towns for garbage sorting, resulting in the building of eight four-class garbage sorting rooms and 2,498 two-class bins indoors and outdoors. A garbage exchange and recycling service station has been established; 15 public toilets in the township have been renovated for a complete overhaul; 168 facilities of various types have been equipped, and more than 500 square meters of walls have been painted. Significant improvements have been achieved in the township, resulting in a desirable living environment that boost the satisfaction and well-being of locals and tourists alike.

2. Increase the collective income to enrich people

In 2020, the five administrative villages of the township registered a total income from their collective economy of 1.8233 million yuan, an increase of 169% over 2014. The per capita

disposable income in rural areas was 25,377 yuan, an increase of 132% over 2014. The township received 1,481,200 tourists and registered an operating income of 23,797,400 yuan in 2020, 16.5 million yuan of which came from the operating income of agritainment and B&Bs.

3. Support cultural tourism for a flourishing industry

The township has now formed an ecological industry cluster with cultural tourism as the pillar and water rescue and quality research and education industries as the supplement. In the township there are 33 B&Bs and 58 sites for agritainment, with more than 3,000 seats for meals and 557 beds, including two gold-ranked B&Bs (high-end standard) and two silver-ranked B&Bs (ordinary standard). The scale of the water rescue industry continues to expand.

Since 2018, more than 120 training courses have been completed in the training base. More than 3,500 people have completed their training, at a total cost of more than 21 million yuan.

The industrial revitalization and the success of the window of the She Township has generated accolades and awards. It has been successively honored with such titles as a provincial-level town with tourism styles and a 4A-level scenic town in Zhejiang Province.

Experience and Inspirations

1. Maximize the cultural theme and messaging

The township is an important showcase for the She culture and traditions. The Libao Village, for example, guided the planning on the concept of a "charming She minority village", and highlighted the positioning of a "fascinating village", to facilitate the construction of the Donggong Shewangzhai project (located at Libao Village) and the overall development of villages.

2. Improve human settlements

Relying on the key tasks outlined in the "Comprehensive Renovation of Small Towns", "Six Sides, Three Improvements, Three Beauties (to achieve the goal of beautiful cities, villages, and houses at the roadside, railway side, waterside, mountain side, city side, and countryside through cleaning, greenery, and embellishment)", "Toilet Revolution", and "Beautiful Village Construction", environmental enhancements have been implemented for the improvement of rural infrastructures, public services and human settlements in the surrounding scenic spots of the villages and the consolidation of the developmental foundation of rural tourism. Activities such as the appraisal of beautiful courtyards and diverse rural residences are also conducted to spark the enthusiasm of villagers and stimulate their passion for beauty. The work on "Five Water Governance (involving sewage treatment, flood control, drainage, water supply, water conservation)" is implemented. As a result, more than 15,000 meters of riverways and more than 45 tons of garbage have been cleared and one fouling river and five small and micro waters have also been controlled. The construction of 4A-level scenic towns has helped the masses of Dajun Township and tourists are benefiting from the development. They have become active partners and participants in "appreciating the culture of others for the prosperity of human civilization" between hosts and guests.

3. Integrate digital technologies

As the first township with 5G coverage in the city, the Dajun Township has launched a smart tour guide system to offer tourists intelligent self-service and also provide a publicity platform for the agritainment and B&Bs. For example, the Fuye Village has developed experiential digital agricultural leisure parks based on its positioning as an "idyllic development". It has provided a modernized agricultural experience in aquaponics, and also created digitally shared vegetable gardens. The Quankeng Village has introduced the city's first sewage treatment system using the Israeli MABR technology. This can adequately meet the demands for sewage treatment during the tourist season. It has built sewage treatment plants in rural landscapes for the use of villagers, visitors and tourists. This has improved the service quality of tourism and achieved the goal of "digital + tourism" and rural revitalization through digital empowerment.

Next Steps

There is still a long way to go for rural revitalization through tourism development. At the threshold of the new era, in adherence to the integration of the industrial development of waters rescue, forest economy and culture-tourism integration with "5G communications + smart ecological governance platform" and "two mountains financial services + rural ecological credit rating system" as the "two wings" of technology and finance, the township will promote the innovative practice of the "Two Mountains Theory", accelerate integrated development, pave the road to prosperity, demonstrate the native ethnic culture and strive to create a new model for the rural revitalization of the She Township.

旅游减贫案例故事（中英文双语版）
Best Practices of Poverty Alleviation through Tourism（Chinese-English Bilingual Edition）

浙江省杭州市淳安县下姜村：
打好脱贫攻坚战，旅游减贫成效明显

收录于《2020世界旅游联盟：旅游减贫案例》

摘要

　　下姜村位于浙江省杭州市淳安县西南部，在2003年至2007年期间，时任浙江省委书记的习近平多次来到淳安县下姜村进行实地考察。如今，这个当年远近闻名的贫困村打了翻身仗，通过改善村庄面貌、培育富民产业等措施，村子成了"绿富美"的典范。从山坞变身产业基地，从贫困村变为美丽乡村，下姜村生动演绎了"绿水青山就是金山银山"的发展理念，为新时代农村如何与绿水青山和谐共荣、农民如何富有安康树立了现实标杆。

挑战与问题

村子贫困的原因可以总结为以下几点。一是区域因素，早在2002年以前，下姜村是个远近闻名的贫困村，曾流传着"土墙房、烧木炭、半年粮，有女莫嫁下姜郎"的民谣。该村地处淳安西南山区，早年从下姜村到县城，乘车需要3小时，交通极为不便。1998年，村民人均收入只有1860元，贫困发生率达到50%以上。村民基本在家务农，由于人均耕地面积少，劳动力严重闲置，全村只有599亩土地，而且多为沿山改造的田地，粮食产量低。二是产业因素，下姜村地处山区，土地分布非常散乱，这使得发展农业难以形成规模化效益。三是意识因素，村民小农意识根深蒂固，开拓创新意识欠缺，对接市场意识不足，对政府的依赖性较强。

措施

1. 积聚发展力量（2002年以前）

1998年村党支部进行了改选，新一届班子带领干部把"整治歪风邪气、发展效益农业、开展村庄整治"作为重要工作来抓，下姜村的基层组织、村庄管理、产业发展等逐步走上有序化道路。

2. 加强新农村建设（2002—2014年）

一是加强基层设施建设，全面推进"三改一建（危房改造、厕所改造、村容村貌改造、建设文化广场或基础设施）"以及拆危拆旧等工作，大力改善村庄面貌，初步奠定了下姜村新农村雏形，先后完成240幢46391平方米的房屋立面整治和墙体美化。落地"二十四节气"景观小品和"下姜村，梦开始的地方"文化，完成隧道口景观改造等。二是培育富民产业，农业产业方面，引进社会资本，成立农业开发有限公司，流转土地近500亩，发展葡萄、草莓、桃子三大现代休闲农业产业，基本形成"七月葡萄、腊月草莓、三月桃花"的"四季果园"。乡村旅游方面，全村共培育民宿23家，床位398个，落地了水上游乐、水上实景演出、石头画坊、狮城酒坊、打铁铺、打麻糍等业态，成功创建国家3A级旅游景区。三是优化村庄治理，探索网格管理，将社会治理的触角延伸到每一个家庭单元，实现村民信息动态掌握、矛盾纠纷动态管控，提高村庄平安指数，让"小事不出村、大事不出镇"。

3. 实施乡村振兴（2014年至今）

启动实施下姜村及周边地区乡村振兴发展工程，编制"1+4"规划，全面推动"五个振兴"，并取得较好成效。一是山更青，水更绿，环境更美丽。全面完成下姜3个自然村的环境整治，建成源塘和薛家源2个市级精品村，"心无百姓莫为官——习近平同志帮扶下姜村"展示馆和下姜村及周边地区乡村振兴发展规划展示馆完成装修布展。二是村更旺，地更肥，业态更丰富。土地从"分散经营"走向"流转经营"，亩均效益提高了。目前下姜村民宿数量达到33家，532个床位。三是心更齐，人更活，思想更解放。不断凝聚干部和群众的发展共识，牢固树立起"破旧立

新""绿水青山就是金山银山"等新思想、新理念。

成效

1. 集体增收，百姓致富

下姜村2019年全年实现农村经济总收入8256万元，较2014年同比增长131.4%。村集体经济收入202.56万元，较2014年增长462.7%。农村人均可支配收入39693元，较2014年增长145.5%。下姜景区全年共接待游客73.3万人次，其中住宿游客5.2万人次，实现旅游经济收入4451万元。下姜村先后获评"全国基层民主法治村""中国美丽休闲乡村""全国生态宜居十佳村"等荣誉，乡村振兴展示馆获评"浙江省社会科学普及基地"。

2. 产业兴旺，生产方式革新

下姜村现形成以乡村旅游产业为支柱，规模效益农业为补充的生态产业集群。截至2019年，村庄共有民宿33家，其中精品民宿6家。这些民宿共提供532个床位，其中精品民宿有107个床位。此外，村庄还设有2000余个就餐座位。2019年下姜人家餐厅和红色培训基地也相继落成。

3. 民生保障、百姓安居

自2014年以来，下姜村强力推进危房治理工作，共拆改十余栋危房，同时已经全面完成村庄外立面整治工程和村庄内部绿化工程。在全面完成村庄主体改造和农户截污纳管之后，下姜村又实施生猪、家禽退养政策，并扎实推进垃圾分类收集。此外，下姜村还建成了一座老年食堂，70周岁以上老人由村庄补贴可便宜就餐，基本建成居家养老机制。

经验与启示

1. 激发主体意识是核心

村庄发展的主体永远是广大群众。在欠发达地区，群众谋发展的主体意识往往不是很强，而群众是村庄脱贫的奋斗者和受益者，激发老百姓对发展的渴望和致富前景的信心尤为重要。在有一部分人享受到发展红利之后，村集体要做好宣传工作。每一个老百姓都有致富的愿望，但是他们缺乏的是致富的信心和致富的技能。村集体要提升产业服务能力，村两委干部要

提高业务水平和服务意识，共同营造一个有利于发展的良好氛围。

2. 推动产业发展是抓手

下姜村脱贫攻坚的成功，关键在于其始终以发展产业为重要抓手。脱贫攻坚的最终目标就是要让村集体富起来，让老百姓的袋子鼓起来。因地制宜制定产业方向是下姜村取得成功的关键。在制定产业前进方向时，下姜村考虑到其地处山区、土地资源匮乏，不能像平原地区一样大规模发展效益农业。同时，结合村庄拥有的红色历史文化和依山傍水、邻近千岛湖的自然资源优势，下姜村决定发展以红色和绿色为主题的乡村旅游。在乡村旅游成为支柱性产业之后，下姜村除了要积极发展本地产业，还要招商引资引进外来主体到本地经营。

3. 紧扣民生福祉是关键

发展的根本目的是增进民生福祉。在村庄总体经济水平得到提升的同时，要做好民生服务工作，社会养老体系的加快构建、人居环境的提升、生态资源的保护都必须作为关键性工作开展。抓好民生工程，对稳定百姓情绪有着很重要的作用，而且对今后的发展有着潜移默化的作用，特别是在农村工作当中，这一点尤为明显，只有百姓的获得感得到了提升，才能更好地开展工作。

下一步计划

一是将下姜村打造成习近平新时代中国特色社会主义思想的教育基地；二是将其打造为浙江省"大花园"建设的关键组成部分；三是致力于构建乡村振兴中三生融合的富丽家园。下姜村与周边村庄实现协调发展、同频共振，"产业、村庄、人口"的融合已经初见成效，"居住、产业、旅游"的共同发展也开始显现。下姜村高水平地实现了全面小康，基本建成了"乡村振兴示范区"。到2020年年底，核心区农村经济总收入达到20亿元；省级现代农业园区建设顺利推进，农林牧副渔总产值达到2.32亿元。核心区农户生活垃圾源头分类率达到100%；村集体经济可分配收入达到450万元以上；规划区内农村居民人均可支配收入达到全省平均水平。

旅游减贫案例故事（中英文双语版）
Best Practices of Poverty Alleviation through Tourism (Chinese-English Bilingual Edition)

Xiajiang Village, Chun'an County, Hangzhou City, Zhejiang Province:

Winning the Battle Against Poverty, and Achieving Remarkable Progress in Poverty Alleviation through Tourism

Included in *WTA Best Practices in Poverty Alleviation through Tourism 2020*

Abstract

Xiajiang Village is located in the southwest of Chun'an County, Hangzhou City, Zhejiang Province. From 2003 to 2007, Xi Jinping, then Secretary of the CPC Zhejiang Provincial Party Committee, paid several visits to Xiajiang Village in Chun'an County. Now, this village, which was well-known for its impoverishment at that time, has brought about an upswing. Due to such measures as improving the appearance of the village and cultivating industries that enrich villagers, it has been built into a "green, rich and beautiful" village. Its transformation from a level ground in the mountains to an industrial base as well as from a poverty-stricken village to a beautiful village vividly interprets the practice of "lucid waters and lush mountains are invaluable assets", and sets a benchmark in practice regarding how rural villages and lucid waters and lush mountains can live in harmony and co-prosperity in the new era, and how to increase income and enhance health of farmers.

Challenges and Problems

The causes resulting in poverty of this village can be summarized as follows. Firstly, regional factors. As early as 2002, Xiajiang Village was a well-known impoverished village. There was a folk song which goes "avoiding marrying a man in Xiajiang Village where houses are built with earth walls, charcoal is used for warm-keeping and cooking, and the food could only last for half a year". The village is located in the southwest mountainous area of Chun'an County. In early years, the transportation was extremely inconvenient and it took 3 hours to travel from Xiajiang Village to the county. In 1998, the per capita income of villagers was only 1,860 yuan, and the poverty headcount ratio reached more than 50%. The villagers basically did farm work at home. Due to the small area of arable land per capita and severely idle labor force, there was only 599 *mu* land across the village, most of which was farmland rebuilt along the mountain, with a low grain yield. Secondly, industrial factors. Located in a mountainous area, this village features scattered distribution of land, making it difficult to form efficient agriculture on a large scale. Thirdly, awareness factors. Villagers have a deep-rooted small peasant mentality, insufficient awareness of pioneering, innovation and market connection, and strong dependence on the government.

Measures

1. Converge powers for development (before 2002)

After re-election of the village party branch in 1998, the new team led various cadres to focus on "rectifying unhealthy tendencies, developing profitable agriculture, and carrying out village remediation" as important tasks, guiding the grassroots organization, village management, industrial development and other aspects of Xiajiang Village gradually onto an orderly track.

2. Enhance efforts in new rural construction (2002-2014)

Firstly, strengthen the construction of basic facilities. Comprehensively promote "three reconstructions and one construction (reconstruction of dangerous houses, reconstruction of toilets, reconstruction of village appearance and environment, construction of cultural squares or infrastructure)", the demolition of old and dilapidated houses and other work, and vigorously improve the appearance of the village, initially laying the new rural prototype of Xiajiang Village. The facade renovation and wall beautification of 240 houses with an area of 46,391 square meters were completed successively. The "Twenty-Four Solar Terms" featured landscape and the culture of "Xiajiang Village: a place where dreams begin" were built, and the landscape transformation of tunnel entrances was completed, etc. Secondly, foster industries that enrich villagers. In terms of agricultural industry, it introduced social capital to establish an Agricultural Development Co.,

Ltd. Nearly 500 *mu* land was transferred to develop three modern leisure agriculture industries of grape, strawberry and peach, basically forming an "orchard in four seasons" with "peach blossom in March, grapes in July and strawberry in December". In terms of rural tourism, a total of 23 homestays with 398 beds were built. A series of commercial activities such as water recreation, water live performances, stone painting workshop, lion city wine workshop, iron workshop, and Fried glutinous pudding making, etc., were launched, successfully creating a national 3A-level scenic spot. Thirdly, optimize village governance. Explore grid management, extend social governance to every family unit, dynamically grasp villagers' information, implement dynamic management and control of conflicts and disputes, and improve the village's safety index, so that "villagers can handle small matters within the village and large matters within the town".

3. Implement rural revitalization (2014 to now)

Initiate and implement the rural revitalization and development project in Xiajiang Village and surrounding areas, and formulate the "1+4" plan to comprehensively promote "rural revitalization in five aspects", delivering good results. Firstly, the mountains are lusher, the water is more lucid,

and the environment is more beautiful. Complete environmental improvement of 3 natural villages in Xiajiang, build two municipal-level boutique villages in Yuantang and Xuejiayuan, and the exhibition hall entitled "Officials with the masses as the center - Comrade Xi Jinping helped Xiajiang Village", and complete the decoration and setup of the rural revitalization development and planning exhibitions of Xiajiang Village and surrounding areas. Secondly, the villager is more prosperous, the land is more fertile and the business format is more diverse. Transform from "decentralized management" of land to "circulation management", increasing the benefits per mu. There are currently 33 homestays with 532 beds in Xiajiang Village. Thirdly, villagers' hearts are linked together, and their mindset is more flexible and liberated. Constantly gather the development consensus of cadres and the masses, and firmly establish new ideas and concepts such as "breaking the old and establishing the new", and "lucid waters and lush mountains are invaluable assets".

Results

1. Income increase of all villagers and the masses

In 2019, Xiajiang Village realized a total rural economic income of 82.56 million yuan, an increase of 131.4% over 2014. The village's collective economic income reached 2.0256 million yuan, an increase of 462.7% over 2014. The rural per capita disposable income was 39,693 yuan, an increase of 145.5% over 2014. The Xiajiang scenic area received a total of 733,000 tourists throughout the year, including 52,000 accommodation tourists, recording a tourism economic revenue of 44.51 million yuan.

Xiajiang Village has been granted the titles of "National Grassroots Democracy Village under the Rule of Law", "China's Beautiful Leisure Village", "One of Top Ten National Ecological and Livable Villages", etc. The Rural Revitalization Exhibition Hall was rated as the "Social Science Popularization Base of Zhejiang Province".

2. Thriving businesses and innovative production modes

Xiajiang Village has now formed an ecological industrial cluster with the "rural tourism industry" as the pillar and scaled profitable agriculture as the supplement. As of 2019, there had been 33 homestays in the village, including 6 boutique homestays; a total of 532 beds, including 107 boutique homestays; and more than 2,000 dining places. In 2019, the Xiajiang Family Restaurant and Red Training Base were completed.

3. People's livelihood and comfortable housing is ensured

Since 2014, Xiajiang Village has vigorously promoted the management of dilapidated houses, with more than ten dilapidated houses demolished and renovated. Moreover, the renovation project of the village facade and the internal greening project have been fully completed. After completing the renovation of the main part of the village and the sewage interception and containment of peasant households, Xiajiang Village also implemented the campaign to stop breeding pigs and poultry, and steadily promoted the classification and collection of garbage. In addition, a canteen for the elderly was built, where old people aged above 70 can eat cheaply with a subsidy from the village. A home-based pension system was basically in place.

Experience and Inspirations

1. The core is to stimulate the subject consciousness

The main body of village development is broad masses. In underdeveloped areas, people often lack the subject consciousness of seeking development. The masses are the strugglers and beneficiaries of poverty alleviation in the villages, so it's particularly important to inspire people's desire for development and their confidence in the prospect of getting rich. After some people have enjoyed the development dividend, the village collective should do a good job in publicity. For every citizen with a desire to get rich, what they lack is the confidence and skills in this regard. It's necessary for the village collective to improve industrial services, and for the cadres of the party branch committee and autonomous committee to improve their business level and service awareness, so as to form a good atmosphere for promoting development.

2. The means is to promote industrial development

The key to the success of getting Xiajiang Village out of poverty alleviation always lies in industrial development. In the final analysis, the fight

an important role in stabilizing people's mood, and has a subtle effect on future development, especially in rural work. Only when people's sense of gain is improved can related work be carried out more effectively.

Next Step

Firstly, build it into an education base for Xi Jinping Thought on Socialism with Chinese Characteristics for a New Era; secondly, take it as an important node in the construction of Zhejiang Big Garden; thirdly, build a prosperous and beautiful village for rural revitalization and integration of life, production and ecology.

Realize coordinated development and resonance at the same frequency between Xiajiang Village and surrounding villages, basically complete the integration of "industry, village and villagers", initially promote common progress in the mode of "residence, employment and tourism", help villagers live a high-level well-off life in all aspects, and basically build a "rural revitalization demonstration zone". By the end of 2020, the rural economic gross income in the core area reached 2 billion yuan; the construction of provincial-level modern agricultural parks were advanced smoothly, and the total output of agriculture, forestry, animal husbandry, side-line production and fishery reached 232 million yuan. The source classification rate of domestic waste from peasant households in the core area reaches 100%; the distributable economic income of the village collective exceeds 4.5 million yuan; the per capita disposable income of rural residents in the planned area reaches the province's average level.

against poverty is to help the village collective get rich, and increase the income of villagers. The key to the success of Xiajiang Village is to determine the industrial direction based on local conditions. When setting the industrial direction of Xiajiang Village, it's necessary to take into account that Xiajiang Village is located in a mountainous area and lacks land resources, unfeasible to develop profitable agriculture on a large scale like a plain area. In light of the revolution genes in its history as well as its natural resource advantages of nestling under a mountain and near a river and adjacency to Qiandao Lake, it's decided to develop the revolution and green rural tourism. After developing rural tourism into a pillar industry, the village should attract investment and introduce external entities to operate locally, in addition to actively developing local industries.

3. The key is to stick closely to people's well-being

The basic purpose of development is to benefit people. While improving the overall economic level of the village, it is necessary to do a good job in provision of people's livelihood services, accelerate the construction of a social pension system, improve the living environment, protect ecological resources and carry out other key work. To implement various projects that can improve people's wellbeing plays

安徽省黄山市歙县卖花渔村：
"盆景+"产业融合新模式赋能乡村振兴

收录于《2022世界旅游联盟：旅游助力乡村振兴案例》

摘要

安徽省黄山市歙县卖花渔村紧密围绕传统产业，积极探索"盆景+旅游""盆景+节庆""盆景+电商"的产业融合新模式，不断拓宽传统盆景产业边界，推动产业升级，坚持非物质文化遗产和创新创意赋能乡村振兴。全力建设有产业、有活力、有颜值、有创意、有乡愁的"新安山居图"村落景区，走出了一条独具特色的乡村振兴之路。

问题与挑战

卖花渔村地处新安江上游皖南山区的丘陵地带，以旅游和盆景产业为主。村庄距离县城约20千米，其中大部分路段为山路，游客游览观光以及盆景买卖运输均较为不便。全村下辖9个村民组236户共641人，土地总面积3800亩（其中国家公益林面积2268亩，占总面积的59.6%），村民人均用地较少，影响苗木的替代式培养，盆景产业发展受到极大限制。

措施

1. 守住乡村魂

为壮大非遗传承队伍，卖花渔村积极实施"名师带徒"育才工程，通过组织名师与徒弟结成教学小组，确保徽派盆景技艺的传承不息。目前村内已组建起一支由86人构成的徽派盆景技艺专业队伍，该队伍融合了老年、中年和青年三代人才。其中徽派盆景技艺国家级传承人1人、省级传承人1人、市级传承人12人和县级传承人15人。同时，为弘扬良好的乡村民风，卖花渔村乡贤积极收集资料撰写村志、村歌以及村规民约，村歌《卖花渔村好风光》荣获"中国村歌十大金曲"金奖。

2. 展现乡村美

近年来卖花渔村按照"快旅慢游"的理念，从项目布局入手，积极整合资金1000余万元，相继完成从卖花渔村至瀹岭坞村循环道的拓宽、卖花渔村到夏坑古道的修复、旅游标识牌的完善、停车场和旅游公厕的建设、村庄环境整治等项目，提升了村庄的整体美观度。同时围绕卖花渔村徽派盆景小镇建设，相继编制了徽派盆景产业发展规划、卖花渔村文旅产业提升策划方案等，在产业发展、公共服务、宣传营销等方面进行综合谋划，进一步优化卖花渔村发展空间格局。

3. 做好"盆景+"模式

为实现盆景产业绿色发展，卖花渔村大力推行"盆景+旅游"模式，重点实施"移一培一"套种培育模式，最大程度利用现有土地资源，并引导村民在裸露山地培育梅桩，让房前屋后增绿添绿。每年春季都有无数游客慕名而来，只为一睹这梅花盛放的美景，卖花渔村万亩梅花也多次获得央视推荐。此外，卖花渔

村还推行了"盆景+节庆"模式，坚持以花为媒，连续成功举办十届梅花摄影节活动，有效促进盆景产业和乡村旅游融合发展，实现产业兴旺、村民增收。2022年梅花艺术节带动民宿农家乐产业收入累计80余万元，盆景收入200万元。为拓宽盆景销售渠道，卖花渔村还积极推行"盆景+电商"模式，以花开盆景专业合作社和协会为纽带，引导盆景生产经营户加入联合经销组织，通过抖音直播、云直播、淘宝销售等方式，将卖花渔村盆景销往全国。目前，村内建有农村电子商务综合服务站点1家，经营网店40余个，盆景网络年销售额突破500万元。

成效

卖花渔村先后获得"全国美丽乡村示范村""全国'一村一品'示范村""全国生态文化村""中国传统村落""安徽省特色景观旅游村""安徽省徽派盆景发源地""安徽省乡村旅游示范村"和"安徽省农村电商示范村"等荣誉称号，卖花渔村徽派盆景技艺先后被列入安徽省首批非物质文化遗产名录和国家级非物质文化遗产代表性项目名录。2021年，卖花渔村经济总收入达3824万元，同比增长5.57%，人均收入达到2.5万元，同比增长8%。村内先后涌现出40多户专业盆景销售户，他们的年销售额突破2300万元。村内现有农家乐和民宿15家，年旅游接待量为8万人次，解决周边村民就业500人次。2022年一季度卖花渔村乡村旅游实现集体经济收入84万元。

经验与启示

1. 以"两山"理论为本，厚植生态文明之基

卖花渔村始终坚持践行"两山"理论，不断夯实生态文明建设基础，推动"绿水青山"向"金山银山"持续转化，建设人与自然和谐共生的中国美丽乡村，为其乡村旅游产业发展提供了重要保障。多年来，卖花渔村以盆景花卉种植为主的高端绿化，从村庄、山地出发，向周边村镇拓展、延伸，形成了点、线、面一体的生态绿色乡村旅游自然景观和人文景观，成为集中展示中国徽派盆景文化的乡村旅游目的地。

2. 以徽州文化为根，厚筑文化传承之魂

博大精深的徽州文化，是卖花渔村中国徽派盆景文化传承与发展的根和魂，与徽派盆景技艺一起融入了广大村民血脉，世世代代传承不息。现有29名国家、省、市、县级徽派盆景技艺传承人，以发挥中华优秀传统文化优势和加强中国徽派盆景文化保护传承为己任，大力实施系列"名师带徒"工程，倾情讲述中国徽派盆景非遗传承故事，集中展现了中国徽派盆景文化的魅力和活力，成为乡村旅游核心吸引物中最为亮丽的一张名片。

3. 以全民共享为核，拓宽融合发展之路

卖花渔村充分利用产业服务团队、村级网格员和致富带头人，积极筑牢农户信息基础和盆景产业发展基础，营造良好的乡村发展环境。卖花渔村以花卉盆景专业合作社为平台，引导调动群众参与乡村旅游发展的主动性、积极性，努力探索"盆景专业合作社+市场+社员"的利益联结机制，通过研发文创产品、培育电商产业、开展技术培训等方式，提升乡村旅游品质、徽派盆景制作技艺，进一步扩大销售渠道，实现村集体经济发展与村民增收双赢。

下一步计划

卖花渔村将进一步发挥乡村模式的可持续性，强化文化、艺术与旅游融合，努力将卖花渔村打造成独特乡村旅游IP。

一是做优文旅产业。围绕非遗传承人各自特点，加快徽派盆景展示园以及精美庭院建设；建设徽派盆景技艺培训研发中心，加强技术交流，拓展盆景产品样式，适度发展小微盆景，增强市场竞争力。

二是突破要素制约。加快推进村循环道拓宽改造，新建停车场，规范进村换乘车辆运营，有效缓解行车堵、停车难问题。采用土地流转、土地入股等形式，加大与周边乡镇合作力度，为盆景产业发展整合更多土地资源。

三是打造乡村旅游综合体。积极践行"双微"（微改造、微创意）提升行动，盘活村集体闲置资产，打造集徽派盆景文化旅游、休闲、餐饮、住宿为一体的乡村旅游综合体。引进特色高端民宿业态，统一规范农家乐服务质量，打造特色服务品牌，大力提升旅游品质，解决"留不住人"的问题。同时，利用线上线下合作的方式，创新丰富卖花渔村梅花节内容，吸引更多的摄影和户外运动爱好者前来走古道、赏梅花、摄美景、品徽韵。

Maihuayu Village, Shexian County, Huangshan City, Anhui Province:

"Potted Landscape +," A New Model of Industry Integration to Empower Rural Revitalization

Included in *WTA Best Practices of Rural Revitalization through Tourism 2022*

Abstract

Focusing on traditional industries, Maihuayu Village of Shexian County, Huangshan City, Anhui Province, actively explores a new model of integrating potted landscape with tourism, festivals and celebrations, and e-commerce industries, constantly expands the boundaries of traditional potted landscape industry and promotes its upgrading, and continues to empower rural revitalization with intangible cultural heritage and creative ideas. It is going all out to build a dynamic, beautiful, nostalgia-evoking mountainous countryside that has thriving businesses and creativity along the Xin'an River, and has blazed a unique path to rural revitalization.

Problems and Challenges

Maihuayu Village is located in the hilly area of the upper reaches of Xin'an River in southern Anhui province, and lives on tourism and the potted landscape industry. The village is about 20 kilometers away from the county seat, and most of the roads leading to it are dirt roads, making it inconvenient for tourists to come or to transport potted plants out of it. Under its jurisdiction are 236 households of 641 people divided into 9 villager groups, living on a land spanning 3,800 *mu* (including 2,268 *m*u of national non-commercial forest, accounting for 59.6% of the total). The per capita land area is so small that replacement of seedlings is restricted, so is the development of potted landscape industry.

Measures

1. Preserve the intangible cultural heritage

In order to cultivate more intangible cultural heritage inheritors, Maihuayu Village actively promotes the "master-apprentice" program, and pairs masters with apprentices to pass down Huizhou-style techniques of potted landscape. At present, the village has a professional team of 86 dedicated to the Huizhou-style potted landscape, including the young, the middle-aged and the old. Among them is one certified by the state, one by the province, 12 by the municipality, and 15 by the county. At the same time, to advocate upbeat social etiquette and civility, the villagers actively collected materials to record the history of the village, write village songs and code of conduct. In particular the village song *The Beautiful Scenery of Maihuayu Village* won the gold medal of "Top Ten Village Songs in China."

2. Show the beauty of the countryside

In recent years, embracing the trend of "arriving tourist attractions faster and staying longer," Maihuayu Village has raised more than 10 million yuan and started to improve the project layout. It has widened the microcirculation road leading to Yuelingwu Village, restored the ancient path to Xiakeng, and improved tourist signs, parking lots

and public toilets for tourists. The overall village environment is better. At the same time, in its drive to become a specialty town of Huizhou-style potted landscape industry, Maihuayu Village has formulated the development plan for the potted landscape industry, the plan for upgrading the cultural and tourism industry, and plans to coordinate industrial development, public services, and marketing efforts, and further optimized the spatial layout of development.

3. Launch the "potted landscape +" initiative

Firstly, "potted landscape + tourism". In order to achieve green development of the potted landscape industry, Maihuayu Village vigorously promotes the interplanting cultivation model of "transferring one, cultivating one" to make maximum use of existing land resources. It nudges villagers to cultivate plum trees in the exposed mountain areas, in front or at the back of their houses. Now its plum trees have covered nearly 10,000 *mu* and when they bloom in spring, they would attract countless tourists. Secondly, "potted landscape + festivals and celebrations". With blossoms as the medium, the village has held ten editions of the plum blossom photography festival in a row, effectively promoting the integrated development of potted landscape industry and rural tourism, leading to the prosperity of the industry and income increase for villagers. In 2022, the Plum Blossom Art Festival generated revenue of over 800 thousand yuan for the B&B and agritainment industry and 2 million yuan from the sale of potted plants. Thirdly, "potted landscape + e-commerce". In order to expand the sales channels, the village, with the help of specialized flower and potted plant cooperatives and associations, guides the potted plants growers to join the joint distribution network and sell the

potted plants to the rest of the country by means of live streaming on Douyin, Cloud Live Streaming and opening stores on Taobao, etc. At present, the village has one comprehensive e-commerce service station, more than 40 online stores, and the annual sales of potted plants online exceeded 5 million yuan.

Results

Maihuayu Village has been awarded such titles as "National Beautiful Demonstration Village", "National Demonstration Village for the 'One Village, One Product' Program", "National Model Village in Ecological Progress", "Traditional Village of China", "Anhui Provincial Tourism Village with Special Landscape", "Birthplace of Huizhou-style Potted Landscape", "Anhui Provincial Demonstration Tourism Village" and "Anhui Rural E-commerce Demonstration Village". Its Huizhou-style potted plant cultivation techniques have been included in the first batch of intangible cultural heritage of Anhui province and the list of national intangible cultural heritage items. In 2021, the village registered an income of 38.24 million yuan, up 5.57% year-on-year, and the per capita income of 25,000 yuan, up 8%. It has more than 40 households specialized in growing potted plants, with annual sales exceeding 23 million yuan. There are also 15 farm stay and B&B service providers, which can receive 80,000 visitors a year and have created 500 jobs for villagers. In the first quarter of 2022, the community collective generated 840,000 yuan from tourism.

Experience and Inspirations

1. Embrace the theory that lucid waters and lush mountains are invaluable assets, and consolidate the foundation for ecological conservation

Maihuayu Village has always adhered to the theory that lucid waters and lush mountains are invaluable assets, constantly consolidated the foundation for ecological conservation, promote the sustainable transformation of "lucid waters and lush mountains" into "invaluable assets", so as to build a beautiful countryside where man live in harmony with nature, and provide an important guarantee for the development of rural tourism. Over the years, the high-end potted landscape industry has stretched from the village, the hills, to surrounding villages and towns, and formed a natural landscape of eco-friendly rural tourism and a cultural landscape, making Maihuayu Village a destination showcasing the essence of Huizhou-style potted landscape.

2. Take root in the huizhou culture and inherit the traditional cultural heritage

The profound Huizhou culture is the root and soul of the Huizhou potted landscape culture that is being inherited and advocated in the village. The Huizhou culture and the Huizhou-style potted landscape techniques are deeply rooted in the village and have been passed down from generation to generation. At present, there are 29 national, provincial, municipal and county-level inheritors of the Huizhou-style potted landscape techniques. They take it as their duty to promote Chinese excellent traditional culture and strengthen the protection and inheritance of the Huizhou-style potted landscape techniques. The village is vigorously promoting the "master-apprentice" program, tells the story of this intangible cultural heritage, shows its charm and vitality, and makes it the trump card of its core tourist attractions.

3. Broaden the path to inclusive development by centering on sharing development fruits with the people

Making full use of the industrial service team, village-level grid workers and entrepreneurship-based poverty relief leaders, the village is actively building the information base of farmers and the development base of the potted landscape industry, to create a good environment for rural development. Via the platform offered by specialized potted landscape cooperatives, the villagers are mobilized to engage in rural tourism. The village is striving to explore the interest linkage mechanism that brings together specialized potted landscape cooperatives, the market and cooperative members. By developing cultural and creative products, cultivating the e-commerce industry and offering technical training, it has improved the quality

of rural tourism and the techniques of Huizhou-style potted landscape, expanded sales channels, boosted the development of the village collective and increased villagers' income.

Next Steps

The village will continue to play to the sustainability of the rural development model, strengthen the integration of culture, art and tourism, and strive to build its reputation as a unique tourist destination.

1. Strengthen the cultural and tourism industry

Catering to the characteristics of the intangible cultural heritage inheritors, it shall move faster to build the Huizhou-style Potted Landscape Garden and exquisite courtyards; build the Huizhou-style potted landscape technology training and R&D center, strengthen technology exchange, diversify the portfolio of potted landscape products, and develop micro and small-sized potted plants as appropriate to enhance market competitiveness.

2. Break away from the constraints of factors

It will accelerate the expansion and renovation of the village's microcirculation roads, build new parking lots, regulate the administration of incoming shuttle vehicles, and effectively ease traffic congestion and address the shortage of parking spaces. By means of land use right transfer and pooling of land as shares, it will strengthen cooperation with surrounding towns and townships, and consolidate more land resources for the development of potted landscape industry.

3. Build a rural tourism complex

The village will actively encourage and promote micro-renovations and micro-innovations, put the idle assets back into use, and build a rural tourism complex that offers Huizhou-style potted landscape tours, leisure, catering and accommodation services. It will introduce high-end B&B services with unique features, standardize the service quality of farm stays, build specialty service brands, and vigorously improve the quality of tourism so that visitors are willing to lengthen their stay and come back. Meanwhile, it will enrich the contents of the Plum Blossom Festival with both online and offline activities, and attract more photography and outdoor enthusiasts to hike along the ancient path, appreciate the beautiful plum blossoms, take photos of beautiful scenery and immerse in the local culture and lifestyle.

旅游减贫案例故事（中英文双语版）
Best Practices of Poverty Alleviation through Tourism (Chinese-English Bilingual Edition)

福建省龙岩市上杭县古田红色旅游区：
红色旅游高质量可持续发展

收录于《2021 世界旅游联盟：旅游助力乡村振兴案例》

摘要

福建省龙岩市古田红色旅游区积极探索红色旅游发展路径，推动旅游区高质量发展，不断完善和丰富红色旅游产品体系、管理服务体系、基础设施体系、公共服务体系，进一步调动广大群众参与红色旅游的积极性，不断增强其满意度，将古田特有的红色文化资源优势有效转化为发展优势，增强红色旅游对当地经济社会发展的辐射带动作用。

挑战与问题

福建省龙岩市古田红色旅游区是著名的古田会议召开所在地。虽然古田红色旅游越来越火爆,但红色旅游开发的深度远远不够,大部分游客到古田仅限于参观古田会议会址。古田旅游需发挥红色文化旅游的优势,依托古田国家5A级旅游景区综合提升项目和红色文化教育培训等举措,将古田打造成中国著名的红色文化研学旅游目的地、教育培训基地和国际红色文化旅游交流中心。同时,推进红色文化产业和绿色生态产业协同发展,带动文旅康养产业跨越式发展。

措施

1. 强化古田旅游品牌打造

一是优化游览环境。古田红色旅游区实施了景区(点)提升改造、古田会议旧址群修葺、景区交通改造提升、景区夜景提升等工程项目,持续建设旅游要素,完善景区服务功能,景区面貌焕然一新。二是探索建设古田梅花山文旅康养试验区。为推进红古田、绿步云深度融合,打造"红绿"交相辉映、城乡融合、农文旅融合发展的现代化文旅康养小城市,2019年11月起,古田红色旅游区创新体制机制,通过公司化运营模式来打造古田梅花山,旨在将其打造成"新时代老区苏区振兴发展样板",进一步提升古田影响力。2020年,梅花山文旅康养试验区的多个项目正式落地。三是构建古田红色旅游和环梅花山生态旅游经济圈。在古田镇原有的基础上优化城市布局,并在古田镇筹划新集镇中心、学校和医院,按县级城市标准打造古田小城市。目前,古田已初步明确三大片区,即古田镇、梅花山区和小池片区,全面发展红色旅游、森林康养、地质旅游、研学培训、温泉养生和度假居养。

2. 强化古田培训品牌打造

一是着力打造专兼职多元体系的师资队伍,强化社会大师资观念,构建"三位一体"的师资格局,借助古田基地合作院校的优质师资力量、教学资源和先进的教学管理经验,实现师资共享。二是加强现场教学点建设,按照"六个有"(有供学习观摩的主场,有报告解读场所,有基本设备,有专兼职解说人员,有文字和影像通稿资料,有规章制度)标准,逐步推进并提升全市100个现场教学点的功能水平,打造现场教学基地集群,并充分挖掘各教学点的听点、看点、悟点和卖点,串点成线,策划不同专题、不同板块的精品培训线路。三是加大对外交流力度,目前,中央和国家机关工委、财政部、公安部、国家公务员局、国防大学等156家部门单位在古田设立了教育培训基地或教学点。四是加快培训基地建设,提升培训承载力,积极推进古田干部学院二期、古田干部学院步云分院、古田红色宾馆、福建农商行古田党校等四个培训基地的建设。五是拓宽培训市场,积极在厦门、广州、深圳、上海等地开设运营中心,2019年承接培训班5196期,学员约24.13万人次,与去年同期相比增加了21.6%。

3. 强化古田研学品牌打造

依托古田国家5A级旅游景区及周边红色、绿色、客家、畲族等文化资源,古田县充分发挥全国爱国主义教育基地、全国中小学生研学实践教育基地、港澳青少年游学基地的品牌优势,着力打造面向全国青少年的综合实践基地,加快推进全国中小学研学营地的建设。目前,已初步形成了以古田县为点向外辐射的研学实践教育网络,规划设计了小学、初中阶段的研学实践教育线路,高中阶段研学线路正在考察中。截至2019年年底,古田县累计为龙岩市境内中小学校提供了40期近3800人次的免费公益研学活动。古田红色培训现已实现对全国31个省、自治区、直辖市的全覆盖，中央各部委、央企、民企、高等院校等160多家单位在古田县设立了教育基地或教学点，每年吸引超过20万人次前来参加培训。截至2019年年底，古田县共接待研学实践教育培训班280余批次，学生约8.5万人次。

成效

红色旅游的发展，迅速带动了古田县当地餐饮、住宿、服务等相关行业的发展，吸引了一大批有实力的企业入驻，其中"四上"（规模以上工业企业，资质等级建筑业企业，限额以上批发、零售、住宿、餐饮业企业，规模以上服务业企业）企业16家，包括文化休闲旅游、研学旅游、党性教育培训、养生休闲、购物、商务会展、餐饮、节庆等8种服务业态，提高了当地群众的生活水平，造福当地百姓。如今千米古田街和万米古田路上，有三星级以上标准酒店3家，中档舒适型宾馆快捷酒店13家，特色红军客栈、农家乐民宿33家，总床位约2000张；各类餐饮店100余家，可同时容纳12000人就餐。沿路沿街100多家商铺琳琅满目，立面统一改造为青砖灰瓦，道路统一铺设为沥青路面，招牌统一用新式材料制成，路灯统一设计为火炬状……呈现出一派欣欣向荣的景象。作为"最美乡村"的五龙村，借助毗邻古田会议会址的优势，结合红色旅游，发展生态和乡村旅游，形势喜人，民宿、农家乐和红军客栈人来人往，热闹非凡。据不完全统计，古田红色旅游实现直接就业1000余人、间接就业5000人；景区群众收入有五成源于旅游。通过发展红色旅游，古田当地形成了一系列旅游产业链，周边村民的收入翻了好几番，村里建起了图书室、篮球场和公园，丰富和方便了村民生活，全村还栽种了油菜花、荷花等，使得四季风景如画，人民幸福安康。

经验与启示

1. 活动创新

开展"走出去、请进来、送上门、勤服务、善创新"等多种多样的教育活动，每年举办10次以上的临时展览，组织宣传小分队巡回宣讲，并派出专业人员开设讲座近500场次。举办奥运火炬传递仪式、激情广

场大家唱、全国青少年青春歌会、全国红色旅游经典巡礼、2021年上杭"红古田"半程马拉松等诸多活动；开展"古田会议万里行"，在新疆昌吉、呼图壁和江苏省茅山新四军纪念馆举办"古田会议——党和军队建设史上的里程碑展览"；在福建省海峡民间艺术馆举办"古田会议90周年红色文化展"；在澳门举办"客家精神文化展"。

2. 内容创新

古田（吴地）红军小镇通过开展"十个一"活动——"当一回红军战士，缅怀革命先烈""听一个红军故事，追忆峥嵘岁月""学一篇主席诗词，陶冶革命情操""唱一首红色歌谣，激发爱国情怀""行一段红军路，重温革命历史""煮一顿红军饭，体验艰苦岁月""打一场模拟战，接受战争洗礼""开一次运动会，激发人体潜能""写一篇红色征文，传承红色基因""领一枚荣誉勋章，争做时代新人"，让中小学生在重温革命历史、体验艰苦岁月的过程中追忆峥嵘岁月，激发爱国情怀，争做时代新人。影视作品《红色摇篮》《古田会议》《古田1929》《寻访铸魂之路——走进古田》《长征路，新故事——古田专题》《古田军号》等，从平凡的视角去挖掘革命故事、老区故事的爱国主义闪光点，从而实现爱国主义教育和好口碑的双丰收。

3. 形式创新

不断创新古田油菜花节活动内容，耗时一个多月开展汉服周、小红军研学周、非遗文化周、红色快闪周、文创集市周等活动，充分挖掘出红色、绿色、古典、民俗、文创等文化内涵。2019年国庆假期期间，景区通过升国旗、观看国庆盛典、唱支红歌给祖国、瞻仰一次古田会议旧址群、听一回革命历史故事、"我和国旗同框"摄影活动、红色主题蜡像馆探索、为毛主席献枝花、"我在圣地古田，为祖国祝福"万人签名等活动掀起爱国热潮，受到广大游客的欢迎。2021年，景区为喜迎建党100周年，特别举办了油菜花季系列活动，其中红歌快闪周尤为引人注目。同时，景区还倾力打造了古田油菜花欢乐谷，古田梅花山的千亩油菜花海以盛情之姿，献礼中国共产党百年华诞，为古田增添了一抹专属的春季亮色，展现出"圣地党旗红，十里菜花香"的乡村振兴诗画胜景。

下一步计划

继续把古田会议这一"金字招牌"用足、用活，充分发挥红色资源与绿色生态优势，推进红色文化产业和绿色生态产业协同发展，实现"红绿"交相辉映，带动文旅康养产业跨越式发展。通过提升红色旅游景区质量，持续促进周边交通设施提升、生活环境改善，带动景区周边乡村居民，在餐饮业、住宿业、娱乐业、交通业、商业、景区运营参与等方面实现创业富民和就业富民。采取切实可行的措施促进红色旅游与乡村旅游融合发展，实现旅游反哺农业，使农户成为旅游商户、农产品变成旅游商品，实现乡村振兴。

旅游减贫案例故事（中英文双语版）
Best Practices of Poverty Alleviation through Tourism (Chinese-English Bilingual Edition)

Gutian Red Tourist Area, Shanghang County, Longyan City, Fujian Province:

High-Quality Sustainable Development of Red Tourism

Included in *WTA Best Practices of Rural Revitalization through Tourism 2021*

Abstract

Through the active exploration of the quality development path of red tourism, the Gutian Red Tourist Area of Longyan City, Fujian Province, has enriched the red tourism products, management services, infrastructure and public services systems. It has enhanced the enthusiasm and satisfaction of the masses to engage in red tourism and transformed the advantages of red cultural resources with Gutian characteristics into developmental advantages for the enhancement of the radiating and leading role played by red tourism on the local economy.

Challenges and Problems

The Gutian Red Tourist Area is the site of the famous Gutian Conference. Despite the popularity of Gutian red tourism, there is still a long way for its development, as most tourists who visit Gutian are limited to exploring the site of the Gutian Conference. Supported by projects such as the comprehensive upgrade of the national 5A-level scenic spot and red culture education and training, Gutian's advantages in red cultural tourism should be leveraged to develop it into China's most famous research red culture destination, education and training base and international red culture tourism exchange center. At the same time, the coordinated development of the red cultural and the green ecological industries should be promoted to drive the forward leap of the culture, tourism, and healthcare industries.

Measures

1. Strengthen Gutian's tourism brand building

Firstly, optimize the tour environment. Projects in scenic spots such as the upgrade of scenic areas, renovation of the former site of Gutian Conference, traffic improvement and the night view beautification have been implemented. Also, continuous tourism construction and improvement of service functions have brought a new look to the scenic area. Secondly, explore the construction of Gutian Meihua Mountain Culture, Tourism and Healthcare Experimental Zone. To promote the in-depth integration of Red Gutian (red tourism development of Gutian Town) and Green Buyun (green ecological development of Buyun Township) and create a modern city with culture, tourism, and healthcare industries featuring "red and green" interplay, urban-rural integration, and integrated development of agriculture, culture and tourism, the system and mechanism have been innovated since November 2019 to build the Gutian Meihua Mountain through corporate operations, develop it into a "model for the revitalization and development of old revolutionary base areas and Soviet areas in the new era", and further enhance the influence of Gutian Town. In 2020, a number of projects in the experimental zone were officially launched. Thirdly, develop Gutian's red tourism and eco-tourism region around Meihua Mountain. The urban layout has been optimized based on the original, aiming to build new town centers, schools and hospitals in Gutian Town. Small cities of Gutian Town have been developed according to county-level city standards. At present, three areas

have been preliminarily identified—Gutian Town, Meihua Mountain Area and Xiaochi Town Area—for the comprehensive development of red tourism, forest recuperation, geological tourism, research and training, hot springs and leisure vacation.

2. Strengthen the Gutian brand building training

Firstly, more efforts have been made to build a diversified system with full-time and part-time teachers, establish the concept of "professional teacher resources" and build a "three-in-one" pattern of teacher qualifications, realize teacher resources sharing by virtue of excellent teachers, quality teaching resources and advanced teaching management experience of colleges and universities in cooperation with Gutian base. Secondly, construction of on-site teaching sites has been strengthened. According to the "six aspects" standards (there is a home field for learning and observation, a place for report interpretation, basic equipment, full-time and part-time commentators, text and video documents, as well as rules and regulations), one site integrating the standards on the six aspects above can be implemented and functions of the 100 on-site teaching sites in the city have been improved, so as to create a cluster of on-site teaching bases, and fully tap their comprehensive potentials, and then plan boutique training routes with different topics and sectors. Thirdly, intensify foreign exchanges. Currently, 156 departments and units including the State Organs Work Committee of the CPC, the Ministry of Finance, the Ministry of Public Security, the National Civil Service Administration, and the National Defence University PLA China have set up education and training bases or teaching sites in Gutian Town. Fourthly, it's important to accelerate the construction of training bases, enhance training capacity, and promote the construction of the four training bases, namely Gutian Cadre College Phase Ⅱ, Gutian Cadre College Buyun Branch, Gutian Red Hotel, and Fujian Rural Commercial Bank Gutian Party School. Fifth, the training market has been expanded to launch operation centers in Xiamen, Guangzhou, Shenzhen, Shanghai and other places. In 2019, 5,196 training courses were undertaken with about 241,300 trainees, a year-on-year increase of 21.6%.

3. Strengthen Gutian's study tour brand building

In reliance on the cultural resources such as red tourism, green development, Hakka culture, and the She Nationality customs of the national 5A-level scenic spot and surrounding areas, the brand advantages of the national patriotism education base, the national primary and secondary school student

research and practice education base, and the Hong Kong and Macao youth study tour base have been leveraged to build a nationwide comprehensive practice base for youth, thereby accelerating the construction of national primary and secondary school research camps. A research and practice education network radiating outwards with Gutian Town as the core has been formed. Research and practice education routes for primary and secondary schools have been designed, and the research routes for high schools are being examined. As of the end of 2019, a total of 40 free public research activities for nearly 3,800 people had been provided to primary and secondary school students in Longyan City. Also, 31 provinces, autonomous regions and municipalities directly under the central government across the country had been covered with training on Gutian red culture. More than 160 units including central ministries and commissions, central enterprises, private enterprises, and institutions of higher learning had set up education bases or teaching sites in Gutian Town, training over 200,000 people every year. Furthermore, more than 280 batches of training courses on research and practice education had been delivered in the town by the end of 2019, offering training to approximately 85,000 students.

Results

The red tourism development has promoted local catering, accommodation, services and other related industries and attracted a large number of powerful companies, including 16 which were above the designated size (namely Industrial enterprises above designated size, construction enterprises with qualifications, enterprises above designated size of wholesale, retail sale, catering trades and hotels, service enterprises above designated size), covering the services in eight different kind of businesses: cultural and leisure tourism, research tourism, and Party education training, health preservation, shopping, commercial conventions and exhibitions, catering, and festivals, benefiting the local people and improving their living standards. Nowadays, there are three standard hotels above three-star level on the one-thousand-meter Gutian Street and ten-thousand-meter Gutian Road, 13 middle-grade comfortable budget hotels, 33 characteristic Red Army inns and agritainment B&Bs, with a total of about 2,000 beds. Also, there are over 100 eateries which can accommodate 12,000 people for dining at the same time. A wide variety of products are exhibited in more than 100 shops along the road and on the streets, with uniformed blue bricks and gray tiles in the facade, uniformed asphalt pavement on the roads, uniformed new materials for shop signs, and uniformed torch shape for street lights, all of which convey prosperity. Adjacent to the former site of the Gutian Conference and relative to the red tourism development, the Wulong Village, the most beautiful village, has developed ecological and rural tourism, achieving satisfactory results and receiving a flood of tourists in B&Bs, agritainment, and Red Army inns. According to an incomplete statistics,

the Gutian red tourism has directly helped in the employment of more than 1,000 people and indirectly employed 5,000 people. 50% of the income of people on the scenic spot is derived from tourism. Through the development of red tourism, the tourism industry chains have been formed in the town, redoubling the income of surrounding villagers. Moreover, libraries, basketball courts, and parks have been built in the village to enrich the lives of villagers. Also, rape flowers and lotus have been planted presenting to portray a picturesque all-season scenery and a happy and healthy life.

Experience and Inspirations

1. Innovate activities

Various educational activities such as "going global, calling in, delivering door-to-door, providing diligent services, and frequent innovation" have been carried out. Also, more than ten temporary exhibitions are held every year, so publicity teams are organized to promote these exhibitions and professionals are dispatched to deliver nearly 500 lectures. It's necessary to hold such activities as the Olympic Torch Relay Ceremony, Passionate Singing on Squares, National Youth Songs competitions, National Red Tourism Classic Tour, and "Red Gutian" Half Marathon in Shanghang County 2021; carry out the activity of "Ten-Thousand-Li Spread of Gutian Conference Spirit" and hold the exhibition Gutian Conference — A Milestone in the History of Party and Army Building in Changji Hui Autonomous Prefecture and Hutubi County of Xinjiang Uygur Autonomous Region, and Maoshan Mountain New Fourth Army Memorial Hall; hold the Red Culture Exhibition commemorating the 90th Anniversary of the Gutian Conference was held at Fujian Strait Folk Art Museum; and the Hakka Spiritual Culture Exhibition was held in Macao.

2. Innovate content

Through the implementation of the following ten activities in the Red Army town of Gutian (Wudi Community), that is, to be a Red Army soldier in memory of revolutionary martyrs; listen to a story of the Red Army in remembrance of extraordinary times; read a poem by Chairman Mao to nurture revolutionary sentiments; sing one red ballad to inspire patriotism; take a walk along the Red Army road to experience the revolutionary history; cook a meal of the Red Army to experience the hardships; stage a simulated battle to receive baptism of the war; hold a sports meeting to stimulate potentials of the human body; write an article related to the Red Army to pass on the red genes; earn a medal of honor as a pioneer of the time. Primary and elementary school students can experience the revolutionary history and recollect the extraordinary hardships of those years to inspire their patriotism in the new era. Film and television shows such as *Red Cradle, Gutian Conference, Gutian 1929, Explore Roads to Soul Building — into Gutian, Long March Road, New Stories — Gutian Special,* and *The Bugle from*

*Gutia*n have explored the highlights of patriotism in revolutionary stories and stories of old areas from an ordinary perspective, hereby acquiring both patriotism education and "good reputation".

3. Innovate forms

To fully explore red, green, classical, folk custom, and creative cultural themed programs, continuous efforts should be made to innovate the content of Gutian Rape Flower Festival, carry out more than one-month activities such as Han Chinese Clothing Week, Little Red Army Research Week, Intangible Cultural Heritage Week, Red Song Flash Week, and Cultural and Creative Market Week. During the National Day in 2019, scenic spots sparked a wave of patriotism through various activities such as flag-raising ceremonies, watching the National Day celebration, singing revolutionary songs in honor of the motherland, paying tribute to the sites of the Gutian Conference, listening to revolutionary historical stories, participating in the "National Flag and I" photography event, exploring wax museums with red themes, laying flowers for Chairman Mao, and taking part in the "I'm in Holy Gutian, Blessing the Motherland" mass signature campaign. These activities were warmly welcomed by tourists. In 2021, the Red Song Flash Week to celebrate the "100th anniversary of the founding of the People's Republic of China" rape flower blossom season activities were held in the scenic area, and more efforts were made to develop Gutian Rape Flower Happy Valley. The rape blossoms throughout the Meihua Mountain in Gutian cordially paid tribute to the centennial birthday of the CPC, adding a touch of exclusive spring color to Gutian Town and presenting a rural revitalization featuring "red Party flag flying on the holy land permeated with profound rape flower fragrance".

Next Steps

To ensure continuous efforts will be made for the full utilization of the golden brand of the Gutian Conference, advantages of both red and green resources should be given full play and the promotion of the coordinated development of the red cultural industry and green ecological industry. This will ensure the "red and green" interplay and the forward leap development of culture, tourism, and healthcare industries. The quality of red tourist attractions will be further boosted to improve surrounding transportation facilities and living environment, drive rural residents around the scenic area to engage in entrepreneurship and employment in catering, accommodation, entertainment, transportation, commerce, and scenic area operations. Last but not least, practical measures will be adopted to promote the integrated development of red and rural tourism, so it can play an agricultural back-feeding role of turning farmers into tourist merchants and agricultural products into tourist commodities for the realization of its rural revitalization goal.

旅游减贫案例故事（中英文双语版）
Best Practices of Poverty Alleviation through Tourism（Chinese-English Bilingual Edition）

江西省婺源县篁岭村：
共享经济领航与复兴"篁岭晒秋"

收录于《2019 世界旅游联盟：旅游减贫案例》

摘要

　　婺源县篁岭村是近年江西省乡村旅游最耀眼的新星，民进基层会员吴向阳主导的篁岭乡村旅游扶贫富民实践破解了乡村旅游产权纠葛引发的深层难题，构建了发展共享的合意空间，实现了乡村旅游从做产品到做产业、做事业的转变。"篁岭模式"复活了行将消逝的古村，复原了传统农耕文明，复兴了乡民的经济自信、产业自信和文化自信，解决了农民就地城镇化、土地经营权集约流转等难题，使篁岭村人均年收入从旅游开发前的 3500 元，提升为 4 万元；户年均收入从 1.5 万元提升为 13 万元。此外，"篁岭晒秋"已成为"中国最美文化符号"之一，为中国乡村旅游的升级发展提供了领航样本。

挑战与问题

篁岭民俗文化村地处江西省婺源县东端,坐落在婺源县主峰石耳山(海拔1260米)之中,始建于明朝宣德年间,已有500多年的建村史,属典型的山居古村。全村古树环抱、梯田簇拥、风景如画,犹如挂在山坡上的盆景。有关篁岭的摄影作品曾多次获得国际国内大奖。然而,由于地质灾害频发,从1978年开始地方政府便不断鼓励村民下迁。在旅游开发之前,篁岭村已陷入缺水缺电、经济凋敝、居民搬离、房屋失修、梯田荒废的窘境,面临着在"半空心化"中逐渐消亡的命运,因此如何处理好生存与发展的关系,成了村落发展的首要任务。

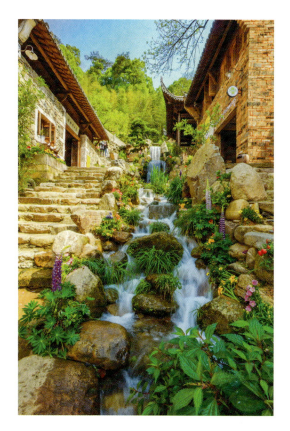

措施

2009年,吴向阳注册婺源县乡村文化发展有限公司,决心投资建设婺源篁岭民俗文化村项目,经过近十年的发展,吴向阳开创了独有的"篁岭模式",并于2018年与中青旅与公司签署战略合作协议,力争将篁岭打造成全国乡村旅游和乡村振兴的标杆,主要措施如下。

1. 通过房屋产权整体置换统合旅游开发经营权

婺源县乡村文化发展有限公司经过与县、镇两级政府协商,投资1200万元,建设安置房68户,老年、单身公寓24套,并配套基础设施,对篁岭村的320名村民进行整体搬迁。2013年,通过招标、拍卖和挂牌,公司获得了古村3.3万平方米建设用地的使用权。在解除地质隐患、改善村民居住条件和农业生产条件的基础上,实现了产权清晰、边界清晰,整体盘活了古村旅游的开发经营权。

2. 通过老建筑异地搬迁复兴古村鼎盛期的风貌

婺源明清徽派老建筑遍布全县各地,2014年,婺源县乡村文化发展有限公司与许村镇政府达成协议,由公司全额出资,将老建筑怡心堂整体搬迁至篁岭进行修缮保护,所有权仍归许村镇政府,公司则拥有经营使用权。开创了老建筑保护利用的"寄养模式"。迄今,篁岭的120多栋老建筑,有20多栋是异地搬迁来的,篁岭因此成为婺源精品老建筑密度最大的村落之一。

3. 通过原住民返迁兼业和就业实现"就地城镇化"

婺源县乡村文化发展有限公司投资的3个多亿绝大多数用于搬迁、修复、营造、做旧、保养等繁杂的"修旧如旧"工程,工程建造期间,平均每天有4万多元工资款注入篁岭和栗木坑、晓容、前段等周边村庄。全手工打磨的篁岭古村,唤醒了沉睡的"婺源三雕"(砖雕、木雕、石雕)工艺,许多工程参与者习得了手艺,劳动的含金量不断提升。一些手艺精湛者迄组建了专门的古建修复队,将兼业变成了专业。

公司流转了村落四周曾经大半抛荒的梯田,雇用

117

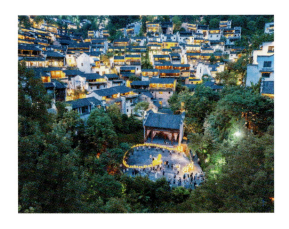

"就地城镇化"描绘了一个崭新的样本。

4. 通过打造"篁岭晒秋"品牌构筑乡土中国符号

篁岭村民通过凿窗支匾晾晒农作物，形成了极富特色的"晒秋"民俗。景区通过复原和发展"篁岭晒秋"民俗，打造了一系列"晒秋产品"，并将"篁岭晒秋"塑造成"中国最美文化符号"的文化现象，使"篁岭晒秋图"和"清明上河图""富春山居图"一样，成为中国文化的核心想象。

当地农民，按公司制定的种植方案，用传统种植方式打造"千亩梯田四季花海"。收获的菜油、辣椒、皇菊、稻谷、果蔬等农产品则定向销售给旅游接待单位，将耕作变成了就业。

篁岭则复原了近300米的"天街"，街旁密布茶坊、酒肆、书场、砚庄、篾铺，吸引村民返迁"天街"经营相关业态。此外，还集结了一批甲路油纸伞、婺源龙灯、龙尾歙砚等非物质文化的遗产传承者，在街里巷间制作传授工艺绝活。通过"整体搬迁、精准返迁、产业融入"三步走策略，每一个利益相关方的利益都得到了有效提升，特别是原住民家庭妇女，她们获得了在家门口就业的机会，成功实现了非农化转型，为

成效

篁岭民俗文化村于2013年开始试营业，2017年游客量首次突破百万大关，先后被评为"中国最美文化符号"和"中外最美外景地"，并荣获多项国家级荣誉，包括国家4A级旅游景区、中国最美休闲乡村、全国特色景观旅游名镇名村示范点和中国乡村旅游模范村等。

"篁岭模式"的减贫效果十分显著。第一，村民有了工资性和经营性的收入。2016年，篁岭景区支付给村民的工资有500余万元，村民旅游创业收入

有600余万元。篁岭村人均年收入从旅游开发前的3500元提升为4万元，户年均收入从1.5万元增长至13万元。此外，景区周边村庄有50余家农户从事农家乐经营，户均年增收5万元。第二，村落精英开始回流，同时吸引了大量的外村甚至外县人员涌入篁岭村寻找就业、创业机会。第三，留守老年人实现了再就业，劳动价值得到了延长。第四，大量农村妇女在景区就业，经济收入增加的同时，家庭和社会地位也得到显著提升。第五，村民通过资源使用费、房产增值、租金上涨等方式获得了资产性收入。

2. 以旅带农，以农促旅

篁岭旅游的发展带动了周边旅游服务的全面提升。当地通过发掘农家民俗生活体验、打造特色农家客栈以及开发农特产品，进一步丰富了篁岭旅游的多样性，增强了其吸引力和竞争力。

3. 参与式扶贫，扶贫扶智

篁岭景区首创"参与式扶贫"，让当地村民参与到旅游发展中，使其从旅游发展中直接受益，而非成为发展的阻力，实现了可持续发展的良性循环。

经验与启示

篁岭开发通过"参与式扶贫"，保障了多数村民的参与权，不仅提高了村民的脱贫能力、开拓了村民的就业视野，为村民带来了实质上的旅游红利，还为乡村旅游的振兴之路带来了启发。主要经验与启示有以下几点。

1. 以特为先，以奇取胜

构建具有生命力的乡村旅游模式，充分挖掘当地生态及文化上的特色，走差异化的发展道路，充分带动地方经济，实现长久的减贫效益。

下一步计划

婺源篁岭景区在旅游精准扶贫过程中，以打造婺源最具民俗特色的文化影视村落为目标，将篁岭古村落打造成特色晒秋民宿，将数万亩梯田变成现代高效农业观光园。通过复兴古村民俗文化、提升乡村文化旅游品质，篁岭成功打造了一个独具特色的文化小镇，为婺源乡村旅游的转型升级探索出了一条新路径。此外，篁岭景区创新式推出"参与式扶贫模式"，让当地村民参与到旅游发展中，成为旅游发展的受益者，实现良性循环，具有全球性借鉴意义。

旅游减贫案例故事（中英文双语版）
Best Practices of Poverty Alleviation through Tourism (Chinese-English Bilingual Edition)

Huangling Village, Wuyuan County, Jiangxi Province:
Revitalizing the Scenery of "Autumn Harvest" through Sharing Economy

Included in *WTA Best Practices in Poverty Alleviation through Tourism 2019*

Abstract

Huangling Village in Wuyuan County has emerged as the brightest new star of rural tourism in Jiangxi Province in recent years. The tourism-empowered poverty alleviation project led by Wu Xiangyang, an ordinary member of China Association for the Promotion of Democracy, has solved the underlying problem of tourism resources ownership by establishing a sharing-economy model of Consensus Space, and shifted the focus of rural tourism from product creation to industry and business nurturing. The "Huangling model" has revived the fading ancient village, revitalized the traditional agriculture civilization, restored villagers' confidence in their local economy, industry and culture, and offered inspirations to the promotion of in-situ urbanization and the transformation of land-use right. As a result, the annual per capita income of villagers was raised to 40,000 yuan from 3,500 yuan while the average annual household income increased to 130,000 yuan from 15,000 yuan after tourism development. The "Autumn Harvest" scenery in Huangling has become one of the most beautiful cultural symbols of China, contributing a case in point of developing and upgrading rural tourism in China.

Challenges and Problems

The Huangling Folk Culture Village is located at the eastern end of Wuyuan County, Jiangxi Province, at an altitude of 1,260 meters among Mont Shi'er, the main peak in Wuyuan County. The village was established during the Xuande period of the Ming Dynasty and has a history of more than 500 years. As a typical mountain village, Huangling Village is surrounded by ancient trees and dotted with terraces, so picturesque that the village is like a bonsai hanging on a hillside. Pictures taken of Huangling have won more than ten domestic and international awards. However, due to frequent geological disasters, villagers have been encouraged by the local government to relocate downhill since 1978. Before tourism development, the ancient village was caught in the dilemma of water and electricity shortage, a withering economy, immigration, collapsing houses, and abandoned terraces. Facing the danger of gradual demise in the semi-hollow state, it is essential to focus on the relationship between survival and growth when it comes to rural development.

Measures

In 2009, Wu Xiangyang registered Wuyuan County Rural Culture Development Co., Ltd. to invest in the project of Wuyuan Huangling Folk Culture Village. With nearly ten years of development, a unique "Huangling model" was established by Wu Xiangyang. In 2018, his company signed a strategic cooperation agreement with China Youth Travel Service, with the aim to make Huangling a benchmark for rural tourism and revitalization. Main measures include the following.

1. Integrate tourism development and management rights through the overall replacement of housing property rights

After consultation with the county and township governments, Wuyuan County Rural Culture Development Co., Ltd. invested 12 million yuan in building 68 resettlement houses, 24 apartments for old people and singles, and supporting infrastructure to provide for the overall relocation of 320 villagers in Huangling Village. Through the process of "bidding, auctioning and listing", the company gained the right to use the 33,000 square meters of construction land in the ancient village in 2013. While eliminating the geological dangers, improving local living standards and farming conditions for villagers, this method has established clear-cut ownerships and boundaries, and revitalized the tourism resources in Huangling Village.

2. Reinvent the style of the ancient village through relocation of old buildings from other places

Hui-style architectures of the Ming and Qing Dynasties are spread over the Wuyuan County. In 2014, agreements were reached between the Wuyuan County Rural Culture Development Company and Xucun township government for the relocation, renovation and protection of "Yi Xin Tang" fully

funded by the company. With the ownership still belonging to the township government and the operation right owned by the company, a new model of "foster care" was created for the protection and management of old buildings. Up to now, over 20 ancient buildings are relocated to Huangling Village. More than 120 exquisite old buildings in Huangling have made it one of the most densely filled villages in Wuyuan County.

3. Realize "in-situ urbanization" by encouraging the return of local people and promoting local employment

The majority of the more than 300 million yuan invested by Wuyuan County Rural Culture Development Co., Ltd. was used for the complicated "restoration to its original state" project, including relocation, restoration, construction, aging treatment, and maintenance. During the construction period, an average of more than 40,000 yuan in wages was injected into Huangling Village and surrounding villages such as Limukeng, Xiaorong, and Qianduan every day. In the renovation process, the long lost craftsmanship of brick carving, wood carving and stone carving were brought alive by the handwork of participants who in turn acquired new skills that made their work more valuable. Some skilled craftsmen even set up a special team for repairing ancient buildings, turning what was a part-time job into a professional practice.

The land-use right of the nearly abandoned terraces was transferred to the company. It formulated planting plans and hired local farmers to use tradition methods to turn the terraces into a sea of flowers in four seasons. The harvested produce, such as pepper, chrysanthemum, rice, fruits and vegetables, is sold to targeted tourist reception sites. In this way, jobs are created through developing farming.

Tianjie (or Paradise Walk), a nearly 300 meters of commercial street was restored, with various shops selling tea, liquor, books, ink stones and bamboo strip products. Villagers were attracted to return home and run businesses at the Tianjie while inheritors of intangible cultural heritages such as Jialu Oil Paper Umbrella, Wuyuan Dragon Lights and Longwei Ink Stone are gathered at the street to demonstrate and promote these traditions. By overall relocation, targeted return and industrial integration, all stakeholders have benefitted, especially local housewives who now have the opportunity to work near their homes doing non-farming activities. This provides a new sample for "in-situ urbanization".

4. Create a symbol of China countryside through the branding of "Autumn Harvest" in Huangling Village

The villagers of Huangling have formed a unique folk custom called "Shaiqiu" (autumn harvest) by cutting windows and supporting plaques to air-dry their crops. By restoring and developing the "Autumn Harvest" folk custom, the scenic area has created a series of autumn harvest products and shaped autumn harvest into a cultural phenomenon known as "The Most Beautiful Cultural Symbol of China", making the "Huangling Shaiqiu painting" a core image of Chinese culture, alongside the *Along the River During the Qingming Festival* and *Dwelling in the Fuchun Mountains*.

Results

Huangling Folk Culture Village began trial operations in 2013 and surpassed one million visitors for the first time in 2017. It has been successively awarded titles such as "The Most Beautiful Cultural Symbol of China" and "The Most Beautiful Location for Foreign Films", as well as numerous national honors, including national 4A-level scenic spot, China's Most Beautiful Leisure Village, National Demonstration Site for Famous Towns and Villages with Unique Landscapes, and China's Model Rural Tourism Village.

The "Huangling model" has a significant effect on poverty alleviation. Firstly, villagers earn wages as well as income from business operations. In 2016, Huangling Scenic Spot Administration paid more than 5 million yuan in wages to villagers who also earned over 6 million from tourism-related businesses. The per capita annual income of Huangling villagers was raised to 40,000 yuan from 3,500 yuan and the average annual income of households increased to 130,000 yuan from 15,000 yuan after tourism development. More than 50

households in the neighboring villages run home inns, which add 50,000 yuan to their annual income. Secondly, capable villagers are attracted back home. Many people from other villages and counties come for employment and business opportunities. Thirdly, the left-behind elderly are re-employed, further increasing their labor value. Fourthly, many rural women are employed in the scenic spots, improving their wealth as well as family and social status. Fifthly, villagers now have more asset income due to resource usage fees, property value appreciation, and higher rent.

Experience and Inspirations

By engaging most of the villagers, Huangling's poverty alleviation efforts not only improve villagers' ability to get out of poverty, expand their horizons for employment and bring them tangible benefits, but also provide inspirations for developing rural tourism. Main experience and inspirations are as follows.

1. Unique resources for success

To ensure the enduring effects of poverty reduction, we need to foster a vibrant rural tourism model, fully tap into the local eco-environment endowment and culture, and take a differentiated path for economic growth.

2. Tourism and peripherals reinforcing each other

Huangling Village's tourism development encourages peripheral services to upgrade, while business operations such as local folk culture experience, home inn and local agriculture products add to the diversity of Huangling's tourist attractions in turn.

3. Participatory poverty alleviation

Huangling Scenic Area pioneered "participatory poverty alleviation" by involving local villagers in tourism development, enabling them to directly benefit from it rather than becoming obstacles to development. This has achieved a virtuous cycle of sustainable development.

Next Step

In the process of targeted poverty alleviation through tourism, Huangling Scenic Spot has been positioned as a beautiful cultural village and filming site, with highlights on the unique autumn harvest custom and homestay houses and the turning of thousands hectares of terrace into modern agriculture sightseeing sites. By revitalizing the folk culture of the ancient village and enhancing the quality of rural cultural tourism, Huangling has successfully created a unique cultural town, exploring a new path for the transformation and upgrading of rural tourism in Wuyuan. In addition, Huangling Scenic Area innovatively introduced the "participatory poverty alleviation model", allowing local villagers to participate in tourism development and become beneficiaries of it, achieving a virtuous cycle. This has global significance for reference.

山东省日照市岚山区官草汪村：
渔文旅融合助力乡村振兴

收录于《2023 世界旅游联盟：旅游助力乡村振兴案例》

摘要

山东省日照市岚山区官草汪村因地制宜，依托优质的海滨沙滩、地道美味的海鲜小吃，以渔村特色精品民宿、民俗文化节庆体验、休闲海钓、特色海鲜品尝等为亮点，大力挖掘打造"渔文化"特色项目。官草汪村建设以海洋渔文化为特色的"吃、住、行、游、购、娱"全要素旅游体系，有效传承和发扬海洋渔文化，培育沿海旅游新业态，实现渔村文化和旅游的完美融合，成为当地一张旅游新名片。官草汪村通过渔业生产和旅游观光结合，实现保护和开发并举，传承和利用并重，形成滨海文化休闲旅游发展新格局。

挑战与问题

山东省日照市岚山区官草汪村北依阿掖山，南临海州湾渔场，总人口3366人，1120户，全村总面积1.5平方千米。官草汪村因地制宜，以滨海渔村风光为主题，结合官草汪渔村的传统建筑、村落格局和历史风貌，由传统的渔业生产村居向新型的滨海休闲旅游村落转型升级。村庄近些年在发展滨海文化休闲旅游产业过程中面临一些挑战和问题：一是特色文化有待挖掘，官草汪村对村庄拥有的文化遗产、特色民俗等资源挖掘力度不足，旅游产品存在同质化问题；二是配套设施仍需完善，5—10月旅游旺季期间游客数量相对较大，超过村庄道路交通、餐饮住宿、安全防护等服务设施现有承载能力；三是人才需求存在缺口，村庄对乡村旅游发展中各类人才的需求显著增加，亟须吸引各类人才到村创业、就业。

措施

1. 突出规划引领

2017年官草汪村完成官草汪渔村发展策划及概念性规划，规划用地总面积360亩，预计投资10亿元。一期官草汪渔港小镇已建成运营，二期内容主要包括龙王庙、山东手造·岚山风物展示体验馆、乡村记忆馆、鱼市、民俗街等。2024年开始进行三期建设，建设内容为青年旅社、海产品加工体验、游船俱乐部等。官草汪的乡村旅游发展主题明确，全方位展示"渔文化民俗游"主题和"海滨海洋游"休闲度假特色，以其浓郁的渔村风情和丰富的海洋文化，成为日照休闲度假的一大品牌。

2. 推进环境整治

官草汪村秉承保护原有生态、尊重村落原始肌理、延续岚山民间传统建筑特征的理念，借助当地山海资源和独特的渔俗文化，对区域内街道两旁的470处房屋立面进行改造，改造凸显旧民居中原有建筑元素，将街道水泥路改造为青石板路，建设具有当地渔俗文化特色的民居建筑。渔村在开发建设中，全面加强生物多样性保护，维护生态系统的生态特性和基本功能，最大限度保障生态旅游持续健康发展。村内各项设施设备符合国家关于环境保护的要求，不造成环境污染、自然资源破坏和其他公害。

3. 丰富旅游产品

官草汪村依托自身资源优势和产业优势，积极开发海洋渔业研学旅行、滨海观光休闲度假游、海钓游、精品民宿游等。在官草汪的渔村观光，推窗见海、景色秀丽，冬季倚窗观雪、坐大炕品渔家饭。官草汪村依托滨海优势和海洋牧场产业优势，积极开发海洋研学旅行课程，吸引大批中小学生参加。官草汪村每年农历六月十三日举办"民俗祭海节"、阳历九月初七举办"渔船首丰归港庆典"等活动，把传统海洋民俗变成旅游吸引力，充分展现渔村民俗特色文化，大力推动乡村旅游文化建设与发展。

成效

据统计，2020年，官草汪村游客接待量超过20万人次，旅游收入9160万元。项目采用"公司+合作社+村民"的发展模式，拓宽了周边村庄居民的就业渠道，为当地创造了460个就业岗位。优先录用贫困户，丰富村民就业渠道。旅游业使人均收入增加10447元。2021年，官草汪村被列入国家乡村旅游重点乡村名录。

经验与启示

1. 立足主题定位

官草汪村人文资源、自然生态资源、海洋渔业资源组合度好,滨海渔文化休闲旅游主题鲜明。官草汪村积极开发海洋渔业研学旅行、滨海观光休闲度假游、海钓游、精品民宿游等,把传统海洋民俗变成旅游吸引力,特色渔村精品民宿蓬勃发展,特色美食层出不穷,民俗祭海节、海虹节、渔船首丰庆典等节庆活动丰富多彩,"渔文旅"吸引力持续增强。

2. 突出项目引领

官草汪村以海洋牧场、渔港小镇项目为引领,积极进行"传统海洋渔业+旅游"的产业转型升级,积极发展海洋休闲旅游经济。村内大力开展海上观光、采摘、垂钓等活动,全村共有2000多个钓点,1个占海近700平方米的大型海上游钓平台,3个大型海上垂钓俱乐部,成为山东省最大的休闲海钓示范基地。渔港小镇一期建成启用,配套完善了民宿、餐饮、文化体验等旅游业态,优化了旅游产业链条。

3. 打造互联营销

官草汪村运用互联网大力开展乡村旅游宣传与营销,利用微信公众平台和快手、抖音等新媒体渠道开展宣传推广和营销,打造乡村旅游品牌,提升乡村整体形象。推出"互联网+服务""大数据+服务""电子信息+服务"等智慧乡村旅游服务,给旅游者提供了优质的旅游体验。

下一步计划

官草汪村将继续依托最美渔村资源,推动滨海文化休闲旅游高质量发展,助力乡村振兴。一是继续完善旅游设施,建设包括龙王庙、文化中心、鱼市、民俗街等设施。二是打造智慧旅游平台,开发并利用岚山旅游APP和一机游日照微信小程序。三是加快全产业链建设,以点带面,扩大辐射范围,把岚山区的渔港村落、安东阿掖旅游度假区、海上碑、多岛海景区、多岛海赶海园、柽柳公园等旅游景区串联起来,打通"吃、住、行、游、购、娱"乡村旅游全产业链,谱写旅游助力乡村振兴新篇章。

旅游减贫案例故事（中英文双语版）
Best Practices of Poverty Alleviation through Tourism (Chinese-English Bilingual Edition)

Guancaowang Village, Lanshan District, Rizhao City, Shandong Province:

Promoting Rural Revitalization through Fishery-Tourism Integration

Included in *WTA Best Practices of Rural Revitalization through Tourism 2023*

Abstract

Guancaowang Village, located in Lanshan District, Rizhao City, is vigorously developing characteristic projects based on local conditions, such as high-quality coastal beaches, authentic and delicious seafood and snacks, with highlights including characteristic boutique homestays in the fishing village, folk culture and festival experiences, leisure sea fishing, and unique seafood offerings. It has built a comprehensive tourist service system covering catering, accommodation, travel, sightseeing, shopping, and entertainment, and featuring the marine fishing culture. It has effectively inherited and promoted the marine fishing culture, fostered new business models in coastal tourism, achieved seamless integration of fishing village culture and tourism, and emerged as a new attraction for the local tourism industry. By combining fishery production with tourism, Guancaowang Village achieves ecological conservation and economic development, places equal emphasis on inheritance and utilization, and fosters a new development momentum for coastal leisure tourism.

Challenges and Problems

Surrounded by Aye Mountain to the north and Haizhou Bay Fishery to the south, Guancaowang Village has a population of 3,366 spread across 1,120 households, covering an area of 1.5 square kilometers. Drawing on local conditions, it positions itself as a scenic coastal fishing village, utilizing the traditional architecture, village layout, and historical style to transform from a traditional fishing village into a coastal leisure tourism destination. In recent years, the village has faced some challenges and problems in developing the coastal leisure tourism industry. Firstly, it still needs to further exploit its characteristic culture. Its cultural heritage, unique folk customs, and other resources await further exploration and optimal utilization, while there is an issue of homogenization among tourism products. Secondly, its supporting facilities still require improvement. During the peak tourist season, which spans from May to October, the village's existing roads, catering and accommodation facilities, as well as safety measures, are inadequate to accommodate the large influx of tourists. Thirdly, there is a shortage of talent. The village has an increasing demand for skilled workers to develop rural tourism, and it is imperative to attract a diverse range of talents to establish businesses and seek employment within the village.

Measures

1. Highlight the leading role of plans

In 2017, Guancaowang Village completed its development plan and conceptual plan, with a total planned land area of 360 *mu* and an estimated investment of 1 billion yuan. The first phase of the Guancaowang Fishing Port Town project has been completed and put into operation, and the second phase is underway, including the Dragon King Temple, the Exhibition and Experience Hall of Handicrafts and Customs in Lanshan and Shandong, the Rural Memory Hall, the Fish Market, and the Folk Street. The third phase of the project has begun in 2024, including a youth hostel, the seafood processing experience, and a cruise club. Guancaowang Village has a clear theme for rural tourism development, that is, fishing culture and folk customs, which will be presented comprehensively. It also highlights the leisure holiday-making characteristics of "seaside marine tour", and has become a major brand of Rizhao City's leisure vacation market with its distinct fishing village style and rich marine culture.

2. Improve the environment

Guancaowang Village preserves the original ecological environment, the original village texture, and the traditional architectural characteristics of Lanshan District, and has transformed the facades of 470 houses on both sides of the streets by making use of local mountain and marine resources and unique fishing culture. The transformation highlights the original architectural elements of the old houses.

Meanwhile the cement roads are covered with flagstones, and residential buildings are built with characteristics of local fishing culture. In the process of development and construction, the fishing village has comprehensively strengthened biodiversity conservation, maintained the ecological characteristics and basic functions of the ecosystem, and ensured the sustainable and healthy development of ecotourism to the greatest extent. All facilities and equipment in the village meet the national environmental requirements and cause no environmental pollution, or damage to natural resources or any other public hazards.

3. Enrich the portfolio of tourist products

Relying on its own resource advantages and industrial advantages, Guancaowang Village actively develops study tours themed on marine fishery, coastal sightseeing and leisure vacation tours, sea fishing tours, and boutique homestay tours. Tourists can enjoy the picturesque view of sea at the window, watch the snow fall in winter, and have a feast of seafood on the kang, a traditional heated bed-stove common in northern China. Leveraging its advantageous location and marine ranching industry, Guancaowang Village actively develops marine educational travel which has attracted a large number of primary and secondary school students to participate. It holds activities such as the Folk Sea Sacrifice Festival on the 13th day of the sixth lunar month, and the Celebration of the Return of Fishing Boats on the seventh day of the ninth month of the solar calendar every year, to attract tourists with traditional marine folk customs, fully display its folk culture, and vigorously promote the development of rural tourism.

Results

According to statistics, in 2020, Guncaowang Village received more than 200,000 tourists and earned 91.6 million yuan in tourism. The project adopts the development model of "companies + cooperatives + villagers", broadens the employment channels of residents in surrounding villages, and has created 460 local jobs. It gives priority to poor households in recruitment, and diversifies the employment channels for villagers. The tourism industry has increased per capita income by 10,447 yuan. In 2021, Guancaowang Village was inscribed on the National List of Key Villages for Rural Tourism.

Experience and Inspirations

1. Stay true to its positioning

Guancaowang Village has a combintion of cultural resources, ecological resources, and marine and fishery resources, and has a clear theme of coastal fishing culture and leisure tourism. It actively develops marine fishery-themed study tours, coastal leisure vacation tours, sea fishing tours, and boutique homestay tours, and attracts tourists with traditional marine folk customs. Its characteristic boutique homestays are booming, specialty dishes emerge one after another, and it has organized a host of festivals including the Folk Sea Sacrifice Festival, the Mussel Festival, and the Celebration of the Return of Fishing Boats, to continuously enhance the appeal of fishery-themed tourism.

2. Highlight the leading role of major projects

Led by the marine ranching and fishing port town projects, Guancaowang Village actively promotes "traditional marine fishery + tourism" for industrial transformation and upgrading, and develops the marine leisure tourism economy. In particular, it

has been vigorously developing marine sightseeing, U-pick and angling businesses. The village has more than 2,000 fishing spots, 1 large marine fishing platform covering nearly 700 square meters of sea area, and 3 large sea fishing clubs, making it the largest recreational sea fishing demonstration base in Shandong Province. The first phase of the fishing port town project was completed and put into use, and supporting homestays, catering facilities and cultural experience were improved, to optimize the tourism industry chain.

3. Promote Internet-based marketing

Guancaowang Village uses the Internet to vigorously promote itself as a rural destination. It uses new-media platforms such as Wechat Official Platform, Kuaishou and Douyin to promote itself, build a rural destination brand and enhance the overall image of the countryside. Smart rural tourist services such as "Internet + service", "big data + service" and "electronic information + service" have been launched to offer a high-quality tourist experience.

Next Steps

Guancaowang Village will continue to leverage its resources as a beautiful fishing village to promote

the high-quality development of coastal leisure tourism and contribute to rural revitalization. Firstly, it will continue to improve tourist facilities, including the Dragon King Temple, the culture center, the fish market, the folk street and so on. Secondly, it will build a smart tourist service platform, and develop and use the "Travel in Lanshan" APP and the "A Mobile Phone Tour of Rizhao" mini-app on Weixin. Thirdly, it will move faster to develop the whole industrial chain, expand the scope of influence, connect the fishing port villages in Lanshan District, Aye Resort in Andong, Haishangbei, Duodaohai Scenic Area, Duodaohai Sea Park, and Tamarix Park, form a whole industrial chain of rural tourism covering catering, accommodation, travel, sightseeing, shopping and entertainment, and write a new chapter of rural revitalization empowered by tourism development.

山东省济宁市泗水县龙湾湖乡村振兴示范区：
新型合伙人机制激活乡村文旅新业态

收录于《2021世界旅游联盟：旅游助力乡村振兴案例》

摘要

山东省济宁市泗水县龙湾湖乡村振兴示范区通过创新"乡村合伙人"机制，打造创客村落、文创小街、儒学讲堂、初心学院等文旅新业态，推动乡村振兴融合发展，形成了绿水青山生态资源与文旅新业态相呼应、生态文明与文化艺术相连接的典型发展模式，走出了一条文旅产业与乡村振兴融合发展的特色道路。

挑战与问题

山东省济宁市泗水县龙湾湖乡村振兴示范区规划面积7.9万亩，辖南仲都村、东仲都村、夹山头村等18村，现有3576户共12255人。示范区内林木覆盖率达54.7%，龙湾湖水域面积达7500亩，山清水秀、生态环境较好。但长期以来，示范区内生态资源利用率不足，村民参与乡村新业态开发的积极性不高，缺少将绿水青山转化为绿色发展的思路和办法。

措施

1. 打造"文创小街"

由村集体牵头，盘活农村闲散宅基地，以租赁形式对房屋进行统一改造，引入等闲谷艺术粮仓等文旅项目，打造具有创客集聚功能的"文创小街"。引入"花筑"等品牌民宿，借助外来优质资源丰富乡村旅游业态。利用当地文化匠人和设计师资源，开展柳编、工艺品制作等培训活动，带动当地农户加盟运营。

2. 创建文创院落

持续开展乡村人居艺术环境提升行动，通过创建文创院落集群，打造新型乡村空间，将乡村生态与创意艺术有机融合，大大提升了乡村气质形象。培育研学旅行产品业态，改造原有民居，建设创客研学基地，打造了龙湾书房、鲁班记忆木工坊、陶艺工坊等创客空间，实现创意活动与艺术村居的深度融合。

3. 创新"乡村合伙人"机制

构建了"基础合伙人—成长合伙人—核心合伙人"晋升机制，进而形成"合伙人招合伙人，合伙人招项目，项目招合伙人，项目衍生项目"的人才与产业联动机制，全面激活乡村人才集聚体制，吸引外部合伙人33人，落地业态40余个，为当地筹集各类资金2.5亿元，带动直接就业300余人。

4. 推行"儒学讲堂＋初心学院"模式

示范区积极推进乡村文化振兴，建设乡村儒学讲堂，开展以孝文化学习为特色的儒学讲解活动，并形成常态化机制；建设了集课堂教学、实践教学、案例教学于一体的泗水县初心学院，打造符合山区特色的教学课程体系，助力乡村文化振兴。

成效

1. 集体经济显著增收

示范区已落地等闲谷艺术粮仓、龙湾湖艺术小镇等文旅项目9个，入驻汇源矿泉水等涉农加工企业6家。区内龙湾湖文化旅游特色小镇2020年累计接待游客逾50万人次，生态采摘等旅游活动农业产值超过600万元，产业融合发展格局逐步形成。

2. 民生状态明显改善

受益于旅游业的蓬勃发展，示范区内南仲都村在2017年实现全面脱贫；2020年，该村已建立旅游采摘大棚74个，年产值达645万元，村民每人每年可获得旅游分红1500元，该村被评为"国家级旅游扶贫试点村"。

3. 环境保护成效显著

通过文旅项目配套，示范区内新增污水处理站2处，新修樱花大道、环湖路等生态旅游道路16.6千米，实施全面亮化工程，村庄生态保护能力和人居环境都得到极大提升。

龙湾湖乡村振兴示范区获批"中国乡村旅游创客示范基地""全国乡村旅游重点村"，入选"山东省美丽村居建设省级试点""山东省政府乡村振兴联系点"等，逐步发展成为独具特色的乡村文旅新业态集聚区和示范区。

经验与启示

1. "乡村合伙人"机制激活市场化运营模式

探索创新"乡村合伙人"机制，利用技术入股、创意合作、直接注资、协助招商、扩充平台等多种形式，激活乡村人才集聚模式，吸引艺术家、行业带头人、非遗传承人等30余位合伙人加入，产业融资规模超过2亿元，以人才振兴推动乡村产业市场化运营。

2. 文化艺术与生态文明有机融合

示范区充分依托原真村落与生态资源，将现代创意艺术、自然生态、村居环境有机融合起来，以文旅新业态推动乡村三产绿色发展，打造"三生三美"的和谐乡村。

3. 文化振兴与产业振兴有机融合

示范区创意落地项目在传承质朴民风的同时，挖掘和谐、共生、孝道、大美等儒家文化，通过精品民宿、创意农业打造具有齐鲁风韵的现代精品乡村，实现文化振兴与产业振兴的有效融合。

4. 文旅发展与民生诉求有机融合

乡村振兴的落脚点是改善民生，区内文旅产业平台在选择合伙人、引进项目、平台发展等多个环节上都引入了"反哺"乡村的元素：通过创造就业、常态化技能培训等活动，提升村民新业态从业能力；通过举办乡村艺术节、成立乡村合唱团等形式，丰富了乡村文化活动；通过开办研学辅导班、文化辅导课，改善村里儿童的受教育环境，在发展文旅产业过程中解决民生诉求。

下一步计划

1. 持续探索乡村合伙人新场景、新机制

加强与高校、研究机构的合作，总结乡村合伙人机制与现代企业经理人制度间的共性与差异，探索通过产品标准化、服务标准化、管理标准化等措施弥补短板，深入研究乡村合伙人机制的适用场景、创新路径、复制条件，提高成功率。

2. 持续扩大优势项目覆盖范围

扩大区内艺术粮仓、乡村文创街区等优势项目的覆盖范围，发挥片区生态环境、人文禀赋等资源优势，形成文旅产业发展合力。力争在三年内实现：落地产业项目60个以上，扶持、培训各类创新创业合伙人超300位，带动就业人数达到4000人以上。

3. 持续推广乡村文旅新业态发展模式

总结文旅新业态在乡村场景中的发展模式，梳理创意文化商业流程与推广潜力，归纳乡村振兴模式化输出的理论体系，逐步开展文旅新业态模式的复制与商业输出，打造乡村振兴集聚区、示范带，形成集群效应。

Longwan Lake Demonstration Zone for Rural Revitalization, Sishui County, Jining City, Shandong Province:

The New Partnership Mechanism Activates the New Type of Business in Rural Cultural Tourism

Included in *WTA Best Practices of Rural Revitalization through Tourism 2021*

Abstract

Longwan Lake Demonstration Zone for Rural Revitalization, Sishui County, Jining City, Shandong Province has formed a typical development mode in which ecological resources are utilized to develop tourism and rural revitalization. The "rural partnership" entails building new types of businesses such as Maker Village, Cultural and Creative Street, Confucianism Lecture and the Original Aspiration Academy, and has pushed for the development of rural revitalization. These developments create a cultural tourism and ecological civilization that links culture, art, and rural revitalization.

Challenges and Problems

The planned area for Longwan Lake Demonstration Zone is 79 thousand *mu* with 18 villages under its jurisdiction. The total population of the 18 villages is 12,255 people from 3,576 households. The forest coverage rate in the demonstration zone reaches 54.7%, while the water covers 7,500 *mu*. It is beautiful as it is surrounded by mountains, its clear waters, and a good ecology. However, some of these ecological resources have not been fully utilized for some time as the villagers here are not too enthusiastic about participating in the development of new forms of business in their community. Further more, they lack the ideas and methods to transform ecological resources such as lucid waters and lush mountains into green development.

Measures

1. Building cultural and creative streets

The demonstration zone will take the lead in redeveloping the use of homesteads and implement the transformation on these buildings by turning them into rental units. Cultural tourism projects such as Leisure Valley Art Granary are introduced to build Cultural and Creative Streets that can gather Makers. Homestay hotels, such as the Floral Hotel, are also introduced to enhance the commercial activities of rural tourism through high-quality external resources. The internal resources of local craftsmen and designers are used to carry out training in crafts and wickerwork manufacturing. This results in local peasant households working together to operate local businesses together.

2. Building cultural and creative clusters

The demonstration zone will work to improve the artistic environment of rural habitats by creating new rural spaces for Creative and Cultural Clusters. This project will organically integrate the rural ecology with creative arts and hopefully enhance the image of the rural areas. The village has created a study tour product system. This will transform the original folk houses and repurpose them as the base for creative artists and establish creative spaces for Longwan Study, Luban's Memory Wood Workshop and Pottery Workshop, all of which are integrated in artistic village dwellings.

3. Innovating the "rural partnership" mechanism

The promotion mechanism of "basic partner -

growing partner - core partner" has been formulated. This partnership has created a linkage mechanism between industry and talents in which "partners recruit other partners, partners attract projects, projects attract new partners, and projects can multiply". This partnership has fully gathered rural talents, attracted 33 external partners, landed more than 40 business models, raised 250 million yuan from various funds for the local area, and driven the direct employment for more than 300 people.

4. Implementing the model of "confucianism lecture + original aspiration academy"

To actively promote the revitalization of rural culture, the demonstration zone has constructed a rural Confucianism Lecture Hall with the goal of conducting lectures on Confucianism's the filial piety values and mores. The demonstration zone has also constructed the Original Aspiration Academy in Sishui Country, which integrates classroom teaching, practical teaching and case teaching. This process creates a teaching curriculum system in line with the characteristics of mountainous areas.

Results

1. The collective economy has significantly increased its income

The demonstration zone has landed 9 cultural tourism projects. These include Leisure Valley, Art Granary, and Longwan Lake Art Town. In addition, 6 agricultural related processing enterprises, including Huiyuan Mineral water, have also been settled in the area. Longwan Lake Cultural Tourism Town in the demonstration zone drew a total of more than 500,000 tourists in 2020. Ecological fruit picking and other tourism activities have produced an

agricultural revenue of more than 6 million yuan. The developmental pattern of industrial integration is gradually formed.

2. People's livelihood has improved significantly

As a result of the tourism industry, South Zhongdu Village in the demonstration zone achieved comprehensive poverty eradication in 2017. By 2020, 74 fruit-picking sheds for tourists have been established, generating 6.45 million yuan each year. The South Zhongdu Village was accordingly named the National-level Tourism Poverty Alleviation Plot Village.

3. Effective environmental protection is achieved

The living environment of villagers has been greatly improved through facilities that were created through cultural tourism projects. Two sewage treatment facilities have been added in the demonstration zone and 16.6 kilometers of ecological tourism avenues have also been built. These avenues — the Cherry Blossom Avenue and Ring Lake Road — included comprehensive lighting projects.

Longwan Lake Demonstration Zone for Rural Revitalization has been approved as a demonstration base for Chinese Rural tourism Creators. These creators are a National-level Key Village of Rural Tourism, a provincial-level pilot area of Beautiful Village Construction of Shandong Province, a contact point for rural revitalization of Shandong Provincial Government and others. It has gradually formed a gathering area of demonstration zone for the development of unique villages in rural cultural tourism.

Experience and Inspirations

1. Activating the market-oriented operation mode with the "rural partnership" mechanism

The demonstration zone has explored innovative "rural partnerships" and activated the gathering of rural talents. This has been done through technical shareholding, creative cooperation, direct capital injection, and assistance in investment. More than 30 partners have joined in the endeavor and more than 200 million yuan has been invested as industrial financing to promote the market-oriented operation in rural industries for talent revitalization.

2. Organic integration of ecological civilization with culture and art

The demonstration zone relies on the original villages for their ecological resources and the organic integration of the village's modern creative arts, natural ecology and the environment. It also promotes the green development of three rural industries, with the new cultural tourism mode and creates a harmonious village of "prosperous production, good ecology, and beautiful life."

3. Organic integration of cultural and industrial revitalization

The culture of the village is fully and effectively integrated into the demonstration zone. Village people are simple and honest folks so this creative

project dives into the Confucian values of harmony, symbiosis, filial piety, and greater beauty. As a result, the village hotels and creative agriculture become more modern with the charm of the Qilu area.

4. Organic integration of developing cultural tourism and improving people's livelihood

Rural revitalization is based on the improvement of people's livelihood. The platform of cultural tourism in the demonstration zone has introduced the back feeding of the rural areas in many ways. For example, by selecting the villagers as participants in the new business model, the development zone is able to create employment and help with the development of new skills for the villagers. Traditional rural cultural activities are enriched by holding rural art festivals and forming rural choirs. Children in the village are educated by running classes that focus on the culture of the village. The demand for a better quality of life is addressed in the process of developing cultural tourism.

Next Steps

1. The continuous efforts to explore new scenarios and mechanisms for rural partners

The demonstration zone will seek to strengthen its agreement with universities and research institutions. They will summarize the commonalities and differences between the rural partnership mechanism and the manger system that is present in modern enterprises. In addition, they will explore measures that make up for shortcomings through product standardization, service standardization, and dive into the applicable scenarios. This exploration project will ultimately serve to seek out new innovative paths, replicate the conditions of rural

partnerships, and improve the success rate of such efforts.

2. Continuous efforts to expand the coverage of advantageous projects

The demonstration zone will expand the coverage of advantageous projects such as art granaries, cultural and creative clusters, and give full play to the ecological environment. It will also utilize humanistic endowments and other resources which will help form a synergistic cultural tourism development. The zone will attempt to reach more than 60 industrial projects within three years. During this time, they will seek to support and train over 300 partners of innovation and entrepreneurship and create 4,000 jobs.

3. Continuous efforts to promote the new type of business in rural cultural tourism

The demonstration zone will summarize the development models of the new business in rural cultural tourism. They will also work to sort out the business process including the potential for promotion and the success rate of the replication and output of new cultural tourism modes. In the end, the demonstration zone seeks to form a cluster effect from the summarization of this new business model.

旅游减贫案例故事（中英文双语版）
Best Practices of Poverty Alleviation through Tourism (Chinese-English Bilingual Edition)

河南省洛阳市洛宁县罗岭乡：
爱和小镇助力乡村振兴

收录于《2022世界旅游联盟：旅游助力乡村振兴案例》

摘要

2015年4月，中国陶瓷艺术大师郭爱和与洛宁县签订了爱和小镇建设协议。爱和小镇把旧窑洞、老房子、大陶缸洛阳三彩釉结合在一起，活态传承文化遗产，以"世外陶源，四季画谷"为诠释核心，积极倡导"艺术扶贫、美育扶贫、教育扶贫、旅游扶贫"，发挥洛阳三彩釉艺术的影响力，并融合地域优势，打造中国乡村艺术公园。爱和小镇将扶贫与艺术、旅游、文化、传统工艺相结合，通过艺术与教育结合推动乡村美育，艺术与旅游融合促进村民增收，助力乡村振兴。

挑战与问题

在爱和小镇项目建设入驻前,罗岭乡交通闭塞、农作物结构单一、房屋破旧,农业生产依赖自然条件,是国家级贫困村。项目建设初期条件艰难,没有水、没有路、没有电,基础设施和硬件设施极为匮乏。同时,当地农民的思想十分陈旧,想要这样一个艺术项目被当地接纳,就需要开展大量思想动员工作,引导村民认识艺术、了解艺术,培养他们发现美、欣赏美的能力,帮助当地农民成为艺术的启蒙者,使他们愿意融入并参与到项目建设中,与项目形成良性互动。

计并烧制了多幅三彩陶艺作品,展现出别具一格的艺术魅力。

3. 打造系列节庆活动

爱和小镇结合四季特色,连续举办油菜花观赏节、向阳花观赏节、三彩中国年、金珠沙梨采摘节等节庆活动。同时,还成功引入第二十六届亚洲影艺联盟洛阳大会、世界书艺全北双年展、洛阳(国际)创意产业博览会洛宁分会场、"艺术乡村山水洛阳"摄影大赛等各类大型活动。这些举措不仅催生了一个充满艺术气息的乡村公园,而且形成了以爱和小镇为核心,辐射并带动周边地区发展的良好局面。

措施

1. 打造"当日"艺术展

罗岭乡人烟稀少,为了吸引游客来到这个美丽的小山村,郭爱和策划了山村里的艺术展"当日"。2015年12月第一届中国"当日"艺术展就在简陋的窑洞里拉开了序幕。通过驻村创作、举行展览、现场拍卖,郭爱和将募集的爱心善款全部捐赠给当地山区用于孩子的美育教育。这一系列举措旨在以文化滋养人心,用美学启迪智慧,促进当地儿童的全面发展。

"当日"艺术展一经举办就引起巨大轰动,人民日报、新华社等中央媒体纷纷关注,这项"24小时公益快闪"的活动,被评为"中国最具关注度艺术大展"。截至2021年12月,中国"当日"艺术展已连续举办七年,参与人数越来越多,活动规模越来越大,在国内艺术界引起了很大的轰动。

2. 打造艺术小镇新面貌

郭爱和带领团队致力于用设计力量改造乡村,他们无偿为洛宁县设计了一套完整的旅游标识系统,并义务为罗岭乡的前河村、韩沟村、卧岭村、皮坡村等地设计并烧制了三彩村标10座;此外,他们还义务指导了洛宁县美丽乡村的建设规划。在爱和小镇,团队将传统三彩陶艺、非遗项目融入当地地域环境,开设了三彩艺陶宝店和三彩釉画烧制技艺扶贫工坊,设

成效

从爱和小镇进驻那天起,罗岭乡村民就得到了踏踏实实的实惠。一是土地流转,爱和小镇承包农户土地430亩,当地农户按照统一规划种植指定农作物,经济收益归农户,观赏效应归景区,每亩还补贴农民50元。二是优先安排有劳动能力的脱贫户到园内务工,聘用脱贫群众23人次,年收入可达2万元以上。三是优先安排脱贫户的大中专毕业学生到洛阳市区三彩艺术博物馆和工作室就业,学习陶瓷制作技艺。

"当日"艺术展共邀请艺术家为洛宁县师生进行大型讲座、授课35次,捐赠作品613幅,共筹集爱心善款154.8万元,为86所中小学挂牌设立"美育教室",为中小学捐赠16个大型户外电子屏,资助6所学校进行校园墙体美化建设,组织了1164人次

的洛宁中小学师生研学活动，捐赠图书超过 6500 册，并发放了 18 万元的"当日"奖学金。

爱和小镇及周边地区每年平均吸引游客超过 10 万人次，带来超过 2000 万元的收入。附近贫困群众经营的农家乐和周边贫困户的农副产品如核桃、柿子、沙梨、苹果等销售也火爆起来，当地村民得到了可观的经济效益。

4. 投入教育

爱和小镇积极强化与国内各大高校的合作，涵盖旅游服务平台构建、创意人才培养以及创新创业等多个领域，现已成为景德镇陶瓷大学、西安美术学院、洛阳师范学院等国内多所高校的创新创业基地、旅游学科建设基地、工艺美术教学科研实践基地、大学生就业见习基地等，这些合作显著提升了爱和小镇的知名度。

经验与启示

1. 智力先行

"授人以鱼不如授人以渔"，当乡村碰上艺术，碰撞的火花可能是我们想象不到的。乡村振兴最重要的是从思想上让政府、群众理解艺术乡村理念，让他们对项目发展有概念、方向，这样才能更好地促进他们融入并推动项目的发展。

2. 因地制宜

合理利用当地资源，因地制宜，走可持续发展之路。不大拆大建，就地取材，同时要注重环保理念，促进项目可持续发展，保护当地生态资源，还乡村自然之美、艺术之美。

3. 国际交流

爱和小镇自开建以来，吸引了国内外艺术大家的目光，众多艺术家多次到爱和小镇进行采风、艺术创作、艺术交流等活动，带动了罗岭乡的知名度和美誉度。

下一步计划

一是持续加大建设力度，完善硬件设施，努力实现打造国家 4A 级旅游景区的目标，并开始建设洛阳市最具代表性的"当日艺术馆"。二是继续承办各大国际性的艺术展、会展、研学等活动，将爱和小镇建设成为一个推广文化与精神文明建设的新高地。同时将在园区建设大师创作营、高端民宿、研学基地等空间，紧跟时代的经济发展步伐，紧密衔接资本市场、艺术市场，打造一个符合乡村振兴之路、符合市场经济的国际化三彩陶艺村。三是持续开展美育教育，坚持举办"小手画三彩"、中国"当日"艺术展等丰富多彩的艺术美育活动，推进乡村建设与当地儿童美育教育。四是根据当地自然环境继续举办花开、节庆类活动，带动周边辐射景区人流量。通过一系列的活动，洛宁县的曝光率和知名度得到了持续提升，这不仅带动了当地农民的就业人数增加，还促进了周边辐射景区的客流量及收入的增长，有力地推动了旅游业在乡村振兴中的助力作用。

Luoling Township, Luoning County, Luoyang City, Henan Province:

The Aihe Town for Rural Revitalization

Included in *WTA Best Practices of Rural Revitalization through Tourism 2022*

Abstract

In April 2015, Chinese ceramic art master Guo Aihe signed an agreement with Luoning County to develop the Aihe Town. The Aihe Town project brings together old caves, old residences, large pottery jars and the Luoyang's tri-colored glaze art, inherits and gives cultural heritage a new life. Positioned as "a pottery heaven and a four-season painting valley", it actively advocates poverty alleviation through art, aesthetic education, education and tourism. It gives full play to the influence of Luoyang's tri-colored glaze art and integrates regional advantages to build a rural art park with Chinese characteristics. Aihe Town combines poverty alleviation with art, tourism, culture and traditional crafts, promotes rural aesthetic education and integrates art and tourism to increase the income of villagers and boost rural revitalization.

Challenges and Problems

Before the Aihe Town project was launched, Luoling Township was isolated from the outside world, the crops were undiversified, the houses dilapidated and the agricultural production depended on natural conditions. It was a state-level impoverished village. In the early days of the project, the conditions were harsh: there was no tap water, roads or electricity, and the infrastructure was very weak. To make it worse, local farmers were very conservative, and it took a lot of effort to convince them that such an art project was necessary for the village, guide them to learn what art was and appreciate beauty, and enlighten them on art, so that they were willing to participate in the project and achieved benign interaction with the project.

Measures

1. The "One Day" art exhibition

To attract visitors to the sparsely populated Luoling Township, Guo Aihe curated the art exhibition titled "One Day" in the beautiful village. The exhibition debuted in December 2015 in a humble cave. Through the creation in the village, holding exhibitions and live auctions, Guo Aihe donated all the charity money raised to the local mountain area for the aesthetic education of children. This series of initiatives aimed to nourish people with culture, enlightened wisdom with aesthetics, and promoted the all-round development of local children. The exhibition became an instant hit and made headlines on the People's Daily and Xinhua News Agency, among the central media outlets. This "24-hour non-profit flash mob event" was rated as the art exhibition with the most attention in China. Till December 2021, the "One Day" Art Exhibition has held seven consecutive editions, with more and more participants and getting bigger in scale. It has become a great sensation in the Chinese art circles.

2. Give the art town a new look

Guo Aihe led the team to transform the countryside with design power. They designed a complete set of tourism sign system for Luoning County free of charge, and designed and fired 10 three-color village signs for Qianhe Village, Hangou Village, Woling Village, Pipo Village and other places in Luoling Township. In addition, they have volunteered to guide the construction planning of beautiful villages in Luoning County. In Aihe Town, the team integrated traditional three-color pottery and intangible heritage projects into

the local environment, set up a three-color pottery treasure shop and a three-color glaze painting firing technology poverty alleviation workshop, designed and fired a number of three-color pottery works, showing a unique artistic charm.

3. Organize festival celebrations

In light of the characteristics of the four seasons, Aihe Town organized the rape flower festival, the sunflower festival, the Sancai-themed Lunar New Year, the pear picking festival, among other celebrations. It also hosted major events including the 26th Congress of Federation of Asian Photographic Art in Luoyang, the World Calligraphy Art Biennale, the 2019 Creative Industry Exposition, and the Luoyang Rural Landscape Photography Competition. It has not only given birth to the rural art park, but also taken the lead in driving local economic growth and the development of surrounding areas.

Results

Since the day the Aihe Town was launched, it has delivered substantial benefits to the villagers. Firstly, in terms of the transfer of land use right, the Aihe Town project contracted 430 *mu* of land, and asked local farmers to grow designated crops as planned. The income generated goes to the farmers while the view of the crops and fields is part of the scenery. A subsidiary of 50 yuan is provided for each farmer for each *mu* of land contracted. Secondly, in recruitment the project team gives priority to those who have just emerged from poverty and have working abilities. It has offered 23 jobs to people who have emerged from poverty, with an annual income of more than 20,000 yuan. Thirdly, it gives priority to secondary-school and college graduates from poverty-stricken households when selecting candidates to work in the Sancai Art Museum and Studio in downtown Luoyang to learn the skills of ceramic making.

The "One Day" Exhibition has invited artists to give lectures to teachers and students in Luoning County. So far they had given 35 lectures, and donated 613 artworks. A total of 1.548 million yuan was raised, and used to open the aesthetic education classrooms in 86 primary and middle schools. It also donated 16 large outdoor electronic screens for local primary and middle schools, sponsored the campus wall beautification in six schools, organized study tours for 1,164 students and teachers of primary and middle schools in Luoning, donated more than 6,500 books, and granted the One Day scholarship of 180,000 yuan.

Every year, more than 100,000 visitors would come to Aihe Town and its surroundings, generating an income of more than 20 million yuan. Local homestays and the walnuts, persimmons, pears, and apples grown by local poor farmers are very popular among consumers, generating considerable income for the villagers.

Experience and Inspirations

1. Education first

There is an old saying in China: "Give a man a fish and you feed him for a day. Teach a man to fish and you feed him for a lifetime." When rural areas meet with art, the sparks thus ignited may be beyond our imagination. The most important thing about rural revitalization is to help the government and the masses understand the concept of art village, so that they will understand what the project is and where it is heading, support and contribute more to the project.

2. Adapt to local conditions

The Aihe Town project makes proper use of local resources and pursues sustainable development according to local conditions. Instead of demolition and construction of buildings on a large scale, it uses local materials and is environment conscious. It promotes sustainable development, protects local ecological resources, and add the beauty of art to the beautiful rural landscape of the village.

3. Promote international exchange

Since the Aihe Town project started, it has attracted the attention of the artists at home and abroad. Many of them have visited Aihe Town many times to draw inspiration, create artworks and exchange with peers, boosting the popularity and reputation of Luoling Township.

4. Increase input into education

Aihe Town strengthens cooperation with domestic colleges and universities in building tourist service platforms, training creators, making innovations and starting businesses. It has become the innovation and entrepreneurship base, tourism discipline development base, arts and crafts teaching, research and field practice base, and internship base of Jingdezhen Ceramic University, Xi'an Academy of Fine Arts, Luoyang Normal University, etc., building up its visibility.

Next Steps

Firstly, Luoning County will continue to step up efforts in infrastructure construction and improve hardware facilities to achieve the goal of building a national 4A-level scenic spot, and start to build the most representative "One Day Art Museum" in Luoyang City.

Secondly, it will continue to host international art exhibitions and other exhibitions, conventions and study tours and become a new high ground for the promotion of culture and raising cultural and ethical standards. At the same time, the park will open master's studios, high-end homestays, study tour base, etc., keep pace with the economic development of the times, closely follow the capital market and the art market, and build an international tri-colored glazed pottery art village that aligns with rural revitalization and the market economy.

Thirdly, it will continue with aesthetic education. It will hold a variety of artistic and aesthetic activities such as tri-colored painting for children and the "One Day" Art Exhibition, and promote rural development and rural aesthetic education.

Fourthly, it will continue to host floriculture-themed events and celebrations based on local natural conditions, to attract visitors to the town and surrounding scenic areas. Through such activities, it hopes to build up the visibility and popularity of Luoning County on an ongoing basis, increase the employment of local farmers and the traffic to and income of surrounding scenic areas, and boost rural revitalization through tourism.

旅游减贫案例故事(中英文双语版)
Best Practices of Poverty Alleviation through Tourism (Chinese-English Bilingual Edition)

湖北省恩施土家族苗族自治州宣恩县:
紧扣"融合",全域旅游发展助力脱贫致富

收录于《2021世界旅游联盟:旅游助力乡村振兴案例》

摘要

　　宣恩县通过农旅融合、文旅融合、体旅融合、工旅融合及数字旅游等产业创新发展模式,借助旅游产业在挖掘资源、改善环境、吸引人流、创造就业等方面的强大能力,依托浙江大学、重庆大学、华中科技大学等高校的专家智库,以县城仙山贡水国家4A级旅游景区为核心,辐射带动周边乡镇,形成主客共享、景城同建、产城共融的全域旅游发展格局。2019年4月20日,宣恩县成功脱贫;10月18日,在世界休闲发展高峰论坛上,宣恩县城仙山贡水旅游区荣获"中国文旅融合创新奖"。2019年,全县游客接待300.88万人次,旅游综合收入14.85亿元,同比分别增长24.2%、26.5%,两项数据增幅均在恩施州八县市中排名第一。2020年4月,宣恩县人民政府与中国农业发展银行恩施州分行签订《支持宣恩县全域旅游政银共建框架协议》,又开启了金融助推旅游的快速发展模式。

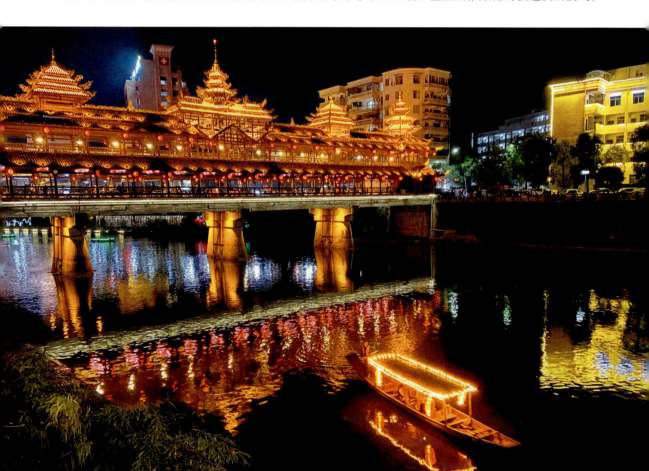

挑战与问题

宣恩县地处鄂西南边陲，在恩施土家族苗族自治州南部，东接鹤峰县，西邻咸丰县，西南同来凤县毗连，总面积2740平方千米，属西部连片贫困地区。宣恩县下辖5个镇4个乡，总人口36.2万人，常住人口30.58万人，其中城镇人口11.22万人，城镇化率36.70%。除土家族、苗、侗族三个人口较多的少数民族，还有彝、回、白、满、壮、蒙古、畲、傣、朝鲜、维吾尔等32个少数民族。

作为国家级贫困县，宣恩面临的首要问题是脱贫。宣恩自然资源得天独厚，有七姊妹山自然保护区和贡水河国家湿地公园，县域范围内的其他旅游项目也都高度依赖自然环境，因此在旅游产业的发展过程中，如何兼顾环境质量并达到脱贫，成为关键。众多少数民族聚居也为宣恩县创造了大量特色鲜明的文化元素，如何将建筑、服饰、美食等民俗文化融入生活，达到保护和传承的双重目的，成为宣恩县高质量发展的需求。

措施

1. 农旅融合——激活资源，带动就业

伍家台贡茶文化旅游区以伍家台万亩生态茶园为载体，以贡茶文化为底蕴，以生态茶园观光和休闲养生为特色，成功创建为国家4A级旅游景区，并建设了伍家台贡茶小镇。同时，以千亩黄金梨基地为载体，挖掘土司文化、茶马古道历史，开发打造黄坪阿尼阿兹休闲旅游区。此外，还以南三镇万亩白柚园为载体，打造白柚观光走廊。通过深入推进农旅融合，全力落实旅游扶贫，为下一步振兴战略奠定基础。

2. 文旅融合——传承文化，提升品位

依托彭家寨"生态、村落、民俗"特征，打造集建筑奇观、村落景观、视觉美观、文化感观为一体的活态博物馆；依托县城仙山贡水旅游区的墨达楼、民俗文化街景点，打造县城开放式景区，凸显国家全域旅游示范区和开放型生态文化旅游区特点。组织彭家寨参加威尼斯双年展。在威尼斯双年展上，中国土家族建筑文化首次向世界揭开神秘面纱。

3. 体旅融合——四季运动，彰显活力

在休闲旅游项目中融入体育元素，如椿木营运动休闲旅游区配套高山滑雪场、锣圈岩休闲旅游区配套高山足球场，还连续11年举办中国内陆河水上运动会、连续7年在五子岩举办高山露营节及赛马会，以及多次举办汽车越野赛等。

4. 工旅融合——多元产业，旅游赋能

椒园生态产业园区企业将生产工艺、品牌产品和企业文化转换成旅游商品。土家爱公司的合渣粉在"湖北礼道"旅游商品创意设计大赛上获农产品土特产类金奖，亚麦食品公司的DIY糕点体验等为游客提供了"先学习再模仿"的"工业品制造体验之旅"。

5. 数字旅游——科技引领，创新体验

引进杭州颐居草堂科技有限公司，搭建"互联网+旅游"的双创平台，在伍家台设置乡村旅游智慧服务中心；搭建"旅游+"电商平台，通过线上流量实现将土特产品向旅游特色商品转型，借助数字经济之城杭州的东西部协作帮扶机遇，通过线上认筹、领养果树等方式，提高宣恩旅游知名度，加快旅游产业转型升级。

成效

宣恩县已有县城仙山贡水旅游区、伍家台景区、七姊妹山国家级自然保护区、贡水河国家湿地公园、狮子关景区、庆阳古街、彭家寨景区、萨玛长潭景区、椿木营滑雪场、锣圈岩景区等10多个旅游景点，县城核心吸引力强，功能完善；乡镇辐射面广，带动性强。

2019年4月20日，宣恩县成功脱贫；10月18日，宣恩县城仙山贡水旅游区荣获"中国文旅融合创

新奖";12月4日,创建"湖北旅游强县"通过验收;2021年10月,宣恩县仙山贡水旅游区景区被列入国家4A级景区名单。2019年,全县游客接待量300.88万人次,旅游综合收入14.85亿元,同比分别增长24.2%、26.5%,两项数据增幅均在恩施州八县市中第一。

3. 产城共融

在旅游产业的带动下,宣恩县逐渐从贫困落后的山城,转变成人气旺、产业兴、体制活的区域旅游强县,在环境保护、文化传承、技术应用、消费体验、项目投资等方面,进一步拉近与东部地区的距离,不断提升旅游产业的富民创收能力。

经验与启示

1. 主客共享

以县城仙山贡水国家级4A旅游景区创建工作为标杆,分布于周边各乡镇的景区配合,全县旅游产业发展从活动组织、休闲体验、就业带动、成果分享等方面,充分践行主客共享理念。

2. 景城同建

全县围绕旅游产业发展,在基础建设、环境整治、团队架构、政策制定等方面,依托浙江大学、重庆大学、华中科技大学等高校的规划设计,集中财政支持和政策杠杆,有目标、有重点地发挥各类产业基础的势能,共同提升整体旅游休闲氛围。

下一步计划

进一步总结前期经验,依托县城全域开放型景区的高质量发展起点和对周边乡镇的辐射带动作用,发挥景城同建政策在提升县城活力和就业接纳方面的能力,通过提升游客总体消费体量、侧重游客自主消费品类和激活居民参与经营三种策略,提升当地居民的参与度和创收能力;通过空间格局锁定、业态比例协调、集散功能支撑和游赏动线引导四种方式,发挥旅游产业发展在改善环境质量方面的作用;通过主动接纳外来文化、挖掘和活化本土文化,实现特色民俗文化的传承和创新。

Xuan'en County, Enshi Tujia and Miao Autonomous Prefecture, Hubei Province:

Alleviating Poverty through Integration and All-For-One Tourism Development

Included in *WTA Best Practices of Rural Revitalization through Tourism 2021*

Abstract

Based on the great function of tourism in tapping resources, improving the environment, attracting people and creating jobs, Xuan'en County is developing all-for-one tourism characterized by host-guest sharing, simultaneous building of tourist attractions and the city and industry-city integration through innovative development modes including agriculture-tourism integration, culture-tourism integration, sports-tourism integration, manufacturing-tourism integration and digital tourism under the support of think tanks of Zhejiang University, Chongqing University, Huazhong University of Science and Technology and other universities. The tourism industry of Xuan'en centers around the Xianshan Gongshui national 4A-level scenic spot in the urban area of the county and covers surrounding towns and villages. On April 20, 2019, Xuan'en County was removed from the list of national poverty-stricken counties. On October 18, 2019, at the World Leisure Development Summit, the Xianshan Gongshui Tourism Area in the urban area of Xuan'en County won the "Chinese Culture and Tourism Integration Innovation Award". In 2019, Xuan'en received 3,008,800 tourists and realized a total tourism income of 1,485 million yuan, which were increased by 24.2% and 26.5% respectively from the year before, both being the largest growth among the eight counties and cities of Enshi Tujia and Miao Autonomous Prefecture. In April 2020, the People's Government of Xuan'en County and the Enshi Branch of Agricultural Development Bank of China signed *The Framework Agreement on Supporting Xuanen's All-for-one Tourism through the Cooperation between Government and Bank*, building the mode of boosting rapid development of tourism with finance.

Challenges and Problems

Located on the southwest border of Hubei Province, Xuan'en County borders Enshi Tujia and Miao Autonomous Prefecture on the south, Hefeng County on the west, Xianfeng County on the east and Laifeng County in the northeast. It covers a total area of 2,740 square kilometers and is a contiguous poverty-stricken areas in the west China. Xuan'en County rules 5 towns and 4 townships and has a total population of 362,000 and a permanent population of 305,800, including 112,200 urban population with an urbanization rate of 36.70%. In addition to the three ethnic minorities with the largest population, Tujia, Miao and Dong, there are 32 other ethnic minorities including Yi, Hui, Bai, Man, Zhuang, Mongol, She, Dai, Korean and Uygur.

As a national poverty-stricken county, the primary task for Xuan'en is poverty alleviation. Xuan'en is blessed with rich natural resources. Not only the Qizimei Mountain Nature Reserve and Gongshui River National Wetland Park but also other tourism projects in the county highly rely on the natural environment. Therefore, it is critical to maintain the environment quality while alleviating poverty in the development of tourism industry. Many ethnic minorities living in the county also create a large number of distinctive cultural elements for Xuan'en County. How to integrate folk customer and culture in architecture, clothing, food, etc. into people's life for protection and inheritance is a problem which needs to be solved by Xuan'en County in order to realize quality development.

Measures

1. Integrating agriculture and tourism to utilize resources and drive employment

Based on the Ten-Thousand-Mu Wujiatai ecological tea garden and tribute tea culture,

Xuan'en successfully builds the Wujiatai Tribute Tea Culture Tourism Resort featuring ecological tea garden sightseeing and leisure wellness into a national 4A-level scenic spot and constructs the Wujiatai tribute tea town. Besides, the Huangping Aniaz Leisure Tourism Resort is built based on the Thousand-Mu gold pear base by exploring the chieftain culture and history of ancient tea-horse road, and a white pomelo sightseeing corridor is built based on the Ten-Thousand-Mu sightseeing white pomelo garden in Nansan Town. The county is making every effort to advance the profound integration of agriculture and tourism to implement the tourism-based poverty alleviation and lay a solid foundation for the future revitalization strategy.

2. Integrating culture and tourism to inherit culture and improve life quality

Based on its characteristics in "ecology, village and folk custom", Pengjiazhai is built into a museum incorporating amazing architecture, village landscape, wonderful scenery and splendid culture. Relying on the Moda Building and the folk custom and culture street in Xianshan Gongshui Tourism Area, an open tourism attraction is built in the urban area, which highlights the characteristics of Xuan'en as the national all-for-one tourism demonstration area and open ecological cultural tourism area.

Pengjiazhai attended the Venice Biennale, unveiling the architectural culture of Tujia in China to the world for the first time.

3. Integrating sports and tourism to display vitality with sports of the four seasons

Sports elements are incorporated in leisure tourism projects, such as establishing mountain ski resort in Chunmuying Sports and Leisure Tourism Area and building mountain football field in Luoquanyan Leisure Tourism Area. Besides, Xuan'en has held the China Inland River Water Games for 11 consecutive years, the mountain camping festival and horse-racing (in Wuziyan) for 7 consecutive years, and automobile cross-country races many times.

4. Integrating manufacturing and tourism to develop diverse industries and create impetus through tourism

The enterprises in Jiaoyuan Eco-industrial Park transform production technology, branded products and corporate culture into tourism commodities. The Hezha powder produced by Tujia Ai won the gold medal in the "Hubei Gift" Tourism Product Creative Design Competition, and the DIY cake-making experience provided by Yamai Food allows tourists to enjoy the "journey of manufacturing industrial products" by "learning and imitating".

5. Developing digital tourism to lead the industry with technology and provide innovative experiences

Working with Hangzhou Yiju Caotang Technology Co., Ltd., Xuan'en builds a "mass entrepreneurship and innovation" platform of "internet + tourism", and sets up a rural tourism intelligence service center in Wujiatai. Besides, a "tourism + e-commerce" platform is established to transform local products into specialty tourism products through online traffic. Taking advantage of the support offered by Hangzhou, the city of digital economy, under the east-west cooperation program, Xuan'en manages to increase the popularity of its tourism through online subscription, fruit trees taking, etc. so as to accelerate the transformation and upgrading of tourism industry.

Results

Xuanen has built more than 10 tourist attractions, including Xianshan Gongshui Tourism Zone, Wujiatai Resort, Qizimei Mountain National Nature Reserve, Gongshui River National Wetland Park, Shiziguan Resort, Qingyang Ancient Street, Pengjiazhai Resort, Sama Changtan Resort, Chunmuying Ski Resort and Luoquanyan Resort. The urban area of the county has strong attraction and complete functions, while the towns of the county have extensive influence over surrounding areas and may provide a strong driving force for their development.

On April 20, 2019, Xuanen County successfully achieved poverty alleviation. On October 18, the Xianshan Gongshui Tourist Area in Xuanen County was awarded the "China Cultural and Tourism Integration Innovation Award". On December 4, the county passed the acceptance review for the creation of a "Hubei Tourism Strong County". In October 2021, the Xianshan Gongshui Tourist Area was listed as a national 4A-level scenic

spot. In 2019, the county received 3.0088 million tourist visits, generating a comprehensive tourism revenue of 1.485 billion yuan, representing year-on-year increases of 24.2% and 26.5%, respectively. Both growth rates ranked first among the eight counties and cities in Enshi Tujia and Miao Autonomous Prefecture.

Experience and Inspirations

1. Host-guest sharing

As reflected in the building of the benchmark project of Xianshan Gongshui, a national 4A-level scenic spot in the urban area, and the scenic spots distributed in surrounding towns, the idea of host-guest sharing is fully implemented in the tourism industry development of the county from event organization, leisure experience, job creation and achievements sharing.

2. Simultaneous building of tourist attractions and the city

Centering around the development of tourism industry, Xuan'en County centrally utilizes financial support and policy leverages to make full use of key various industrial bases in a targeted manner to jointly enhance the overall tourism and leisure environment relying on the planning and design provided by Zhejiang University, Chongqing University, Huazhong University of Science and Technology, etc. in infrastructure construction, environmental improvement, team structure and policy making.

3. Industry-city integration

Driven by the tourism industry, Xuan'en has gradually changed from a poor and backward mountain city into a regional key tourism county with great popularity, prosperous industry and efficient systems. In terms of environmental protection, cultural heritage, technology application, consumption experience, project investment, etc., it has further narrowed the gap with eastern China region and is working to improve the ability of tourism industry to increase people's income.

Next Steps

Based on a further review of its experience already accumulated, Xuan'en will fully utilize the function of the policy of "simultaneous building of tourist attractions and the city" in increasing economic vitality and employment opportunities relying on the open tourism area in the urban area, which is a good starting point for quality development, and its driving forces for surrounding towns. By increasing the consumption by tourists, stressing autonomous consumer goods of tourists and encouraging residents to participate in business, it will increase the involvement and income-generating ability of local residents. Besides, it will give full play to the role of tourism industry development in improving environmental quality by locking spatial pattern, coordinating business size, supporting distribution function and adjusting tourist routes. Active efforts will be made to accept foreign culture, explore and activate local culture to realize the inheritance and innovation of characteristic folk culture.

旅游减贫案例故事（中英文双语版）
Best Practices of Poverty Alleviation through Tourism（Chinese–English Bilingual Edition）

湖南省张家界市武陵源区：
"世界自然遗产旅游+"的脱贫之路

收录于《2021世界旅游联盟：旅游助力乡村振兴案例》

摘要

　　脱贫攻坚以来，湖南省张家界市武陵源区围绕"把景区旅游效益辐射到乡村中去""把农民带进旅游产业链上来""把游客带到农户家中去""把农民带到旅游致富路上来"四大路径，探索出以"四带动、四转变"为特征的旅游扶贫模式：实施核心景区带动，促进农业向旅游业转变；实施乡村民宿带动，促进农村向乡村旅游目的地转变；实施旅游企业带动，促进农民向旅游从业者转变；实施旅游产品带动，促进农产品向旅游商品转变。武陵源区实现了经济社会在质量和数量上的双重飞跃，实现了从"养在深闺"到享誉世界、从偏僻山区到宜居宜游、从"靠山吃山"到生态优先的转变，将旅游产业发展与精准扶贫有机结合，为贫困群众打开了致富之门。

挑战与问题

武陵源区位于湖南省西北部武陵山脉中的张家界市境内，1988年5月经国务院批准设立为县级行政区，总面积397.58平方千米，其中核心景区217.2平方千米。建区初期，由于自然、历史、文化等各种因素，全区5万多人口大多在温饱线上挣扎，年人均收入不足200元，脱贫攻坚的任务艰巨而繁重。1992年，联合国教科文组织将武陵源作为中国首个"世界自然遗产"列入世界遗产名录。武陵源区以此为契机，开始大力发展旅游业，走上了乡村振兴之路。

措施

1. 绘就产业发展新蓝图

武陵源区通过做优做强乡村旅游、农业、文创三大带贫产业，绘就"旅游+扶贫"产业发展蓝图，出台了《武陵源区乡村旅游发展实施指导意见》《武陵源区产业精准扶贫规划》等一系列政策文件，投入财政产业扶持资金逾1.5亿元，调动特色民宿、农家乐、农业龙头企业、农民专业合作社、文创企业等带贫主体的积极性，撬动社会投资逾30亿元，通过打造武陵源峰林峡谷特色民宿体验区和实施"一县一特""一乡一业""一村一品""一户一产"等带贫项目，培育带贫主体强劲的造血功能，确保贫困人口真正脱贫。

2. 发展乡村旅游

武陵源区充分利用秀丽的山水风景和浓厚的民俗文化，大力发展乡村旅游，让农民变成旅游从业者，实现农村"内循环"，抓住乡村旅游"点、线、面"布局，通过推出乡村旅游精品路线和特色民宿，为当地农民提供"家门口就业"的机会，确保了旅游产业发展红利有效释放、真金白银尽快"落袋"。目前，"张家界市—中湖乡—天子山"和"张家界市—协合乡—索溪峪—张家界村"两条精品线路上有特色民宿、农家客栈、农家乐700多家，带动8000多位农民从事乡村旅游服务业，每年带动农民增收逾2000万元。

3. 发展农业产业

武陵源区将创新产业扶贫模式融入"创建湖南省农村一二三产业融合发展示范县"之中，建成鱼泉贡米、天子山剁辣椒、湘阿妹菜葛、武陵源头茶叶4个省市级产业园，培育发展省级农业龙头企业1家、市级农业龙头企业11家、农民专业合作社76家。龙头企业产业链融合、农业功能融合、农业渗透融合走上良性轨道，带动建档立卡贫困户大力发展优质水稻、精品果蔬、绿色茶叶、特色养殖等扶贫农业产业，近年来脱贫户享受"区、乡、村"三级产业累计分红资金逾1000万元。如菜葛产业，近年来武陵源区整合扶贫资金2000万元支持菜葛种植、产品提质和品牌创建发展，全区葛根种植面积4000亩，直接受益农民达5000多人，每年帮助2300名脱贫户实现增收，年人均增长超过1000元。

4. 发展文创产业

走"文旅融合发展，产业带动扶贫"的特色路子。武陵源区投入扶贫资金491万元引进乖幺妹土家织锦产业，其产品涵盖艺术品收藏、居家装饰、服装、服饰和实用类产品600多种，申请专利122件，公司累计培训土家织锦技师1200多人次，现有产业工人180多名，是目前武陵山片区最大的土家织锦研发中心和生产基地，带动索溪峪街道1463名脱贫人口致富；投入扶贫资金410万元引进扶持熊风雕塑产业做大做强，流转土地86.5亩，在索溪峪街道双文村打造湘西第一个兼具人文历史价值、民俗风情的雕塑公园，使其成为湘西最专业的写生、创作、实习、培训、接待基地，解决了4个村31户脱贫户的务工就业问题。

5. 健全发展机制

武陵源区建立健全"全域旅游+扶贫"。"四跟

四走"（资金跟着贫困户走，贫困户跟着能人走，能人跟着产业项目走，产业项目跟着市场走）产业扶贫带动机制，"劳动务工型、土地流转型、订单收购型、入股分红型、种养托管型、合作帮扶型"等产业帮扶模式也得到广泛运用，产业扶贫变输血为造血，贫困户和村集体长期获得产业发展红利。据统计，2020年武陵源区农村居民年人均可支配收入达15621元，同比人均增收逾1200元。各村级组织在农民自愿的基础上，采取反租倒包、租赁承包、土地入股等多种形式流转土地，发展特色民宿、旅游店铺、特色产业，增加村级集体经营性收入；并依托项目优、发展快、前景好的产业主体，以土地使用权等资源形式参股，增加村集体股份合作收入。协合村、李家岗村、土地峪村等5个村与张家界湘阿妹食品有限公司签订菜葛土地流转协议，公司统一经营管理，每年村产业分红资金3万元；双文、双星、田富、金杜4个村资金入股熊风雕塑产业园，每年村集体分红32万元。

成效

2016年，武陵源区率先在湖南省整区脱贫，2017年、2018年、2019年连续三年持续巩固，武陵源区旅游扶贫之路越走越宽广。据统计，全区农村居民年人均可支配收入由2015年的10000元，增加到2020年的15621元，全区人民最大限度地享受到了旅游发展的红利。武陵源区充分利用世界自然遗产资源大力发展旅游产业，将产业扶贫与精品景区、特色城镇、美丽乡村"三位一体"的全域旅游进行高质

量融合，成为"首批国家全域旅游示范区"，每年带动农民增收逾4亿元，其中5119名脱贫人口增收总额逾4000万元。

经验与启示

1. 注重农民技能提升

武陵源区编印《武陵源区产业扶贫技能培训资料汇编》和《武陵源区产业发展实用技术手册》，采取技术单位、龙头企业、合作社相结合的方式，对全区扶贫产业进行"点对点""一对一"的巡回培训。2016年以来，累计组织各类产业技能培训班200多期，培训农民2万余人次，其中贫困户8000多人次。

2. 注重乡村品牌培育

天子山剁辣椒、湘阿妹菜葛、禾田居茄子、天门红茶、天子绿茶等16个产品获得绿色食品认证；系列扶贫产品获得专利13件；湘阿妹菜葛获评"国家葛根种植标准化示范区"；"天子名翠"和"鱼泉贡米"

获评湖南省著名商标；金毛猴红茶获评米兰世博会金奖；"两品一标"认证面积和基地创建面积所占耕地面积的比例，均位居全省前列。

3. 注重农业产品营销

除了积极参加农博会、展览会、年货节、扶贫日等活动，武陵源区还以多种形式促进线下产品的销售，并通过众创空间、供销云商、农村淘宝等电商企业和智慧武陵源、微信、抖音、京东等电商平台促进线上销售。各经营主体紧跟科技新前沿，瞄准消费新趋势，将"互联网+""生态+"等现代新理念引入生产经营活动，创新生产方式、经营方式和资源利用方式；将"旅游+产业"的边界扩展到更广的范围，实现生产、生活、生态共赢。

下一步计划

脱贫攻坚取得全面胜利、实现全面小康后，武陵源区在新的历史起点上提出了"把武陵源美丽乡村打造成武陵山片区乡村振兴的样板"目标，大力实施乡村产业提质、乡村建设升级、人居环境整治提升、公共服务保障行动、乡风文明培育行动、乡村治理示范6大行动26项工程100项重点任务。力争到2025年，实现农业总产值达10亿元，乡村旅游接待430万人次、综合收入66亿元，农村居民年人均可支配收入逾25000元的新目标。

Wulingyuan District, Zhangjiajie City, Hunan Province:

Road to Poverty Alleviation through "World Natural Heritage Tourism +" Model

Included in *WTA Best Practices of Rural Revitalization through Tourism 2021*

Abstract

Wulingyuan District, Zhangjiajie City, Hunan Province, has explored a poverty-alleviation model through tourism based on four major paths: promoting the extension of tourism benefits from scenic spots to rural areas; encouraging farmers to participate in the tourism industry chain; attracting tourists to visit farmers' homes; and helping farmers achieve prosperity through tourism.

It has also become a core scenic spot in the agriculture-to-tourism transformation. It has also served as a model for rural B&Bs in driving the transformation of rural areas into tourist destinations. Furthermore, it has become a model for tourism enterprises in the transformation of farmers into tourism practitioners. Additionally, the village also serves as a model in the transformation of agricultural products into tourist commodities. The district has changed significantly as its economy, quality and way of life have undergone an unprecedented change from little-known to world-renowned. The village used to be a remote mountainous area, but it has transformed into an ideal living and travel destination. It has shifted its focus from exploiting local resources to prioritizing ecological conservation. As a result, it has realized the organic integration of tourism industry development and targeted poverty reduction, offering poverty-stricken people the opportunity for a more prosperous life.

Challenges and Problems

Located in Zhangjiajie City in Wuling Mountain of northwestern Hunan Province, Wulingyuan District was established by the approval of the State Council in May 1988 with a total area of 397.58 square kilometers. It includes core scenic spots of 217.2 square kilometers. In the early days of the district's establishment, a majority of the population of more than 50,000 were impoverished. People were struggling for food and clothing and lived off an annual average income of less than 200 yuan. The task of poverty alleviation was arduous and onerous. In 1992, Wulingyuan was inscribed by UNESCO as China's first World Natural Heritage Site. Capitalizing on this prestigious badge of honor and recognition, Wulingyuan District began to develop its tourism industry and took on the mission of rural revitalization.

Measures

1. Deploy industrial development

The district has drawn up a blueprint for the development of "tourism + poverty alleviation". This will be done by strengthening the three poverty-reduction industries of rural tourism, agriculture and cultural and creative industries. It has created policy documents, such as *Guiding Opinions on the Implementation of Rural Tourism Development in Wulingyuan District* and *Targeted Poverty Alleviation Plan through Industrial Development in Wulingyuan District*. In addition, it has invested heavily with the financial support funds of more than 150 million yuan to stimulate the building of characteristic B&Bs, agritainment, leading agricultural enterprises,

farmers' professional cooperatives, cultural and creative enterprises and other poverty-reduction entities. By leveraging the social investment of up to 3 billion yuan the district has created a distinctive homestay experience zone in the Wulingyuan Peak Forest Canyon and implemented poverty-alleviation projects such as "One County, One Specialty", "One Town, One Industry", "One Village, One Product", and "One Household, One Livelihood". This is to ensure that the impoverished people are lifted out of poverty.

2. Develop rural tourism

The district has made full use of its stunning landscape and rich folk culture to develop rural tourism. This also entails turning farmers into tourism practitioners and realizing the "inner recycle" in rural areas. To accomplish this, it launched boutique routes and incorporated rural tourism into the layout, scaling it up from micro to macro. The village characteristic B&Bs provide local farmers with job opportunities and ensure that they can obtain dividends from industrial development and increase their income. At present, there are over 700 characteristic B&Bs, farm inns, and agritainment along the two boutique routes of "Zhangjiajie City – Zhonghu Township – Tianzi

Mountain" and "Zhangjiajie City – Xiehe Township – Suoxi Valley – Zhangjiajie Village". This helps over 8,000 farmers engage in rural tourism services and increases their annual income to more than 20 million yuan.

3. Develop agricultural industries

It has incorporated the poverty alleviation model through innovative industries. This was done through the initiative of "creating demonstration counties with integrated development of rural primary, secondary and tertiary industries in Hunan Province". Four provincial and municipal industrial parks on Yuquan Gongmi, Tianzishan Chopped Pepper, Xiang A Mei Caige (a new type of vegetable, cultivated from pachyrhizua angulatus), and Wuling Yuantou Tea were built. In addition, a leading agricultural enterprise at the provincial level, 11 leading agricultural enterprises at the municipal level, and 76 farmers' professional cooperatives were also developed. The integration of leading enterprises' industrial chains with agricultural functions and agricultural penetration was a guaranteed path to follow. The archived impoverished households were motivated to develop quality rice, boutique fruits and vegetables, green tea, special breeding and other poverty-alleviation agricultural industries. In recent years, households that were lifted out of poverty have enjoyed a cumulative dividend of more than 10 million yuan in the three-tier industry in the "village, township, and district." For example, in recent years, the district has integrated the poverty-alleviation funds of 20 million yuan to support Caige planting, product quality improvement, brand creation and development. The planting area of Pueraria lobata in the region is 4,000 *mu*, benefiting more than 5,000 farmers and lifting 2,300 people out of poverty every year, with the annual per capita income increase of more than 1,000 yuan.

4. Develop cultural and creative industries

The village has followed the path of "integrated development of cultural and tourism, and industry-driven poverty alleviation". It invested the poverty-alleviation funds of 4.91 million yuan to introduce the Guaiyaomei Tujia brocade industry. These products cover more than 600 kinds of art collection, home decoration, clothing, costume and practical products. The company has also applied for 122 patents and trained more than 1,200 Tujia brocade technicians. With more than 180 industrial workers, it's currently the largest Tujia brocade R&D center and production base in Wuling Mountain area as it helps 1,463 people in Suoxiyu Sub-district rise out of poverty and make some money. It invested the poverty-alleviation funds of 4.1 million yuan to introduce and support the vigorous development of Xiongfeng sculpture industry, with the transferred land area of 86.5 *mu*. The first sculpture park featuring cultural history and folk customs has been built in Shuangwen Village, Suoxiyu Sub-district, which is the most professional sculpture park in western Hunan Province. A base for sketching, creation, internship, training and reception has also been constructed.

5. Improve the development mechanism

The district has established and improved the "all-for-one tourism + poverty alleviation". In addition, the "Four Follows (Funds follow the poor, the poor follow the capable people, the capable people follow the industrial projects, and the industrial projects follow the market)" poverty alleviation mechanism driven by industrial development has also been implemented. The industrial assistance models characterized by "labor work, land transfer, order purchase, dividend sharing, planting and breeding trust, and cooperative assistance" have been widely applied. The poverty alleviation through industrial development has transformed the model from continuous supply to self-upgrading. This means that the impoverished households and village collective can obtain long-term dividends from industrial development. Statistically, the per capita disposable income of rural residents in the district reached 15,621 yuan in 2020, a year-on-year increase of more than 1,200 yuan. Based on farmers' voluntary efforts, village-level organizations have adopted various forms of land transfer, such as subcontracting, lease contracting and pooling of land as shares to develop characteristic B&Bs, tourist shops and other local industries that would increase the operating income of the village collective. The village has relied on industry entities with excellent projects, rapid development and bright prospects. Because of this, it has participated in shares in the form of resources such as land use rights to increase joint stock income of the village collective. Five villages, including Xiehe Village, Lijiagang Village, and Tudiyu Village have signed the Caige land transfer agreement with Zhangjiajie Xiang A Mei Food Co., Ltd. The company has conducted a unified operation and management over village industries with an annual dividend from industries of 30,000 yuan. The four villages of Shuangwen, Shuangxing, Tianfu and Jindu have invested in Xiongfeng Sculpture Industrial Park, generating an annual dividend for the village collective of 320,000 yuan.

Results

In 2016, the district took the lead in reducing the poverty levels in Hunan Province. It continued to consolidate its poverty alleviation achievements for three consecutive years from 2017 to 2019. According to statistics, the per capita disposable income of rural residents in the district increased from 10,000 yuan in 2015 to 15,621 yuan in 2020. This means that local people enjoyed the maximum benefits of tourism development. The district has made full use of world natural heritage resources to develop the tourism industry based on the high-quality integration of poverty alleviation through industrial development and the all-for-one tourism featuring boutique scenic spots, characteristic towns, and beautiful villages. It has become the first batch of national all-for-one tourism demonstration zones, which increased local farmers' income by more than 400 million yuan each year. Overall, 5,119 people were lifted out of poverty and the village income increased by more than 40 million yuan.

Experience and Inspirations

1. Improve farmers' skills

The district compiled and printed *Skills Training Materials Collection on Poverty Alleviation through Industrial Development in Wulingyuan*

District and *Practical Technical Manual on Industrial Development in Wulingyuan District*. It has adopted a combination of technical units, leading enterprises and cooperatives to provide "one-to-one" itinerant training on poverty-alleviation industries in the region. Since 2016, it has organized more than 200 training courses on various industrial skills, offering training to more than 20,000 farmers, including more than 8,000 impoverished households.

2. Develop rural brands

A total of 16 products, including Tianzishan Chopped Chili, Xiang A Mei Caige, Hetianju Eggplant, Tianmen Black Tea, Tianzi Green Tea, were granted Green Food Certification. Thirteen patents were granted to a series of poverty-alleviation products. Xiang A Mei Caige was awarded "National Caige Planting Standardization Demonstration Zone," "Tian Zi Ming Cui" and "Yu Quan Gong Mi" were awarded the famous trademarks of Hunan Province, and Golden Monkey Black Tea was awarded the Gold Medal of Expo Milano 2015. The certifications of green food, organic agricultural products, and geographic agro-product indications, as well as their base establishment were ranked first in terms of the proportion of arable area in the province.

3. Promote agricultural products

In addition to actively participating in the Agricultural Expo, exhibitions, New Year's Shopping Festivals, and Poverty Alleviation Day, Wulingyuan District is also promoting online sales through various forms. Furthermore, it facilitates online sales via e-commerce enterprises such as maker spaces, supply and marketing cloud commerce, and Rural Taobao, as well as e-commerce platforms including Smart Wulingyuan, WeChat, Douyin (TikTok), and JD.com. All business entities have kept up with new frontiers in science and technology by staying on top of new consumption trends. They have introduced modern concepts of "internet +" and "ecology +" into production and business activities, and innovated production methods, operational and resource utilization. The extension of the boundary of "tourism + industry" into a wider range has achieved a win-win situation in production, life and ecology.

Next Steps

Poverty alleviation has been achieved and the local villagers attained a prosperous standard of living, the district aims at "making the beautiful village into a model for rural revitalization in the Wuling Mountain area" a new historical starting point. They will implement 26 new projects and 100 key tasks. These will take place in the six key activities: the improvement of rural industrial quality, the upgrading of rural construction, the improvement of human settlements, the support for public services and the cultivation of rural traditions and customs. By 2025, it hopes to achieve a total agricultural output value of 1 billion yuan, with a rural tourist reception of 4.3 million people, a comprehensive income of 6.6 billion yuan, and a per capita disposable income for rural residents of more than 25,000 yuan.

广东省肇庆市封开县：
贺江碧道画廊景区建设粤桂省际廊道美丽乡村示范带

收录于《2022 世界旅游联盟：旅游助力乡村振兴案例》

摘要

2018 年，广东省提出在省际边界地区打造 5 条乡村振兴示范带。贺江碧道画廊景区位于肇庆市封开县，属于粤桂省际廊道美丽乡村示范带核心区，其打造了"广信文化""潇贺古道""茶船古道"融合的文化商旅古驿道。项目分四期：一期完成总体规划设计及开展民生设施建设；二期提升廊道风貌；三期发展全域旅游；四期创建国家 4A 级旅游景区。贺江碧道画廊现已达到国家 4A 级旅游景区验收标准，仅 2021 年五一期间，贺江碧道画廊共接待游客 4.99 万人次，实现旅游收入 0.15 亿元。

挑战与问题

广东省肇庆市封开县是岭南地区的古首府、广府文化的发源地,也是潇贺古道与茶船古道的重要流经地。随着历史车轮的不断向前,岭南的政治与经济中心、广府文化中心逐步转移至珠江三角洲地区,位于广东省际边界的封开县在经济上逐渐走向边缘化。在贺江碧道画廊景区建设以前,封开县拥有的蛇曲地貌、贺江"九曲十八湾""江下竹林"等独特景观尚未被充分挖潜,历史文化品牌不够突出,沿线村庄景观杂乱,旅游业发展缓慢,旅游设施配套严重不足,缺乏特色文旅产业项目,村民经济收入水平普遍较低。如今的粤桂省际廊道美丽乡村示范带涉及的12个行政村中,曾有贫困户277户、贫困人口686人,属于乡村发展的薄弱地区。

措施

1. 打造三大历史文化名片

当地组织编制《省际廊道(肇庆段)美丽乡村示范带提升规划及风貌提升设计指引》系列规划项目,引领景区建设遵从"以路为廊""以水为链"的理念,将陆道、水道、赛道、碧道、古驿道、绿道"六道合一",合称为"贺道",有着取位于贺江畔和庆贺、庆祝等吉祥寓意。积极发挥自然本底优势,深入挖掘古驿道历史文化,高标准建设两广源流博物馆,在建筑中充分体现广府特色,打造"广信文化""潇贺古道""茶船古道"融合的文化商旅古驿道。

2. 提升贺江碧道画廊景区沿线风貌

2019年底,广东省投入1800万元专项资金建设贺江(潇贺古道)沿线绿道,以"低成本、见效快、有特色"为原则,以打造"干净、整洁、统一、有序"的乡村环境为目标,根据《省际廊道(肇庆段)美丽乡村示范带提升规划及风貌提升设计指引》,重点从打通沿江视线通廊、打造重要项目节点、提升建筑风貌三方面提升景区沿线风貌。2020年初,励志新村碧道示范段和建筑风貌提升示范点建成,取得显著成效。

3. 引进市场参与景区建设

封开县引进华侨城集团投入约8200万元建设励志新村竹荪基地、上下罗田茶文化园、上律两广农副产品交易中心等现代农业项目,并谋划以"贺江福来,广信封开"为主题的文旅产业,策划古道茶文化体验廊、西畔村古建筑群"旅拍+精品民宿"、大洲村非物质文化街等项目,同时通过举办"乡村骑士"等体

育赛事聚集人气，构建"文旅 + 体育"的贺道画廊骑行之旅，充分做到以景区兴产、兴村。

成效

1. 达到国家 4A 级旅游景区验收标准

贺江碧道画廊景区总面积 42.46 平方千米，核心游览面积 13.12 平方千米，共有 10 个旅游节点；配置 6 个观光巴士停靠站、1 个巴士枢纽站、17 个停车场、11 个大型旅游厕所、南北 2 个游客中心；在餐饮和住宿产品方面，有农家乐 15 间，以及可容纳上百名游客休憩的大规模民宿 1 间。

2. 带动村民就业增收

截至 2022 年，贺江碧道画廊景区内已建成封开青年创业孵化基地和两广青年创业服务中心，成立公司 9 家、专业合作社 27 个、家庭农场 36 个、电商平台 2 个、扶贫车间 3 个，通过"合作社/经营体 + 基地 + 农户 + 电商"模式推动杏花鸡、竹荪、食用菌、兰花、单丛茶等种养示范基地建设。景区 2021 年度接待游客 81.08 万人次，实现旅游收入 2.75 亿元，春节期间接待游客数在全肇庆景区中排名第二，新开放景区中排名第一。2019 年，封开县农村人均可支配收入 15703.6 元，2020 年封开县农村人均可支配收入 16856.3 元，同比增长 7.3%。

经验与启示

1. 保护生态环境是前提

在景区建设过程中，封开村牢牢抓住美丽乡村的两个核心要素：一个是绿水青山，即要有良好的自然生态；另一个是乡土情结，即乡村要体现岭南乡村特色。

2. 挖掘历史文化是基础

围绕"广信文化""潇贺古道""茶船古道"三大历史文化名片，封开县强调文化的再现和体验。一

是深入挖掘古驿道的历史文化；二是结合省际廊道示范带建设，高标准建设两广源流博物馆；三是在建筑中充分体现广府岭南特色。

3. 落实产业振兴是关键

封开村坚持市场化思维，把产业打造贯穿省际廊道示范带建设始终，将廊道建设作为产业运营项目来谋划打造。贺江碧道画廊现已形成了以现代农业和观光农业为核心的产业体系，形成了强大的产业牵引力。

4. 编制建设规划是措施

封开村探索出一种综合村庄规划、风貌整治设计、道路景观设计、碧道设计、片区概念设计、建筑设计等多类型、不同深度的复合型、实施型规划，同时在编制过程中广泛听取县、镇、村民意见，过程实时纠偏。

下一步计划

贺江碧道画廊景区作为广东省五条省际廊道美丽乡村示范带之一，以规划最为超前、特色最为鲜明、效果最为优异、影响力最为突出的成绩，从中脱颖而出。下一步景区将从"示范带效应"逐步走向"全域旅游"兴旺发展，在广东省"一核一带一区"的全域旅游发展思路指导下，通过谋划封开中线公路以及环贺江乡村旅游公路，连接贺江碧道画廊与封开国家地质公园旅游资源，如龙山景区、大斑石、千层峰等，使各景点串珠成链。同时，通过创建全域旅游示范区辐射周边区域，如往北可接怀集寻源谷文旅项目，往东可达德庆盘龙峡，使更多的人文自然美景融入贺江碧道画廊景区，推动肇庆市全域旅游发展。

Fengkai County, Zhaoqing City, Guangdong Province:

Developing the Hejiang River Green Corridor into the Beautiful Countryside Demonstrantion Belt of the Guangdong-Guangxi Inter-Provincial Corridor Demonstration

Included in *WTA Best Practices of Rural Revitalization through Tourism 2022*

Abstract

In 2018, Guangdong Province proposed to build five demonstration belts for rural revitalization along its provincial boundary. The Hejiang River Green Corridor scenic area, the core area of the Beautiful Countryside Demonstration Belt of the Guangdong-Guangxi Inter-provincial Corridor, is located in Fengkai County, Zhaoqing City. The scenic area development project integrates Guangxin Culture, the Xiaohe Ancient Path, and the Ancient Navigation Route for Tea Trade. The project was implemented in four phases: in Phase I, the scenic area completed the overall planning and design, and the construction of livelihood facilities; in Phase II, the corridor look was improved; in Phase III, all-area-advancing tourism was promoted; and in Phase IV, materials were prepared for the application for the status of the national 4A-level scenic spot. So far, the Hejiang River Green Corridor has reached the acceptance standard for national 4A-level scenic spots. It received 49,900 tourists during the May Day holiday of 2021 alone, generating a tourism income of 15 million yuan.

Challenges and Problems

Fengkai County is the ancient capital of Lingnan region, the birthplace of Guangfu Culture, and also an important stopover of the Xiaohe Ancient Path and the Ancient Navigation Route for Tea Trade. As time passed, the political and economic center of Lingnan and the cultural center of Guangfu gradually moved to the Pearl River Delta region, and Fengkai, a county on the provincial boundary, also gradually slipped into the economic periphery. Before the Hejiang River Green Corridor was built, Fengkai's meandering terrace, the winding mountain road and the bamboo forest along the Hejiang River, were largely unknown to outsiders, so were its history and cultural heritages. The village look along the river was messy and chaotic. The tourism growth was slow, with a severe shortage of supporting facilities and cultural and tourism products with local characteristics. And villagers were generally poor. In the 12 administrative villages involved in the Beautiful Countryside Demonstration Belt of the Guangdong-Guangxi Inter-Provincial Corridor, there used to be 277 households of 686 people living below the poverty line, making them a weak link in rural development.

Measures

1. Highlight three historical and cultural heritages

The local government organized the compilation of the plan series entitled *Guidelines for Upgrading Planning and Design of the Beautiful Countryside Demonstration Belt of the Inter-provincial Corridor (Zhaoqing Section)*, to guide the scenic area to string the roads, waterways, race courses, green belt, ancient path, etc. together under the umbrella name "He Path" – here "He" refers to the Hejiang River and also in Chinese means celebrating. It gives full play to its natural endowments and digs deep into the historical and cultural value of the ancient post road. It has built a high-standard museum dedicated to the birthplace of Guangdong and Guangxi cultures, fully reflecting the characteristics of Guangfu. It is reviving the ancient path that integrates Guangxin Culture, the Xiaohe Ancient Path, and the Ancient Navigation Route for Tea Trade.

2. Enhance the landscape along the Hejiang River Green Corridor

At the end of 2019, Guangdong Province invested 18 million yuan for greening along the Hejiang River (Xiaohe Ancient Path), to create a "clean, tidy, uniform and orderly" rural environment at "low cost, with instant effect and local characteristics". In accordance with the *Guidelines for Upgrading Planning and Design of the Beautiful Countryside Demonstration Belt of the Inter-provincial Corridor (Zhaoqing Section)*,

the priority is to improve the landscape along the scenic area by opening up the visual corridor along the river, developing major projects at key nodes and beautifying the buildings. At the beginning of 2020, the Lizhi New Village demonstration section of the Corridor and architectural beautification demonstration site were completed, producing significant results.

3. Introduce market forces to participate in scenic area development

Fengkai County has introduced Overseas Chinese Town Group to invest about 82 million yuan in modern agricultural projects including the Lizhi New Village Bamboo Mushrooms Production Base, the Shangxia Luotian Tea Cultural Park and the Shanglv Liangguang Agricultural and Sideline Products Trading Center. It was planning to develop the cultural and tourism industry themed on the Hejiang River and Guangxin Culture, with such projects as the tea culture experience corridor on the ancient path, the ancient building complex at Xipan Village where photo-shooting tour and video services and boutique homestays are available, and the intangible cultural heritage street

at Dazhou Village. It has hosted sport events such as "Rural Equestrians" to attract crowds, and launched cycling tours that combine culture, tourism and sports. The scenic area was fully tapped for the development of industries and the village.

Results

1. Meet the acceptance standards for national 4A-level scenic spots

The scenic area covers 42.46 square kilometers, including the core sightseeing area of 13.12 square kilometers. There are 10 major tourist nodes, 6 tourist bus stops, 1 bus hub, 17 parking lots, 11 large tourist toilets and 2 tourist centers – one in the north and the other the south. As to catering and accommodation

services, there are 15 farmstays and one homestay big enough to accommodate more than a hundred tourists.

2. Promote employment and increase the income of villagers

In the scenic area, as of 2022, there is a youth entrepreneurship incubation base and a service center for young entrepreneurs from Guangdong and Guangxi, nine companies, 27 specialized cooperatives, 36 family farms, two e-commerce platforms and three workshops for poverty alleviation. The cooperatives/operators, production bases, farmers and e-commerce platforms have worked together to develop demonstration bases for the raising of Xinghua chickens, and the cultivation of bamboo mushrooms, edible fungi, orchids and Dancong tea trees. In 2021, it received 810,800 tourists and generated a tourism revenue of 275 million yuan. During the Spring Festival holiday, it ranked second among scenic spots in Zhaoqing City and the first among newly opened scenic spots in terms of the number of tourists received. The per capita disposable income in rural areas of Fengkai County was 15,703.6 yuan in 2019, and 16,856.3 yuan in 2020, up 7.3% year on year.

Experience and Inspirations

1. Ecological conservation is the prerequisite for development

While developing the scenic area, Fengkai County has firmly grasped two core elements of the beautiful countryside: One is the lucid waters and lush mountains, which means having a good natural ecology; the other is native land complex, which means that the countryside should reflect the characteristics of Lingnan rural areas.

2. Uncovering the historical and cultural heritage is the foundation

Focusing on the three historical and cultural heritages of Guangxin Culture, the Xiaohe Ancient

Path, and the Ancient Navigation Route for Tea Trade, Fengkai County emphasizes the reproduction and experience of culture. Firstly, it dug deep into the historical and cultural value of the ancient post road. Secondly, it built a high-standard museum dedicated to the birthplace of Guangdong and Guangxi cultures while developing the Inter-Provincial Corridor Demonstration Belt. Thirdly, it fully incorporated the characteristics of Lingnan culture in buildings.

3. Developing local industries is the key

Adhering to market-oriented thinking, Fengkai County has been developing local industries throughout the whole process of developing the Inter-Provincial Corridor Demonstration Belt which is advanced as an industrial operation project. At present, along the Hejiang River Green Corridor, there has formed an industrial system with modern agriculture and sightseeing agriculture at the core, with strong stimulus effects for other industries.

4. Prepare the development plan

Fengkai County tried to formulate a comprehensive, feasible development plan that covers village planning, landscape improvement design, roadside landscape design, Green Corridor design, conceptual design of functional zones and architectural design, and listened to the opinions of villagers, township and county authorities, and made corrections timely in this process.

Next Steps

As one of the five beautiful countryside demonstration belts of the inter-provincial corridor in Guangdong Province, the Hejiang River Green Corridor stands out from the others with its future-oriented planning, distinct characteristics, remarkable effect and prominent influence. In next steps, it will gradually evolve from "the demonstration belt effect" to "all-area-advancing tourism". Following Guangdong's guidelines for the development of all-area-advancing tourism, concentrated in "one core, one belt, one zone", Fengkai County plans to build a middle highway and a ring road along the Hejiang River, connect the Hejiang River Green Corridor with the tourism resources of Fengkai National Geological Park, such as Longshan Scenic Area, Dabanshi and Qiancengfeng, and string the scenic spots together like beads. Meanwhile, it will build a demonstration zone for all-area-advancing tourism, which can be accessed from Xunyuan Valley of Huaiji in the north and Panlong Gorge of Deqing in the east, so as to include more cultural and natural tourist attractions into the Hejiang River Green Corridor scenic area, and promote the development of all-area-advancing tourism in Zhaoqing City.

广西壮族自治区河池巴马瑶族自治县：
充分发挥生态优势，打造特色旅游扶贫

收录于《2020世界旅游联盟：旅游减贫案例》

摘要

广西壮族自治区巴马瑶族自治县不仅是巴马长寿养生国际旅游胜地的核心区，也是革命老区和深度贫困县。2019年全国"两会"期间，习近平总书记听取广西工作汇报时说："利用良好的生态优势，可以发展旅游、康养和其他生态型产业。你们巴马是长寿之乡，百岁老人很多，这些都是发展生态产业很好的条件。"巴马把生态资源优势转化为脱贫攻坚的强大动力，牢固树立"越是贫困地区越要坚持高质量发展，越是贫困地区越要走开放发展之路"的理念，主动作为，抢抓机遇，坚持把旅游发展和脱贫攻坚同步规划，一体推进，引进龙头企业，打造全域旅游，成功实现了"旅游做加法，贫困做减法"。截至2019年年底，巴马精准脱贫攻坚战取得了决定性胜利，贫困发生率降至1.24%，整县达到脱贫摘帽标准。

挑战与问题

巴马瑶族自治县位于广西西北部,县域面积1976平方千米,辖10个乡镇,103个行政村和4个社区,聚居着瑶、壮、汉等12个民族,总人口30.5万人,少数民族占总人口的85.2%,其中瑶族人口占17.46%。这是一个集"老、少、边、山、穷"于一体的新时期国家级贫困县,全县共有50个贫困村,14573户贫困户,64710名贫困人口,贫困发生率为25.5%,属深度贫困县。

然而,独特的地理位置,丰富的历史积累,也造就了巴马县特殊的旅游资源,主要包括:原始森林、天坑群、水晶宫、百魔洞、百鸟岩、赐福湖等自然旅游资源;红七军二十一师师部旧址、韦拔群牺牲地旧址教育基地、"龙田精神"发源地龙田村等红色旅游资源;仁寿源、长寿岛、田园风光、民族风情、实景演艺等人文旅游资源。旅游业是巴马第三产业中的支柱产业,在参与全县脱贫攻坚、助力减贫方面发挥了重要作用。

措施

1. 规划带动项目,打造"硬件"过硬的旅游营商环境

巴马瑶族自治县委托专业团队编制《巴马县全域旅游总体规划设计》《巴马大健康产业发展规划》《巴马饮用水产业规划》,绘制巴马县域空间信息与旅游资源"一张蓝图"。河池至百色、贺州至巴马等多条高速公路陆续建成通车或启动建设,城际高铁、民用机场建设纳入布局规划,区域内公共交通、给水排水、污水和垃圾处理等基础设施不断完善,高端星级酒店综合体等重大项目建设加快推进,旅游营商环境日臻完善。

2. 发挥"旅游+"作用,打造"信用为本"的旅游人文环境

"旅游+养生",建成了赐福湖君澜度假酒店、世纪养生园、百魔洞养生度假区等一批精品酒店和度假场所;"旅游+农业",培育了那澜湾、华昱三生

农场、德农万川等一批农业生态观光乡村旅游业态；"旅游＋文化"，以瑶族文化为基础，推出民族文化探索、体验游项目，建成了巴优瑶寨、文钱射弩文化展示馆等；"旅游＋体育"，举办了巴马国际马拉松赛、男子篮球赛、"7＋1"足球联赛等一系列赛事活动。在推动"旅游＋"融合发展的同时，巴马还致力于构建"积极向上的经济生态、风清气正的政治生态、优秀自信的文化生态、团结和谐的社会生态、山清水秀的自然生态"，通过打造"五位一体"信用体系，将诚信建设融入旅游管理机制，建立"黑名单"制度，促进文旅业规范发展，树立巴马旅游的行业口碑。

3. 整治结合修复，打造"美丽家园"的旅游生态环境

通过实施"青山""蓝天""碧水""净土"工程，加强石漠化生态治理、河域综合整治和土壤修复，实施盘阳河流域生态环境保护条例，推进山水林田湖草系统治理项目，以及强化城乡综合整治，创设民族特色街区，提高乡村污水集中处理率，让自然环境与人居环境完美融合，探索"生态与发展互动共赢"路径，打造"望看得见山，看得见水，记得住乡愁"的"美丽家园"。

成效

1. 旅游软硬件条件不断优化

在县与县之间、县城与山区之间、景区与景区之间，巴马的公共交通日趋便利，枢纽地位不断得到加强。

2. 巴马的品牌影响逐步提升

随着中国—东盟传统医药健康旅游国际论坛（巴马论坛）和巴马国际马拉松赛事的连续成功举办，进一步丰富了巴马旅游元素，增强了"世界长寿之乡"的品牌号召力。

3. 康养旅游助力扶贫发展格局日益显现

通过"旅游＋大健康"，旅游减贫的"造血功能"得到充分印证，当地旅游企业以高端酒店、自然奇观、实景演出、特色美食、文博游览、民俗体验、乡村野趣、非遗工艺、养生民宿等多种经营方式，拉动大量贫困人口实现就业增收，群众生产生活条件极大改善，贫困山区面貌焕然一新，旅游经济增长所带来的获得感、幸福感得到了显著提高。

经验与启示

1. 坚持富民增收的宗旨

坚持把富民增收作为发展旅游的出发点和落脚点，增强旅游产业的辐射联动效应，鼓励城乡居民特别是贫困农民积极参与旅游服务，尽力为群众搭建创业就业平台，让老百姓获得更多实惠。

2. 坚持融合发展的路径

突破一产、二产和三产的界限，推进旅游与农业、工业、商业、文化、体育、交通、扶贫等相关部门和

行业的融合，通过部门联合、产业融合为旅游发展创造新的亮点和经济增长点，形成多点支撑、全面发展的"大旅游、大市场、大产业"格局。

3. 坚持生态优先的理念

生态资源是巴马的最大财富、最大优势、最大品牌，生态线就是巴马的生命线。巴马旅游需充分发挥生态优势，以实际行动践行"两山"理论。尊重自然、传承历史、绿色低碳，是巴马生态文明建设和旅游开发的关键所在；治山理水、依山傍水、显山露水，是巴马生态文明建设和旅游开发的主要方向。

4. 坚持多元共建的模式

巴马旅游扶贫模式主要包括：景区开发带动辐射模式，累计带动3.68万农民实现了直接或间接就业；旅游项目投资拉动模式，引导贫困地区农民采取土地流转、房屋资产入股分红、门票分红等方式实现增收，共带动4个乡镇48000多人，其中贫困人口22168人；当地成功人士引领模式，通过当地企业家回乡投资创业，形成"旅游公司+农户"的发展模式，以土地入股、就业、分红等方式助力精准脱贫；村集体自主开发模式，成立以发展产业为主体的专业合作社，截至2020年，有5个重点旅游扶贫村注册成立旅游开发合作社，通过种植食用菌、五谷杂粮、动物养殖等项目，实现旅游生产脱贫。

下一步计划

继续重视发挥好旅游减贫、旅游致富的独特作用，巴马旅游将始终坚持"世界眼光，国际标准"，全面启动"巴马国际长寿养生旅游胜地"建设，做到高起点规划、高品质建设、高水平管理、高定位营销，以国际知名的康养旅游胜地为目标指向，加快推动由单一景区景点的观光游向融合大健康概念的新时代康养旅游转变，增强旅游减贫的循环"造血"功能，为精准扶贫注入新动能，推动新发展，创造新辉煌，引领"广西的巴马""中国的巴马"向"世界的巴马"嬗变。

Bama Yao Autonomous County, Hechi City, Guangxi Zhuang Autonomous Region:

Give Full Play to Ecological Dominance and Create Featured Tours for Poverty Alleviation

Included in *WTA Best Practices in Poverty Alleviation through Tourism 2020*

Abstract

As the core area of Bama international tourist attraction for longevity and health maintenance, Bama Yao Autonomous County in Guangxi is also an old revolutionary base area and a deeply impoverished county. During China's "Two Sessions" in 2019, President Xi Jinping, when listening to the work report regarding Guangxi, said "Good ecological dominance can be used to develop tourism, health maintenance and other ecological industries. Known as a longevity village, Bama has a number of centenarians, offering good conditions for the development of ecological industry". Bama has translated the advantages of ecological resources into a strong driving force for poverty alleviation and firmly established the concept that "the poorer the region, the more important it is to pursue high-quality development and to take the path of open development". Bama acts proactively, seizes the opportunity, adheres to synchronized planning of tourism development and poverty alleviation, promotes integration, introduces leading enterprises and creates all-area-advancing tourism, achieving "tourism development and poverty alleviation". By the end of 2019, Bama's targeted poverty alleviation campaign had seen a decisive victory, with the poverty incidence dropping to 1.24% and the whole county shaking off poverty.

Challenges and Problems

Located in Northwest Guangxi, Bama Yao Autonomous County, covering an area of 1,976 square kilometers, has jurisdiction over 10 townships, 103 administrative villages and four communities. The county is populated by 12 ethnic groups, including Yao, Zhuang and Han, with a total population of 305,000. Ethnic minorities account for 85.2% of the total population, of which Yao population makes up 17.46%. It was a state-level poverty-stricken county in the new era, with "the old, the young, the border, mountains, and poor". The county had a total of 50 poverty-stricken villages, 14,573 poverty-stricken households and 64,710 poor people, with the poverty incidence of 25.5%. For these reasons, it was a deeply impoverished county.

Nevertheless, its unique geographical location and rich historical accumulation have also created special tourism resources, which mainly include: natural tourism resources, such as primitive forest, karst landforms, crystal palace, limestone caves, underground river karst cave and Cifu Lake; "red tourism" resources, including the site of the communist 21st Division Headquarters of the 7th Column, the educational base of the site where Wei Baqun died, cradleland of "Longtian Spirit" — Longtian Village; humanistic and cultural tourism resources, such as Longevity Museum — Renshouyuan, longevity island, idyllic scenery, national customs and live-action performance. The tourism industry is the pillar industry of Bama, and plays an important role in poverty alleviation and reduction in the whole county.

Measures

1. Promote projects with planning to create a favorable tourism business environment

A professional team was entrusted to work out the *Overall Planning and Design of All-area-advancing*

Tourism in Bama County, *Development Planning for the Massive Health Industry of Bama*, *Planning for the Drinking Water Industry of Bama*, and draw a blueprint of spatial information and tourism resources of Bama. A number of expressways, including Hechi-Baise Expressway and Hezhou-Bama Expressway, have been open to traffic or started construction; the construction of intercity high-speed rails and civil airports has been incorporated into the layout plan; the infrastructure of public transportation, water supply and drainage, sewage disposal and other facilities in the region has been constantly improved; the construction of major projects, such as high-end starred hotel complexes has been accelerated, and the tourism business environment is improving day by day.

2. Give full play to the role of "tourism +" and create a "credit-based" tourism cultural environment

In terms of "tourism + health maintenance", a batch of boutique hotels and vacation spots, including Narada Resort & Spa Cifu Lake, Bama Century Health Park and Bama Baimodong International Health Resort; as for "tourism + agriculture", a batch of business types of village tourism featuring ecological sightseeing agriculture has been developed, including Nalanwan Farm, Huayu Sansheng Farm and Denong Wanchuan Farm; in terms of "tourism + culture", projects, such as ethnic culture exploration and experience tour, were launched based on Yao culture, and Bayou Yao Village and Wenqian Shennu Cultural Exhibition Hall were built; as for "tourism + sports", a series of events were held, including Bama International Marathon, men's basketball match and "7+1" league football match. While promoting the integrative development of "tourism +", Bama is also committed to building "positive economic ecology,

clean and upright political ecology, excellent and confident cultural ecology, united and harmonious social ecology, and picturesque natural ecology". Through building the "Five-sphere Integrated Plan" for the credit system, it integrates the construction of honesty and faithfulness into the tourism management mechanism and establishes a "blacklist" system to promote the regulated development of cultural tourism and build the reputation of Bama in the tourism industry.

3. Combine remediation with restoration, and create a tourism ecological environment of "beautiful home"

Through the implementation of "green mountains", "blue sky", "clear water" and "unpolluted soil" projects, Bama has made efforts to strengthen ecological management of stony desertification, comprehensive regulation of drainage basin and soil remediation; implement the regulations on ecological and environmental protection for Panyang River Basin; promote the projects of a holistic approach to conserving mountains, rivers, forests, farmlands, lakes, and grasslands; strengthen comprehensive improvement of urban and rural areas; build blocks with ethnic characteristics; increase the rate of centralized treatment of rural sewage; integrate natural environment with the living environment; explore the path that "ecology and development are mutually beneficial"; build a "beautiful home" which can see the mountain, see the water, feel the homesick.

Results

1. Software and hardware of tourism have been optimized constantly

Bama can be easily accessible by public transport between counties, between county town and mountainous areas, and between scenic areas. In this way, its position as a hub is constantly consolidated.

2. Bama's brand influence has been improved gradually

As the China-ASEAN International Forum on Traditional Medicine and Health Tourism (Bama Forum) and Bama International Marathon were held successfully, Bama's tourism elements have been further enriched, enhancing the brand appeal of "The Home of Longevity in the World".

3. Health tourism contributes to gradual emergence of the pattern of poverty alleviation and development

Through "tourism + health", the impetus of poverty alleviation through tourism has been fully confirmed. Local tourism enterprises have helped a large number of poor people achieve employment and higher income by means of diversified business patterns, including high-end hotels, natural wonders, live-action performances, featured delicious food, cultural and museum tours, experience of folk customs, rural experience, intangible cultural heritage process, and homestays for health maintenance. In this way, the production conditions and living standards of people have been greatly improved, and the poor mountainous areas have taken on a new look, and the sense of gain and happiness brought by tourism economic growth has been significantly improved.

Experience and Inspirations

1. Adhere to the purpose of enriching people and increasing their incomes

Bama will continue to take "enriching people and increasing their incomes" as the starting point and goal of tourism development, increase the interactive effect of the tourism industry, and encourage urban and rural residents, especially poor farmers, to take an active part in tourism services, and make the greatest efforts to build a platform for people to start their own businesses and find jobs, so as to deliver more tangible benefits to the people there.

2. Stick to the path of integrated development

Bama breaks through the boundaries of primary industry, secondary industry and tertiary industry, to promote the integration of tourism with relevant departments (concerning agriculture, industry, commerce, culture, sports, traffic and poverty alleviation) and industries. In this way, new highlights and economic growth points have been created for tourism development and economic growth through cooperation between departments and industry integration, thus forming a pattern of "great tourism, great market and great industry" with multiple support and all-around development.

3. Insist on the concept of ecological priority

Ecological resources are Bama's greatest wealth, advantage and brand, and the ecological line is the lifeblood of Bama. Bama makes the best of ecologic dominance in tourism and takes concrete actions to practice "Two Mountains" theory. The key to Bama's ecological progress and tourism development is to respect nature, inherit the history and advocate green and low-carbon development. The main direction of Bama's ecological progress and tourism development is to protect the environment.

4. Pursue the mode of multiple co-constructions

Bama's mode of poverty alleviation through tourism mainly includes the following aspects. (1) The mode of scenic area development with an influence on surroundings: This model has offered direct or indirect jobs to a total of 36,800 farmers. (2) The tourism project investment driving mode: This model has led farmers in poor areas to increase their income by means of land transfer, dividends on housing assets, and dividends on entrance tickets. A total of more than 48,000 people from four townships and towns benefited, 22,168 of whom were poor. (3) The leading mode of local successful people: through the return of local entrepreneurs to invest and start businesses, a development mode of "tourism company plus peasant household" is formed, and targeted poverty alleviation is promoted by means of land investment, employment and dividends. (4) The independent development mode of village collective: specialized cooperatives with the development industry as the main body has been established. As of 2020, five key tourism poverty alleviation villages have registered tourism development cooperatives, which have realized poverty alleviation through tourism by means of planting edible mushrooms, whole grains, animal breeding and other projects.

Next Steps

Bama will continue to attach importance to the unique role of tourism in poverty reduction and wealth creation. Moreover, Bama will always insist on "global vision and international standards" and launch the construction of "Bama international longevity and health tourism resort" in an all-around way to achieve planning at a high starting point, high-quality construction, high-level management and target marketing. Aiming to become a global famous health tourism resort, Bama will accelerate the transformation from a sightseeing tour of a single scenic spot to health tourism in the new era integrating the concept of great health and enhancing the circular impetus of poverty reduction through tourism, thus injecting new impetus into targeted poverty alleviation, promoting new development, creating new brilliance, and leading the transformation of "Bama of Guangxi" and "Bama of China" to "Bama of the world".

旅游减贫案例故事（中英文双语版）
Best Practices of Poverty Alleviation through Tourism (Chinese–English Bilingual Edition)

海南省琼中黎族苗族自治县红毛镇什寒村：
构建多方共建、融合发展的什寒模式

收录于《2021世界旅游联盟：旅游助力乡村振兴案例》

摘要

海南省琼中黎族苗族自治县什寒村依靠天然生态环境、资源禀赋、民族风情等独特优势，通过农旅融合、文旅互动，推动形成"政府＋公司＋农民合作社＋农户＋品牌＋基地"多方共建、"产业发展＋生态保护＋文化传承＋环境整治＋休闲旅游＋高效农业＋品牌农业"融合发展的什寒模式，重点发展养蜂、益智和铁皮石斛种植、农家乐等一批有区域特色、有竞争优势的旅游业态，加快什寒村从"有旅游、有产品"向"有旅游、有产品、有产业"升级，从乡村脱贫走向乡村振兴。

挑战与问题

海南省琼中黎族苗族自治县什寒村坐落于黎母山和鹦哥岭之间的高山盆地中,海拔800多米,村内交通不便,曾是琼中较偏远、较贫困的村庄之一。然而,什寒村天然在生态环境、资源禀赋、民族风情等方面具有独特优势,因此,解决什寒村的交通问题、充分利用什寒村的现有资源开发适合其发展的旅游产业、解决旅游发展投入所需资金等问题迫在眉睫。

措施

1. 紧扣农旅融合,促进产业实现转型升级

一是调整优化农业产业结构。根据什寒村的实际情况,因地制宜,引导农户大力发展"短、平、快"农业特色产业,种植益智2600多亩,发展养蜂2000多箱,采取"龙头企业、专业合作社、村集体经济、种养大户+基地+农户"等四种产业扶贫模式,引导成立了群生养蜂专业合作社,推动农户抱团发展。二是加快发展体验型休闲农业。县旅游总公司结合什寒村现有的农业特色产业,开发经营蜂蜜采割、割稻捞鱼、蓝莓采摘等农事体验项目,促进农业与旅游业融合发展。

2. 实施文旅互动,黎苗特色文化有效彰显

一是深入挖掘黎苗文化元素。什寒村黎苗文化底蕴深厚,在深入挖掘什寒黎苗婚俗、"三月三"黎苗节庆等黎苗生活习俗的基础上,不断融合外来文化精华,推动什寒形成具有地方特色、民族风格鲜明、兼具现代时尚感的独特黎苗文化。二是抓好旅游宣传策划包装工作。挖掘黎苗语言文化元素,打造什寒"奔格内"("奔格内"是黎语"来这里"的意思)旅游文化品牌,使其成为琼中乡村旅游对外宣传的新名片。

3. 完善旅游要素,村民参与度不断提升

挖掘黎苗传统特色饮食,引导有条件的农户经营黎苗农家乐,打造什寒黎苗特色长桌宴,开发三色饭、竹筒饭、山鸡、野生芭蕉芯、白花菜、鱼茶等原生态特色美食。结合黎苗文化,将黎族的甘工鸟和苗族的牛角等黎苗图腾元素融入民宿建筑,并按公寓式酒店规格对民宿进行装饰,打造民族风情

浓厚、简约舒适的"奔格内"民宿休憩场所。引导农户参与乡村游项目开发,大力发展户外探险游、自驾车游、骑行游、户外露营、森林科考等项目。支持农户开发"什寒山珍"系列旅游产品,对铁皮石斛、蜂蜜、灵芝、山兰米等农家特色农产品进行包装和推销。不定期举办篝火晚会表演原生态黎苗歌舞,引导村民创作水平高、品质精的民俗歌舞,使之成为什寒游客的必看节目。

4. 创新经营模式,完善旅游扶贫长效机制

积极探索产业帮扶方式,推动形成"政府+公司+农民合作社+农户+品牌+基地"多方共建、"产业发展+生态保护+文化传承+环境整治+休闲旅游+高效农业+品牌农业"融合发展的经营管理新模式,重点发展养蜂、益智和铁皮石斛种植、农家乐等一批有区域特色、有竞争优势的旅游业态,加快什寒从"有旅游、有产品"向"有旅游、有产品、有产业"升级,不断增强"自我造血"功能。

5. 注重资金整合,加强旅游配套

以开展交通扶贫为契机,利用什寒村山地坡缓、植被丰富、田园景观优美等自然条件,修建进山旅游观光公路和国家步道,配套完善自行车绿道、木栈道、乡村巴士、自驾车营地、指示标识等设施,构建"慢游"旅游出行体系。坚持"政府主导、企业参与、金融支持、依靠群众"的共建原则,结合富美乡村建设,统筹整合专项扶贫资金,大力改善什寒村的环境卫生、村容村貌、村道户道、景观景点、文化广场、游客咨询中心等基础设施建设,为发展乡村旅游奠定了良好基础。

成效

什寒村成功的产业转型升级,使村民的收入不再依靠单一的种植收入,而是可以通过合作社分红、土地分红、开农家乐、民宿务工等方式增加个人经济收入,提高村民生活水平。

什寒村曾经是琼中较偏远、较贫困的村庄之一,2009年,村民人均纯收入仅为946元;2020年,村民人均纯收入达到18000元,较2009年增长了约18倍。目前,村庄旅游从业人员已达436人,占全村人口的97.6%。

经验与启示

1. 生态保护是前提

"绿水青山就是金山银山",保护生态环境是实现旅游扶贫的重要前提。什寒村在旅游开发过程中,始终坚持以"居民零动迁、生态零破坏、环境零污染"为宗旨,以"村民不失业、不失地、不失居"为基础,不搞大拆大建,用原生态的自然环境、优美的田园风光吸引八方来客,实现"增资产、增就业、增收入"的目标。

2. 规划先行是基础

规划是行动的先导。坚持把什寒旅游扶贫摆在首要位置,高起点、高标准狠抓什寒村发展规划的编制和实施,先后出台《什寒村委会联手扶贫规划》《什寒村危房改造实施规划》《什寒村村庄建设规划》等文件,为什寒村建设和发展提供了全方位的支持和保障。

3. 改革创新是动力

改革是推进"三农"发展的强劲动力。在县委、县政府的领导下,村民积极利用集体或个人闲置土地、民房或劳务等资源入股企业、合作社,以参股的形式分享农村改革红利,建立了政府、企业、村民利益联结机制,不断增加自身收入。

4. 黎苗文化是依托

在什寒村的乡村旅游开发过程中,通过宣传引导,村民逐渐认识到黎苗文化的价值,开始重新审视黎苗婚俗、原生态歌舞表演、传统手工艺等非物质文化遗产,并对其加以充分保护和利用,实现文化效益和经济效益双促进、双发展。

一是硬件提升。狠抓环境整治,继续完善基础设施,增设非物质遗产展示馆、会议厅、旅游商品展厅等服务功能区。深挖文化内涵,完善什寒村旅游娱乐设施建设,结合农业旅游、文化旅游开发趣味性强、参与性强的旅游产品。

二是软件提升。加强乡村旅游人才培养,开展乡村旅游从业人员教育培训,切实提升村民素质及参与乡村旅游经营的能力,夯实旅游扶贫人才基础。依托当地黎苗文化,加强民族特色技艺培训,在实现非物质文化遗产保护的基础上增加旅游的情趣。强化乡村旅游的标准化管理,构建"吃、住、行、游、购、娱"等方面的标准化管理和从业人员的日常规范化管理,为乡村旅游持续发展提供良好环境。

三是市场资本化运作。抓好与旅游企业的合作,利用PPP模式,以农村资源变资产、资金变股金、农民变股民的"三变"改革试点为手段,发挥政府指导和企业市场化运作的双重优势,积极撬动社会资本,加大对什寒乡村旅游重点项目的开发和投入,增强什寒的旅游接待能力,提高什寒的旅游服务水平,实现乡村振兴。

下一步计划

"什寒模式"开创了旅游扶贫新模式,琼中黎族苗族自治县将持续依托"旅游+"计划,从以下方面着手,不断加以完善。

旅游减贫案例故事（中英文双语版）
Best Practices of Poverty Alleviation through Tourism (Chinese-English Bilingual Edition)

Zahan Village, Hongmao Town, Qiongzhong Li and Miao Autonomous County, Hainan Province:
Form a Zahan Model with Co-Construction and Integrated Development

Included in *WTA Best Practices of Rural Revitalization through Tourism 2021*

Abstract

Endowed with the unique advantages of a natural ecological environment, rich resources and ethnic customs, Zahan Village, Qiongzhong Li and Miao Autonomous County, Hainan Province is a unique model created by a multi-party co-construction of "government + companies + farmers' cooperatives + peasant households + brands + bases" and integrated development of "industrial development + ecological protection + cultural inheritance + environmental improvement + leisure tourism + high-efficiency agriculture + brand agriculture" through the integration of agriculture and tourism and interaction between culture and tourism. It develops tourism industries with regional attributes and competitive advantages, such as beekeeping, *Alpinia oxyphylla* Miq. and *Dendrobium officinale* planting and agritainment, all of which have accelerated the progression from the "tourism and products" stage to the "tourism, products and industries" stage for Zahan Village, and moved from rural poverty alleviation to rural revitalization.

Challenges and Problems

Located in the mountain basin between Limushan and Yinggeling, Zahan Village, with an elevation of more than 800 meters, Qiongzhong Li and Miao Autonomous County, Hainan Province, is inconvenient for transportation, and was one of the remotest and poorest villages in Qiongzhong. However, endowed with unique advantages of natural ecological environment, rich resources and ethnic customs, measures have to be taken to solve the problems in traffic, the means to use existing resources to develop tourism industries suitable for village development and obtain the required investment fund for tourism development.

Measures

1. Adhering closely to the integration of agriculture and tourism, promoting the transformation and upgrading of industries

Firstly, adjust and optimize the agricultural industry structure. Based on the local conditions in Zahan Village, farmers are guided to develop agricultural industries with a short maturation period and grow more than 2,600 *mu* of *Alpinia oxyphylla* Miq. and feed more than 2,000 boxes of bees. Also, it has to establish professional beekeeping cooperatives to promote the common development of farmers through the four models of poverty alleviation through industrial development of "leading enterprises, professional cooperatives, village collective economy, big specialized households of crop and animal productions + bases + peasant households". Secondly, accelerate the development of experience-based leisure agriculture. The tourism company of the county combines the existing attributes of Zahan's agricultural industries to develop and operate agricultural experience projects such as honey collecting, ice harvesting, fishing and blueberry picking, promoting the integrated development of agriculture and tourism.

2. Implementing cultural tourism interaction, effectively showcasing the unique culture of Li and Miao ethnic groups

Firstly, utilize more Li and Miao cultural elements. Zahan Village has a rich Li and Miao cultural heritage, including wedding traditions and the "March 3rd" Festival. Integrate the ethnic elements of their traditional heritage with local customs and modern fashion to showcase the unique fusion of cultures. Secondly, scale up the tourism promotion, planning and marketing. The language and cultural elements of the Li and Miao groups should be explored to create the "Bengenei" (means "come here" in Li language) brand of Zahan Village. Such a brand should be developed into a new marketing slogan to popularize rural tourism in Qiongzhong.

3. Enrich tourism products for more extensive participation of villagers

The traditional special diet of the Li and Miao ethnic groups should be explored to encourage more Miao and Li agritainment among peasant households,

develop the Li and Miao long table banquet with unique features of Zahan, and exploit ecological specialties such as three-color rice, bamboo-tube-cooked rice, pheasant, wild banana stem, wild spider flower and fish tea (fermentative fish with steamed sticky rice, a cuisine similar to sushi). Combining Li and Miao cultures, totems such as the Gangong Bird symbolizing the Li nationality and the horns symbolizing the Miao nationality are added to the building of homestays which are decorated according to the specifications of apartment-style hotels, in an effort to develop a simple and comfortable "Bengenei" homestay with strong ethnic characteristics. Farmers are encouraged to develop rural tourism projects, and conduct outdoor adventure tours, self-driving tours, cycling tours, outdoor camping, forest scientific surveys and other projects. Great supports are provided for farmers to exploit the tourism products of "Zahan Mountain Treasures", to package and sell specific agricultural products such as *Dendrobium officinale*, honey, *Danoderma lucidum* and Shanlan rice. Bonfire evening parties are held from time to time to stage original Li and Miao performances. Villagers are guided to create high-level and quality folk songs and dances, which have become a must-see program for tourists in Zahan Village.

4. Develop new business models and create a viable long-term poverty alleviation through tourism program

The ways and channels for effective industrial assistance have been explored along with new business models featuring multi-party co-construction of "government + companies + farmers' cooperatives + peasant households + brands + bases" and integrated development of "industrial development + ecological protection +

cultural inheritance + environmental improvement + leisure tourism + high-efficiency agriculture + brand agriculture", and tourism industries with regional characteristics and competitive advantages have been developed, such as beekeeping, *Alpinia oxyphylla* and *Dendrobium officinale* planting and agritainment. As a result, all these accelerate the progressions from the "tourism and products" stage to the "tourism, products and industries" stage.

5. Highlight fund integration for advanced tourism supporting facilities

Based on the opportunity of poverty alleviation through transportation development, and the natural qualities such as gentle slopes, rich vegetation and beautiful pastoral landscapes, tourist roads and national trails were built and supporting facilities including bicycle greenways, wooden plank roads, rural buses, self-driving camps and signs were equipped to build a "slow travel" system. By adhering to the co-construction principle of "government leading, enterprise participation, financial support, and mass-oriented" concept and taking into account the construction of rich and beautiful villages, special poverty-alleviation funds were integrated to improve the construction of infrastructure such as sanitation, village appearance, roads, scenic spots, cultural squares and tourist information centers, thereby laying a sound foundation for tourism development.

Results

The successful industrial transformation and upgrading of Zahan Village has provided more channels to increase villagers' income and improve their living standards, including cooperative and land dividends, agritainment operation and working in homestays.

Zahan Village, with its remote location, was once one of the poorest villages in Qiongzhong. In 2009, the per capita net income of farmers was only 946 yuan. In 2020, however, the per capita net income of villagers reached more than 18,000 yuan, with an increase of nearly 18 times compared to 2009. A total of 436 villagers have been engaged in the tourism business, accounting for 97.6% of the village's population.

Experience and Inspirations

1. Ecological protection is a prerequisite

"Lucid waters and lush mountains are invaluable assets", and protecting the ecological environment are important prerequisites for poverty alleviation through tourism. During the tourism development of Zahan Village, the tenet of "no resident resettlement, no ecological damage, and no environmental pollution" is strictly followed to guarantee that the jobs, lands and homes of the villagers are not damaged. Large-scale demolition and construction are not advocated, and original ecological environments and charming pastoral scenery are developed to attract visitors from all over the world, thereby increasing tourism assets, and job opportunities, expanding the villagers' revenue streams.

2. Planning is the foundation

Planning drives the action. With poverty alleviation through tourism in Zahan Village as the priority, the preparation and implementation of its development plan involved top-quality blueprints in documents such as the *Zahan Village Committee's*

Joint Poverty Alleviation Plan, the *Implementation Plan on Zahan Village Dilapidated House Reconstruction*, and the *Zahan Village Construction Plan*. They were successively issued and provided comprehensive support throughout the entire process of planning and construction.

3. Reform and innovation are engines of transformation

Reform drives the development of "agriculture, rural areas and farmers". Under the leadership of the county party committee and the county government, villagers used collective or individual idle land, private houses or labor services and other resources to invest in enterprises and cooperatives, and gain dividends from rural reform in the form of equity participation. The benefit of the coupling mechanism between government, enterprises and villagers is established, resulting in an increase in their income.

4. Li and Miao culture is the basis

During the tourism development of Zahan Village, villagers gradually realized the value of the Li and Miao culture through publicity and guidance. They were inspired to re-examine the intangible cultural heritage such as wedding customs, original ecological performances and traditional handicrafts. More importantly, they were motivated to protect and make full use of them, thereby advancing the development of cultural and economic benefits.

Next Steps

Since the "Zahan Model" has created a new model of poverty alleviation through tourism, the following aspects will be further improved based on the "tourism +" plan in Qiongzhong Li and Miao Autonomous County. Firstly, upgrade the hardware. More emphasis should be put on environmental governance to improve infrastructure, and service function zones including intangible heritage exhibition halls, conference halls and tourist product

exhibition halls should be added. Moreover, cultural connotations should be further utilized to improve the entertainment facilities in Zahan Village, and highly interesting and participatory tourism products should be developed based on both the agriculture-tourism integration and the culture-tourism interaction.

Secondly, upgrade the software. The training of rural tourism talents should be strengthened. Education and training for rural tourism practitioners should be provided to improve the villagers' skills in rural tourism operation, nurturing the talents in poverty alleviation through tourism. More training on ethnic Li and Miao cultural skills should be offered. Tourism development should be premised on the protection of intangible cultural heritage. Moreover, the standardized management of rural tourism should be strengthened to develop a standardized management of "catering, accommodation, transportation, travel, shopping and entertainment", including the daily standardized management of employees to ensure a sustainable development.

Thirdly, manage and operate market capitalization. Cooperation with tourism companies should be pursued and implemented. Pilot reforms to turn rural resources into assets, capital into equity, and farmers into stockholders should be conducted through the PPP model, to give full play to the dual advantages of government guidance and enterprise market operation, leading to more social capital to flow into the village. Development and investment in key rural tourism projects, reception capacity and tourism service level for rural revitalization will likewise improve.

旅游减贫案例故事（中英文双语版）
Best Practices of Poverty Alleviation through Tourism（Chinese-English Bilingual Edition）

重庆市武隆区仙女山街道荆竹村：
一二三产"+旅游"助推乡村蝶变

收录于《2022世界旅游联盟：旅游助力乡村振兴案例》

摘要

　　重庆市武隆区仙女山街道荆竹村是一个"旅游景区+田园综合体+特色小镇+美丽乡村+特色产业园"的全新融合发展村。近年来，荆竹村坚持以"活化乡村，留住乡愁"为目标，大力发展一二三产"+旅游"，大胆探索"旅游+N、N+旅游"的核心发展模式，积极推进农旅、林旅、文旅、商旅融合发展，聚焦长远式乡村振兴蓝本，深耕乡村生态文明体系，坚持以"两山论"为主线发展乡村特色旅游，全面带动周边村民和脱贫户致富增收，助推荆竹村乡村振兴。

挑战与问题

荆竹村距武隆城区22千米,全村面积34平方千米,辖8个组、565户、2084人。荆竹村位于亚高山型丘陵地带,海拔高度在800米至1300米之间。当地喀斯特地貌导致土壤蓄不住水,种不了庄稼,当地村民只能种植对土质要求不高的烟草。然而,种植烟草会导致土地板结,越种土壤越贫瘠,从而形成一个死循环。村内青壮年逐渐流失,村庄"空心化"严重,亟待发展新型产业模式打破发展约束。

措施

1. 组建"乡宿联盟"

其一,由政府、村社、龙头企业共同成立"乡宿联盟",争取项目资金和农担贷款,用于村民房屋改建,使其达到中端精品农家乐标准。其二,由"乡宿联盟"引入重庆民宿产业联盟,成立仙女山服务中心,把先进的民宿经营经验和其他旅游业态经营经验通过荆竹夜校形式传授给当地村民,带动参与村民共同发展乡村旅游,打造乡村精准扶贫和农家乐旅游接待样板。其三,组建"乡宿联盟"电商平台,结合直播带货、"土货"网红,用新手段为村民增收,与物流公司合作,成立荆竹村电商网点,解决了物流快递问题,为村内乡村旅游注入新活力。

2. 扩宽"增收渠道"

一是壮大休闲农业。提档升级现有30个高山水果采摘园,向集观光、休闲、教育培训于一体的综合休闲农业园发展。同时,搭建仙女山绿色水果销售平台,助推产品销量提升,实现当季水果售罄。二是推动传统农业改造提档升级。持续发展烤烟种植,推进荆竹现代烟草种植示范区项目向科技化种植、休闲观光、教育培训方向发展;发展高山蔬菜种植,积极推进有机蔬菜基地建设;保持厚朴、玄参等中药材在地种植面积,规划建设"百草园"中药基地项目。

3. 挖掘乡村文化

一是坚持旅游开发利用与保护并重。建立非遗文化传习所,保护和传承乡村非遗、民俗、乡村艺术;对蜡染、竹编、木叶吹奏、老咸菜制作、棕编制作、土陶传统制作、老醋传统制作、豆腐干传统制作、天然蜂蜜传统酿制、剪纸、碗碗羊肉等文化活动和非遗项目进行现场展示和体验,让游客零距离感受乡村特色文化的魅力。二是保留"原汁原味",留住村魂。利用当地的老房子、古柴火灶、方桌竹椅、铜茶壶与青瓷杯等打造"归原茶馆",向游客展示20世纪80年代的农村民居风格和生活;改造"无有图书馆",布置村史文化书籍和图册,村民和游客可以在此了解荆竹村的历史和文化。

成效

荆竹村产业发展和村民生活水平都有极大变化。

人居环境得到进一步提升,"小洋房"数量明显增多;产业发展融入了旅游元素,从传统农业发展模式向农旅融合发展模式转变,丰富了荆竹村特色产业布局;吸引了更多游客和投资者到访荆竹村,带动荆竹村乡村旅游品牌发展和招商引资;村民的衣食住行各个方面都有质的飞跃。据统计,全村流转用地 2400 余亩,全村年接待游客约 50 万人次。村民人均收入从 5 年前的 8000 多元,上升到 18000 多元,40 余户特困户摘掉了贫困的帽子。

经验与启示

1. 重视可持续发展

乡村在发展过程中,不仅要考虑产业规模、项目绩效,更要在村内可持续发展上做文章。荆竹村在发展的同时,一方面重视解决乡村用水、用电、交通等问题;另一方面因地制宜组建了由社会资本、村民、政府和运营商共谋发展的"乡宿联盟",通过打造旅游品牌 IP,进而带动农产品销售和加工,带动当地就业和发展,增强了村内发展活力。

2. 增强可持续发展能力

荆竹村以田园、庄园、乐园"三园模式"为发展思路,对应"自然、乡邻、文创"的理念,力图为古老村庄注入更多的活力。坚持"原汁原味"发展,留住村魂,力争打造一幅恬淡、自然、浪漫的田园图景。同时,坚持项目的乡村性、在地性和创造性,保持原

乡生态、复合产业、跨界生活,构建理想生活模式,营造新型"生产、生活、生态"的场景,让村庄增强自己的生命力,实现可持续发展。

下一步计划

荆竹村将持续坚持"两山论"发展初心,持续深挖旅游资源,实施"旅游+"战略,大力谋划旅游研学、户外体验、农旅观光、亲子体验等创新旅居模式。通过自然、人文、旅居、康养、游乐五大艺术生活场景,构建"旅游景区+田园综合体+特色小镇+美丽乡村+特色产业园"的全新融合发展村,进一步辐射带动周边三产融合,带动农民增收,促进产业转型,助力乡村振兴。

Jingzhu Village, Xiannushan Sub-district, Wulong District, Chongqing City:

The Primary, Secondary and Tertiary Sectors "+ Tourism" Driving the Transformation of the Countryside

Included in *WTA Best Practices of Rural Revitalization through Tourism 2022*

Abstract

Jingzhu, a village in Xiannushan Subdistrict, Wulong District of Chongqing City, is a brand-new integrated development village that combines the scenic area with the rural complex, the specialty town, beautiful countryside and specialty industrial parks. In recent years, with the goal of "injecting vitality into the countryside and arousing rural nostalgia", it has vigorously promoted the integrated development of primary, secondary and tertiary sectors and tourism. It boldly explores the core development model of "tourism + N, and N + tourism", and actively promotes the integrated development of tourism and agriculture, forestry, culture and commerce. With a focus on creating a blueprint for long-term rural revitalization, it works hard on building a working system for promoting rural ecological progress, and adheres to the theory that "lucid waters and lush mountains are invaluable assets" while developing rural tourism with local characteristics. It has driven the development of surrounding villages and increased the income of households which have been lifted out of poverty, thus contributing to local rural revitalization.

Challenges and Problems

Jingzhu Village is 22 kilometers away from the downtown of Wulong District, and covers a territory of 34 square kilometers. It is home to 565 households of 2,084 people, divided into eight villager groups. The village is located in the subalpine hilly area, with the altitude between 800 and 1,300 meters. The local karst topography is not good for water absorption in soil, and is too dry to grow crops; it can only grow tobacco which can survive the poor soil quality. However, the soil will harden after growing tobacco, and the more tobacco it grows, the poorer the soil quality will be, hence a vicious cycle. What's worse, as the young and middle-aged fled for cities, the village was seriously hollowed out and was in urgent need of a new industrial development model to break the development constraints.

Measures

1. Form the rural homestay alliance

Firstly, the government, the village collective and the leading enterprises jointly set up the rural homestay alliance, to seek for project funds and guaranteed rural loans for the reconstruction of idle houses to meet the standards of middle-end agritainments. Secondly, the Chongqing Homestay Industry Alliance was introduced into the village via the rural homestay alliance, and the Xiannushan service center was set up to share good practices of homestay management and other tourism businesses to local villagers via the Jingzhu Night School. The villagers were mobilized to jointly develop rural tourism, and built a model for targeted poverty alleviation and tourist-friendly agritainments. Thirdly, the rural homestay alliance set up an e-commerce platform to sell local specialty agricultural products at live-streaming sessions, and increase the income of villagers via the new means. It also works with the logistics company to set up an e-commerce service site in the village, which solves the express delivery problem for the villagers and injects new vitality into rural tourism.

2. Expand income sources

Firstly, expand leisure agriculture. The existing 30 alpine U-pick orchards were upgraded to become leisure agricultural parks offering a diversity of services including sightseeing, leisure, education and training. At the same time the Xiannushan organic fruit sales platform was set up to help sell local fruits. All the fruits of the season are sold out on this platform. Secondly, promote the transformation and upgrading of traditional agriculture. It continued to develop the cultivation of flue-cured tobacco, and develop cultivation, leisure tourism, education and training projects in Jingzhu Modern Tobacco Cultivation Demonstration Zone. It also developed the cultivation of alpine vegetables, and actively promoted the development of organic vegetable bases. The existing cultivation area of Magnolia officinalis, Radix Scrophulariae and other Chinese medicinal herbs was maintained. It also planned to build a traditional Chinese medicinal herb base called Baicaoyuan.

3. Explore the village's cultural heritage

Firstly, pay equal attention to tourism development, utilization and protection of cultural heritage. An intangible cultural heritage center was established to protect and inherit rural intangible cultural heritage, folk customs and rural art. On-site displays and experience activities were organized for local specialty products and intangible cultural heritage items including batik, bamboo weaving, leaf whistling, the making of pickled vegetables, palm fiber weaving, earth pottery making, vinegar making, the making of dried bean curd, natural honey brewing, paper cutting, and the cooking of bowls of mutton, so that visitors could feel the characteristic charm of rural culture at zero distance. The second is to keep the "original flavor" of the village. The Guiyuan Teahouse features old houses, ancient firewood stoves, bamboo chairs and square tables, copper teapots and celadon cups, to represent to visitors the way of life in rural residences in the 1980s. The Wuyou Library was renovated and displayed books and atlases on the history and culture of the village, where villagers and visitors could learn about the history and culture of Jingzhu Village.

Results

Jingzhu Village has seen tremendous changes to its industrial landscape and living standards. The living environment has been much improved, and the number of modern houses has obviously increased. Tourism elements are integrated into industrial development, and it is transitioning from the traditional agricultural development model to the integrated development mode of agriculture and tourism, and has diversified its specialty industries. More tourists and investors are coming, which builds up Jingzhu's brand as a tourism village and attracts investment from outside. Villagers have seen substantial improvement in their living

standards ranging from clothing, food, housing and transportation. According to statistics, the village has transferred the land use right for more than 2,400 *mu* of land, and receives about 500,000 tourists every year. The per capita income has increased from more than 8,000 yuan five years ago to more than 18,000 yuan, and more than 40 households have been lifted from poverty.

Experience and Inspirations

1. Value sustainable development

In the process of rural development, it's important to not only consider the industry scale and project performance, but also work hard to promote sustainable development within villages. In its pursuit of development, Jingzhu Village has worked hard to solve the problems with water and electricity supply and improve transport conditions. Meanwhile, based on local conditions, it establishes a rural homestay alliance that brings together social capital, native villagers, local government and operators for common development. By building its own tourism brand, it drives the sales and processing of agricultural products, promotes local employment and development, and injects vitality into the development of the village.

2. Enhance the capacity for sustainable development

Jingzhu Village bases its development upon farmland, manors and paradise, corresponding to the concepts of "nature, neighborliness and the cultural & creative industry", and strives to inject more vitality into this ancient village. It will keep the "original flavor" and the soul of the village, strive to create a tranquil, natural and romantic pastoral landscape. At the same time, it stresses that the projects must be rural, local and creative, to keep the original ecological environment, integrate industries and build a cross-sector lifestyle. It will build an ideal way of life and new scenes of "production, lifestyle, and ecological conservation", so that the village can enhance its vitality and ensure sustainable development.

Next Steps

Jingzhu Village will continue to adhere to the theory that "lucid waters and lush mountains are invaluable assets", tap its tourism resources, implement the "tourism +" strategy, vigorously plan the development of study tours, outdoor experiences, sightseeing agriculture, parent-child tours and other new tourism products. By developing five lifestyle scenes themed on nature, culture, resorts, wellness and entertainment, it will strive to build itself into a brand-new integrated development village that combines the scenic area with the rural complex, the specialty town, beautiful countryside and specialty industrial parks. It will continue to drive the integrated development of the primary, secondary and tertiary industries in the surrounding areas, increase farmers' income, promote the transformation of industries, and boost rural revitalization.

四川省眉山市丹棱县幸福村：
农文旅融合"古村模式"赋能乡村振兴

收录于《2022世界旅游联盟：旅游助力乡村振兴案例》

摘要

四川省眉山市丹棱县顺龙乡幸福村抓住"古村落"文化、农耕民俗、自然生态主线，以"质朴原乡"为主题，将观光度假、农事体验、民俗文化、休闲游憩、乡村民宿、研学旅游、节庆活动等农文旅产品自然地融入古村之中，构建"幸福古村"新乡村生活方式。整合"公司、合作社、原住村民、新村民"等多方力量，构建起"公司+合作社+村民"的共建共享模式，探索出城乡融合的乡村振兴发展路径。村民通过土地房屋参股、提供服务、销售产品等方式，为古村乡村旅游发展赋能。发展乡村旅游以来，村民人均可支配收入从11080元增长到39880元；幸福村从"藏在深山无人知"到如今引起国际社会广泛关注，实现了经济效益和社会效益双丰收。

挑战与问题

幸福村处于半山腰，海拔600米至900米，距县城约12千米，其中约6千米为盘山公路，道路较为崎岖。村内民居依山而建，农田多为梯田，人均可利用农田不足1亩，农业生产条件较为落后。村内保持着传统农耕方式，经济类农业发展较为滞后；村民守着"绿水青山"，却不知如何换来"金山银山"；村内青壮年为改善生活，纷纷外出务工，村落逐步失去了活力，"空心村"问题愈发突出。

措施

1. 守住古村底蕴

一是保留古韵。幸福村森林覆盖率达80%，依山而建，临溪而立，曲径通幽，溪水潺潺，土墙青瓦的川西民居院落散布其中，错落有致。在开发过程中，始终坚持"旧物新用、修旧如旧"。二是保留生态。村内散布着千年银杏夫妻树、清代赵桥、大寨梯田、盐铁古道等近30个自然人文景观。开发中坚持"布新景适旧景、以新景衬旧景"。

2. 打造质朴原乡

一是尊重村落灵魂。不搞"腾空"，充分保留原住村民以及其生产生活习惯，保留传统农耕文化、民俗文化、知青文化以及唢呐等民间艺术，开展各类民俗文化活动展示和体验，体现乡土风情，守住乡愁记忆。二是尊重原乡建筑。恢复完善"堂屋""仓库"等农村传统特色设施，呈现犁、耙、风桶、石磨、蓑衣等传统农耕生产生活用品，打造"质朴原乡"。

3. 拓宽发展路径

一是村集体按照一定比例从收益中提取古村落保护基金，之后按贡献参与度向社员分红，破解古村落保护与发展可持续难题。村民通过开展经营性项目和土地流转、劳务、合作社分红等，获得良好收益，2021年人均可支配收入达39880元。二是

通过成立产业专业合作社、旅游专业合作社、旅游管理有限公司和旅游管理协会等机构，形成新的建设营运管理模式，激发村民的主动参与性，推动农旅融合良性发展。

4. 契合时代需求

一是提升游览服务。古村顺应市场需求，完善网上预订、线上景区等功能，邀请金牌导游、专业摄影师等行业大咖开展"云旅游"直播活动；通过"网上商店"实现旅游商品"云销售"。利用"丹棱文旅""大雅丹棱""幸福古村"等微信公众号、抖音号、视频号，携手国际在线、中国旅游报、蜀韵文旅等媒体，构建古村新媒体宣传矩阵。二是深耕产品打造。将休闲、度假、体验作为古村产品定位，打造休闲度假业态；以"幸福里"公共文化空间为载体，开展花艺、读书分享会、手工制作等体验活动；以苔藓博物馆为核心，开发亲子研学、自然科普、农事体验等旅游产品，做好细分市场。

成效

幸福村依照古村肌理脉络，总投资约2.6亿元，精巧布局6处精品民宿，打造幸福里公共文化空间、石磨豆坊、私房菜、文创体验空间等20余处特色业态，建成游客中心1处，旅游厕所6个，停车位500余个，游步道37千米，形成"两环两纵"游览线路。幸福村作为联合国教科文组织"历史村镇的未来"国际会议参观点，接待了世界各地的嘉宾和游客。幸福村共计接待游客突破150万人次，实现旅游总收入约1.8亿元。

经验与启示

1. 充分发挥示范引领作用

编制《丹棱县幸福古村旅游提升方案》《幸福古村景区总体规划》，以及《丹棱县顺龙乡幸福古村传统村落保护发展规划》，明确古村"质朴原乡"定位，探索"两山转化"的实现路径。幸福村，项目建设采取示范引领、分期建设的方式有序推进，在循序渐进中，赢得原住村民的支持，获取村民的认同感，实现与原住村民和谐共处，构建良性的发展环境。

2. 始终坚持"保护开发"理念

遵循"旧物新用、修旧物旧、资源活化"方式，提升古村落整体气质。通过古居古桥修葺、古渠古道修缮、古树古石保护、古物古事挖掘，留住悠久的历史印记；举办迎亲、唢呐、农耕等系列民俗体验活动，传承最纯粹的民俗文化；实现在保护中开发，在开发中传承，进一步凸显古村的山脉、水脉、地脉、文脉和人脉，打造"记得住乡愁"的"质朴原乡"，用原乡灵魂和魅力实现"近者悦、远者来"，促进保护传承和发展能力提升。

3. 探索实践共建共享机制

成立国有幸福古村发展有限公司，做好村落的规划、建设和市场运营；引进"新村民"50余人，开

展艺术创作、业态指导、社区营造;整合"公司、合作社、村民"三方力量,构建起"三位一体"的共建共享模式,实现古村落协调有序发展。

4. 创新业态适应市场需求

发挥原住村民的技艺特长,实现"民与企"合作,植入石磨豆坊、小院咖啡、私房菜等新业态,打造场景化消费体验产品。实施文化下乡,打造"幸福里"公共文化空间,通过市场化运营,为古村营造展览、教育、阅读与店铺等新场景,实现多维度的当代乡村

新生活与价值流动。依托在地演艺特色,将农耕、民俗故事等进行丰富的展示和演绎,建立唢呐体验基地、文创体验馆、青苔博物馆,开发自然研学、民俗体验等"沉浸式"产品,打造旅游的深度体验感。

下一步计划

以创建省级全域旅游示范区为统揽,着力推进以幸福村为核心的省级旅游度假项目建设;凸显幸福村农文旅融合发展标杆典范的作用,为乡村振兴提供可普遍适用的先进经验。整体提升幸福村业态产品,加快打造乡村精品民宿,推进峡谷水域展示区以及游船码头建设,建设村史博物馆,设置常态化演艺场所,拉长古村游线;重点对智慧景区建设、研学旅行、文化活化等方面进行改善、提升、创新,进一步增强业态产品市场吸引力;实现幸福村模式的带动、促进和辐射作用的全新飞跃。

Xingfu Village, Danling County, Meishan City, Sichuan Province:

The "Ancient Village Model" Integrating Agriculture, Culture, and Tourism to Empower Rural Revitalization

Included in *WTA Best Practices of Rural Revitalization through Tourism 2022*

Abstract

Xingfu Village in Shunlong Township, Danling County, Meishan City of Sichuan Province, based on its "ancient village" culture, farming customs and natural ecology, has proposed the slogan of "rustic homeland", and integrates sightseeing and holidaymaking, farming experience, folk customs, leisure and recreation, homestays, study tours, and celebrations to create a new rural lifestyle of its own characteristics. It integrates multiple forces such as companies, cooperatives, natives and newly-arrived residents, and has established a model for companies, cooperatives and villagers to work with each other and share development fruits, and explored a path for rural revitalization and development featuring urban-rural integration. The villagers invest in companies and cooperatives with their land use right or idle dwellings, provide services or sell products to contribute to rural tourism. The development of rural tourism has increased the per capita disposable income from 11,080 yuan to 39,880 yuan, and brought Xingfu, once a little-known ancient village, international attention and both economic and social benefits.

Challenges and Problems

The village is located in the middle of the mountain, 600-900 meters above sea level and about 12 kilometers from the county seat, and about 6 km of the road is winding through mountains, making it difficult to access. The residential houses are all in the mountains, and the farmland is mostly terraced fields, with less than 1 *mu* of usable farmland per capita. The farming conditions are relatively backward and the farming method outdated. The yield of cash crops is small. Though the ecological environment is great, the villagers did not know how to capitalize on it. As a result, the young and middle-aged people have flocked out to cities to make a living. The village gradually became listless and increasingly hollow.

Measures

1. Preserve the rural legacy

Firstly, keep the ancient village's timelessness. The village's forest coverage rate reaches as high as 80%. It is located in the mountain, run by streams, and scattered with residential houses made of earth walls and grey-green roof tiles commonly seen in the western part of Sichuan. It has adhered to the development principle of "giving old items a new purpose, and repairing the old items as they were". Secondly, protect the ecological environment. The village is proud of its nearly 30 natural and cultural heritage sites, including thousand-year-old ginkgo trees, a bridge built in the Qing Dynasty, terraced fields, and the ancient path for transporting salt and iron goods. Another development principle —"adapting new tourist attractions to existing ones and complementing existing tourist attractions with new ones" is followed.

2. Build up the brand of "rustic homeland"

First is to respect the tradition and legacy of the village. Instead of vacating, it allows the villagers to stay where they are and live and farm the way they like. Not only the traditional way of farming, but also folk customs, the legacy of *zhiqing*, and the folk art of Suona are preserved. Various activities have been staged to show folk customs and give visitors a first-hand, memorable experience with the country life. The second is to keep the original buildings intact.

Traditional rural facilities such as main halls and barns are restored and improved. And farming tools such as ploughs, harrows, blowing driers, stone mills and coir raincoats are on display to create "rustic homeland".

3. Broaden development paths

Firstly, after deducting a certain proportion of profits for the ancient village conservation fund, village collectives distribute dividends to members according to their contribution and participation, thus solving the problem of sustainable conservation and development. The villagers make good money by doing business, receiving payment for land circulation, their labor and dividends from cooperatives. The per capita disposable income reached 39,880 yuan in 2021. Secondly, specialized industrial cooperatives, tourism cooperatives, tourism management companies and tourism management associations are established, under a new operating and management model which stimulates the active participation of villagers, and promotes the integrated development of agriculture and tourism.

4. Meet the needs of the times

The first is to improve tourist services. The village responds to the market demand by improving its online reservation system and online tours. It also invited top-rated tour guides, professional photographers and other key opinion leaders (KOL) to live-streaming sessions and give the audience a virtual tour in the village. It has also opened online stores to sell tourism products. It has launched such public accounts as "Danling Wenlv", "Daya Danling", and "Xingfu the Ancient Village" on Weixin and Douyin, and worked with CRIOnline, *China Tourism News*, *Shuyun Wenlv* and other new media outlets to build up the village's visibility and reputation. Secondly, develop high-quality tourism products. The village develops tourism products with focus on leisure, holidaymaking and experience. At the public cultural space Xingfuli, experiential activities such as flower arranging, reading clubs and DIY are organized. With the moss museum at the core, tourism products such as parent-child study tours, natural science popularization and farming experience are developed to appeal to niche markets.

Results

Based on the original texture of the ancient village, Xingfu Village has developed six boutique homestays, with an investment of about 260 million yuan, in addition to more than 20 characteristic business forms including the public cultural space Xingfuli, the stone-mill bean shop, private-home kitchens, and cultural and creative experience space. There is one tourist center, six tourist toilets, more than 500 parking spaces and a pedestrian path of 37 kilometers, forming two ring and two vertical tourist routes. As a designated place to visit for attendees of the UNESCO Conference on the Future of Historic Villages and Towns, Xingfu Village received conferees and visitors from around the world. So far, it has received more than 1.5 million tourists and generated tourism revenue of about 180 million yuan.

Experience and Inspirations

1. Give full play to the leading role of demonstration projects

The *Tourism Promotion Plan for Xingfu Ancient Village in Dangling County*, the *Master Plan for Scenic Spots of Xingfu Ancient Village* and the *Conservation and Development Plan for the Traditional Dwellings of Xingfu Ancient Village in Shunlong Township, Dangling County* are formulated, clarifying Xingfu's positioning as a place with "rustic homeland" and exploring the path of translating lucid waters and lush mountains into invaluable assets. The village advances projects in an orderly manner and in stages with demonstration projects playing the leading role, and in this process, wins the support of native villagers, so as to realize harmonious coexistence with them and create a favorable environment for development.

2. Always adhere to the concept of "conservation and development"

While improving the village environment as a whole, it follows the principles of "giving old items a new purpose, repairing old items as they were, and putting idle resources into good use". It has repaired ancient houses and bridges, ancient ditches and roads, protected ancient trees and rocks, and uncovered ancient relics and more of the village history, to preserve its memories and marks of the passage of time. It organizes wedding ceremonies, Suona performance and farming experiential activities to advocate its folk customs. By promoting development and conservation side by side, it

highlights its mountains, waters, land, culture and people, and creates a "rustic homeland" that benefits local community and attracts visitors from afar. In this course, its abilities of conservation, inheritance and development have improved.

3. Explore a mechanism for collaboration and sharing development fruits

The state-owned Xingfu Ancient Village Development Co., Ltd. was founded to take charge of village planning, development and marketing. The village has attracted more than 50 new arrivals who are engaged in artistic creation, business mentoring and community building. It has established a model for the company, cooperatives and villagers to work with each other and share development fruits. Coordinated and orderly development of the village is realized.

4. Introduce new business forms to meet market demands

Native villagers who have skills and expertise work with enterprises, to develop new business forms such as the stone-mill bean shop, courtyard cafe and private-home kitchen, and develop new scenario-based consumption products. To rejuvenate local culture, it has built the public cultural space Xingfuli and introduced new scenarios such as exhibitions, education, reading and shops through market-oriented operations, to create a new rural lifestyle in multiple dimensions and facilitate value flow. Based on the characteristics of local performing arts, it has adapted local farming and folklore stories to the stage, opened a Suona experience base, an artistic creation experience hall and a moss museum, and developed immersive tourism products such as study tours in nature and folk customs experience, to create an immersive rural lifestyle experience.

Next Steps

Aimed to build itself into a provincial-level demonstration zone for all-area-advancing tourism, the village will work hard to build a provincial-level tourism resort with it at the core, highlight its demonstration role for promoting the integrated development of agriculture, culture and tourism, and share its good practices of reference value for rural revitalization. It will improve its overall tourism economy and products, accelerate to develop boutique homestays, build the exhibition areas in canyon waters, docks for sightseeing boats, a village history museum and permanent performance venues, and extend the tourist routs. The focus will be on improving and upgrading the application of intelligent technology to scenic spots, study tours, and cultural inheritance to enhance the market attractiveness of its tourism products and promote the Xingfu Model to more areas.

旅游减贫案例故事（中英文双语版）
Best Practices of Poverty Alleviation through Tourism（Chinese-English Bilingual Edition）

四川省阿坝藏族羌族自治州九寨沟县：
全域旅游促进乡村脱贫奔小康

收录于《2021世界旅游联盟：旅游助力乡村振兴案例》

摘要

自脱贫攻坚以来，九寨沟县充分依托生态优势和九寨沟国家5A级风景名胜区旅游资源优势，不断创新旅游扶贫新模式，以全域旅游为方向，构建"一主两核三带"新布局，优化旅游产业结构，走出了一条生态旅游发展齐头并进的新路子，实现了从"木头财政"到"旅游财政"、从"资源大县"到"旅游强县"、从"深度贫困"到"小康富裕"的重大转型。自1953年建县以来，全县GDP增长了122倍，财政收入增加了118倍，以旅游业为主导的第三产业对GDP贡献率逾60%，成为全国首批"中国旅游百强县市"。

挑战与问题

九寨沟是中国重要生态屏障和水源涵养地，属于川滇森林及生物多样性保护国家重点生态功能区，是四川省第二大林区。与此同时，九寨沟县也曾是四川88个贫困县之一，是"三区三州"深度贫困县，是四川省脱贫攻坚"高原藏区"的主战场。九寨沟的旅游业过度依赖于九寨沟风景区，如何打破单一业态、单一景区的模式，如何借助旅游消费转型升级倒逼供给侧结构性改革，让更多困难群众享受到旅游业发展带来的红利，便成为九寨沟县探索的方向。

措施

九寨沟县充分发挥旅游优势，不断创新旅游扶贫机制，以全域旅游为方向，以"一主两核三带"为路径，优化旅游产业结构、促进转型升级，走出了一条"旅游+"的新路径。

1. 推进景区景点建设

对照省级旅游扶贫示范区创建标准，打造12个旅游扶贫重点村，落实停车场、旅游漫道、旅游厕所、观景台、农副产品销售点、游客接待中心等旅游基础服务设施的"六小工程"项目建设。截至2021年，九寨沟县已成功创建"四川省旅游扶贫示范区"，成功创建6个"四川省旅游扶贫示范村"、107户"四川省乡村民宿达标示范户"，初步形成"一核多点"彼此带动的全域旅游格局。

2. 推动农旅产业融合

实施"九寨沟+"品牌培育计划，明确双河镇河坝村和罗依坝村、白河乡太平村、勿角镇苗州村、黑河镇达舍寨村、南坪镇双龙村5个农旅融合示范园为九寨沟县现代农业产业融合示范园区。着手打造大录乡油菜大地景观基地和黑河镇七里村甜樱桃采摘园，完善步道、观景台、旅游厕所、标识标牌等旅游配套设施，为第三产业扶贫打下基础。

3. 促进手工旅游发展

充分挖掘县域内特有的饮食文化和手工技艺，探索旅游产品订单式加工模式，引导九寨祥巴、阿布氇孜、奉巫餐饮等公司共同打造一个旅游商品研发基地，发掘旅游食品和旅游手工艺品等特色旅游商品；培育旅游商品企业和品牌，开发"小九九"系列文创产品180多种；定向选择200余名贫困群众派发旅游商品生产订单，持续带动其增收。

4. 培育发展旅游服务产品

依托九寨沟景区的优势资源，全县共开业藏（农）家乐39家。发挥乡村旅游发展优势，成功将罗依乡九寨庄园建设成为"四川省乡村旅游创客基地新业态示范品牌"。截至2021年，已接待县内外游客3600余人次，实现经济收入40余万元，间接带动贫困人口参与就业900余人，拓宽了贫困群众增收渠道。

5. 打造旅游精品线路

立足"全域九寨"深度游工程，成功推出环神仙池一日游、秦川文化白马藏族风情一日游 2 条全域九寨休闲度假游线路。以柴门关驿站、罗依产业园区自驾游营地、白河乡太平农庄及县城周边特色农家乐为载体，向游客提供食宿等旅游接待服务，在九环沿线设置以游客体验为主的水果采摘点，带动周边群众发展乡村旅游增收致富，推动九寨环线旅游由景点旅游向串珠式全域旅游、由传统观光游向"旅游+"综合立体游的转变。

成效

九寨沟县依托全域旅游走上了致富路。2019 年，九寨沟县累计接待游客 185.51 万人次，实现旅游综合收入 17.6 亿元。2020 年，全县通过旅游脱贫人数逾 5500 人，占全县脱贫总人数 5638 人的 97%。截至 2021 年，九寨沟县已成功引进项目 20 余个、协议投资近 200 亿元；全县共有星级酒店 11 家、非星级酒店 88 家，乡村客栈 700 余家，（藏）农家乐 14 家，演艺场所 10 家，餐饮 2230 家，超市 572 家，带动数万人就业创业。

经验与启示

1. 串珠成线，破解景区高度集中"窘境"

坚持多点布局全面提升，加快构建以九寨风景名胜区为核心、多景区互为支撑、多点多级发展的全域旅游格局。一是推进景点建设。将全县科学划分为全域旅游发展示范带、休闲度假旅游发展带、生态文化旅游培育带，全力打造县域内其他景区景点，促进全域旅游高质量发展。二是提升基础设施水平。全力构建"对外畅达、内部通达"的立体综合旅游交通体系；落实对停车场、旅游厕所、游客接待中心等"六小工程"的建设，塑造美丽乡村新面貌。三是打造精品旅游线路。立足全域九寨深度游工程，精心设计全域旅游专线，实现 A 级景区"串珠成线"，运营好县域旅游线路。

2. 深度融合，多维提升旅游综合"质感"

积极推动农旅、文旅、体旅等产业融合发展。一是实施差异发展。鼓励旅游饭店、地方餐饮品牌、旅行社实施品质化建设，支持旅游市场主体开发丰富多彩的旅游新业态。引导企业打造旅游商品研发基地、旅游创客基地等新业态示范品牌。二是丰富开发模式。深入挖掘民族民俗文化，积极筹办系列节庆活动，推动6大类种养基地和5个农旅融合示范园建设，精心打造集"农业+文化"创意、特色饮食体验和观光旅游于一体的"农业+文化"创意基地。三是坚持招大引强。多举措强化全域旅游宣传推介，先后举办了文化旅游联盟品牌战略发布会、文旅发展联盟大会、"文旅品牌之夜"等系列活动，以优质旅游资源吸纳高质企业入驻。

3. 精准衔接，助推贫困群众搭上"便车"

坚持"旅游、扶贫发展"大扶贫模式，多举措促进贫困群众持续增收。一是壮大集体产业。按照"村有支柱产业、户有致富项目、人有一技之长"的要求，以小额贴息贷款、产业发展基金为保障，以九寨沟旅游市场为支撑，积极发展优势中药材和特色种养殖业，120个村全覆盖建立集体经济，成功创建省级旅游扶贫示范村6个，彻底消灭"空壳村"。二是打造村企同盟。通过"百企联百村、百企圆百梦"等活动，动员组织宾馆饭店、藏（农）家乐、演艺市场、旅行社等旅游企业积极参与脱贫攻坚，在就业创业、项目投资、农特产品宣传销售、从业人员技能提升等方面发挥帮扶作用，增强贫困村、贫困户的"造血"功能。

下一步计划

以全域旅游发展为目标，深入推进乡村振兴工作。一是科学制定乡村旅游建设详规，合理布局产业要素，实现乡村产品的全域化。二是打造特色"农旅+文旅"新业态，拓宽乡村关联产业融合渠道，不断延伸农业产业园区、农产品基地、农产品加工、传统手工业制造、农产品销售平台、乡村文创产品融合等特色业态，带动乡村旅游消费。三是进一步完善乡村交通枢纽网，规划建设产业路、生态路、文明路、致富路。四是加大对乡村旅游从业人员服务技能的培训力度，并建立本地外出人员联络机制，发掘一批"田秀才""土专家""乡创客"和能工巧匠，为乡村振兴汇聚人才。

旅游减贫案例故事（中英文双语版）
Best Practices of Poverty Alleviation through Tourism (Chinese-English Bilingual Edition)

Jiuzhaigou County, Aba Tibetan and Qiang Autonomous Prefecture, Sichuan Province:

All-Area-Advancing Tourism Drives Rural Poverty Alleviation and Prosperity

Included in *WTA Best Practices of Rural Revitalization through Tourism 2021*

Abstract

Since the initiation of poverty alleviation efforts and with full reliance on its ecological advantages and the tourism resources of the national 5A-level scenic spot of Jiuzhaigou, the Jiuzhaigou County continues to innovate the poverty alleviation through tourism model. Its new paradigm puts Jiuzhaigou Scenic Area squarely at the core. With all-area advancing tourism as the guiding framework, it has put into motion "the Jiuzhaigou Scenic Area as the mainstay, enhancing the core driving force of Zhangzha Charming Town and Nanping Livable Town, and building All-Area-Advancing Tourism Development Demonstration Belt, Leisure Vacation Tourism Development Belt, and Ecological Cultural Tourism Fostering Belt" concept.

They have optimized the tourism industry structure and embarked on a new eco-tourism development parallel to its goal of realizing a major transformation from "timber finance" to "tourism finance", "large resources county" to "strong tourism county" and "extreme poverty" to "well-off and prosperous". Since the county was established in 1953, its GDP has increased 122 times and its financial revenue 118 times. The tourism-dominated tertiary industry has contributed more than 60% to the GDP, leading to Jiuzhaigou County being recognized as the national first batch "Top 100 Tourism Counties and Cities in China".

Challenges and Problems

Jiuzhaigou is a major national ecological screen and water conservation area that belongs to the national key ecological function zone for forest and biodiversity conservation in Sichuan and Yunnan provinces. It is the second largest forest zone in Sichuan Province. As the main battleground in poverty alleviation in the "Plateau Tibetan Area" in Sichuan Province, the county was one of 88 poverty-stricken counties in Sichuan Province. It was also one of the counties with extreme poverty in Tibet Autonomous Region, the four southern administrative districts of Xinjiang Uygur Autonomous Region, Tibetan areas of Qinghai, Sichuan, Yunnan and Gansu provinces, Linxia Prefecture, Liangshan Prefecture and Nujiang Prefecture. Since its tourism industry is overly dependent on the Valley Scenic Area, the county has been exploring ways to break away from the single business and single scenic area model and pivot to the supply-side structural reform through the transformation and upgrading of tourism consumption. This economic shift allows villagers who are facing financial difficulty to benefit and share in the dividends from tourism development.

Measures

The county has given full play to its tourism advantages and continued to innovate the mechanism of poverty alleviation through tourism. With the all-area-advancing tourism as the direction and Jiuzhaigou Scenic Area as the mainstay, it has optimized its tourism industry structure, facilitated transformation and upgrade and embarked on the path of "Tourism +". This was accomplished by enhancing the core driving force of Zhangzha Charming Town and Nanping Livable Town and building an All-area-advancing Tourism Development Demonstration Belt, Leisure Vacation Tourism Development Belt and an Ecological Cultural Tourism Fostering Belt.

1. Accelerate the construction of scenic spots

In compliance with the standard requirements for the construction of provincial tourism poverty alleviation demonstration zones, 12 key villages have been built to implement the construction of "Six Small Projects" which include the following: parking lots, tourist roads, tourist toilets, viewing platforms, agricultural and sideline products points of sale, tourist reception centers and other basic tourism service facilities. As of 2021, the county has successfully established the "Sichuan Province Tourism Poverty Alleviation Demonstration Zone", six "Sichuan Province Tourism Poverty Alleviation Demonstration Villages" and 107 "Sichuan Province Rural Homestays Standardization Demonstration Households", initially forming an all-area-advancing tourism pattern driven by "one core and multiple points".

2. Promote the integration of agricultural and tourism industries

The brand development plan of "Jiuzhaigou +" has been implemented and the five agricultural and tourism integrated demonstration parks in Heba Village and Luoyiba Village of Shuanghe Town, Taiping Village of Baihe Township, Miaozhou Village of Wujiao Town, Dashezhai Village of Heihe Town, and Shuanglong Village of Nanping Town have been earmarked as the county's modern agricultural industries integration demonstration zones. Great efforts have been made to construct a ripe produce landscape base in Dalu Township and a sweet cherry-picking garden in Qili Village, Heihe Town. All these are designed to pave the way for poverty alleviation through a tertiary industry and to improve tourism at supporting facilities that include trails, viewing platforms, tourist toilets and increase brand awareness through logos and signage.

3. Promote the development of artisanal tourism

Great efforts have been made to optimize the county's unique cooking culture and craftsmanship. Also, work has been done to explore the order-based processing model of tourism products and guide companies such as Jiuzhai Xiangba Culture and Art Co., Ltd., Abu Luzi Tibetan Restaurant, and Fengwu Catering Co., Ltd. to build a tourism product research and development base. Progress has been achieved to develop special products like tourism food and handicrafts and cultivate tourism commodities enterprises and brands that will create more than 180 kinds of cultural and creative products like the "Small Ninety-Nine" series. The county has also guided over 200 impoverished people on distribution orders for tourism commodities production. Implementation of these measures has ensured the continuous growth of income for poor households.

4. Foster and develop tourism service products

With the Jiuzhaigou Scenic Area and its superior resources as the base, the Jiuzhaigou County has opened a total of 39 Tibetan-styled agritainment industries. Capitalizing on the proven advantages of

rural tourism development, it has transformed the Jiuzhai Manor in Luoyi Township into a new business form demonstration brand of rural tourism maker base in Sichuan Province. As of 2021, the township has received over 3,600 visitors from inside and outside of the county, resulting in over 400,000 yuan income for the people. With such measures implemented, it has indirectly driven more than 900 impoverished people to be employed, thus broadening the channels for the poor to grow their income.

5. Develop boutique routes of tourism

Based on the "All-area-advancing Jiuzhai" in-depth tour project, the county has introduced two routes of all-area-advancing Jiuzhai leisure and vacation tour such as a one-day tour around the Fairy Pool and one-day tour of Qinchuan Culture Baima Tibetan Customs. With the Chaimenguan courier station, the self-driving camp in the Luoyi Industrial Park, the Taiping farm village in Baihe Township and special agritainment around the county as the carriers, it has provided tourists with food, accommodation and other tourism reception services. Along the ninth ring road from Chengdu to Jiuzhaigou, experiential fruit picking points for tourists have been set up to motivate those living in the surrounding areas to increase their income through rural tourism. With such measures implemented, the transformation of the Jiuzhai Ring Tour from scenic spot to all-area-advancing tour by stringing various scenic spots together has been realized. Also, it has been successfully converted from a traditional sightseeing tour into a "Tourism +" comprehensive three-dimensional tour.

Results

Based on the all-area-advancing tourism, the county has embarked on a road to progress. In 2019,

it cumulatively received 1.855 million visitors that generated a comprehensive revenue of 1.76 billion yuan. In 2020, more than 5,500 people moved out of poverty through tourism. They account for 97% of 5,638 people lifted out of poverty in the county. As of 2021, over 20 projects have been introduced, with an agreed investment of nearly 20 billion yuan. Currently, the county boasts 11 starred hotels, 88 non-star hotels, over 700 village inns, 14 Tibetan-styled agritainment enterprises, 10 performing art venues, 2,230 restaurants and 572 supermarkets, resulting in tens of thousands of people being employed or starting their own businesses.

Experience and Inspirations

1. Leverage the high concentration of scenic spots by stringing various scenic spots together

It has upheld the comprehensive improvement of multi-point layout and accelerated the construction of an all-area-advancing tourism pattern with Jiuzhaigou Scenic Area as the core. Furthermore, multiple scenic spots that support each other and multi-point and multi-level developments have also begun. The first step is to promote the construction of scenic spots. The whole county has been divided into All-Area-Advancing Tourism Development Demonstration Belt, Leisure Vacation Tourism Development Belt and Ecological Cultural Tourism Fostering Belt to build other scenic spots and facilitate the high-quality development of all-area-advancing tourism. Secondly, upgrade the infrastructure level. Great efforts should be made to build a three-dimensional comprehensive transportation system of "externally unblocked, internally accessible" and implement the construction of "Six Small Projects", including parking lots, tourist toilets and tourist reception centers to create an appealing new look for the village. Thirdly, build boutique tourism routes. Based on the all-area-advancing Jiuzhai in-depth tour, an all-area-advancing tourism special route should be designed to string all A-level tourist attractions together for a smooth and seamless operation of the county tourism route.

2. In-depth integration to enhance the comprehensive "quality" of tourism in all aspects

The integrated development of industries of such industries agricultural, cultural and sports tourism will be proactively promoted. Firstly, we will implement differential development. Tourism restaurants, local catering brands and travel agencies should be encouraged to implement quality construction. Tourism market players should be supported to develop diverse new tourism businesses. Secondly, enhance and fine-tune development models. The national folk culture should be explored, festival activities should be organized, the construction of six major planting and breeding bases and five agricultural tourism integration demonstration parks should be boosted. Additionally, an "agriculture + cultural" creativity base that integrates "agriculture + culture" creativity, special food experiences and sightseeing tourism should be created. Thirdly, secure

the introduction of big or powerful enterprises. Multiple measures should be taken to expand and elevate the publicity and promotion of all-area-advancing tourism. Events and activities like the cultural tourism alliance brand strategy conference, the cultural tourism development alliance conference and the cultural tourism brand night should be held, with a view to attracting high-quality enterprises to establish their operations in the county as sign on as partners for quality tourism resources.

3. Precise connection helping poor people catch an "express of getting rich"

The "tourism facilitating poverty alleviation development" model should be held high and various measures should be adopted to promote the sustained income growth of poverty-stricken people. Firstly, the collective industry should be strengthened. With the support of the Jiuzhaigou tourism market and through small sums and interest loans from industrial development funds, we will develop superior traditional Chinese herbs, special planting and breeding industries as required by "a pillar industry for each village, a program of getting rich for each household, and a professional skill for each person". Efforts should be made to build the collective economy in all 120 villages under its jurisdiction and create six provincial tourism poverty demonstration villages completely eliminating "hollow village". Secondly, build village-enterprise alliance. In adherence to the tenets of "enterprises partnered with villages to help the poor realize their dreams", hotels and restaurants, Tibetan-type agritainment enterprises, performing arts venues, travel agencies and other tourism businesses should be organized and coordinated in poverty alleviation. Relevant assistance for employment and entrepreneurship, project investment, publicity and sales of agricultural and sideline products and the improvement of skills of the locals must be provided. Impoverished villagers must be motivated and inspired to practice self-reliance to improve their standard of living and move out of poverty.

Next Steps

Rural revitalization will be further facilitated by all-area-advancing tourism development. Firstly, a detailed plan of rural tourism development will be scientifically formulated. Industrial elements will be logically arranged, and rural production should be integrated. Secondly, special "agricultural tourism + cultural tourism" new businesses will be created. The integration channel for rural correlative industries will be broadened. Also, agricultural industrial parks, agricultural product bases, agricultural product processing and traditional handicraft manufacturing, agricultural product sales platforms and rural cultural creative products, and other special business forms will be extended to drive rural tourism consumption. Thirdly, rural transportation hub networks will be further improved and the industrial road, ecological road, civilized road and the road to economic enhancement will be planned and developed. Fourthly, service skills training for rural tourism practitioners will be intensified. A communication system for local migrant workers will be established. Farming technicians, farming experts, local business operators and skillful craftsmen will be trained and pooled together for rural revitalization.

旅游减贫案例故事（中英文双语版）
Best Practices of Poverty Alleviation through Tourism（Chinese-English Bilingual Edition）

贵州省黔南布依族苗族自治州荔波县朝阳镇洪江村：
艺旅融合探索乡村扶贫新路径

收录于《2021世界旅游联盟：旅游助力乡村振兴案例》

摘要

贵州省荔波县洪江村结合村落资源提炼出了"非遗洪江、艺术洪江、匠人洪江、生态洪江"的发展定位，围绕废旧房、闲置地、贫困户做文章，实现了从废旧房到文创房、从闲置地到生财地、从贫困户到示范户、从"空心村"到网红村的蜕变。洪江村以乡土文化为灵魂，以乡村田园为图景，以生态农业为基础，以艺术扶贫为抓手，以旅游富民为目标，以村民闲置老房和传统村落遗存为媒介，探索出了一条艺术扶贫新路径。

挑战与问题

洪江村共有9个自然寨，2014年建档立卡贫困户为168户651人，贫困发生率高达29%，是一个典型的深度贫困村。洪江村基础设施建设薄弱，村庄环境脏乱，道路狭窄，且因资金短缺，无法改善基础条件。洪江村地貌以山地、高山为主，耕地面积少，全村耕地面积仅有924亩，人均耕地面积不足1亩，农业机械化和产业化难度大，大部分山地荒坡不适宜种植经济树种，村民收入主要来自外出务工。由于大量劳动力外流，村内仅剩老弱病残留守，缺乏活力和创新，洪江村成为"空心村"。留守老人大多思想观念保守，难以接受新思想和新事物，拒绝学习新知识和新技能。

措施

洪江村围绕荔波县全域旅游发展战略，结合村落资源提炼出了"非遗洪江、艺术洪江、匠人洪江、生态洪江"的发展定位思路。

1. "废旧房"变"文创房"

利用村内闲置的干栏式建筑，结合"集体经营性建设用地试点"等政策，邀请世界各地的艺术家来到洪江，对复建老房进行艺术工作坊兼居室改造，全面激活闲置破败老房。截至2021年，已收储老房屋及宅基地使用权81宗，宅基地面积1.86万平方米；入驻洪江村的艺术家有88人，其中以认养30年方式入驻的有11人，以有偿使用方式入驻的有77位；改造修复老房48栋，使艺术和乡村在洪江村发生了奇妙的"化学反应"。

2. "闲置地"变"生财地"

充分利用黔南州农村集体建设用地使用权制度改革试点村政策，积极探索集体建设用地有偿使用和农村宅基地退出补偿机制，提高土地利用率。村委会引进哈尔滨显著医生集团，并与企业合作建立洪江康养基地，激活自然资源。

3. "贫困户"变"示范户"

按照"支部+公司+农户"的产业扶贫推进模式，聚焦贫困户，坚持在推动产业兴旺过程中推进"志智"双扶，把贫困户培育成脱贫示范户。引进企业发展蔬菜、大蒜、蚕桑等产业850亩，全村187户群众在土地流转中受益；组建房屋修复队7支80人，其中贫困户48人，每天每人200元务工费，月人均收入逾3000元。艺术家工作室提供房屋保洁、安保等就业岗位逾70个。

4. "空心村"变"网红村"

着力推进文艺扶贫试点建设，主动保护和传承民族文化、乡土文化资源。著名艺术批评家贾方舟、当代艺术家李向明、艺术家崔国泰等来自国内外的艺术家，齐聚洪江进行艺术创作，村中先后举办中国—东盟教育交流周之2020洪江论坛暨洪江当代艺术邀请展，写生中国走进洪江艺术展，国际动漫走进洪江艺术展等大型艺术活动，中央、省及州媒体平台报道100余次，先后吸引美国、法国、德国、瑞典等国内外艺术家到访，实现了生态经济和文化经济的融合发展。

成效

洪江村的探索与坚持，有力推进了农村文旅产业经济的发展。近年来，洪江村年接待游客7万人次，旅游年收入300万元，旅游带动村民就业173人，基本建成15个艺术家工作室、46家民宿客栈，2020

年已实现全村脱贫。艺术家进驻后，与村民共同生活，逐步加强互动、彼此滋养，重塑传统村落的人文价值观和产业链，让洪江村传统村落遗存的艺术活化起来。随着艺术家的到来以及当地土布文化的布艺培训班的开展，洪江村的旅游产品由单一的山水风景，转向以多元文化支撑为主。如今，群落式的洪江村布依族干栏式建筑风貌，如艺术交流中心、土语南居艺术活动广场、雁西书院文艺交流中心、小梅摄影写生馆、国泰当代美术馆等，已成为洪江村一道亮丽的风景线。

经验与启示

洪江村的成功实践证明：保护乡村农耕文化独特性、保住乡村文化根脉、增强群众文化自信、深化农业农村改革，对乡村振兴至关重要。

1. 独特的文化魅力是吸引艺术家的核心要素

洪江村展现了贵州农耕文明的独特价值，滋养出具有贵州特色的耕读文化、山地文化和乡土文化。这些文化所体现的多样性、包容性、审美性特点，与艺术家追求艺术创作的愿望高度契合，使他们在情感上找到了归属感。

2. 促进乡村振兴要保住乡村文化根脉

洪江村的探索证明：乡村原始风貌和优秀传统文化本身就是一笔财富，蕴藏着发展的优势和资源。这启示我们：一是在村庄规划上，要更加注重保护村庄原有的历史风物遗存，让村庄更具人文情怀，为保护、传承、弘扬文化留下足够空间。二是在村庄建设过程中，要坚决杜绝大拆大建，充分挖掘和整理村庄历史文化遗存和非遗技艺，进行合理改造，既保留历史痕迹，又融入现代便利和审美元素，实现文化的活态化传承和发展。

3. 促进乡村振兴要提高农民文化自信

洪江村村民通过与艺术家的融洽相处和耳濡目染，其生活方式和精神面貌发生了显著变化。这启示我们：一是要深入挖掘和整理本村的文化遗存，并通过展示让村民从文化艺术价值的角度重新认识村庄的存在意义。二是要发挥好群众的主体作用，鼓励村民积极参与村庄文化的传承与保护，从参与中培养文化自觉和文化自信。三是要讲好乡村发展故事，唤起浓郁乡愁，让村民看到村庄的发展前景，让更多年轻人愿意留下来建设美丽乡村。

4. 促进乡村振兴要深化农业农村改革

洪江村抓住有利契机，用改革创新的办法盘活自身资源，取得了初步成果。这启示我们：一是要在盘活利用村民闲置宅基地和农房上下功夫，在保障村民权益的前提下探索宅基地退出机制和"三权分置"改革，实现资源再利用，实现效益最大化。二是要在农业产业革命上下功夫，积极探索农业产业结构调整，多样化发展助推农民增收。三是要推动农文旅融合发展，将农事活动体验、农耕文化体验与乡村旅游发展相结合，为农村发展注入新动力。

下一步计划

洪江村将在未来工作的开展中探索三种模式，创建三个示范。一是探索艺术家与扶贫相结合模式，创建艺术扶贫示范；二是探索当代艺术与乡村文化相碰撞模式，创建乡村文化振兴示范；三是探索文化与旅游深度融合的发展模式，创建文旅融合示范。

Hongjiang Village, Chaoyang Town, Libo County, Qiannan Buyi and Miao Autonomous Prefecture, Guizhou Province:

Integration of Art and Tourism Explores a New Model of Rural Poverty Alleviation

Included in *WTA Best Practices of Rural Revitalization through Tourism 2021*

Abstract

Based on village resources, the brand positioning of "intangible cultural heritage, art, craftsmanship, and ecology" has been determined for the development of Hongjiang Village, Libo County, Guizhou Province. Focusing on abandoned houses, idle land, and impoverished households, it has achieved the transformation of abandoned houses into cultural and creative houses, idle land into wealth-generating sites, impoverished households into demonstration households, and a "hollow village" into an internet-famous village. With rural culture as the soul, rural pastoral landscape as the blueprint, ecological agriculture as the foundation, poverty alleviation through art as the means, enriching people through tourism as the goal, and idle old houses and remains of traditional villages as media, the village has explored a new path for poverty alleviation through art.

Challenges and Problems

There are nine natural villages in the village. In 2014, there were 651 people from 168 archived impoverished households with a poverty incidence of 29%, making it severely impoverished. The infrastructure construction in Hongjiang Village was weak, the village environment was dirty and chaotic, the roads were narrow, and due to a shortage of funds, it was impossible to improve the basic conditions. Mostly dominated by mountain land and high mountains, with a small arable land area of 924 *mu* and a per capita arable land area of less than one *mu*, the village was not a suitable place for an economic forest development. Agricultural mechanization and industrialization were impossible to attain. Many villagers chose to work outside for their livelihood. Due to a large outflow of labor, only the elderly, weak, and sick remained in the village, lacking vitality and innovation, making Hongjiang Village a "hollow village". Most left-behind elderly people had conservative ideological concepts, found it difficult to accept new ideas and things, and refused to learn new knowledge and skills.

Measures

Centered on the development strategy of all-area-advancing tourism in Libo County, and on the basis of village resources, the positioning of promoting "intangible cultural heritage, art, craftsmanship, and ecology" has been determined for the development of Hongjiang Village.

1. Transform abandoned houses into cultural and creative houses

Through the utilization of idle stilt style architecture and combining policies such as the "pilot project for collective management construction land", artists from all over the world were introduced to revitalize and renovate the old houses and living rooms into art workshops, and living rooms. As of 2021, 81 old houses and homestead use rights have been purchased and stored which covers an area of 18,600 square meters. A total of 88 artists have settled in the village, 11 of whom have owned their houses for 30 years, and 77 of whom have paid for the use. Additionally, 48 old houses have been renovated and restored with the amazing results of art and village integration in full display.

2. Transform idle land into wealth-generating sites

To improve the land utilization rate, the policies for pilot villages on rural collective construction land use rights system reform in Buyi and Miao Autonomous Prefecture of Qiannan were leveraged. Mechanism for the paid use of collective construction

land and compensation on the withdrawal of rural homesteads were also explored. The village committee has introduced Harbin Significant Doctor Group and cooperated with enterprises to establish Hongjiang Health and Wellness Base, activating natural resources.

3. Transform impoverished households into demonstration households

In accordance with the poverty alleviation model through industrial development of "Party branches + companies + peasant households", and focused on impoverished households, a change of attitude and educational support were also required to achieve industrial prosperity and transform impoverished households to demonstration households. Enterprises were introduced to develop industries such as vegetables, garlic, and sericulture which covered an area of 850 *mu*. 187 village households benefited from the land transfer. Seven house repair teams with 80 people were set up, 48 of whom came from impoverished households. Each could earn 200 yuan per day, with a monthly per capita income of more than 3,000 yuan. The artists' studios provided at least 70 jobs such as house cleaning and security.

4. Transform a "hollow village" into an internet-famous village

Efforts have been made to promote the construction of pilot projects for poverty alleviation through literature and art to protect and pass on its national culture and local cultural resources. Famous art critic Jia Fangzhou, contemporary creator and artist Li Xiangming, artist Cui Guotai and other artists at home and abroad gathered in the village for creative endeavors. Large-scale art events were held: the China-ASEAN Education Cooperation Week — The Hongjiang Forum 2020 & Hongjiang Contemporary Art Invitation Exhibition, Sketching China into Hongjiang Exhibition and International Animation into Hongjiang Art Exhibition. Publicity coverage from national, provincial and prefecture-level media platforms exceeded 100, enticing domestic and foreign artists from the United States, France, Germany, and Sweden, etc., achieving the integrated development of ecological and cultural economies.

Results

The exploration and persistence of Hongjiang Village have effectively promoted the development of rural cultural and tourism industry economy. In recent years, the village welcomed 70,000 tourists annually, with the annual tourism income of 3 million yuan. A total of 173 villagers have been engaged in tourism, and 15 artists' studios and 46 homestays have been built. The village has been lifted out of poverty by 2020. After the settling in the village, the artists live together with villagers for more interaction and better understanding of each other. This practice has reshaped humanistic values and the traditional village's industrial chain. It has also revitalized the legacy art here. With the arrival of artists and the fabrics training courses established

according to the local textile culture, tourism products in the village have shifted from solely featuring natural landscapes to being supproted by a diverse cultural foundation. Currently, the clustered architectural style of the Buyi Nationality in Hongjiang Village, such as the Art Exchange Center, Tuyu Nanju Art Activity Plaza, Yanxi Academy Literature and Art Exchange Center, Xiaomei Photography and Sketching Gallery, and Guotai Contemporary Art Museum in the village, etc., has become a beautiful scenic line in Hongjiang Village.

Experience and Inspirations

The village's successful preliminary practice proves that protecting the uniqueness of rural farming culture, preserving the roots of rural culture, enhancing the cultural confidence of people, and deepening the reform of agriculture and rural areas are vital to rural revitalization.

1. Unique cultural charm is the core element of attracting artists

Hongjiang Village showcases the distinctive value of Guizhou's agricultural civilization, nurturing a culture of farming and reading, mountain culture, and rural culture with Guizhou characteristics. The diversity, inclusiveness, and aesthetic qualities embodied in these cultures align closely with artists' aspirations for artistic creation, allowing them to find a sense of belonging emotionally.

2. Preserve the roots of rural culture for rural revitalization

The exploration of the village has proven that the original rural landscape and excellent traditional culture are a fortune, containing advantages and resources for development. It has enlightened us a lot. Firstly, the original historical heritage should be protected in village planning to develop a more humanistic village, and further protect, inherit

and carry forward the village culture. Secondly, large-scale demolition and construction should be eradicated in village construction to tap historical and cultural relics and intangible cultural heritage for reasonable transformations, which can preserve the historical traces, and also integrate modern convenience and aesthetic elements, thus achieving the inheritance and development of cultural liveliness.

3. Enhance the farmers' cultural confidence in rural revitalization

Through harmonious interaction with artists and being influenced by them, the lifestyle and spiritual outlook of Hongjiang villagers have undergone significant changes. This enlightens us: Firstly, it is essential to deeply excavate and organize the cultural relics of the village and showcase them, allowing villagers to rediscover the significance of their village from the perspective of cultural and artistic value. Secondly, the main role of the masses should be fully utilized, encouraging villagers to actively participate in the inheritance and protection of village culture, fostering cultural awareness and confidence through participation. Thirdly, it's important to convey the rural development story, evoking a strong sense of nostalgia, allowing villagers to see the development prospects of the village, and encouraging more young people to stay and build a beautiful countryside.

4. Expand the rural agricultural reform for revitalization

The village has taken advantage of its opportunities and revitalized its resources through reform and innovation with tentative results. This tells us that firstly, more efforts should be made to revitalize idle homesteads and the villagers' idle houses and explore the withdrawal of homesteads and the system of "separating rural land ownership rights, contract rights, and management rights" on the premise of protecting the villagers' rights and interest for resource reuse and maximum benefits. Secondly, more emphasis should be placed on the agricultural industrial revolution for the structural adjustment of the agricultural industry and diversified resources to increase the villagers' income. Thirdly, the integrated development of agriculture, culture and tourism should be highlighted to find new ways to integrate agricultural, farming culture and rural tourism experiences for rural development.

Next Steps

In its future endeavors, Hongjiang Village will explore three models and establish three demonstrations. Firstly, it will explore the model of integrating artists with poverty alleviation, creating a demonstration of art-driven poverty alleviation. Secondly, it will explore the model of contemporary art colliding with rural culture, creating a demonstration of rural cultural revitalization. Thirdly, it will explore the development model of deep integration of culture and tourism, creating a demonstration of cultural and tourism integration.

旅游减贫案例故事（中英文双语版）
Best Practices of Poverty Alleviation through Tourism (Chinese-English Bilingual Edition)

云南省丽江市玉龙纳西族自治县白沙镇玉湖村：
生态立村、旅游富村、文化兴村

收录于《2021世界旅游联盟：旅游助力乡村振兴案例》

摘要

云南省丽江市玉龙县玉湖村坚持以实现共同富裕为出发点和落脚点，以构建"小康玉湖、生态玉湖、魅力玉湖、和谐玉湖"为目标，实施"生态立村、旅游富村、文化兴村"三大战略，创新发展机制，通过盘活旅游业和发展养殖业，带领全体村民走上致富路。

挑战与问题

云南省丽江市玉龙纳西族自治县白沙镇玉湖村下辖9个村民小组，村民383户，人口1465人，其中农业人口1385人，劳动人口732人，全村面积77.78平方千米。玉湖村的基础设施不完善，优质高产高效农业匮乏，2003年，玉湖村经济总收入仅为234万元，旅游收入仅为18万元。村民年人均纯收入仅为937元，人均有粮300多千克，吃粮靠返销、花钱靠贷款、生产靠救济，是丽江市典型的后进村。

措施

1. 创新发展机制

玉湖村遵循"依法、自愿、有偿"的原则，通过转让、出租、转包、入股、互换等方式，创新农村土地流转机制。鼓励村民以荒地入股，栽种时出力出肥，由村合作社投资苗木、管理经营，见效后村民按入股面积分红，合作社适当提成，切实增加村民收入。此外，通过成立旅游开发合作社，组织全体村民合作开发，共享旅游发展的成果。在收益分配上，将总收入按适当比例划分为旅游促销费、个人所得、管理人员工资、办公经费、基础设施建设资金、教育基金、特困救济金和年底全员再次分配金，每家每户都参与旅游经营，全村形成"人人参与旅游，个个忙于做事，集中精力挣大钱，专心致志奔小康"的良好局面。

2. 盘活旅游业

玉湖村充分发挥自然景观和民族文化资源优势，着力发展具有纳西古村落与纳西民族文化特色的乡村旅游，目前已形成特色民居建筑群、洛克故居、黑白水古战场遗址、白沙细乐、东巴文化、民风民俗等文化旅游项目。辖区内乡村民宿发展较好，旅游产品体系日渐成熟，基础设施和公共服务不断完善，形成了以玉湖旅游合作社为主，以村民自发参与的旅游客栈、旅游餐饮、旅游购物为辅的旅游产业格局。

3. 发展养殖业

玉湖村充分利用和整合3万多亩草地和草坡资源，通过品种改良、草场建设、扶持专业大户等措施，大力发展牛、羊等畜牧养殖业。同时，进一步做好"水文章"，加强水源地保护和水源区水利设施建设。在建成玉湖水库、加紧建设文海水库的基础上，修建若干梯级小水库和小水塘坝、小围堰等，利用水质好、气候冷凉等特点，发展虹鳟等高端水产养殖业，并将其培育成重点产业。

成效

玉湖村经济收入从2003年的234万元增加到2020年的1600万元，旅游总收入从2003年的18万元增加到2020年的逾1200万元，村民年人均纯收入从2003年的937元增加到2020年的10000元以上。截至2021年，全村参与旅游服务的人员接近800人。玉湖村先后被评为中国传统村落、中国少数民族特色村寨、中国美丽休闲乡村、全国乡村旅游重点村等，成为丽江市"生态、文化、旅游、和谐"的示范村，吸引了众多的国内外游客。

经验与启示

玉湖村坚持以实现共同富裕为根本出发点和落脚点，实施"生态立村、旅游富村、文化兴村"三大战略。

1. 生态立村

玉湖村加强生态环境保护，以环保制度、旅游发展、项目建设、绿色产业、整治村容村貌"五个带动"为重点，使玉湖村从生态文明建设中受益和发展。玉湖村结合自身实际，优先把改善乡村环境、提高群众生活质量作为建设重点，先后投入300多万元，完成了2500米柏油路建设、710米村道硬化、3000多米的兴玉渠建设；修建了停车场、管理房、环保厕所、景观水系；实施了全村人畜饮水工程，使村民都喝上了清洁甘甜的自来水。村内还实施了123户庭院美化和厕所净化工程，新建了村卫生室，并由村集体出资让每位村民参加新型农村合作医疗。同时，玉湖村通过教育基金保障，加大教育投入，创办农民夜校，开展旅游服务技能及种养实用技术培训，提升村民的旅游服务意识和科技知识水平。

2. 旅游富村

玉湖村以全村共同致富为目标，创新合作开发模式，成立旅游开发合作社，组织全体村民共同参与旅游开发，共享发展成果。玉湖村重点开发了以"沿着洛克足迹，走进玉龙雪山"为主题的骑马徒步生态观光旅游项目，村民在合作社统一调度和安排下，以户为单位，轮流参与。在收益分配上，总收入按适当比例划分，确保每家每户都能参与旅游经营，全村老少均能参加年终分红。

3. 文化兴村

玉湖村梳理与重构纳西文化，从"生产生活、精神信仰、文化艺术"三大方面入手，打造"纳西文化+"模式，推进文旅融合发展。通过产业思维重塑文化特色、以目的地思维提升吸引力，构建"1+1+4+10+X"乡村旅游体系，即：1个特色马经济（骑马体验、场景演绎、马术培训）、1个创意旅拍（全球旅拍第一目的地）、4大导流项目（好好生活雪山音乐节、小小骑士茶马古道基地、低空飞行基地、自然博物探索基地）、10大非遗院落（白沙细乐院、纳西婚俗院、东巴纸艺院、东巴木雕院、纳西小吃街、网红游客中心、沉浸式街区演绎、高端主题民宿、纳西风情民宿、野奢营地）、X个旅游配套设施。

下一步计划

玉湖村将坚持"生态优先、绿色发展"理念，把农旅融合作为乡村全面振兴的关键抓手，以农促旅、以旅兴农。深入挖掘自然生态、历史文化、民俗民居等特色资源，以"旅游+、+旅游"为突破点，完善旅游基础设施，创新旅游产品开发，助推经营主体不断做大做强；打造自然博物探索基地、小小骑士茶马古道基地、旅拍基地、东巴文字院、白沙细乐院、精品民宿等玉湖村乡村振兴项目，让游客"进得来、留得下、记得住"，让美丽乡村真正红火起来，推动乡村振兴，真正实现"生态美、产业兴、百姓富"的有机统一。

Yuhu Village, Baisha Town, Yulong Naxi Autonomous County, Lijiang City, Yunnan Province:

Village Development through Ecology, Tourism and Culture

Included in *WTA Best Practices of Rural Revitalization through Tourism 2021*

Abstract

In adherence to the pursuit of common prosperity and with the goal of building a well-off, ecological, glamourous and harmonious village, the Yuhu Village, Yulong County, Lijiang City, Yunnan Province, has implemented the strategies of village development through ecology, tourism and culture (underlying the village through ecology, enriching the village through tourism, and revitalizing the village through culture), developed a new mechanism, and helped all the villagers become prosperous through the invigoration of the tourism industry and development of the breeding industry.

Challenges and Problems

There are nine village groups in Yuhu Village, Baisha Town, Yulong Naxi Autonomous County, Lijiang City, Yunnan Province, with a land area of 77.78 square kilometers and a population of 1,465 from 383 rural households, including an agricultural population of 1,385 and 732 people for the labor force. The village lacked rural infrastructure and had limited high-quality, high-yield and high-efficiency agriculture. In 2003, the total economic income of the village was only 2.34 million yuan, of which 180,000 yuan was tourism income. The local farmers' per capita net income was only 937 yuan, while the food per capita more than 300 kilograms. It was an impoverished village, mainly due to its reliance on back selling for food, financial loans and government production relief.

Measures

1. Develop a new mechanism

The new rural land transfer mechanism was developed on the basis of the "lawful, voluntary, and paid" principle through transfer, leasing, subcontracting, shareholding, and exchange. Farmers were encouraged to invest in shares through the wasteland and contribute human labor and fertilizers for planting. Village cooperatives were responsible for the investment in nursery stocks and their operation. Farmers would then earn dividends according to their invested land area. Appropriate commissions were given to cooperatives, increasing the income of farmers. All villagers were organized to share in the outcome of tourism development through the establishment of tourism development cooperatives. Income and expenses were categorized into tourism promotion expenses, personal income, salaries of managerial staff, office expenses, funds on infrastructure construction, funds on education and relief funds on extreme poverty. Income distribution and year-end redistribution of funds for all staff were determined based on a fair and proportional calculation. This ensures the involvement of households in tourism operations, with each villager engaged in the work so he can earn money and enjoy a moderately prosperous life.

2. Invigorate the tourism industry

The Yuhu Village strived to develop rural tourism in conjunction with the ancient Naxi villages and Naxi ethnic culture. The latter's favorable natural landscape and ethnic cultural resources have led to the creation of cultural tourist attractions,

including typical native residential buildings, the Former Residence of Rock, the Battlefield Site of Heibaishui in Lijiang City, Baisha Xiyue (ancient music of the Naxi Nationality), Dongba Culture, and folk tradition and customs. The village boasted a sound rural homestay development, gradually maturing tourism product system and constantly improving infrastructure and public services. It has developed a tourism industry framework with tourism cooperatives as the mainstay, supplemented by tourism inns, catering and spontaneous shopping by villagers.

3. Develop the breeding industry

More than 30,000 *mu* of grassland and grass slope resources were fully utilized and integrated. Cattle, sheep and other stockbreeding were developed through species improvement, grassland construction and support for large and specialized family operations. The protection of water source regions and the construction of water conservancy facilities in source areas were reinforced. With the construction of Yuhu Reservoir and Wenhai Reservoir, a number of small cascade reservoirs, small dams, small cofferdams, etc., were also built. The high-end rainbow trout aquaculture was successfully developed into a key industry due to the area's excellent water quality and cold climate.

Results

The village income increased from 2.34 million yuan in 2003 to 16 million yuan in 2020. Total tourism income increased from 180,000 yuan in 2003 to over 12 million yuan in 2020, while the villagers' per capita net income increased from 937 yuan in 2003 to more than 10,000 yuan in 2020. As of 2021, nearly 800 villagers has been engaged in tourism services. More admirably, the village has won many honors such as Chinese Traditional Villages, Chinese Ethnic Minority Style Villages, Beautiful Leisure Villages in China, and National Key Villages in Rural Tourism. It has become a demonstration village for "ecology, culture, tourism and harmony" in Lijiang City, attracting many local and foreign tourists.

Experience and Inspirations

In adherence to the pursuit of common prosperity, Yuhu Village has implemented the strategy of village development through ecology, tourism and culture.

1. Ecology as the underpining for tourism development

Yuhu Village has strengthened ecological environmental protection, focusing on "five drives" including environmental protection systems, tourism development, project construction, green industries, and village appearance improvement, benefiting and developing from ecological civilization construction. Combining its actual conditions, Yuhu Village prioritizes improving the rural environment and enhancing the quality of life for its residents. It has invested over 3 million yuan to complete the construction of 2,500 meters of asphalt road, 710 meters of village road hardening, and more than 3,000 meters of Xingyu Canal. Additionally, parking lots, management buildings, eco-friendly toilets, and landscape water systems have been built. The village has implemented a drinking water project for both humans and livestock, ensuring all villagers have access to clean and sweet tap water. The village has also carried out courtyard beautification and toilet purification projects for 123 households, built a new village clinic, and collectively funded each villager's participation in the new rural cooperative medical scheme. Meanwhile, Yuhu Village has increased educational investment through an education fund, established a farmers' night school, and conducted training on tourism service skills and practical farming techniques to enhance villagers' tourism service awareness and scientific knowledge.

2. Enriching the village through tourism

Aiming for common prosperity, Yuhu Village has innovated a cooperative development model by establishing a tourism development cooperative, organizing all villagers to participate in tourism development and share the benefits. The village has focused on developing an eco-tourism project themed "Following Rock's Footsteps into the Yulong Snow Mountain", where villagers participate in rotation by household under the cooperative's unified scheduling

and arrangement. In terms of profit distribution, the total income was divided in appropriate proportions to ensure every household could engage in tourism operations, and all villagers, young and old, could participate in year-end dividends.

3. Revitalizing the village through culture

The reconstruction and understanding of the Naxi culture allow the Yuhu Village to promote integrated cultural development. It is dedicated to the development of a "Naxi culture +" derived from three aspects of "production and life, spiritual belief, culture and art". An industry mindset is adopted to reshape tourism products and their brand allure while staying true to their native characteristics and build a "1 + 1 + 4 + 10 + X" rural tourism system as follows: one characteristic horse-related economy (horse-riding experience, scene interpretation, equestrian training), one creative photo-shooting tour (Top 1 destination for travel photography worldwide), four diversion projects ("Enjoy Life" Snow Mountain Music Festival, "Little Knights" Ancient Tea Horse Road Base, Low-Altitude Flight Base, Natural Museum Exploration Base), 10 intangible heritage yards (Baisha Xiyue Yard, Naxi Wedding Customs Yard, Dongba Paper Art Yard, Dongba Wood Carving Yard, Naxi Snack Street, Internet-famous Tourist Center, Immersive Block Interpretation, High-end Themed Homestays, Naxi Style Homestays, Luxury Camps), and X supporting projects for tourism.

Next Steps

In compliance with the concept of ecological priority and green development, the village will take the integration of agriculture and tourism as the key to overall rural revitalization. Characteristic resources such as natural ecology, historical culture, folk customs and folk residences will be extensively utilized. Tourism infrastructure will be improved, and new tourism products will be developed with "tourism + , + tourism" as a breakthrough for the facilitation of stronger and more sophisticated business entities. Rural revitalization projects such as the Natural Museum Exploration Base, "Little Knights" Ancient Tea Horse Road Base, Travel Photography Base, Dongba Characters Yard, Baisha Xiyue Yard and boutique homestays will be developed, providing convenient access to tourists and leaving them with enduring favorable impressions. A flourishing development can be achieved in this beautiful village, and rural revitalization can be advanced to attain the organic unity of "beautiful ecology, prosperous industry, and rich people".

旅游减贫案例故事（中英文双语版）
Best Practices of Poverty Alleviation through Tourism（Chinese-English Bilingual Edition）

西藏自治区拉萨市尼木县卡如乡卡如村：
"核乡寻忆"沟域休闲项目模式

收录于《2021世界旅游联盟：旅游助力乡村振兴案例》

摘要

西藏自治区拉萨市尼木县卡如村通过采取"公司＋合作社＋农户"的运营模式，构建了政府主导、企业运营、合作社参股、农牧民增收的"三位一体"产业扶贫模式，积极增加内生动力，挖掘旅游资源。"核乡寻忆"沟域休闲项目按照"完善配套、提升供给、产业融合、振兴乡村"的原则，夯实了产业振兴基础，以文旅产业为抓手，带动当地村民就业，促进了产业、生态、组织、文化和人才的全面发展，实现精准扶贫。2018年10月，卡如村实现全面脱贫，迈上了乡村振兴的新征程。

挑战与问题

西藏自治区拉萨市尼木县卡如村地处雅鲁藏布江中游北岸的高山峡谷地带，是拉萨市的"西大门"，境内有318国道通过，是从日喀则进入拉萨的必经之地，距离县政府20千米，平均海拔3920米。卡如村下辖3个自然组，2018年全村共有110户558人，其中劳动力264人，残疾人12人，低保户9户34人。全村耕地面积为299.6亩，人均仅有0.54亩。全村草场面积为69415.2亩，林地面积为134亩，全村牲畜有1300头。当地农牧业不发达，收入渠道少，劳动力流失严重。

措施

1. 促进农旅融合

运用"自营+合作"方式，推动特色农产品销售，与卡如村建档立卡贫困户签订合作协议，打造藏家桃树茶园和老阿妈青稞酒坊，以客源引导的方式向外推广高原特色农副产品，推进农业现代化发展。充分挖掘当地文旅资源，积极保护森林、湿地等生态旅游资源，大力发展乡村旅游，开发精品旅游线路，以大力发展旅游业。建成以百亩桃园、游客接待中心、非遗展示中心、卡如温泉驿站和千年核桃树为内容的卡如村"核乡寻忆"沟域休闲区。

2. 创新项目建设

在北京援助资金的支持下，卡如村大力发展沟域经济，推动传统农业与文化旅游产业融合发展。卡如村"核乡寻忆"沟域休闲区集休闲农业、森林观光、民俗体验、文化旅游、天然温泉、餐饮住宿等功能于一体，为游客提供"吃、住、行、游、购、娱"的全方位配套服务。该项目旨在保护和传承藏地原乡文化，将卡如村打造为尼木县全域旅游的重要节点，发展文旅产业，以促进精准扶贫和当地农牧民的可持续发展。

3. 挖掘传统文化

尼木县素有"拉萨的作坊"之称，是传统手工艺人的栖息地，拥有藏靴、藏陶、藏鼓等8个非遗项目（国家级3个、自治区级5个），其中尼木藏香、雪拉藏纸、普松雕刻被誉为"尼木三绝"。卡如村积极发展特色民族手工艺文化，引入尼木县国家级、自治区级非遗传承人及其代表性作品，在满足游客体验需求的同时培养非遗传承人，真正实现对西藏非遗文化的保护、传承、发扬和创新。

4. 加强设施建设

近年来，为适应尼木县全域旅游、乡村旅游发展的需要，尼木县不断完善交通、住宿、公共环境等各项基础设施。卡如村投资2500万元，用于村容村貌和基础设施的改造，并实施了"厕所革命"、污水集中处理、垃圾分类管理等措施，全面提升村庄环境。截至2021年，卡如村已建成1个游客中心，并配备1个可容纳40辆自驾车的停车场，以及一定数量的旅游厕所，所有设施均以服务游客为宗旨。

成效

卡如村"核乡寻忆"项目通过"公司+合作社+农户"的运营模式，构建了政府主导、企业运营、合作社参股、促进农牧民增收的"三位一体"产业扶贫模式。2018年，该项目为59户建档立卡贫困户和边缘户以及项目所在地的24户村民分红，总额达32万余元。此次分红以"真金白银"的方式增强了贫困户脱贫致富的信心。自一、二期项目建成以来，持续

为合作社提供分红收益,其中老阿妈青稞酒坊和格桑小院民宿每年各分红 2.4 万元,并为当地群众提供了 26 个就业岗位,其中卡如温泉驿站解决 13 人就业、卡如村景区解决 13 人就业,每人每月平均工资 2800 元。自卡如沟域经济项目运营以来,2018 年向当地贫困户分红 30 万元,2019 年分红 50 万元,2020 年分红 30 万元,成功帮助 11 户 51 人脱贫。

3. 以产业为抓手,巩固扶贫成效

项目建设通过文化旅游业与农业融合发展的模式,有效优化了区域产业结构,形成了以"三产消化一产、带动二产,一、二产反哺支撑三产发展"的产业闭环,夯实了区域"产业振兴"的基础。在产业发展过程中,针对本地村民开展职业技能、服务意识、服务规范等方面的培训,促进本地村民就业技能的提升和思想意识的改变,实现"扶贫、扶智和扶志"相结合,进一步巩固扶贫成果。

经验与启示

1. 以村民为中心,打造宜居乡村

项目建设应以提升村容村貌和基础配套设施水平为基础。生态宜居是实现乡村振兴的关键,也是发展乡村旅游的根本。通过对村民住房实施"三改一整",全面改善生活环境,构建人与自然和谐共生的乡村发展新格局,最终实现"百姓富、生态美"的目标。

2. 以市场为导向,完善项目供给

项目定位为区域级旅游聚集点,以市场需求为导向,完善项目配套,形成了以"民俗接待区"为先导、以"森林度假区"为延展、以"驿站休闲区"为重心的多层次文旅产品。其中,"民俗接待区"以乡风乡貌民俗体验为基础;"森林度假区"依托尼木国家森林公园,突出体现高原独特的生态风貌;"驿站休闲区"在充分结合温室种植的基础上,挖掘天然温泉和本地特色餐饮,打造综合性休闲服务区。

下一步计划

1. 大力提升综合配套水平

围绕"吃、住、行、游、购、娱"六要素,推进卡如温泉驿站二期项目建设,提升硬件设施水平。完善卡如村农旅功能要素,提升服务接待水平,做到"食有特色、住有条件、行有基础、游有内容、购有商品、娱有活动"。

2. 大力提高优质服务水平

紧紧围绕游客需求,持续完善"核乡寻忆"景区和温泉驿站的饮食、住宿、购物等生活服务,优化文明引导、紧急救护等志愿服务,在游客旅游全过程中提供无微不至、体贴周到的服务。

3. 大力提升宣传力度

依托雅江河谷、卡如温泉、卡如千年核桃古树、卡如桃林种植基地、赤朗国家森林公园等优质资源,邀请知名网络媒体加大旅游宣传推广力度;与旅游景区加强合作,积极利用"两微一端"及抖音、快手等社交媒体,开展线上线下联动宣传,扩大卡如村的知名度和吸引力。

Karru Village, Karru Township, Nyêmo County, Lhasa City, Tibet Autonomous Region:

"Memory in Walnut Town" Leisure Valley Project Model

Included in *WTA Best Practices of Rural Revitalization through Tourism 2021*

Abstract

Karru Village, Karru Township, Nyêmo County, Lhasa City, Tibet Autonomous Region, has adopted the "companies + cooperatives + peasant households" framework to create a "trinity" of poverty alleviation model through industrial development with the government playing the dominant role. The project, however, is run by enterprises with the participation of cooperatives to increase the income of villagers and herdsmen. This setup is expected to enhance the endogenous influence of the villagers and motivate them to proactively explore tourism resources. The "Memory in Walnut Town" Leisure Valley Project adheres to the principle of "improving supporting facilities, upgrading supplies, integrating industries and achieving rural revitalization". It enhances the foundation for the revitalization industry, focuses on the cultural and tourism industry and powers the employment of local villagers. This project also promotes industrial, ecological, organizational, cultural and talents development for targeted poverty alleviation. In October 2018, Karru Village was lifted out of poverty and embarked on a new journey of rural revitalization.

Challenges and Problems

Karru Village is located in the alpine and gorge region on the north bank of the middle reaches of the Yarlung Zangbo River. Known as the "Western Gateway" of Lhasa, the village is traversed by National Highway 318, making it a crucial passage from Shigatse to Lhasa. It is 20 kilometers away from the county government and has an average altitude of 3,920 meters. In 2018, there were 558 people in 110 households, with 264 in the labor force, 12 disabled, and 34 people from 9 low-income household. The arable land of the whole village is 299.6 *mu*, only 0.54 *mu* per capita. The grassland area spans 69,415.2 *mu*, while the forested area covers 134 *mu*. The village also has 1,300 livestock. Local agriculture and animal husbandry were underdeveloped, with limited income opportunities and severe labor shortages.

Measures

1. Promote the integration of agriculture and tourism

By adopting a "self-operation + cooperation" model, the sales of distinctive agricultural products were promoted. Cooperation agreements have been signed with registered impoverished households in Karru Village to establish the Tibetan Peach Tree Tea Garden and the Old Mother Highland Barley Winery. This agreement also called for the exportation of the characteristic agricultural and other derivative products produced on the plateau as well as guiding customers for agricultural modernization. Local cultural and tourism resources were fully tapped, with active efforts to protect ecological tourism resources such as forests and wetlands. Rural tourism was vigorously developed,

and premium tourism routes were created to boost the tourism industry. The "Memory in Walnut Town" Leisure Valley in Karru Village has been completed, featuring a hundred-acre peach garden, a tourist reception center, an intangible cultural heritage exhibition center, the Karru Hot Spring Station, and a thousand-year-old walnut tree.

2. Innovative project development

With Beijing's financial assistance, the village worked hard to develop its valley economy and integrated the traditional agriculture and cultural tourism industries. "Memory in Walnut Town" Leisure Valley Project in Karru Village refers to a culture-tourism ecological leisure area that integrates leisure agriculture and contains the following: forest sightseeing, folk custom experience, cultural tourism, natural hot spring, catering and accommodation, a full range of tourist-supporting services of "catering, accommodation, transportation, sightseeing, shopping, and entertainment". It is designed to enhance the protection, preservation and development of Tibetan native culture by building an important node of the whole-region tourism in Nyêmo County. Also, it will develop the cultural tourism industry to promote targeted poverty alleviation and sustainable development for the benefit of local peasants and herdsmen.

3. Explore traditional culture

As the "workshop of Lhasa", Nyêmo County gathers traditional craftsmen and boasts intangible cultural heritages, three of which are on the national level. Of these, five are on the autonomous region level, including Tibetan boots, Tibetan pottery and Tibetan drums. Among them, as well are the Nyêmo Tibetan incense, Xuela Tibetan paper and Pusong carving which are collectively known as the "three wonders of Nyêmo". The village cultivated its

characteristic national handicrafts and representative work by nurturing successors from Nyêmo County to its cultural heritage. It also promoted the legacy, protection and innovation of Tibetan intangible cultural heritage.

4. Strengthen facility construction

To meet the development needs of the whole region and the county's rural tourism, the village worked in recent years to improve various infrastructure such as transportation, accommodation and public environment. The village has invested 25 million yuan to improve its appearance and infrastructure, implement the "toilet revolution" and conduct a centralized sewage treatment and classified garbage management. As of 2021, to serve tourists in the country, it has built a tourist center, a parking lot for 40 self-driving vehicles, and a number of tourist toilets.

Results

The project has adopted the operation mode of "companies + cooperatives + peasant households" to create a "trinity" of poverty alleviation model through industrial development with the government playing a leading role. This is operated by private enterprises with the participation of cooperatives, resulting in the increase of the income of peasants and herdsmen. In 2018, 59 recorded poor households, marginal households and 24 households in the project' site received dividends totaling more than 320,000 yuan. The dividend is given in "genuine gold and silver", leading them to gain confidence in their ability to improve their standard of living. Since the overall completion of Phase Ⅰ and Phase Ⅱ, the project has provided dividend income for cooperatives. The highland barley distillery and Gesang Courtyard Homestays have received a dividend of 24,000 yuan each year, provided 26 jobs for local people, including 13 in Karru hot springs station and 13 in Karru scenic spot, with an average monthly salary of 2,800 yuan per person. Since the project's operation, local impoverished households received profit-derived dividends of 300,000 yuan in 2018, 500,000 yuan in 2019 and 300,000 yuan in 2020. A total of 51 people from 11 households were successfully lifted out of poverty.

Experience and Inspirations

1. Focus on Villagers to Create a Livable Countryside

The project construction should be based

on improving the village's appearance and the level of basic supporting facilities. Ecological livability is the key to achieving rural revitalization and the foundation for developing rural tourism. By implementing the "three reforms and one renovation" for villagers' housing, the living environment will be comprehensively improved, creating a new pattern of rural development where humans and nature coexist harmoniously, ultimately achieving the goal of "prosperous people and beautiful ecology".

2. Market-Oriented Approach to Enhance Project Supply

The project is positioned as a regional-level tourism hub, guided by market demand, to improve project facilities. It forms a multi-level cultural and tourism product system, with the "Folk Reception Area" as the lead, the "Forest Resort Area" as the extension, and the "Post Leisure Area" as the focus. Among them, the "Folk Reception Area" is based on rural customs and folk experiences; the "Forest Resort Area" relies on the Nyêmo National Forest Park, highlighting the unique ecological features of the plateau; and the "Post Leisure Area" combines greenhouse cultivation with natural hot springs and local cuisine to create a comprehensive leisure service zone.

3. Leverage Industry to Consolidate Poverty Alleviation Achievements

The project construction effectively optimizes the regional industrial structure through the integrated development of cultural tourism and agriculture, forming an industrial closed loop where "the tertiary industry absorbs the primary industry, drives the secondary industry, and the primary and secondary industries support the development of the tertiary industry". This solidifies the foundation for regional "industrial revitalization". During the industrial development process, vocational skills, service awareness, and service standards training are provided to local villagers, promoting the improvement of their employment skills and changes in their mindset. This achieves a combination of "poverty alleviation, intellectual empowerment, and motivation enhancement", further consolidating the results of poverty alleviation.

Next Steps

1. Improve comprehensive supporting facilities

We shall focus on the six elements of "catering, accommodation, transportation, sightseeing, shopping, and entertainment". In addition, we will build the hot springs station as Phase II of the project and upgrade facilities in the process. Meanwhile, we shall improve the functional elements of agricultural tourism in Karru Village, standardize its service and reception to fulfill the goal of "characteristic food, comfortable living conditions for all as well as transportation foundation, meaningful journey, abundant goods and colorful activities".

2. Enhance quality service

To keep the tourists' needs top of mind, we will continue to improve living services such as catering, accommodation and shopping in the scenic spots. Hot spring stations and voluntary services such as cordial guidance will provide tourists excellent all-around services

3. Increase publicity

Based on excellent resources such as Yajiang Valley, Karru hot springs, Karru walnut tree of thousands of years, Karru peach planting base and Chi Lang National Forest Park, we shall invite KOLs of well-known internet media for publicity and promotion. Also, we will strengthen cooperation with tourist attractions, and actively utilize social media platforms such as Weibo, WeChat, and official apps, as well as Douyin and Kuaishou, to conduct integrated online and offline promotional campaigns, thereby enhancing the visibility and appeal of Karru Village.

旅游减贫案例故事（中英文双语版）
Best Practices of Poverty Alleviation through Tourism（Chinese-English Bilingual Edition）

陕西省延安市黄龙县白马滩镇：
研学旅游激活乡村经济

收录于《2022 世界旅游联盟：旅游助力乡村振兴案例》

摘要

陕西省延安市黄龙县白马滩镇紧紧围绕"生态立镇、文旅带动、项目支撑、全面振兴"的发展战略，以"旅游+"推动一二三产业融合发展，成功打造神道岭、神峪川、石门峡漂流、印象圪崂、美丽尧头、秀美白西等景区景点，使白马滩镇成为乡村体验游、休闲度假游、健康养生游的首选之地，形成以"两山理论"和"延安精神"研学游为支撑的全域旅游发展格局。

挑战与问题

白马滩镇距县城 43 千米，区域总面积 476 平方千米。全镇辖 7 个村委会、48 个村民小组，总人口 8350 人，其中农业人口 6580 人。受地形地质条件限制，人均耕地面积仅为 2.3 亩，主导产业以农副产品核桃、毛栗子、蜂蜜为主，由于市场波动、品种杂乱，加之农民思想保守等原因，农业收入较低，群众主要依靠外出务工获取收入。近年来，随着白马滩镇旅游业的快速发展，部分农民已享受到旅游发展带来的红利，但红利效应有限，尚不足以吸引大多数外出青年回乡创业。因此，推动农旅融合，带动更多群众增收致富，已成为当前亟待解决的问题。

措施

1. 坚持规划引领

坚持"市场导向、全域统筹、规划引领、项目支撑"的原则，下功夫搞好全镇文化旅游发展的顶层设计。编制完成《白马滩镇文化旅游"十四五"发展规划》，并制定创建石门峡国家 4A 级旅游景区、神峪川濠水源省级旅游度假区等专项规划，形成上下衔接、相互支撑的规划体系。

2. 改善村容村貌

全力推进村子环境整治及洁化、绿化、美化工程，将当地传统的石头文化、农耕文化、水景文化融入村庄改造中。新建污水处理站 4 个、污水收集站 1 个、铺设排污管网 15500 余米；建成标准化旅游公厕 7 座；完成全镇 2215 户改厕；拆除乱搭乱建 32 处，带动全镇向美丽田园式生活迈进。

3. 丰富旅游内容

在印象圪崂国家 3A 级景区成功举办第五届漂流艺术节暨首届啤酒音乐会、旅游黄金月周末文艺演出及陕西省第四届山地自行车越野赛等系列活动 20 余场次；组建了白马滩乡土导游团队，挖掘整理赵氏孤儿、妙善公主舍身救父、东周古寨等历史传说；组建猎鼓展演队伍，在旅游景点轮流展演，提高景区吸引力；打造镇区特色小吃一条街，集中整合街道餐饮门店，提高餐饮标准和服务水平；做精做细文玩核桃、蜂蜜、毛栗子等旅游商品和纪念品，并在景区、景点及电商销售平台出售。

4. 提升研学品质

"两山理论"点燃绿色经济发展，针对绿色研学旅游，推出"印象圪崂—美丽尧头—山水碾子湾—秀美白西—神道岭景区"精品旅游路线，开展"绿水青山就是金山银山"的生动展示；针对红色研学旅游，推出"马武山—尧头民俗村史馆—白马滩校史馆—白西党史文化墙"等旅游路线，追忆红色岁月，讴歌伟大的延安精神。

5. 创新宣传营销方式

多渠道加强信息互通共享，建立与周边旅行团的精准对接，提供优质旅游产品供给和旅游优惠政策；在省体育场、各大商场、车站 LED 显示屏播放白马滩镇文化旅游宣传片，吸引更多游客关注；成立宣传推介代表团，每年至少两次走进大学校园、周边各大企业，开展文化旅游精准推介，并建立合作关系，成为企业文化、高校文化和各类社团活动的实践教学基地和团建基地；借助"秀美古镇白马滩"微信公众号、抖音、快手、新闻媒体等各类宣传平台，探索建立政府搭台、企业主导、线上线下融合、游客参与互动的全方位宣传推广合作模式，全面展现白马滩镇乡村文化旅游新风貌。

成效

近年来，白马滩镇以"全域旅游示范区"创建为契机，不断提升旅游服务体系标准化建设，印象圪崂、神道岭两个国家3A级旅游景区游人如织，石门峡漂流越发红火，漂流艺术节、乡村旅游节等旅游节庆活动常态化开展，"美丽尧头—印象圪崂—东周古寨"精品乡村旅游线路成为全国驴友的"打卡地"。按照"周周有活动、场场都精彩、天天能发团"思路，举办黄龙县乡村旅游节、白马滩镇漂流艺术节等系列活动20余场次，全年接待游客40万人次，带动全镇精品民宿、特色餐饮、食品销售、流动摊贩等新业态有序发展，多元化富民产业发展格局日趋完善。据统计，2021年群众人均享受旅游红利达3200元，实现旅游综合收入3250万元。

经验与启示

1. 创新经济发展思路

"绿水青山就是金山银山"，依托农村广阔天地，打造连接城乡的产业融合大平台。通过农旅融合，白马滩镇系统解决了游客怎么引进、游客怎么留住、怎样带动当地经济发展三大难题，创造了"看得见蓝天白云、望得见青山绿水、记得住村韵乡愁"的综合田园韵味休闲旅游度假村，形成了"春有花、夏有景、秋有果、冬有绿"的全季乡村旅游新格局。

2. 盘活各类闲置资源

按照土地相关管理办法，依法收回两年之内批而未建的农村宅基地、村庄周围群众挤占集体土地，归村集体所有，有效解决村集体无发展用地的问题。按照"旅游产业支撑、主导产业提升、特色产业补充"的发展思路，推行"村委会+合作社+农户"的发展模式，打造核桃、樱桃等采摘园100亩，羊肚菌种植园20亩、中蜂养殖科普园等村集体经济项目，推动全镇"生产型"农业向"生态型"农业转变，推进产业兴旺。

3. 提升生态宜居品位

以"美丽乡村·文明家园"创建为载体，注重突出特色，将生态保护、风情民俗、耕读文化、移风易俗、平安创建等元素融入村庄建设。为让群众和游客记住白马滩发展历史，记住乡愁，动员全镇收集捐赠农耕机具200余件，建设濠水流域耕读文化室外展示博物馆，使"农耕文化"这一主题更加凸显、完整；通过绘制生态保护、民俗风情、勤劳节俭、孝老爱亲、移风易俗等墙绘作品，简洁的文字配以生动的画面，成为传播精神文明的一道美丽风景线，真正实现了山美、水美、人更美的目标。

下一步计划

下一步，白马滩镇将紧紧围绕全镇"生态立镇、文旅带动、项目支撑、全面振兴"发展战略，紧扣"千年古镇，濠水人家"旅游发展主题，着力打造以历史文化深度游、生态乡村绿色游、休闲康养体验游、"两山理论"和"延安精神"研学游为支撑的全域旅游发展格局。加大力度提升基础设施。建设白西村游客服务中心、6千米沿河环形步道、生态停车场、自驾车露营地和标准化公厕。加快推进精品民宿建设，通过引进社会资本和改造升级现有民居打造高端民宿。加强文化旅游队伍建设，采取"考核+绩效"方式，用事业和待遇留人，加大乡土导游培养，讲好"新时代白马滩故事"。

Baimatan Town, Huanglong County, Yan'an City, Shaanxi Province:
Stimulating the Rural Economy with Study Tours

Included in *WTA Best Practices of Rural Revitalization through Tourism 2022*

Abstract

Baimatan, a town of Huanglong County in Yan'an of Shaanxi Province, closely follows the development strategy of "building an eco-friendly town, and driving rural revitalization in all respects with the cultural and tourism industry and the support of projects". It adopts the "tourism+" policy to promote the integrated development of the primary, secondary and tertiary industries. It has successfully developed such tourist attractions as Shendao Ridge, Shenyuchuan, Shimen Gorge drifting, Impression of Gelao, Beautiful Yaotou and Picturesque Baixi, making Baimatan Town the first choice for rural experiential travel, leisure travel and wellness-themed tours. It has formed the development pattern of all-area-advancing tourism supported by the theory that "lucid waters and lush mountains are invaluable assets" and study tours themed on the Yan'an spirit.

Challenges and Problems

Baimatan Town is 43 kilometers away from the county seat, and covers a total area of 476 square kilometers. It governs 7 village committees and 48 village groups, with a total population of 8,350, including an agricultural population of 6,580. Due to topographical and geological factors, the per capita cultivated land is only 2.3 *mu*. The dominant industry used to be the production and sale of agricultural and sideline products such as walnuts, chestnuts and honey. Because of market fluctuation, a motley portfolio of products and the conservative mind of locals, the income from agriculture was low, and the main source of income came from migrant workers. With the rapid development of tourism in the town, farmers have benefited from it, but to a limited extent; the benefit was not big enough to attract most of the young migrant workers to return home to start businesses. Therefore, it was an urgent need to benefit more people and increase their income through the integration of agriculture and tourism.

Measures

1. Plan in advance

Great efforts were made to ensure sound top-level design for the town's cultural and tourism development that is "market-oriented, coordinated town-wide, guided by plans, and supported by projects". It formulated the 14th Five-Year Development Plan for the Cultural and Tourism Industry in Baimatan Town, as well as special plans for building Shimen Gorge into a national 3A-level scenic spot and the development of Jushuiyuan provincial tourist resort in Shenyuchuan, and formed a set of plans that vertically aligns with and support each other.

2. Improve the village's appearance

It went all out to improve, clean, green and beautify the village environment, and incorporated the traditional stone culture, farming tradition and waterscape into the renovations. It has added four sewage treatment stations and one sewage collection station; laid more than 15,500 meters of sewage pipelines; built seven standardized tourist toilets; renovated toilets for all the 2,215 households; and demolished 32 illegal buildings, leading the town toward a beautiful idyllic life.

3. Enrich tourism content

The Impression of Gelao National 3A-Level Scenic Spot has hosted more than 20 events including the 5th Drifting Festival cum the 1st Beer Concert, weekend performances of the Travel Golden Month and the 4th Shaanxi Mountain Bike and Cross Country Race. The Baimatan local tour guide team was set up and they combed through such folk legends as "The Orphan of Zhao", "Princess

Miaoshan Sacrificing Her Life to Save Her Father", and the ancient village of the Eastern Zhou Dynasty. The hunting drum performance team was also set up to perform at tourist attractions in turn and enhance their appeal to tourists. There is a snack street that gathers eateries, and improve the catering standard and service level. Tourist commodities and souvenirs such as antique walnuts, honey and chestnuts are developed, refined and sold at scenic spots and on e-commerce platforms.

4. Improve the quality of study tours

The theory that "lucid waters and lush mountains are invaluable assets" has ignited the development of the green economy. Baimatan Town has launched a boutique route of green study tours, stringing Impression of Gelao, Beautiful Yaotou, Nianziwan, Pituresque Baixi, and Shendao Ridge Scenic Area, putting the theory into practice. There is another route for study tours themed on the CPC heritage, connecting Mawu Mountain, Yaotou Folk Customs and Village History Museum, Baimatan School History Museum, and Baixi Bulletin Wall on the Party History, recalling the revolutionary years and praising the great Yan'an spirit.

5. Employ new marketing methods

Baimatan Town strengthened information exchange and sharing through multiple channels, forms targeted partnerships with tour groups in surrounding areas, and provides high-quality tourism products and preferential policies. Promotional videos on cultural and tourism resources in Baimatan Town are aired on the LED screens set up at the provincial stadium, major shopping malls and stations to attract more tourists' attention. The destination marketing team organizes at least two roadshows to promote Baimatan's

cultural and tourism resources a year on college campus and at office buildings nearby at least twice a year. Through partnerships, Baimatan Town has become a field practice base for universities and a team building base for companies and social groups. Via its official public account on Weixin, Douyin and Kuaishou and other media platforms, it is exploring an online-offline collaborative marketing model initiated by the government, led by enterprises and participated by tourists, to show the new landscape of rural cultural and tourism in Baimantan Town.

Results

In recent years, while striving to build into a demonstration zone for all-area-advancing tourism, Baimatan Town has constantly improved the standardization of its tourism services. Impression of Gelao and Shendao Ridge, two national 3A-level scenic spot, have attracted an endless stream of tourists. Shimen Gorge drifting has become more and more popular, and the drifting and art festival, rural tourism festival and other events are carried out on a regular basis. The boutique rural tourist route "Beautiful Yaotou – Impression of Gelao – Ancient Village of Eastern Zhou Dynasty" has gained

popularity and become a must-visit for backpackers from across the country. In line with the goal of "staging activities every week, making sure every event is well organized and receiving tour groups on a daily basis", it organized more than 20 events including the Huanglong Rural Tourism Festival and Baimatan Drifting Festival, and received 400,000 visitors throughout the year. It has driven the orderly development of new business forms such as high-quality homestays, specialty catering, food sales and street vendors, and improved the development pattern of diversified industries. According to statistics, in 2021, the per capita dividend from the tourism industry reached 3,200 yuan and the comprehensive tourism income 32.5 million yuan.

Experience and Inspirations

1. Adopts a new approach to economic development

"Lucid waters and lush mountains are invaluable assets." With its vast countryside, Baimatan Town strives to build a large platform for the integration of urban and rural industries. Through the integration of agriculture and tourism, Baimatan Town has systematically solved three major problems: how to attract and retain tourists, and how to drive local economic development through tourism. It has built a comprehensive idyllic leisure resort that allows the people to be close to mountains and waters and recall their rural roots with fond memories, and formed a new pattern of all-year-round rural tourism with spring blossoms, summer view, autumn fruits and a green winter.

2. Put various idle resources into effective use

In accordance with relevant land administration measures, the village collectives have retrieved rural residential land that has been approved for residence construction but remained unoccupied in the past two years and the collective land that skirts villages and is occupied without permission. This has effectively solved the problem of the lack of land for development in villages. In pursuit of development that is supported by the tourism industry, upgraded by leading industries and supplemented by specialty industries, it adopts the development model that brings together the village committees, cooperatives and rural households. The village collectives have built 100 *mu* of walnut and cherry U-pick orchards, and 20 *mu* of common morel plantation, the breeding and science-popularization park dedicated to morel mushrooms and the eastern honeybee. Baimatan is transforming the "production-oriented" agriculture to ecological agriculture and promoting the prosperity of industries.

3. Create an eco-friendly, livable countryside

While building a "beautiful countryside and civilized homeland", Baimatan Town highlights its characteristics, and incorporates elements of ecological conservation, folk customs and folklore, the farming-reading culture, the transformation of outdated customs and habits, and public safety into the development of villages. To better communicate the development history of Baimatan Town to residents and tourists and arouse their rural nostalgia, the whole town was mobilize to collect and donate more than 200 farm machines and tools, and a museum for the outdoor display of the farming-reading culture in the Jushui basin is built, highlighting and completing the theme of farming culture. The village walls are painted with pictures themed on ecological protection, folklore and folk customs, diligence and thrift, filial piety and respect for the elderly, and the transformation of outdated customs and habits, matched with concise captions. They have become an eye-appealing highlight in public communication of social etiquette and civility. The goal of not only improving the ecological environment, but also advancing social etiquette and civility in the countryside is truly realized.

Next Steps

In next steps, Baimatan Town will closely follow the development strategy of "building an eco-friendly town, and driving rural revitalization in all respects with the cultural and tourism industry and the support of projects". Positioned as "A millennium-old ancient town by the Jushui River", it will strive to create a development pattern of all-area-advancing tourism supported by immersive travel themed on local history and cultural heritage, ecological rural tours, leisure, wellness-themed experiential travel, and study tours themed on the theory that "lucid waters and lush mountains are invaluable assets" and the Yan'an spirit. More efforts will be made to upgrade infrastructure. It will build a tourist service center at Baixi Village, a 6-kilometer ring footpath along the river, an ecological parking lot, a self-driving campsite and standardized public toilets. It will move faster to develop boutique homestays, and introduce social capital to upgrade existing homestays into high-end ones via renovation. It will build a stronger team of professionals in the cultural and tourism industry. It will adopt the "assessment + performance-based bonus" method and attract and retain people with job prospects and competitive pay; step up to train local tour guides and tell the stories of Baimatan in the new era.

旅游减贫案例故事（中英文双语版）
Best Practices of Poverty Alleviation through Tourism（Chinese-English Bilingual Edition）

甘肃省临夏回族自治州临夏市妥家村：
全域全季旅游助力乡村振兴

收录于《2023世界旅游联盟：旅游助力乡村振兴案例》

摘要

甘肃省临夏回族自治州临夏市南龙镇妥家村在和美乡村建设中立足北临大夏河、南靠凤凰山和近郊区的优势，突出休闲静谧主题，全力发展全域全季节旅游，打造"悠游南龙·金色草滩"文旅品牌，并通过土地流转入股实现村民就近就业，带动群众增收致富。

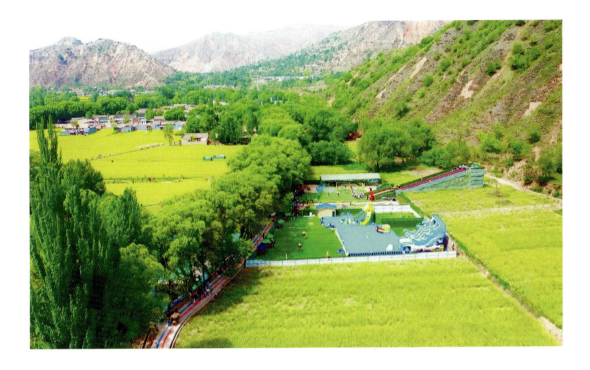

挑战与问题

妥家村位于临夏市东南部，东接南龙山，西邻大夏河，是一个回族、汉族和东乡族杂居的多民族村落。全村有村民小组6个、农户313户、村民1499人，耕地面积520亩，人均耕地面积0.26亩。妥家村交通基础设施薄弱，基础配套设施不足，专业人才匮乏，村民民俗文化传承与开发的观念意识薄弱，村庄经济发展滞后。

措施

1. 完善基础建设

妥家村依托现有旅游资源，按照连点成线的发展思路，一方面完成5条乡村道路及游客服务中心、大型停车场、公共厕所等配套设施建设；另一方面，以农村"五改"为抓手，统筹做好村庄绿化、美化和亮化，利用老物件、老照片、村民全家福等乡愁元素对群众房屋、特色建筑、沿街商铺外围墙面进行装饰，使村庄内涵和自然环境更好地融为一体，率先在全市完成省级乡村示范村建设。

2. 丰富旅游项目

妥家村充分利用金色草滩的自然风景，精心打造风铃长廊、观景亭、云梯云镜、黄酒坊等网红打卡点；综合开发100亩紫斑牡丹、百合、油菜花、芍药、观赏玫瑰等特色花卉景点，"赏花经济"成为激活乡村旅游的重要引擎；不断丰富卡丁车、网红桥、彩虹滑道、水上乐园等亲子娱乐项目内容，全力打造集田园观光、亲子娱乐、露营烧烤、红色记忆、农耕体验于一体的沉浸式乡村旅游综合体和亲子研学基地。

3. 提升村民福利

妥家村通过不断完善基础设施和开发旅游项目，极大改善了人居环境品质和群众生活质量。在此基础上，为了进一步提升村民幸福感，妥家村充分发挥党建引领作用，聚焦辖区老年人"吃饭难"的问题，积极探索老年人助餐服务体系，建设运行妥家村关心关爱幸福食堂，除此之外，还同步提供阅读、娱乐、休闲等服务，确保村民老有所依、老有所乐。

成效

2019年以来，妥家村利用"党建+乡村旅游+餐饮服务"的发展模式，依托凤凰山文旅景区建设规划，开拓思路，成立了临夏市金色草滩休闲农业观光旅游农民专业合作社，年经营收入实现30万余元，累计接待游客上万人。2023年五一期间，妥家村接待游客1.2万人次，增加旅游收入30余万元，带动就业100余人，人均增收2000余元。

经验与启示

1. 深耕当地优势旅游资源

妥家村依托凤凰山文旅景区建设规划，积极争取项目资金，实施金色草滩二期项目建设，增设水上乐园、中小学生素质拓展基地、彩虹滑道等一批独特、新颖的旅游项目，提升改造景区各项旅游基础设施。通过鼓励本村投资和招商引资，集中发展农家乐等餐饮产业，全面提高景区各项服务质量。

2. 充分激发群众的内生动力

妥家村村民积极投身于全村产业发展中，调整农业种植结构，开展特色种植和养殖业，如蜂蜜、花卉、油菜花等。妥家村通过金色草滩旅游品牌建设，一并打造以"金色草滩"为名片的菜籽油、黄酒、蜂蜜等农产品和手工制品的旅游产品系列。

3. 不断丰富乡村旅游文化内涵

妥家村在景区注入农耕文化、怀旧文化和乡愁文化元素，打造一批农耕文化小品景观及历史展示景观，提升景区文化底蕴。妥家村依托优美的田园风光和古朴的农耕情调，为游客提供"吃农家饭、干农家活、看农家景、购农家物"的沉浸式体验。

下一步计划

下一步，妥家村将认真学习贯彻党的二十大精神，找准金色草滩乡村旅游发展的着力点，积极探索"城市游+乡村游、昼游+夜游、景点游+人文游、美食游+季节游"相结合的新型旅游模式。不断提升风铃长廊、风车长廊、观景亭、水系景观、紫藤长廊、网红景观等景区景点服务质量，持续发展壮大乡村旅游产业，让妥家村金色草滩景区逐步形成春季能看花、夏季能避暑、秋季能采摘、冬冬能戏雪，集赏景、游玩、美食于一体的旅游发展格局。

Tuojia Village, Linxia City, Linxia Hui Autonomous Prefecture, Gansu Province:

Promoting Rural Revitalization through the Development of All-Area-Advancing and All-Season Tourism

Included in *WTA Best Practices of Rural Revitalization through Tourism 2023*

Abstract

In its drive to build a harmonious and beautiful village, Tuojia Village of Nanlong Town, Gansu Province, leverages its proximity to the Daxia River in the north, the Phoenix Mountain in the south, and its closeness to the suburban area. It highlights the themes of leisure and tranquility and makes every effort to develop all-area-advancing tourism and all-season tourism. It has created the cultural and tourism brand "Leisure Travel to Nanlong Mountain and the Golden Grassland", created jobs for the villagers and increased their income through land use rights transfer and shareholding schemes.

Challenges and Problems

Tuojia Village is located in the southeast of Linxia City, bordering Nanlong Mountain to the east and Daxia River to the west. It is a multi-ethnic village inhabited by Hui, Han and Dongxiang people. The village has a population of 1,499 people of 313 households which are divided into six villager groups, and a cultivated land area of 520 *mu*, 0.26 *mu* per capita. Tuojia Village had a weak transportation infrastructure, and lacked supporting facilities and professionals. The villagers lacked the awareness to inherit and develop folk culture, and the village economy was lagging behind.

Measures

1. Improve infrastructure

To string the existing tourism resources, on the one hand, Tuojia Village has completed the construction of five rural roads and facilities including the tourist service center, large parking lots, and public toilets. On the other hand, while advancing the transformation of water pipelines, toilets, roads, kitchens and houses in rural areas, it coordinated efforts to increase its green coverage, and beautify and light up the village. It used old objects, old photos, villagers' family portraits and so on to decorate the outer walls of residential houses, characteristic buildings, and storefronts, to better integrate the cultural heritage of the village and the natural environment. It is the first in the city to be recognized as a provincial-level demonstration village.

2. Enrich the contents of the tourism industry

Tuojia Village has made full use of the natural scenery of the golden grassland, and has created popular photo spots such as the Wind Chime Corridor, the viewing pavilion, the cloud ladder, the cloud mirror, and the yellow wine shop. It has planted 100 *mu* of purple spotted peonies, lilies, canola flowers,

Chinese herbaceous peonies, ornamental roses and other specialty flowers, and the flower appreciation economy has become an important engine driving rural tourism. It continues to enrich the content of parent-child entertainment projects such as go-karts, the photogenic bridge, the rainbow slide, and the water park, and makes every effort to build an immersive rural tourism complex and a parent-child study tour base where visitors can enjoy the rural scenery, parent-child entertainment, and camping & barbecue, red tourism, and farming experience.

3. Improve the welfare of villagers

Through continuous efforts to improve infrastructure and tourism projects, Tuojia Village has greatly improved the living environment and quality of life. On this basis, in order to further enhance the sense of happiness of villagers, it gave full play to the guiding role of Party building, focused on the meal problem faced by the elderly in its jurisdiction, actively explored the meal service system for the elderly, and put into operation the Care and Happiness Canteen in the village. In addition, reading, entertainment, leisure and other services are also provided to ensure that elderly villagers have access to what they need to enjoy their life.

Results

Since 2019, under the development model of "Party building + rural tourism + catering service" and under the guidance of the *Phoenix Mountain Scenic Area Development Plan*, Tuojia Village has broadened its mindset and established the Linxia Golden Grassland Farmers' Cooperative for Leisure Agriculture and Tourism. It has received more than ten thousand tourists with an annual operating income of more than 300,000 yuan. During the Labor Day holiday in 2023 alone, it received 12,000 tourists, generated more than 300,000 yuan in tourism income, and created more than 100 tourism-related jobs, with

the per capita income rise by more than 2,000 yuan.

Experience and Inspirations

1. Tap local advantageous tourism resources

Following the *Phoenix Mountain Scenic Area Development Plan*, Tuojia Village worked actively to secure project funds, implemented the second phase of the Golden Grassland project, and added a number of unique and novel tourism projects such as the water park, outdoor education base for primary and secondary school students, and rainbow slide, and upgraded various tourism infrastructure in the scenic area. By encouraging villagers to invest and attracting external investment, it focuses on the development of agritainment and catering services, and has comprehensively improved various services in the scenic area.

2. Fully stimulate the inner drive of the people

The villagers actively participate in the industrial development of the village. They adjusted the planting mix, and are planting specialty flowers and canola flowers, and raising bees for honey. Through the branding of the Golden Grassland, Tuojia Village has launched a series of tourism products, including rapeseed oil, yellow wine, honey and other agricultural products and handicraft products under the brand.

3. Continuously enrich the cultural connotation of rural tourism

Tuojia Village added agricultural culture, nostalgic culture, and homesickness culture to the scenic area, and built a number of farming-themed landscapes and historical heritage display landscapes, to enhancehe the cultural content of the scenic area. With its beautiful scenery and simple farming life, Tuojia Village provides tourists with an immersive rural experience covering catering, farming experience, scenery appreciation, and shopping.

Next Steps

In the next step, Tuojia Village will earnestly study and implement the guiding principles of the 20th National Congress of the Communist Party of China, identify the focus of rural tourism development in Golden Grassland, and actively explore a new tourism model featuring "city tour + rural tour, day tour + night tour, attraction-themed tour + culture-themed tour, food tour + seasonal tour". It will continuously improve the service quality of tourist attractions such as the Wind Chime Corridor, Windmill Corridor, viewing pavilion, water system landscape, Wisteria Corridor, and viral tourist attractions. It will continue to develop and expand the rural tourism industry, and turn the Golden Grassland scenic area into a destination where people can enjoy beautiful scenery and delicious food and have fun, with blooming flowers in spring, coolness in summer, fruit and vegetable picking in fall, and playing snow in winter.

宁夏贺兰山东麓葡萄酒产业园区管理委员会：
葡萄酒文旅融合模式

收录于《2021 世界旅游联盟：旅游助力乡村振兴案例》

摘要

宁夏回族自治区葡萄酒产业的综合发展，在带动产区村民脱贫致富、农业增效、企业获利等方面发挥了巨大的作用，它将宁夏本土文化、葡萄酒文化、"绿进沙退"治沙文化等与旅游产业发展相结合，是一、二、三产业有机结合的特色产业。宁夏贺兰山东麓葡萄酒产业园区管理委员会为葡萄酒产业提供创新内生动力，走出了独特的葡萄酒文旅融合创新开发助力乡村振兴之路，不仅有效突破了发展瓶颈，还形成了一系列引领产业发展的三产融合创新模式。

挑战与问题

宁夏贺兰山东麓产区在酿酒葡萄种植方面有着得天独厚的自然地理环境。作为受欧盟保护的中国首批地理标志，宁夏贺兰山东麓葡萄酒已经被编入《世界葡萄酒地图》。自2014年宁夏贺兰山东麓葡萄酒产业园区管委会成立，截至2021年，产区已有建成投产的酒庄101家，酿酒葡萄种植面积49.2万亩，年生产优质葡萄酒1.3亿瓶。在国际、国内广泛关注贺兰山东麓产区的情况下，如何高效发挥葡萄酒产业一、二、三产业高度融合的特质，做好葡萄种植、酿造生产和文旅体验融合发展，满足市场多元需求，实现产业高效可持续发展，成为管委会面临的主要挑战。

措施

1. 聚集葡萄酒产业发展人才

葡萄酒产业融合创新发展，需要从业人员既具有一定的葡萄种植和葡萄酒酿造储存专业知识，又能对当前文旅市场热门趋势拥有敏锐的嗅觉，更需要有接轨国际著名产区发展模式的国际化视野，所以它对人才的整合与创新能力要求非常高。管委会广泛吸引来自浙江大学、复旦大学、南开大学、中山大学、美国普渡大学等国内外近30名专家，共同为宁夏葡萄酒产业综合开发提供智力支持。

2. 建立葡萄酒产业发展智库

创新宁夏本地与东部沿海城市的联动机制，探索建设葡萄酒指数研究院，研究发布产业指数、消费指数、品牌指数和葡萄酒文旅指数等指数体系；制定葡萄酒旅游服务标准，开发葡萄酒文化创意产品；开展葡萄酒产业链延伸的模式和策略研究、葡萄酒旅游融合创新的机制和模式研究、葡萄酒旅游市场研究、葡萄酒旅游融合创新的产品和服务设计、葡萄酒康养目的地研究等，全面推动和促进宁夏贺兰山东麓葡萄酒产业向文旅融合的方向高质量创新发展，提升葡萄酒产业竞争力。

3. 建立葡萄酒产业发展联盟

贺兰山东麓葡萄酒虽然在全球主要消费国有相当大的知名度，但主流产品价格偏高，在银川、中卫等宁夏本地市场和国内其他地区的消费量不大，且酒庄及周边文化旅游设施和服务配套相对滞后，现有葡萄酒相关的文化旅游体验活动以采摘、品酒和酒窖参观游览为主。在文旅市场消费以休闲度假和亲子体验为主的情况下，管委会积极联系沙坡头旅游景区、黄河宿集、镇北堡西部影视城等主要旅游和度假景区，以及张裕摩塞尔十五世酒庄、志辉源石酒庄、西鸽酒庄等主要旅游酒庄，加强合作，丰富和提升葡萄酒旅游产业体验型产品与服务的内容与质量。

成效

产业园区葡萄酒产业综合开发的观光旅游模式、亲子休闲模式、节事驱动模式、经销商接待体验模式等逐渐成为全国范本，张裕摩塞尔十五世酒庄、志辉源石酒庄、巴格斯酒庄、贺东庄园、米擒酒庄、玉泉国际酒庄、森淼兰月谷酒庄等7家酒庄被评为A级景区的旅游酒庄，并在农村环境治理、农民就业增收、农业增产提效等方面发挥了显著的作用。葡萄酒产业综合开发提供的就业岗位已超过12万个。

管委会联合产区酒庄创新推出了一系列推广行动，如在本地产区举办国际葡萄酒旅游博览会，在外部客源市场举办葡萄酒品鉴体验推广会，在互联网渠道设立葡萄酒虚拟体验展厅，最大限度地确保产区信息的立体化展示。贺兰山东麓产区酒庄接待游客数量逐渐成为自治区休闲旅游接待量的重要组成部分，志辉源石酒庄、张裕摩塞尔十五世酒庄等旅游酒庄的游客年接待量增长率始终保持在 20% 左右。

培训中心、贺兰红酒庄、贺兰山东麓葡萄酒教育学院等，探索建设葡萄酒工业旅游基地、文商旅综合体、研学基地、酒庄民宿、酒庄设计酒店等文旅新业态，将闽宁镇打造成贺兰山东麓葡萄酒全产业链聚集展示中心，使其成为集历史观光、文化体验、文创产品展示、研学教育、品酒活动等于一体的产区文化地标。

经验与启示

1. 确定发展思路

宁夏将发展葡萄酒产业作为脱贫的根本之策，依托这一"紫色名片"发展特色优势产业，因地制宜，把发展葡萄酒产业同加强黄河滩区治理、加强生态恢复结合起来，提高技术水平，增加文化内涵，加强宣传推介，打造知名品牌，不断增加附加值，提高综合效益。用葡萄酒文旅高质量发展模式，为乡村脱贫和振兴提供引领示范。

2. 明确发展模式

产业园区依托中国（宁夏）国际葡萄酒文化旅游博览会永久会址、红酒一条街、中国酒业协会葡萄酒

下一步计划

2021 年，国务院批准《宁夏国家葡萄及葡萄酒产业开放发展综合试验区建设总体方案》，该试验区是国务院批准设立的我国西部第一个国家级农业类开放试验区。目标到 2025 年，贺兰山东麓酿酒葡萄基地总规模达到 100 万亩，年产葡萄酒 3 亿瓶以上，实现综合产值 1000 亿元。为确保实现发展目标，管委会将在自治区党委和政府的领导下，进一步发挥产区资源、政策优势，加强与东部沿海地区高校和市场的联动，推动"葡萄酒+文旅"产业融合发展，整合贺兰山东麓的史前文化、农耕文化、西夏文化、黄河文化和移民文化，做强做透"葡萄酒+文旅"产业链，形成具有中国特色的葡萄酒产业综合开发示范样本。

旅游减贫案例故事（中英文双语版）
Best Practices of Poverty Alleviation through Tourism（Chinese-English Bilingual Edition）

Ningxia Helan Mountain East Foothill Wine Industry Park Management Committee:
"Integration of Wine and Cultural Tourism" Model

Included in *WTA Best Practices of Rural Revitalization through Tourism 2021*

Abstract

The wine industry in the Ningxia Hui Autonomous Region has achieved comprehensive development and played a prominent role in lifting villagers in the wine region out of poverty. It has improved agricultural efficiency and increased profit from enterprises. The industry integrates Ningxia's local culture, wine culture, and sand containment through "afforestation for desertification control". Rural tourism development has organically created a new enterprise which is a combination of the primary, secondary and tertiary industries. Ningxia Helan Mountain East Foothill Wine Industry Park Management Committee has provided the endogenous push for innovation in the wine industry. It blazed a unique path to rural revitalization through the integration of wine cultural tourism. It has not only effectively broken through development bottlenecks, but also formed a series of integrated innovation models of the tertiary industry that lead industrial development.

Challenges and Problems

The Ningxia Helan Mountain East Foothill Region boasts a unique natural and geographical environment for wine production and grape planting. As one of the first geographical indications protected by the European Union in China, the Ningxia Helan Mountain East Foothill Wine has been included in *The World Atlas of Wine*. From the establishment of Ningxia Helan Mountain East Foothill Wine Industry Park Management Committee in 2014, as of 2021, 101 wineries have been built and put into production in the region, with a grape planting area of 492,000 *mu*, and an annual production of 130 million bottles of quality wine. The attention the village has received has led to more challenges for it. In the context of widespread attention to the Ningxia Helan Mountain East Foothill Region both internationally and domestically, how to efficiently leverage the highly integrated characteristics of the grape industry's primary, secondary, and tertiary industries, achieve integrated development of grape planting, brewing production, and cultural tourism experience, meet diverse market demands, and achieve efficient and sustainable development of the industry has become the main challenge faced by the management committee.

Measures

1. Assemble talents for wine industry development

The development of this industry requires that employees possess certain expertise in grape planting, winemaking, and storage, as well as a keen sense of the current popular trends in the cultural and tourism market. They also need an international perspective that aligns with the development models of internationally renowned wine producing regions. Therefore, it has very high requirements for the integration and innovation ability of talents. The management committee has widely attracted nearly 30 experts from home and abroad, including Zhejiang University, Fudan University, Nankai University, Sun Yat-sen University, and Purdue University in the US, to jointly provide intellectual support for the comprehensive development of the wine industry in Ningxia Hui Autonomous Region.

2. Establish a think tank for wine industry development

The management committee has developed a new linkage mechanism between Ningxia and other cities. The goal of this project is to establish a wine index research institute that would study index systems, consumption index, and brand index. The management committee has also formulated wine tourism services and has developed wine cultural and creative products. In addition, it has conducted research into the model and strategy of wine industry chain, extension and the mechanism, of wine tourism integration and innovation. The goal of this is to promote the high-quality innovative development of Ningxia wine industry at Helan Mountain East Foothill into the cultural tourism integration and enhance the competitiveness of the wine industry.

3. Form alliances for wine industry development

The Ningxia Helan Mountain East Foothill Wine is well known in major consumer countries worldwide. However, the prices of its mainstream products were relatively high in the local Ningxia markets such as Yinchuan City and Zhongwei City.

The cultural tourism and supporting service facilities of wineries were not as advanced as they should be. However, the industry of wine tasting, grape picking and winery visits were considered major rural tourism experiences. The management committee has contacted major tourist consumption markets such as Shapotou Tourist Attraction, Huanghe Suji, and Zhenbeipu Western Film Studio, as well as major tourist wineries such as Chateau Changyu Moser XV, Yuanshi Vineyard and Xige Estate for better cooperation and to enhance the experience-oriented products and services of the wine tourism industry.

Results

The models, developed based on the wine industry in the Ningxia Helan Mountain East Foothill Region, have become national models for sightseeing, parent-child leisure, festival driven events, and dealer reception experience. Chateau Changyu Moser XV, Yuanshi Vineyard, Chateau Bacchus, Chateau Hedong, Chateau Miqin, Chateau Yuquan, and Chateau Senmiao Moon Valley, have been rated A-level tourist attractions. These seven tourists' wineries played a prominent role in rural environmental governance, farmers' employment, income increase, agricultural production and efficiency growth. The comprehensive development of the grape industry has provided more than 120,000 job opportunities.

The management committee, in collaboration with wineries in the production area, has launched a series of innovative promotion actions. For example, they have held wine expos and tasting experiences. The management committee has established relations with external customer markets and set up virtual experience halls to ensure the three-dimensional display of informing the public about the project. The tourists reception of wineries in the Ningxia Helan Mountain East Foothill Region has gradually become an important part of leisure tourism reception of the autonomous region. And the growth rate of the annual reception of wineries such as Yuanshi Vineyard and Chateau Changyu Moser XV is maintained at about 20%.

Center of China Alcoholic Drinks Association, Chateau Helanhong, and the Helan Mountain East Foothill Wine Education College. The goal is to build Build Minning Town into a gathering and exhibition center for the entire wine industry chain of the Helan Mountain East Foothill Wine. This spot will also be the wine region's cultural landmark that integrates historical sightseeing, cultural experiences, cultural and creative product displays, study tour education, and wine tasting.

Experience and Inspirations

1. Determine development ideas

Ningxia regards the development of the wine industry as the fundamental strategy for poverty alleviation, relying on this "purple business card" to develop characteristic advantageous industries, adapting to local conditions, combining the development of the wine industry with strengthening the governance of the Yellow River beach area and ecological restoration, improving technological level, increasing cultural connotation, strengthening publicity and promotion, creating well-known brands, continuously increasing added value, and improving comprehensive benefits. The model of high-quality development of wine and cultural tourism is adopted to guide rural poverty alleviation and revitalization.

2. Clarify development models

The industry park has explored new cultural and tourism business modes such as the wine industry tourism bases, culture, business and tourism complexes, research bases, winery homestays, and winery design hotels. This was done in reliance on the China (Ningxia) International Wine Culture and Tourism Expo, a red wine street, the Wine Training

Next Steps

In 2021, the State Council approved the *General Plan for the Construction of the Ningxia National Open Development Comprehensive Pilot Zone for the Grape and Wine Industry.* It was the first national-level agricultural open pilot zone in Western China that was approved by the State Council. By 2025, the total scale of wine brewing at the base of the Helan Mountain East Foothill is expected to reach about 1 million *mu*, generating more than 300 million bottles of wine with a value of 100 billion yuan. The management committee will work to achieve this goal by giving full play to the resources in the wine region and policy advantages and strengthened interactions with colleges and universities. It will also promote the integrated development of the "wine+cultural tourism" industry. By integrating the prehistoric culture, farming culture, Xixia culture, Yellow River culture, and immigration culture, the committee aims to strengthen and deepen the "wine + cultural tourism" industry chain, creating a comprehensive development demonstration model for the wine industry with Chinese characteristics.

旅游减贫案例故事（中英文双语版）
Best Practices of Poverty Alleviation through Tourism (Chinese-English Bilingual Edition)

新疆维吾尔自治区喀什地区塔什库尔干塔吉克自治县瓦尔希迭村：

塔吉克高原山村化茧成蝶

收录于《2023 世界旅游联盟：旅游助力乡村振兴案例》

摘要

新疆维吾尔自治区喀什地区塔什库尔干塔吉克自治县瓦尔希迭村近年来依托得天独厚的旅游资源，大力发展旅游业，通过打造集塔吉克文化、旅游、民宿于一体的民俗村，带动农牧民持续增收，推进乡村振兴。

挑战与问题

新疆喀什地区塔什库尔干县瓦尔希迭村位于阿拉尔金草滩、石头城遗址等旅游景区附近，生态环境脆弱，土地贫瘠，农业投入产出率较低，产业发展基础薄弱，市场经济发育度不高。然而，其独特的高原风光和人文风情，吸引着疆内外游客前来旅游观光。"彩云人家"民宿区目前已有27家民宿户，但因为地处帕米尔国家5A级旅游景区核心区，区域面积非常有限，接待游客的入住率完全达到饱和，发展空间非常有限。另外，塔吉克农牧民世代依赖畜牧业，对近几年兴起的旅游业还存在陌生感，参与旅游业的热情需要进一步提高，在旅游接待过程中的服务、语言等都需要系统培训。

措施

1. 打造网红民宿

2019年，瓦尔希迭村"两委"积极协调54万元帮扶资金，将27户村民房屋改造成民宿，打造"彩云人家"民宿旅游示范点。2022年，瓦尔希迭村成立了塔什库尔干塔吉克自治县瓦尔希迭村旅游服务物业管理有限责任公司，帮助村民将自家民宿进行集中托管和网上推介。截至2023年，瓦尔希迭村已经陆续打造上百家民宿、农家乐、牧家乐，并全部纳入村旅游公司统一宣传、统一管理、统一接待。为了规范旅游市场，村里统一制作了住宿和餐饮收费标准，并张贴在所有民宿旅游户的醒目位置，做到收费公开透明、合理合规。村里还聘请专业人士对全村旅游户进行系统培训，规范接待标准，提升服务水平。同时，为了让游客更好地体验塔吉克族文化，当地积极组建了家庭式的演出队，在茶余饭后为游客表演歌舞，丰富了旅游内容。

2. 种植特色雪菊

瓦尔希迭村谋划发展高原雪菊特色种植，驻瓦尔希迭村"访惠聚"工作队全程参与幼苗采购、培育栽种、丰收采摘、阴干晾晒等环节，帮助注册了"关民情·高原雪菊"商标，委托文创公司制做包装礼盒及宣传材料，通过微信朋友圈、抖音直播等平台拓宽销售渠道。在工作队的培训和指导下，村里一批年轻的塔吉克族主播已能熟练地进行直播带货，他们把直播间设在盛开的雪菊地里，以银装素裹的慕士塔格峰为背景，迅速打开了高原雪菊的销路。

3. 提高服务品质

瓦尔希迭村实行精细化和差异化管理，针对不同游客的不同需求在打造"彩云人家"民宿旅游房间时，

既设置了酒店式的标准间，同时也保留塔吉克族传统的"通铺炕"。同时，为了进一步提升旅游接待服务水平，瓦尔希迭村积极组织旅游从业人员参加自治县举办的民宿旅游户培训，同时鼓励想参与旅游创收但普通话水平不高的农牧民参加多轮普通话培训，从而达到能够与游客沟通的标准。

成效

2019年，瓦尔希迭村"两委"积极协调54万元帮扶资金，将27户村民房屋改造成民宿，打造"彩云人家"民宿旅游示范点，当年旅游创收18万元，解决了280多人的就业问题，旅游业成为富民支柱产业。2020年，27户"彩云人家"实施民宿风貌加固改造，牧家乐新增12户。2021年，瓦尔希迭村共接待游客4000余人次，收入51万元，比2020年增加29万元。雪菊销售额达几十万元，惠及69户村民，户均增收数千元。

区，成为集住宿、餐饮、旅游咨询、观光于一体的民俗村。

2. 全域旅游是产业融合的驱动力

仅盯着"彩云人家"单独一个区域去发展旅游，发展空间十分有限，要把全村纳进来，结合村里得天独厚的自然风光和原生态的塔吉克房屋，培训更多的农牧民开展旅游接待，推动旅游全域式发展，助力瓦尔希迭乡村振兴。

经验与启示

1. 民宿是发展旅游的着力点

瓦尔希迭村重点打造的"彩云人家"民宿旅游示范点作为帕米尔国家5A级旅游景区的一部分，景区基础设施完善，民宿和牧家乐旅游户数量初具规模。村庄旅游环线已经形成，环线内植被覆盖率高，自然景色迷人，紧邻阿拉尔国家湿地公园和石头城遗址景

下一步计划

为了积极响应中央一号文件精神，聚焦产业促进乡村发展，不断扩大旅游辐射面，瓦尔希迭村将与新疆新旅投营地投资有限公司合作，在瓦尔希迭村建立塔什库尔干全域自驾营地网络主营区，并在夏拉夫迭村、夏布孜喀拉村与谢尔那甫村分设温泉度假、餐饮、自驾宿营配套营地，搭建塔什库尔干全域自驾营地网络体系。拟搭建的自驾网络营地包含住宿、餐饮、车辆租赁和维护等多项服务，建成后不仅能为往来塔什库尔干的自驾游客提供优质的餐饮住宿和丰富的民俗文化体验，还将带动瓦尔希迭村更多农牧民就业增收，让更多农牧民吃上"旅游饭"，生活更加幸福美满。

Warxidi Village, Taxkorgan Tajik Autonomous County, Kashgar Prefecture, Xinjiang Uygur Autonomous Region:

The cocoon-to-butterfly transformation of a Tajik village on the Pamir Plateau

Included in *WTA Best Practices of Rural Revitalization through Tourism 2023*

Abstract

In recent years, Warxidi Village of the Xinjiang Uygur Autonomous Region has been vigorously developing its tourism industry by leveraging its unique tourism resources and has turned itself into a folk village integrating Tajik culture, tourism and homestays to increase the income of farmers and herdsmen and promot rural revitalization.

Challenges and Problems

Warxidi Village is located near tourist attractions such as Aral Golden Meadow and The Stone City. Its ecological environment is fragile, the land barren, the agricultural input and output rate is low, the industrial development foundation is weak, and the market economy is underdeveloped. Its unique plateau scenery, culture and customs, however, are magnets for tourists from home and abroad. At present, there are 27 homestays in the "Caiyun Renjia" homestay area, but because it is located in the core area of the national 5A-level scenic spot of Pamir, it is small in area, the homestay occupancy rate is full, and the development space is limited. In addition, Tajik farmers and herdsmen have lived on animal husbandry for generations, and the emerging tourism industry has been a novelty to them. They need to be further motivated to participate in the tourism industry and need systematic training on service and language skills for the reception of tourists.

Measures

1. Develop homestays and promote them on the Internet

In 2019, the Party branch committee and the village committee of Warxidi Village actively coordinated 540,000 yuan of assistance funds to transform 27 villagers' houses into homestays and build the "Caiyun Renjia" homestay demonstration site. In 2022, Warxidi Village established the Tashkurgan Tajik Autonomous County Walxidi Village Tourism Service Property Management Co., Ltd. to help villagers manage their homestays and promote them online. As of 2023, Warxidi Village has successively built more than a hundred homestays, farm stays and yurt stays, and all of them have been promoted and managed by and all the guests received by the tourism company. In order to better regulate the tourism market, the village has set uniform accommodation and catering rates, and posted them in a conspicuous position in all homestays, so as to make sure that the charges are transparent, reasonable and compliant. The village hired professionals to provide systematic training for the households engaged in the tourism business and reception standards were set to improve services. Meanwhile, to show the tourists the Tajik culture, the village actively organized households to form a performance troupe to entertain the tourists with singing and dancing and enrich the tourist experience.

2. Plant the plateau snow chrysanthemums

Warxidi Village plans to develop the plateau snow chrysanthemum cultivation industry. The "Fang

Hui Ju" team stationed in Warxidi Village participated in the whole process of seedling procurement, planting, cultivation, picking, and drying, helped register the trademark "Guan Min Qing: Plateau Snow Chrysanthemums", commissioned a cultural and creative company to make packaged gift boxes and prepare publicity materials, and expanded sales channels through Weixin Moments, Douyin Live and other platforms. Thanks to the training and guidance of the team, a group of Tajik youngsters in the village can live-stream skillfully. They live-streamed in the blooming snow chrysanthemum field, against the snow-covered Muztag Ata in the distance, which immediately opened up the market for the plateau snow chrysanthemum.

3. Improve the service quality

Warxidi Village implemented detail-oriented and differentiated management. To meet the different needs of different tourists, there were not only hotel-style standard rooms but also the traditional Tajik kang (a shared sleeping platform) for guests to choose from in the Caiyun Renjia homestays. At the same time, in order to further improve the level of tourist reception services, Warxidi actively organized tourism practitioners to participate in the training programs held by the autonomous county and encourages farmers and herdsmen who wanted to make money from tourism but did not have the Mandarin Chinese proficiency required to participate in several Mandarin Chinese training programs, to equip them with the basic communication skills.

Results

In 2019, the Party branch committee and the village committee of Warxidi Village actively coordinated 540,000 yuan of assistance funds, transformed 27 houses into homestays and built the "Caiyun

Renjia" homestay demonstration site. The project generated 180,000 yuan in income that year, created more than 280 jobs, and made tourism a pillar industry for increasing villagers' income. In 2020, 27 of the homestays reinforced their buildings and enhanced their style, and 12 new yurt stays were added. In 2021, Warxidi Village received more than 4,000 tourists and earned 510,000 yuan, an increase of 290,000 yuan. The sales volume of snow chrysanthemums reached hundreds of thousands of yuan, benefiting 69 rural households and increasing their income by thousands of yuan each.

Experience and Inspirations

1. Homestays are the focus of tourism development

As part of the national 5A-level scenic spot of Pamir, the "Caiyun Renjia" homestay demonstration site, which Warxidi Village has made a particular effort to develop, now has sound infrastructure and a considerable number of homestays and yurt stays. The village has formed a tourist ring road with massive vegetation coverage and charming natural scenery. Close to Aral National Wetland Park and The Stone City, it has become a folk village offering services ranging from accommodation, catering, tourist information and sightseeing.

2. All-area-advancing tourism is the driving force of the integrated development of industries

Relying on "Caiyun Renjia" alone will limit the space for tourism development space, so it is important to engage the whole village, make use of the unique natural scenery and authentic Tajik houses, train more farmers and herders on tourist reception, promote the development of all-area-advancing tourism, and contribute to the rural revitalization of Warxidi Village.

Next Steps

In active response to the guiding principles of the No.1 Document of the CPC Central Committee, Warxidi Village will focus on developing rural industries to promote rural development, and continuously expand the influence of the tourism industry. It will cooperate with Xinjiang New Travel Investment Campsite Investment Co., Ltd to build the main campsite of the Taxkorgan self-driving camp network in Warxidi Village, and set up spa resorts, catering facilities and self-driving campsites in Xialafudi Village, Xiabuzkala Village and Shernav Village, to form a network of self-driving camps covering all of Taxkorgan. The proposed self-driving camp network will offer a wide range of services including accommodation, catering, activities, vehicle rental and maintenance. It will not only provide high-quality catering and accommodation services and a rich folk culture experience for self-driving tourists, but also promote local employment and increase the income of more farmers and herders in Warxidi Village, and benefit more farmers and herdsmen with tourism development so that they can have a happier and better life.

中国旅游集团：
对口帮扶香格里拉，打造标杆项目

收录于《2020世界旅游联盟：旅游减贫案例》

摘要

香格里拉是云南乃至全国极具潜力的旅游目的地，是国家重点推广的12条黄金线路之一，是集观光、休闲、度假、探险、科考于一体的大旅游区域，是具有世界范围影响力的国际旅游品牌。同时，香格里拉也面临着生态脆弱、基础薄弱等问题，不适合发展大的项目，因此更应注重现有资源和文化的开发、挖掘。

旅游减贫案例故事（中英文双语版）
Best Practices of Poverty Alleviation through Tourism (Chinese-English Bilingual Edition)

挑战与问题

香格里拉市地处滇、川、藏三省区交汇处和"三江并流"世界自然遗产腹地，是茶马古道要冲，平均海拔3459米，素有"动植物王国""天然高山生物园"等美誉，有"世界的香格里拉"旅游品牌。香格里拉是多民族共居、多宗教并存、多文化共荣的高原县级市，是国家级贫困县，2017年列入国家"三区三州"集中连片深度贫困地区云南藏区三县市之一。2018年，全市有贫困乡镇4个、贫困村45个。如今，全市已全面脱贫。

香格里拉在文化旅游产业发展中存在以下三个方面的短板。一是香格里拉旅游品牌影响力不足，虽已具备一定知名度，但推广手段相对滞后，缺乏讲好"香格里拉故事"的条件。二是文化与旅游结合不够紧密，缺乏对文化内涵的挖掘，文化元素作为旅游灵魂内核的作用不突出。三是旅游产业结构调整的步伐较为缓慢。香格里拉的旅游仍以自然景观为主，向休闲度假、康体养生、文化体验、科普教育等多元化方向转型的效果不明显。

措施

中国旅游集团充分发挥旅游主业优势，坚持精准扶贫，将旅游资源与企业全产业链立体化嫁接，通过品牌传播、产品策划、路线开发、文化挖掘、人才培养、专业运营"六位一体"的旅游扶贫方式，有效激活香格里拉地区文化旅游产业发展的内生动力。

1. 传播"香格里拉动人故事"，助推旅游品牌价值提升

中国旅游集团联合香格里拉市举办"迪庆·香格里拉端午赛马节暨中国旅游集团首届'时光之礼'香格里拉旅游文化节"；举办香格里拉首届旅游业发展论坛、旅游推介会等，并借助中央级主流媒体进行宣传，讲好香格里拉故事；制作发行香格里拉旅游扶贫特刊，深度挖掘当地的文化、美食、旅游资源。集团

下属《旅行家》杂志制作发行了长篇扶贫专刊《香格里拉返乡人》，与央视电影频道强强联手制作了公益项目"脱贫攻坚战——星光行动"，还促成香格里拉扶贫馆在京东商城正式上线，打造了"电影+电商、线上+线下"的创新扶贫模式。

2. 开发"香格里拉旅游路线"，助力旅游产品和服务提升

中国旅游集团推出香格里拉"时光之礼"旅游路线，打造了囊括香格里拉独克宗古城、普达措国家公园、松赞林寺等景点的高原风光和传统民族文化风情特色旅游线路。在2018年已上线十余条精品扶贫线路的基础上，中国旅游集团又推出3—4条与当地文化特色相结合、带有文化体验、注重品质服务的精品跟团游产品，通过与当地高端民宿紧密合作，研发轻奢产品。2020年年初，中国旅游集团在香格里拉推出酒店单项、一日旅行、接力式自由行、省内一地游、跨省连线游5个产品类型，亲子游、文化体验游、自然生态游、轻徒步游、健康体验游、赏花游、自驾游、低空飞行游8个主题类型的中高端旅行产品10余条。

集团研发中端特色主题旅行产品,与迪庆圣景、香格里拉旅行社两家当地旅行社合作,研发完成网红打卡、健康生态、非遗文化3个主题的8条特色主题目的地参团产品。

3. 援助"香格里拉非遗产品",深挖旅游文化深度和内涵

在独克宗古城1300多年的历史中,建塘锅庄是本地区藏民的祖先在日常生活和劳作中发明和创作的文化遗产。集团将其作为文化体验项目推广,使民族文化得以有效传承。

4. 培养"香格里拉旅游人才",夯实旅游产业发展基石和激发潜力

集团投资200万元,在迪庆藏族自治州民族中等专业学校开办酒店管理专业,培养50名酒店餐饮类人才。2020年,集团进一步投资300万元举办中国旅游集团精品旅游班,培养高素质店长级旅游专业运营人才20余名。

5. 助销"香格里拉农特产品",创新旅游农特产品消费模式

集团助力香格里拉开创直播带货销售新模式,建立扶贫商品线上商城,以集中采购模式为旅游消费产品打开销路。

6. 助推"香格里拉产品和服务平台",提升旅游品质

集团成立中国旅游集团迪庆香格里拉旅游投资发展有限公司,以旅游景区、乡村旅游、酒店、旅游文化地产的投资、健康及养老产业等旅游产业的投资开发建设和经营管理为经营重点。

成效

集团充分发挥企业优势,逐年加大帮扶力度,从2016年至2019年年底,先后支持帮扶各类资金近1900万元,并深入实践"教育+产业"一体两翼精准扶贫开发模式,将香格里拉市贫困发生率降到0.38%。2019年4月,香格里拉市退出贫困县行列。

2019年,香格里拉市被评选为"中国旅游百强县市",实现全年接待旅游者1651.40万人次,其中,海外旅游者68.83万人次,比上年同期增加1.97%;实现旅游收入199.32亿元,其中旅游外汇

收入26.18亿元，比上年同期增加34.3%。机场旅客吞吐量突破60万人次。香格里拉逐步形成了具有核心竞争力的中高端特色旅游产品体系，擦亮了"中国旅游集团品牌"。中国旅游集团注重文化与旅游产业相结合，打造了"以旅游促文化，以文化促旅游"双赢发展模式，深入挖掘了香格里拉旅游文化内涵。

通过帮扶办学，提升了市旅游干部、乡村旅游从业人员的旅游理论应用能力、经营管理水平和服务基本技能，有效推动了香格里拉旅游人才建设。

经验与启示

1. 注重顶层设计，形成体系化

紧密围绕助力打造"世界级的旅游目的地"这一目标，逐步发力，形成体系化、全面化的旅游扶贫工程。

2. 因地制宜，树立标杆项目

打造"时光之礼"旅游路线品牌，立足非遗文化打造"尼西土陶"和"建塘锅庄"品牌。

3. 注重扶"志"和"智"结合，致力铲除致贫根源

造血性的扶贫更有利于当地的长期性发展，应夯实人才基础。

4. 发挥主业优势，创造性开展精准扶贫工作

比如旅游路线的开发，可充分发挥下属旅行服务事业群的策划和组织优势；比如非遗文化的宣传，可充分发挥旗下媒体优势。

5. 符合市场客观规律，坚持市场化运作

坚持市场化的运作模式，对旅游产品、非遗文化产品进行挖掘、扶持、包装、推广，成熟一个扶持一个。

下一步计划

1. 发挥旅游主业优势，打造标杆项目

中国旅游集团将充分发挥旅游主业的优势，创建旅游扶贫示范项目，以点带面，探索可复制的旅游扶贫模式。

2. 创新旅游"企地共建"模式

进一步发挥旅游骨干企业的优势，糅合当地的旅游扶贫要素，与上海对口支援香格里拉的扶贫资源合作，联合打造精品民宿项目，推动地方经济发展。

3. 推动扶贫工作与集团发展战略相结合，发挥平台公司的优势

将旅游扶贫工作与落实集团大滇西战略紧密结合，围绕"大滇西旅游环线"，与地方政府、行业领先企业合作，深度挖掘当地自然资源和人文资源，将大香格里拉打造成"世界级综合旅游精品目的地"，建立长短结合、标本兼治的旅游扶贫长效机制，巩固脱贫成果。

China Tourism Group:
Provide Counterpart Support to Shangri-La and Build a Benchmarking Project

Included in *WTA Best Practices in Poverty Alleviation through Tourism 2020*

Abstract

As a tourist destination with great potential in Yunnan and even the whole country, Shangri-La is one of the 12 hot travel routes promoted by the state, a large tourist area integrating the functions of sightseeing, leisure, vacation, adventure and scientific research and an international tourism brand with worldwide influence. However, Shangri-La is also facing such problems as the fragile ecology and weak foundation, which is not suitable for the development of large projects. Therefore, the focus should be put on the development and exploration of existing resources and cultures.

Challenges and Problems

Shangri-La City is located at the intersection of Yunnan, Sichuan and Tibet, the hinterland of the world natural heritage site—"Three Parallel Rivers of Yunnan Protected Areas" and a major crossroad of the Ancient Tea Horse Road. With an average elevation of 3,459 meters, it's known as the "Kingdom of Animals and Plants" and "Natural Alpine Biological Garden", and has the tourism brand of "Shangri-La of the World". Shangri-La is a county-level city on a plateau where multiple nationalities live together, many religions coexist and multiple cultures co-prosper. It was a national poverty-stricken county and was listed as one of the three counties and cities in Tibetan areas of Yunnan in contiguous poor areas with "a priority in the national poverty alleviation strategy" in 2017. In 2018, there were four poverty-stricken towns and 45 poverty-stricken villages in the city. Up to now, the whole city has been completely lifted out of poverty.

In the development of the cultural tourism industry in Shangri-La, there are weaknesses in three aspects: (1) The influence of the Shangri-La tourism brand needs to be enhanced. Although it has certain influence, its promotion methods are relatively lagging, which makes it difficult to tell a "good story of Shangri-La"; (2) The culture and tourism need to be further integrated, there is a lack of exploration into cultural connotations, and the role of cultural elements as the core of tourism soul is not effectively exerted; (3) The pace of structural adjustment in the tourism industry is slow. The natural landscape is still the main part of the tourism industry in Shangri-La, without an obvious effect of transforming the tourism product structure from sightseeing-oriented to the compound type including leisure and vacation, health and wellness, cultural experience, science popularization education, etc.

Measures

China Tourism Group has given full play to the advantages of its main business in the tourism industry and adhered to targeted poverty alleviation, and has integrated tourism resources with the entire industry chain of the enterprise in a three-dimensional manner. Through the "six in one" tourism poverty alleviation approach of brand promotion, product planning, route development, cultural exploration, talent cultivation, and professional operation, it has effectively activated the endogenous driving force for the development of the cultural tourism industry in the Shangri-La region.

1. Tell the "Touching Story of Shangri-La" and improve the value of its tourism brands

China Tourism Group organized the "Diqing·Shangri-La Dragon Boat Horse Racing Festival & First 'Gift of Time' Shangri-La Tourism Culture Festival of China Tourism Group" jointly with Shangri-La City; organized the first Shangri-La Tourism Development Forum, tourism promotion event and other activities, and relied on the central

mainstream media to tell a good story of Shangri-La; produced and distributed the special issue of Shangri-La on poverty alleviation through tourism, and explored local culture, food, and tourism resources in depth. The Group's *Traveler* magazine produced and distributed the poverty alleviation feature entitled *People Who Return to Hometown in Shangri-La*, and jointly produced the public welfare project "Poverty Alleviation Campaign—Starlight Action" with CCTV 6. It also contributed to the official launch of the Shangri-La Poverty Alleviation Museum on JD.com, creating an innovative poverty alleviation model of "movie + e-commerce, and online + off line".

2. Develop the "Shangri-La Tourist Route" and provide high-quality tourism products and services

The "Gift of Time" Shangri-La tourism poverty alleviation route was launched, and a tourist route featuring plateau scenery and traditional national cultural customs were created, including the Dukezong Ancient Town, Potatso National Park, Songzanlin Monastery and other scenic spots. On the basis of more than ten high-quality poverty alleviation routes launched in 2018, China Tourism Group has also launched 3-4 boutique group tour products that combine local cultural characteristics, provide cultural experiences, and focus on quality services. Through close cooperation with local high-end homestays, they have developed light luxury products. At the beginning of 2020, five product categories including the hotel single service, day trip, relay-style free trip, one-place tour within the province, intra-provincial trip, and more than 10 mid- and high-end tourism products under eight themes of parent-child tour, cultural experience tour, natural ecological tour, light walking tour, health experience tour, flower tour, self-driving tour, and low-altitude flight tour were launched. The Group developed mid-end tourism products with featured themes, and cooperated with two local travel agencies—Diqing Shengjing and Shangri-La Travel Agency to develop products in eight featured theme destinations under three themes of online celebrity recommendation, health ecology, and intangible cultural heritages.

3. Disseminate the "Intangible Heritage Products of Shangri-La" and explore the connotation of its tourism culture in depth

In the history of Dukezong Ancient Town for more than 1,300 years, the ancestors of local Tibetans invented and created the cultural heritage—Jiantang Guozhuang in their daily life and work. The Group has listed it as a cultural experience project to effectively inherit the national culture.

4. Train "Shangri-La tourism talents", consolidate the foundation for the development of the tourism industry and stimulate its potential

The Group invested 2 million yuan to open a hotel management major in Diqing Tibetan Autonomous Prefecture Ethnic Secondary Vocational School and train 50 hotel catering talents. In 2020, the Group further invested 3 million yuan to hold China Tourism Group's boutique tourism class, cultivating more than 20 high-quality store manager-level tourism professional operation talents.

5. Boost the marketing of "Special Agricultural Products of Shangri-La" and innovate the consumption model of special agricultural tourism products

The Group assisted Shangri-La in creating a new model of live-streaming sales, establishing an online shopping mall for poverty alleviation products, and opening up sales channels for tourism consumption products through centralized procurement.

6. Improve the quality of tourism services with the "Shangri-La Product and Service Platform"

The Group established China Tourism Group Diqing Shangri-La Tourism Investment Development Co., Ltd. focusing on the investment, development, construction, and management of tourism industries such as tourist attractions, village tourism, hotels, tourism and cultural real estate, as well as the healthcare and pension industries.

Results

The Group has given full play to its corporate advantages and increased its assistance amount year by year. From 2016 to late 2019, various funds amounting to nearly 19 million yuan in total had been provided, and the targeted poverty alleviation development model driven by "One Body and Two Wings" of "education + industry" had been deeply implemented, reducing the poverty headcount ratio of Shangri-La to 0.38%. In April 2019, Shangri-La City withdrew from the list of poverty counties.

In 2019, Shangri-La was rated as one of "Top 100 Tourism Counties and Cities in China", receiving 16.514 million tourist visits throughout the year, of which 688,300 were overseas tourists, a YoY growth of 1.97%; the tourism income was 19.932 billion yuan, of which the foreign currency earnings were 2.618 billion yuan, a YoY growth of 34.3%. The passenger throughput of the airport exceeded 600,000 person-time.

Shangri-La has gradually formed a mid- to high-end characteristic tourism product system with core competitiveness, polishing the "China Tourism Group brand". China Tourism Group focus on the combination of culture and tourism industry, creating a win-win development model of "promoting culture through tourism and promoting tourism through culture", and deeply exploring the cultural connotation of Shangri-La tourism.

By providing assistance in running schools, the city's tourism cadres and practitioners in village tourism have improved their application ability of tourism theories, management level and basic service skills, effectively promoting the construction of tourism talents in Shangri-La.

Experience and Inspirations

1. Pay attention to the top-level design and establish relevant systems

Stick closely to the goal of building a "world-class tourist destination", gradually exert efforts to form a systematic and comprehensive project of poverty alleviation.

2. Set up a benchmark project based on local conditions

Build the "Gift of Time" tourism route brand, and based on intangible cultural heritage, create the "Nixi Pottery" and "Jiantang Guozhuang" brands.

3. Pay equal attention to "ambition" and "intelligence" support and strive to eradicate the root causes of poverty

"Blood-making" poverty alleviation is more conducive to local development in the long term. So it's necessary to consolidate the talent base.

4. Give full play to the advantages of the main business and implement targeted poverty alleviation work in an innovative way

For example, give full play to the planning and organizational advantages of the subordinate tourism service business group to develop tourist routes; and rely on its media to disseminate the intangible cultural heritages.

5. Observe the objective law of the market, and adhere to market-oriented operation

Adhere to the market-oriented operation model, and explore, support, package, and promote tourism products and intangible cultural products, and support one by one upon maturity.

Next Steps

1. Give full play to the advantages of the main business in the tourism industry to create benchmark projects

China Tourism Group will give full play to the advantages of its main business in the tourism industry, build the demonstration project of poverty alleviation through tourism and explore the replicable model of poverty alleviation through tourism that promotes work in all areas by drawing upon the experience gained on key points.

2. Create an innovative tourism model featuring "enterprise-local co-construction"

Further exploit the advantages of key tourism enterprises and integrate local elements for poverty alleviation through tourism. For example, it will cooperate with Shanghai's poverty alleviation resources to support Shangri-La, jointly create boutique homestay projects, and promote local

economic development.

3. Further integrate the poverty alleviation work with the Group's development strategy, and give full play to the advantages of platform companies

Integrate the work of poverty alleviation through tourism closely with the implementation of the Group's strategy for western Yunnan, cooperate with local governments and the market leaders in related industries centering on the "Western Yunnan tourist loop", dig deeper into local natural resources as well as human resources to build great Shangri-La into a "world-class comprehensive tourism boutique destination", and establish a long-term mechanism of poverty alleviation through tourism that focuses on both short-term and long-term development and addresses both symptoms and root causes to consolidate the results of poverty alleviation.

旅游减贫案例故事（中英文双语版）
Best Practices of Poverty Alleviation through Tourism（Chinese-English Bilingual Edition）

中山大学：
旅游脱贫的"阿者科计划"

收录于《2020世界旅游联盟：旅游减贫案例》

摘要

阿者科村地处云南红河哈尼梯田世界文化遗产核心区内，是元阳县典型的贫困村，村内经济发展缓慢，传统生产生活方式难以为继。2018年1月，中山大学保继刚教授团队到元阳梯田开展元阳哈尼梯田旅游区发展战略研究，项目团队选择阿者科村作为试点，专门为阿者科村单独编制了"阿者科计划"。项目团队带领村民大力发展乡村旅游，使全村实现旅游脱贫。

挑战与问题

阿者科村位于云南省红河州元阳县新街镇，在云南红河哈尼梯田世界文化遗产核心区内，海拔1880米，全村共64户479人。村寨有210年历史，因其保存完好的"四素同构"生态系统（森林、村寨、梯田、水系）、独特的哈尼传统民居（蘑菇房）聚落空间景观，和悠久的哈尼传统文化底蕴，成为云南红河哈尼梯田申遗的五个重点村寨之一，同时也被列入第三批中国传统村落名录。

阿者科村拥有丰富的景观资源，是游客向往的理想目的地，但对村民来说，这里却是他们几代人努力想要摆脱的枷锁——封闭落后严重制约了村庄的发展。阿者科村曾是元阳县典型的贫困村，村内经济发展缓慢，村民人均年收入仅3000元，传统生产生活方式难以为继，大量人口外出务工，村落空心化日趋严重。

措施

1. 科学规划，发展乡村旅游

保继刚教授团队根据扎实的现场调研和丰富的理论研究成果，确定了阿者科村发展乡村旅游的方向。整个计划预计在三年内完成，主要通过驻村团队带领村民发展乡村旅游，实现脱贫攻坚、遗产保护和旅游接待的三大任务。项目团队希望在三年内完成对本村运营团队的培育，三年后正式移交，实现村民自管自治。

2. 统筹管理，村民有序参与

项目团队提出在阿者科村实行内源式村集体企业主导的开发模式，团队派出博士生和硕士生，协同元阳县指派的青年干部，领导村民成立阿者科村集体旅游公司。公司组织村民整治村庄，经营旅游接待，村民对公司经营进行监管。按照分红规则，旅游经营所得收入三成归村集体旅游公司，七成归村民。归村民的分红又分为四部分，即传统民居保护分红

40%、梯田保护分红30%、居住分红20%、户籍分红10%。项目团队重视对村民的能力培训，包括普通话、外语和电脑技术培训，同时也在日常工作中培养和强化村民的旅游服务意识与技能。

3. 建立规则，守住保护底线

为保护古村、留住乡愁，项目团队明确保护利用规则。一是不租不售不破坏。公司成立后不允许村民出租、出售或者破坏传统民居，违者视为自动放弃公司分红权。二是不引进社会资本。公司不接受任何外来社会资本投入，而支持本地村民创业就业。三是不放任本村农户无序经营。公司对村内旅游经营业务实行总体规划与管理，严控新开餐馆和商店，尽可能保持村落原真性。四是不破坏传统。公司尽力恢复传统生产生活设施，进行旅游体验产品创意开发，使传统焕发新生。

4. 传承创新，开发活态产品

项目团队领导公司开发阿者科村深度体验游项目，现已推出自然野趣、传统工艺、哈尼文化等主题性体验活动，游客按需"点单"，公司实现菜单式管理。游客进入阿者科村，既能欣赏壮观的梯田风光和传统的哈尼村寨，又能亲身体验哈尼家庭真实淳朴的生活。

5. 精准营销，打造旅游品牌

项目团队充分利用阿者科村的资源优势，利用新媒体渠道宣传阿者科村乡村旅游，向游客全方位展示万亩梯田的壮美风光和百年古村的活态人文风韵。驻村项目团队为阿者科村开设的抖音号播放量达一千多万次，点赞量达46万次，不断更新的抖音视频正在

吸引越来越多的游客慕名而来拜访阿者科村。

成效

1. 收入稳定增加

驻村项目团队为阿者科村打造了传统村落观光项目和深度定制游项目（人均消费300元），经过全村努力，第一年创收超60万元，村民已收到分红30余万元，直接帮助全村23户贫困户脱贫。阿者科村的乡村旅游发展在项目团队带领下实现了开门红，让每一户村民实实在在享受到了保护遗产和发展旅游带来的好处。

2. 村民参与日益增加

发展乡村旅游以来，公司为建档立卡贫困户村民创造就业岗位16个。项目团队带领村民参与旅游业务的经营和管理，村民得到了实惠，对游客的态度发生了改变。作为东道主，他们以更热情的方式招待远道而来的客人。"阿者科计划"的实施，不仅吸引了游客，还让一些外出务工的青年返乡。

3. 人居环境逐渐提升

公司雇请村民打扫村寨，同时还通过村规民约引导村民积极做好门前"三包"工作，定期开展村内大扫除。公司还顺利完成道路交通、旅游公厕、污水处理、传统民居室内改造等工作。相比之前的"脏乱差"，如今的阿者科村更加宜居宜业。"阿者科计划"让乡

村的人居环境在旅游发展的机遇下获得持续显著的改善。

4. 传统得以保护

在发展乡村旅游之前，部分村民将传统民居出租给外地经营者后搬出村寨，传统村落的核心人文内涵丢失；发展乡村旅游后，公司引导村民不再将房屋出租，而是继续留住在村里，规避了当下旅游型村落发展的常见陷阱，即人口置换产生的"文化空巢"现象。传统技艺和民俗文化被项目团队打造成独具特色的主题性旅游体验项目，得到市场的广泛认可。

5. 丰富的游客体验

原来村内基本没有旅游接待设施，游客到村内只是拍照观光，参与不到更深层次的文化活动，旅游体验较为单一。发展乡村旅游后，公司开设一系列主题性体验活动，对外实行预约定制，带动村民承接精品旅游团，挖掘哈尼村寨的生态与文化，游客获得日益丰富的旅游体验。"阿者科计划"主张发展体验式深度旅游，以替代性旅游形式促进文化交流。

6. 丰富的教育文娱活动

项目团队目前已初步完成村史馆的筹建工作，馆内设有阿者科村历史文化展厅、旅游体验活动场地、图书阅览室、蘑菇房住宿体验点、茶室、公共交流空间等。项目团队安排公司员工轮流在村史馆值班管理，同时招募大学生义工成立阿者科学社，长期组织辅导村内留守儿童，在村史馆开展文娱活动、读书、绘画、电影等分享沙龙，激发儿童的学习兴趣、培养良好的

学习习惯，并加强其对哈尼传统文化的认知。

经验与启示

1. 社会科学理论指导实践

在"阿者科计划"中，保继刚教授运用20年的研究成果指导旅游减贫实践工作，以规避诸多发展陷阱，做到科学指导。例如，"阿者科计划"中将旅游吸引物权的学术概念落地，在整体方案设计上提出一直被忽略的旅游吸引物用益权，将用益权归还于村民。全体村民成为旅游发展的利益主体后，更加主动地保护作为旅游吸引物的文化景观资源，从而实现保护与发展的协同并进。

2. 发展乡村旅游不一定要引入外部资本

阿者科村的人居居住面积小，村寨的污水处理池也无法承接大规模餐饮产品。经过综合测算和评估，项目团队认为阿者科村的承载能力决定了其不能发展大众旅游，也就无须引入资本大搞建设。如果引进外部资本，外来经营者很有可能挤占本地居民的旅游参与机会。因此，"阿者科计划"规定，不允许外来资本进入阿者科村，转而采取技术援助的方式，培养本地村民参与旅游发展，以少量的启动资金，选择轻投资、高回报的发展方式。

3. 培训村民参与旅游

计划的要旨除了社区增权，还有社区赋能。项目团队长年居住在村，从决策到执行的手把手培训，增强了村民参与旅游的能力，从而实现村民自管自治。这需要先将培训方案本地化，并鼓励村民参与培训方案的制定，才能更好地让村民理解和执行培训方案。培训采取"做中学"的方式，项目团队指导村民在具体接待游客的过程中实践并反馈，促进村民更好地理解旅游服务要求。

4. 保护细则与分红绑定

"阿者科计划"将古村落的保护主体和受益主体都定义为本村村民，权利与义务统一，以期村民享受旅游分红的同时自发保护村落景观。这一规则体现了管理学的绩效考评思想，而非绝对的平均主义。只有当村民做到了相应的保护工作，才能得到相应比例的保护分红。

下一步计划

一是完善公司章程制度与村规民约。继续在实践工作中完善治理规则和培养契约精神，结合正式的公司章程制度和非正式的村规民约，实现协同治理路径引导的有序发展。二是加快村民管理团队培育。加快培育具有领导能力和管理能力的本地村民能人，并坚持对村民开展旅游接待知识和技能的培训。三是继续丰富村内旅游产品和业态。挖掘阿者科村的文化资源，打造传统村落精品文化旅游产品，丰富已有的产品体系的形式、种类和层次，坚持推进文化与旅游融合发展，创新产品设计，拓展旅游项目，丰富游客体验。四是拓展旅游宣传渠道。在维持现有的宣传平台（微信公众号、抖音）良好运营的基础上，将线上和线下的资源整合开展营销，不断创新形式，拓展渠道，大力推广阿者科村的旅游品牌。

旅游减贫案例故事（中英文双语版）
Best Practices of Poverty Alleviation through Tourism (Chinese-English Bilingual Edition)

Sun Yat-sen University:
Tourism-based Poverty Alleviation Project "Azheke Plan"

Included in *WTA Best Practices in Poverty Alleviation through Tourism 2020*

Abstract

Azheke Village is located at the core area of a UNESCO World Cultural Heritage Site— Hani Rice Terraces at Honghe, which is a typical poverty-stricken village in Yunnan Province. As a village with slow economic development, Azheke had difficulty in developing its economy with traditional production mode and lifestyle. In January 2018, the research team led by Professor Bao Jigang from Sun Yat-sen University carried out the research on the strategy of developing tourism at Hani Rice Terrace of Yuanyang County. They launched a pilot project at Azheke Village and especially compiled "Azheke Plan" for the village. The residential project team led villagers to develop rural tourism, which helped the whole village basically get out of poverty.

Challenges and Problems

Azheke Village is located at Xinjie Town, Yuanyang County, Honghe Prefecture, Yunnan Province, which is inside the core area of the UNESCO World Cultural Heritage Site, Hani Rice Terraces at Honghe. It is at an altitude of 1,880 meters, and is home to 64 households and 479 people. The village has a history of 210 years. Due to its well-preserved four-in-one ecological system (forest, village, terraces and drainage), distinctive traditional Hani dwellings (Hani mushroom house) and profound traditional Hani cultural heritage, it is one of the five important villages contributing to the successful application of Hani Rice Terraces for world cultural heritage, and also among the third batch of China's Traditional Villages.

Azerke Village has abundant landscape resources and is an ideal destination for tourists. However, for the villagers, it was a shackle that several generations had been striving to break free from — the serious constraints of isolation and backwardness on the development of the village. Azheke Village was a typical poverty-stricken village in Yuanyang County where the per capita income was only 3,000 yuan. People could hardly live in traditional production mode and lifestyle. Plenty of people went out to make a living, and the hollowing out of villages was becoming increasingly serious.

Measures

1. A scientific plan for the development of rural tourism

Professor Bao Jigang and his team determined the development orientation of tourism in Azheke Village on the basis of down-to-earth on-site research and abundant theoretical research results. The whole plan was projected to be completed in three years, with research teams leading villagers to develop rural tourism and accomplish three tasks: poverty alleviation, cultural heritage protection and tourism reception. The project team expected to train the local operation team in three years. And then, this project would be officially handed over to villagers for independent governance and management.

2. Coordinated management and orderly participation of villagers

The project team put forward the development mode of an endogenous rural collective company at Azheke Village. They sent doctoral and graduate students to help young cadres from Yuanyang County and jointly established Azheke Village Collective Tourism Company together with villagers. The company is engaged in organizing villagers to regulate the village and manage tourism reception while villagers can supervise its operation. According to the rule of profit share, 30% of tourism income is attributed to the tourism company and 70% to villagers. The villagers' part would be divided into four parts: 40% for traditional dwellings protection, 30% for terrace protection, 20% for resident population and 10% for household registered population. The project team paid much attention to the training of villagers, including Mandarin, foreign languages and computer skills. At the same time, they developed and reinforced villagers' sense of tourism services and skills in daily work.

3. Rules and underlying principles of protection

In order to protect the ancient village and guard the hometown of local villagers, specific regulations were made on protection and utilization. Firstly, no rent, sale or destruction. After the establishment of the company, villagers shall not be allowed to rent, sell or destroy traditional dwellings. Violation will be regarded as a voluntary waiver of profit sharing. Secondly, no introduction of social capital. The company shall not receive any social capital investment so as to support local villagers' entrepreneurship and employment. Thirdly, disorderly operation of local villagers is not allowed: The company shall make overall planning and management of tourism operation. The number of new restaurants and stores is under strict control so as to protect the authenticity of the village as much as possible. Fourthly, don't destroy traditions. The company shall make efforts to restore traditional production and living facilities, develop innovative tourism-experiencing products and revive the traditions.

4. Inheritance, innovation and development of dynamic products

The project team led the company to develop in-depth tours in Azheke Village. Now they have offered wild natural tours, traditional handicraft experiencing tours, Hani culture experience tours and other theme activities. Tourists "order" routes

according to their own needs, and the company will offer services based on personalized choices. Visitors to Azheke Village can not only enjoy the magnificent terraces and traditional Hani Village, but also experience the real and simple life of Hani families.

5. Targeted marketing and building of tourism brand

The project team made full use of the resource advantages in Azheke Village, used new media to promote rural tourism here, and showed visitors the magnificent terrace and dynamic local customs and practices in an all-round way. The residential project team opened an official Douyin (TikTok) account for Azheke Village, which has been viewed for over 10 million times, and they have received likes from viewers 460 thousand times. The updated Douyin videos are attracting more and more visitors to Azheke Village.

Results

1. Steady growth of incomes

The residential project team has developed the project of traditional village sightseeing and the project of in-depth customized tours (per capita consumption of 300 yuan) for Azheke Village. With the efforts of the whole village, the revenue of the first year exceeded 600,000 yuan, villagers received dividends of over 300,000 yuan, and 23 poverty-stricken households got rid of poverty as the direct result. Under the guidance of the project team, rural tourism of Azheke Village realized a good start, and every household in the village benefited from the heritage protection and tourism development.

2. Growing sense of participation of villagers

Since the start of rural tourism in the village, the company has created 16 jobs for villagers of registered poverty-stricken households. The project team led villagers to participate in the operation and management of tourism business, which benefited the villagers a lot and changed their attitude towards visitors. As the host, they welcome guests who come from afar with hospitality. One year after the implementation of "Azheke Plan", not only did the number of visitors increased, but some young people who worked outside even returned.

3. Gradual improvement of living environment

After the company was established, it employed villagers to clean the village, and guided villagers to shoulder up their own responsibilities in village regulations and regularly sweep up the village. The company also successfully completed the task of renovating roads, public toilets, sewage treatment systems and traditional residences. When compared

to the dirty and disordered village before, the village is now more comfortable for living and doing business. "Azheke Plan" continuously improved the living environment of the village by virtue of utilizing opportunities for tourism development.

4. Traditions are protected

Before developing rural tourism, some villagers rented their residences to others and moved out of the village. As a result, the core cultural connotation of the traditional village was lost. After the village began to develop rural tourism, the company guided villagers to stop renting their houses to others and continue to live in the village, avoiding a common trap in the current development of tourism-driven villages, that is, the "cultural empty nest" phenomenon caused by population replacement. The project team has transformed traditional skills and folk culture into projects of themed tourism experience with special creativity, which have been increasingly recognized in the market.

5. Varied tourist experiences

In the past, there were barely any tourist reception facilities in the village. Tourists could only take pictures and go sightseeing in the village instead of deeply participating in cultural activities. The tourist experience was relatively dull. Now the company has launched a series of themed experience activities, implemented the mode of appointment and customization, and led villagers to undertake premium tour groups which desire to experience the ecology and culture of Hani villages in depth. Tourists can gain increasingly varied experience in the village. "Azheke Plan" advocates the development of experience-based in-depth tourism, and promotes cultural exchange through alternative forms of tourism.

6. Colorful education and entertainment activities.

The project team has initially completed the preparation for the construction of the village history museum, which includes the village's history and culture exhibition hall, tourism experience activity site, reading room, mushroom house experience point, teahouse, and public communication space. The project team arranges for company employees to take turns on duty in the village history museum, and college student volunteers are recruited to establish the Azheke Academy. For a long time, left-behind children in the village have been guided to carry out cultural and entertainment activities, and reading, painting, and film sharing salons in the village history museum, which stimulates their interest in learning, develops their good learning habits and strengthens their knowledge about traditional Hani culture.

Experience and Inspirations

1. Theories of social sciences guide the practice

In "Azheke Plan", Professor Bao Jigang utilized his research results from the past 20 years to guide the practice of tourism-based poverty alleviation to avoid many development traps and provide scientific guidance. For example, the academic concept of tourism attraction property rights has been implemented in the plan. In the design of the overall plan, the long-neglected concept of tourism attraction property rights has been proposed, and the rights of use have been returned to villagers. As all villagers become the main beneficiaries of tourism development, they proactively protect the cultural landscape resources which are tourist attractions, thus realizing the coordinated development of protection and development.

2. Introduction of external capital is not a must for the development of rural tourism

The living area in Azheke Village is small, and its sewage treatment tank doesn't have the capacity to treat sewage from large-scale catering products. According to a comprehensive calculation and evaluation, the village's capacity determines that it is not suitable for developing mass tourism, so there's no need to introduce capital for mass construction. If external capital is introduced, foreign operators are likely to squeeze out the opportunities for local residents to participate in tourism. Therefore, "Azheke Plan" provides that no external capital is allowed to be introduced to Azheke Village. Instead, technical assistance is accepted to support local villagers to

participate in tourism development with a small amount of start-up capital and in the development mode of light investment and high return.

3. Villagers are trained to participate in tourism

The essence of the plan encompasses not only community empowerment but also community capacity building. The project team lives in the village all the year round, trains the villagers from decision-making to execution, and enhances their ability to participate in tourism, thus realizing independent management and governance. This requires localizing the training program first and then encouraging villagers to participate in the preparation of the training program, so they can better understand and implement it. The training adopts the "learning by doing" approach. The project team guides villagers to practice and provide feedback in the specific process of receiving tourists, so as to help the villagers better understand the requirements of tourism services.

4. Binding protection rules with dividends

The "Azheke Plan" defines both the protection and benefit subjects of ancient villages as local villagers, so the rights are aligned with obligations. It is expected that the villagers will protect village landscapes spontaneously while receiving dividends from tourism. This rule reflects the performance evaluation concept in management, rather than absolute egalitarianism. Only when villagers have done the corresponding protection can they get the corresponding proportion of dividends.

Next Steps

Firstly, the company's statute and village regulations will be improved. Governance rules will be improved and the spirit of the contract will be further developed in practice. The formal statute system of the company will be combined with the informal village regulations to achieve an orderly development guided by collaborative governance. Secondly, the cultivation of the villager management team will be accelerated. The cultivation of local villagers with leadership and management capabilities will be accelerated, and training on tourism reception knowledge and skills for villagers will continue to be organized. Thirdly, more varied tourism products and business activities will be launched in the village. Cultural resources of Azheke Village will be tapped into to create premium cultural tourism products in this traditional village, and enrich the forms, types and levels of the existing product system. The integrated development of culture and tourism will continue to be promoted with innovative product designs, expanded tourism projects, and varied tourist experiences. Fourthly, tourism promotion channels will be expanded. On the basis of the good operation of existing promotion platforms (WeChat public account, Douyin), both online and offline resources will be integrated to do marketing in more innovative forms and varied channels, and vigorously promote the brand of Azheke tourism.

旅游减贫案例故事（中英文双语版）
Best Practices of Poverty Alleviation through Tourism（Chinese-English Bilingual Edition）

携程集团：
携程度假农庄助力乡村振兴

收录于《2023世界旅游联盟：旅游助力乡村振兴案例》

摘要

携程度假农庄是携程集团2021年3月启动的落地乡村旅游振兴战略的具体行动。截至2023年5月，全国已上线23家携程度假农庄，分布于11个省、自治区。携程度假农庄落地乡村，不仅为目的地乡村带来客流，同时也带来了更先进的旅游产业运营理念和方式，带动目的地乡村民宿转型升级，更吸引了一批年轻人返乡就业，持续赋能乡村振兴。

挑战与问题

携程集团董事局主席梁建章先生在走访考察了多个亟待扶持的乡村旅游目的地后,发现大多数乡村虽然拥有优质的旅游资源,但普遍存在基础设施不足、人才短缺、规划缺失和资金匮乏等问题。尤其是很多乡村旅游目的地没有承接旅游度假的住宿设施,部分乡村尽管能提供有限的住宿产品,但住宿体验不佳。

措施

1. 提供选择性的农庄落地模式

作为一个全新的乡村休闲度假产品,携程度假农庄分为两种运营模式。一是自营模式。由携程出资建设和运营管理,选址主要考量目的地是否有扶贫需求,是否具备相应的农业、旅游、文化等资源。二是联营模式。携程集团联合目的地政府、国企或其他单位,共同打造特色乡村民宿,通过新型装配式建筑民宿集群引入、闲置农房民宿改造、原有民宿升级改造等措施,打造高品质五星级住宿产品,完善目的地住宿生态,提升旅游接待能力,为游客提供特色舒适的住宿体验,同时带动当地整体旅游增收,实现旅游富民。

2. 实施专业化的农庄运营管理

携程度假农庄逐步形成"安全+服务""产品+营销""品牌+生态"的模式,以农庄为核心,逐步形成"微度假区",吸引更多社会资本和头部品牌进入,为游客提供舒适的特色住宿体验,打造吃、住、行、游、购、娱一体化的高端度假生态。

3. 构建高质量的乡村旅游产品体系

一是聚焦乡村旅游目的地的特色优质旅游资源,定制研发乡村特色主题旅游线路,将乡村康养、家庭亲子、田园旅居、民俗体验、休闲农庄、乡村民宿/度假村、亲子/自然教育基地、文创商品、非遗工艺、特色美食等，串联成可预订的旅游线路产品，重点打造一批农业生态观光游、民宿文化体验游、乡村康养休闲游、农耕生活体验游、乡村主题研学游、美丽乡村休闲游等乡村深度体验类产品线路。二是深度挖掘乡村目的地特色民俗文化、优选特产等，为乡村目的地定制设计特色文创伴手礼，打造专属品牌标识。依托平台搭建集品牌宣传、产品展示、产品预订于一体目的地文创特产品牌旗舰店，拓宽特产、伴手礼等产品的销售通路。

4. 打造全方位的目的地营销推广

一是携程依托社区海量优质内容和优质用户，配合主题线路产品挖掘输出优质 PGC、UGC 内容，打造覆盖吃、住、行、游、购、娱的全方位在地旅游攻略，激发用户的出行灵感，加速其出行决策。二是携程依托全媒体资源平台，定制目的地乡村振兴 3 年营销战略规划，逐步实现"品牌认知—内容种草—消费转化"的传播策略，从基础阵地逐步建设、爆款活动流量导入到优质内容持续输出、四季主题营销常态转化，持续力推乡村目的地旅游及周边产品，助力乡村目的地快速出圈，从而带动当地旅游知名度和整体旅游收入双增长。

成效

自携程的乡村旅游振兴战略启动以来，以携程度假农庄为核心，开展一系列周边民宿产业帮扶、产品线路打造、旅游人才培训、目的地整体营销等活动，对当地产生了实际带动作用。截至 2023 年，23 家携程度假农庄，共吸纳所在地区的村民就业达 200 余人，本地村民占农庄员工总数的 80% 以上。例如，自 2021 年 7 月携程度假农庄安徽金寨大湾店上线以来，重点帮扶指导了周边 5 家民宿，带动周边民宿平均价格上涨 30%。2021 年，安徽省六安市全年旅游收入 337 亿元，全年旅游人次 4220 万人，同比增长 16.20% 和 14.67%。安徽金寨大湾店本地员工人均增收 6900 元/年。2022 年，安徽金寨大湾店庄与大湾村供销社达成合作，一次性采购农副产品 60 余万元；通过向当地农户采购肉蛋禽蔬等食材、与洗涤厂合作布草清洁等方式，共带动当地收入总计 123 万元。安徽金寨大湾店共举行 6 场民宿技能专场培训，上门指导周边民宿 18 次，并在店内组织了 83 次集中统一培训，累计培训 498 人次。

经验与启示

1. 盘活目的地文化资源

作为非标准住宿产品,乡村民宿的服务已逐渐超越单纯的住宿需求,而逐渐成为连接游客与目的地文化的新桥梁。携程度假农庄联合各地非遗传承人、文旅部门、博物馆、民俗馆、文化馆、创意集市等多个合作方,融合农耕文化、非遗文化、节气文化,已研发设计约20项民俗体验活动,包括非遗体验、农耕体验、农作物采摘、手作工坊等。

2. 注重智库建设

携程集团联合国内外知名高校、权威机构等行业专家智库,建立乡村振兴学院,开发多种适合乡村旅游产业发展的基础课程,提供产学研一体化的旅游人才培养服务,设立乡村旅游创新人才千人计划,形成可持续的乡村振兴创新机制。同时,携程集团以乡村振兴特派员、乡村振兴专家顾问团等方式,深入乡村当地实地考察探访,从专业角度为乡村目的地文旅发展提供建议与思路。

3. 促进人才培养

携程度假农庄乡村振兴学院培训体系由店内员工培训体系、周边民宿帮扶体系两大部分组成。通过一整套完善的店内员工培训体系和考核机制,提升员工的专业技能,以满足高品质用户对休闲度假服务的标准和需求。同时,以农庄为孵化点,引入更多的专家智库资源,通过实践培训向当地农民传授服务、运营等方面专业技能。通过组织民宿行业沙龙、周边民宿走访帮扶等形式,分享酒店和民宿的运营管理经验,涵盖服务提升、硬件改造、价格调整、卫生指导、特色餐饮、产品上线等方面,致力于打造人性化、特色化、专业化的服务品质。

下一步计划

民宿产业在促进农村一二三产业融合发展上的作用日益凸显,乡村民宿正从乡村旅游的补充性产品转变为核心吸引力。作为一家扎根实体的互联网公司,携程始终将社会责任与时代要求紧密结合,坚持社会价值和商业价值的有机统一,助力合作伙伴实现更大增长。未来,携程将再接再厉,积极履行社会责任,积极打造以携程度假农庄为代表的高端乡村民宿,在探索自身价值的同时,紧密围绕国家乡村振兴的宏伟目标,构建更美好的旅游生态,让乡村旅游真正成为推动乡村振兴的金钥匙。

旅游减贫案例故事（中英文双语版）
Best Practices of Poverty Alleviation through Tourism (Chinese-English Bilingual Edition)

Trip.com Group:
Country Retreats Launched to Boost Rural Revitalization

Included in *WTA Best Practices of Rural Revitalization through Tourism 2023*

Abstract

    The Trip.com Country Retreats program is a concrete action taken by Trip.com Group in March 2021 to promote the Rural Tourism Revitalization Strategy. As of May 2023, Trip.com Group had launched 23 country retreats in 11 provinces and autonomous regions. It has brought not only the tourist flow but also advanced tourism operation philosophies and methods to the destination villages. This has driven the transformation and upgrading of local homestays and attracted a significant number of young people to return to their hometowns for employment, continuously empowering rural revitalization.

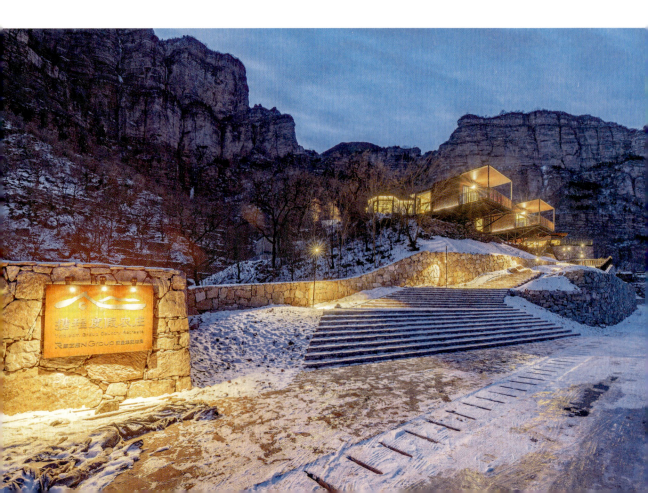

Challenges and Problems

After visiting many rural destinations in urgent need of assistance, Mr. Liang James, Board Chairman of Trip.com Group, found that most villages, despite their high-quality tourism resources, were short in infrastructure, manpower, planning, and capital. In particular, many rural destinations did not have accommodation facilities to serve tourists and vacationers, and even in some villages which do have such facilities, the accommodation experience was poor.

Measures

1. Provide two operating models to choose from

As a new rural leisure and holidaymaking product, the Trip.com Country Retreat program offers two business model. One is the self-owned business models, where Trip.com invests in the construction and operation management. While selecting the project site, the company mainly considers whether the destination has poverty alleviation needs, and whether it has the necessary agricultural, tourism, cultural resources, and so on. The other is the joint operation model, under which Trip.com Group works with destination governments, state-owned enterprises or other units to build characteristic country homestays, and turn them into the Trip.com Group Country Retreat – the high-quality five-star accommodation product – by introducing clusters of new prefabricated homestay buildings, renovating idle farmhouses and homestays, and upgrading existing homestays. In this way, it has helped improve the destination's accommodation services and increase its tourist reception capacity. It also provides tourists with a characteristic and comfortable stay, and meanwhile increases local tourism income on the whole and enriches the villagers.

2. Implement professional operation and management

The Trip.com Country Retreat program has gradually formed the models featuring "safety + service", "product + marketing" and "brand + ecology". With the country retreat as the core, the "micro-resort" has come into being, attracting more social capital and leading brands to join and provide tourists with a unique and comfortable accommodation experience, and to create a high-end resort that offers a wide range of services covering catering, accommodation, transportation, sightseeing, shopping and entertainment.

3. Build a portfolio of high-quality rural tourism products

Firstly, with a focus on the high-quality tourism resources with the destination's rural characteristics, Trip.com Group has customized and developed rural-themed tourism routes that string such services and facilities for health preservation, family and parent-child activities, sojourning, folk custom experience, leisure farms, homestays/resorts, parent-child/nature-based education bases, cultural and creative

products, intangible cultural heritage, specialty food, etc. The focus will be on creating a series of in-depth rural experience product lines, such as agri-ecotours, homestay-based cultural experiences, rural wellness and leisure tours, farming experience tours, rural-themed study tours, and beautiful countryside leisure tours. Secondly, by deeply exploring the characteristic folk culture and selecting specialties of rural destinations, Trip.com has designed customized characteristic cultural and creative souvenirs for rural destinations, and designed special brand logos for them. On the Trip.com platform, a flagship store is launched to display and sell cultural and creative products from the destinations, promote brands, provide product reservation service, and thus broaden the sales channels of cultural and creative products and souvenirs.

4. Promote the destinations via various channels all around

Firstly, Trip.com, with its massive high-quality content and users, digs out and publishes high-quality PGC and UGC content about themed tourism routes, and produces comprehensive travel guides covering catering, accommodation, transportation, entertainment, sightseeing and shopping services and facilities, to inspire the users so that they will make travel decisions more quickly. Secondly, relying on its all-media platform, Trip.com has customized the three-year marketing plan for rural revitalization of each destination, and gradually established the public communication strategy of "brand recognition-content dissemination-conversion to consumption". From gradual base building and traffic diversion from popular activities to the continuous production of high-quality content and all-season marketing, it continues to promote rural destination tourism and sideline products, and helps rural destinations quickly win recognition, thereby building up the visibility and increasing the overall tourism revenue of the destinations at the same time.

Results

Since Trip.com launched the Rural Tourism Revitalization Strategy, with these country retreats as the core, it has organized a series of activities such as assistance to surrounding homestays, developing products and routes, training tourism specialists, and destination marketing, delivering a positive effect on the project areas. So far the 23 country retreats have provided jobs to more than 200 local villagers who account for more than 80% of their staff. For example, since Trip.com Group opened its Country Retreat Dawan in Jinzhai, Anhui, in July 2021, it has helped five homestays nearby, and thanks to it, the average room charge of nearby homestays has increased by 30%. In 2021, the annual tourism revenue of Liu'an City, Anhui, reached 33.7 billion yuan, and the annual number of tourists was 42.2 million, a year-on-year increase of 16.20% and 14.67% respectively. The average income of local employees in Country Retreat Dawan increased by 6,900 yuan per year. In

2022, Country Retreat Dawan partnered with Dawan Village Supply and Marketing Cooperative and purchased from the latter agricultural and sideline products worth more than 600,000 yuan at one go. It also purchased meat, eggs, poultry and vegetables from local farmers, and outsourced linen cleaning to local laundry factories, contributing 1.23 million yuan to local revenue. Country Retreat Dawan has held six homestay skills training workshops, made 18 visits to surrounding homestays to offer on-site guidance, and organized 83 in-house training sessions, benefiting a total of 498 participants.

Experience and Inspirations

1. Make good use of the cultural resources in destinations

Homestay is a non-standard accommodation product, and users are increasingly expecting more from it other than accommodation services. Rural homestays have become a new bridge connecting tourists and the destination culture. Together with various partners such as inheritors of intangible cultural heritage, culture and tourism authorities, museums, folk customs exhibition halls, culture centers, and creative fairs, and drawing inspiration form the farming culture, intangible cultural heritage and solar term culture, the Trip.com Group Country Retreat program has developed and designed about 20 folk customs experiential activities, covering intangible cultural heritage experience, farming experience, picking agricultural produce, and DIY workshops, etc.

2. Develop think tanks

Trip.com Group, together with experts and think tanks affiliated with well-known universities

and authoritative institutions at home and abroad, has established the Rural Revitalization Academy, developed a variety of basic courses suitable for the development of the rural tourism industry, and trained tourism specialists through cooperation with universities and research institutes. It has also launched the Thousand Innovative Talents Program for Rural Tourism and formed a vigorous innovation mechanism for rural revitalization. At the same time, Trip.com Group has sent commissioners and expert advisory groups to conduct field surveys in rural areas and provide professional suggestions and ideas for the development of rural destinations.

3. Promote talent training

The training system of the Trip.com Country Retreats Rural Revitalization Academy is composed of two parts: in-house staff training and assistance to surrounding homestays. Trip.com has developed a sound comprehensive set of in-house staff training systems and assessment mechanisms, to help local employees improve their professional skills and meet the service standards and needs of high-quality users for leisure and vacation products. Then with the country retreat as the incubator, it has introduced more experts and think tanks to train local farmers on professional skills in service and operation. It has also organized industry salons, visits to surrounding homestays, etc., to share its hotel and homestay operation and management experience, including how to improve services, transform the hardware environment, adjust prices, improve hygiene, prepare specialty dishes, and launch products, etc., to deliver humanized, characteristic and professional services.

Next Steps

The homestay industry is playing a growing role in promoting the integrated development of primary, secondary and tertiary industries in rural areas. Rural homestays are evolving from supplementary tourism products to core attractions. As an Internet company rooted in the real economy, Trip.com believes that its greatest social responsibility is to always respond to the call of the times, align social value and business value, and help partners achieve greater growth. In the future, Trip.com will continue to fulfill its social responsibilities, actively build high-end rural homestays represented by its country retreats, continue to explore and realize its own value, and build a better tourist service ecosystem to serve the national goal of rural revitalization, and turn rural tourism into a golden key to rural revitalization.

途牛旅游网：
天津桐画精品民宿助力乡村振兴

收录于《2023 世界旅游联盟：旅游助力乡村振兴案例》

摘要

桐画是途牛旅游网旗下民宿品牌，以"一店一品"为品牌特色，在设计和运营上充分融合目的地的自然环境、人文历史、建筑风格、旅游资源和客群特征等元素，是途牛助力乡村旅游业态发展的重要举措。2021年，途牛将桐画精品民宿落地天津蓟州区西井峪村，将传统农家院深度改造为高质量的乡村民宿。在天津桐画精品民宿发展的带动下，当地乡村旅游成功从农家乐升级为"民宿+X"的深度乡村度假体验。

挑战与问题

天津市蓟州区西井峪村地处中上元古界国家级自然保护区内，采石和运输是西井峪村村民唯一的经济来源。2005年因环保需求关闭采石厂后，从2005年至2015年，村里开设了30多家农家乐。随着乡村旅游市场逐渐由观光向休闲、度假复合型转变，游客越来越关注乡村的住宿品质和游玩体验。西井峪村的农家乐因卫生环境、接待服务等品质上的"痛点"，大部分经营困难，最终倒闭。当地村委会清晰认识到发展精品民宿的重要性，开始寻求与专业旅游团队的合作。西井峪村面临的主要挑战是如何结合本村旅游发展规划，充分发挥专业团队的优势，整合本地资源，拓展多元旅游业态，推动乡村民宿提质升级，从而提升游客体验，实现可持续发展。

措施

1. 盘活闲置农居

天津桐画精品民宿所在的西井峪村靠近北京和天津交界处，地理位置优越，是承接京津冀周边游需求的优质目的地。村内原有大量老旧空置房屋，途牛将其中六处院落进行改造：一处改造为餐厅，提供地道的品质农家菜；其余五处院落分别设计为日式、地中海和中国传统民居等不同风格，各具特色，在当地民宿中独树一帜。

2. 突出设计特色

在民宿建筑设计方面，天津桐画精品民宿巧妙融合了西井峪村独特的"石头"元素，并进行了创新改良，兼具实用性和观赏性。房屋保留了部分老石墙，在墙体中增加保温材料，在墙体外部增设玻璃隔窗，住客可以像欣赏画卷一般直观地感受"石头村"的文化魅力。改造后的老墙还能起到保温和防蚊的作用，这一巧思引发了村里诸多民宿效仿。

3. 提升民宿品质

天津桐画精品民宿在室内设计和布草方面，通过精选软硬件设施提升用户入住体验。每套民宿都有独立小院和会客厅，配备现磨咖啡机、品牌洗护用品、戴森吹风机、自动马桶，让客人享受五星级酒店的入住体验。天津桐画精品民宿给西井峪村带来更多客流，有效带动了西井峪村整体旅游服务接待规范的提升，成为当地民宿行业的标杆和乡村旅游的新地标。

4. 邀请媒体体验

2021年9月，途牛邀请《中国旅游报》《北京青年报》《新京报》、品橙旅游、闻旅派、《北京商报》等多家北京区域的主流媒体及旅游行业媒体到访西井峪村，开展三天两晚的沉浸式体验活动。媒体团深度体验天津桐画精品民宿，走访周边景点，并与村委书

记、村镇旅游公司负责人、民宿经营者、民宿工作人员等进行了深度采访。媒体团主动发布了10余篇相关专题报道，有效提升了项目的社会关注度，增强了消费者认知。

5. 扩大线上宣传

天津桐画精品民宿积极拓展线上营销渠道，通过短视频平台开展常态化宣传。民宿管家将西井峪村的优美风光、特色民俗通过直播间与粉丝实时分享，其中网红打卡点"西崖远眺"累计获得超20万次点赞，形成良好的品牌效应。通过"民宿+X"模式，天津桐画精品民宿成功吸引研学游、摄影游、亲子游等多元化客群，有力推动了西井峪乡村旅游的创新发展。

成效

天津桐画精品民宿为当地带来了多重积极影响。第一，促进了当地旅游客流增长。天津桐画精品民宿开业期入住率超过50%，开业半年入住率突破95%，2023年第一季度营收环比增长79%，已成为当地民宿行业的标杆。第二，有效带动了村民就业。天津桐画精品民宿的管家和后勤保障岗位九成是当地村民，通过专业化培训，具备酒店管理和服务知识。第三，切实提高了村民收入。民宿的入驻使村内房产价值大幅提升，2020年西井峪村里每套宅院的年租金只有2万元，到了2023年，每套宅院年租金在10万元左右。同时，民宿管家团队积极探索直播带货模式，严格筛选本地优质农特产品，通过线上平台将核桃油、蘑菇酱、蓟县蜂蜜等特色产品销往全国，为村民开辟了增收新渠道。

经验与启示

1. 坚持乡村民宿的可持续发展

在民宿选址上，充分考虑乡村资源禀赋、客源市场及交通条件，因地制宜；在改建过程中，注重保护村落历史风貌，避免大拆大建，通过"微改造"合理

利用自然环境与人文景观资源,突出"石头村"的独特文化;同时,注重本地人才培养,依托企业自营的四川青城山桐画酒店的资源及成熟管理经验,强化民宿管家专业化培训,激励村民参与乡村民宿相关岗位,推动乡村民宿健康可持续发展。

2. 打造标准化高质量乡村民宿品牌

致力于塑造桐画乡村精品民宿IP,以"一店一品"为品牌特色,在设计和运营上充分融合目的地的自然环境、人文历史、建筑风格、旅游资源及客群特征,打造高标准民宿集群。通过树立行业标杆,推动西井峪村民宿群高质量发展,提升整体旅游服务规范,促进客流量增长。

3. 深耕"民宿+X"乡村产业融合发展

以村民、村委、游客三方满意度为核心指标,拓展"民宿+"特色产品,开展特色文化体验、农副产品销售等活动,促进资源联动发展,聚焦打造美好生活消费新场景,培育旅游消费新业态,为村民持续增收提供更多渠道,为游客提供多元化的选择与体验,实现乡村产业融合发展。

下一步计划

随着发展乡村民宿相关政策及措施的不断推进,乡村民宿将迎来高质量发展新阶段。途牛将"民宿+X"作为乡村振兴工作的重点,积极探索"持续做、长期做、深入做"的共赢发展新模式。途牛将持续以乡村民宿为着力点,充分发挥互联网平台在数字化、整合营销以及产品创新和服务品质方面的核心优势,持续升级乡村旅游产品。通过提升民宿品质,整合当地特色生态与休闲农业,实现乡村、民宿、景区的有机联动,为乡村产业的可持续发展开拓更多空间,通过农文旅融合新业态有效提升乡村品牌价值,为提质乡村旅游作出积极贡献。

Tuniu.com:
Tianjin Tonghua Boutique Homestay Contributes to Rural Revitalization

Included in *WTA Best Practices of Rural Revitalization through Tourism 2023*

Abstract

Tonghua is a homestay brand owned by Tuniu.com. It stands out with "one homestay, one design", and its design and operation fully integrate the destination's natural environment, culture, history, architectural style, tourism resources and customer group profiles. It plays an important role in the effort of Tuniu.com to develop rural tourism. In 2021, Tuniu.com introduced Tonghua Boutique Homestay to Xijingyu Village, Tianjin's Jizhou District, transforming traditional farmhouses into high-quality rural homestays. Driven by the development of Tianjin Tonghua Boutique Homestay, the local rural tourism industry has been upgraded from the farmhouse business to a "homestay + X" rural vacationing experience.

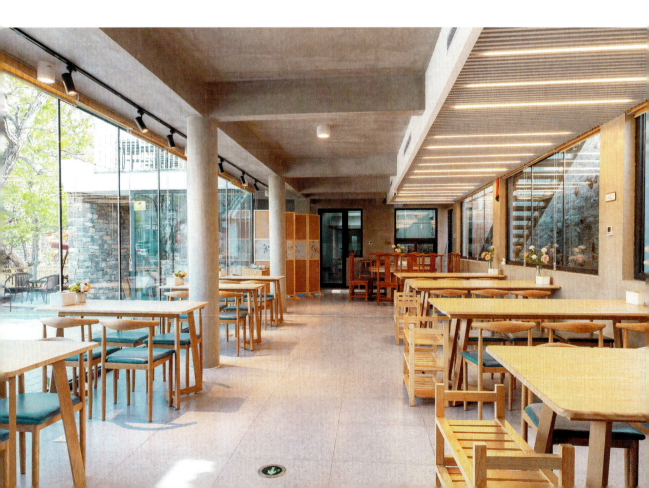

Challenges and Problems

Xijingyu Village is located in the protected area of the Middle and Upper Proterozoic National Nature Reserve, and local villagers used to live on only quarrying and transportation. After the quarry was shut down in 2005 for environmental reasons, more than 30 farmstays emerged in the village from 2005 to 2015. As the rural tourism market gradually shifts focus from sightseeing to the combination of leisure and vacation, tourists are attaching more and more importance to the quality of accommodation and visit experience. Most of the farmhouses in Xijingyu Village had to close down after failing to address their pain points such as sanitation and reception services. This brought home to the village committee the importance of developing boutique homestays and they began to seek cooperation with professional tourism teams. The primary challenge facing Xijingyu Village is how to integrate the village's tourism development plan, fully leverage the strengths of professional teams, consolidate local resources, diversify tourism offerings, and promote the quality enhancement and upgrading of rural homestays, thereby improving visitor experiences and achieving sustainable development.

Measures

1. Put idle farmhouses into good use

Tianjin Tonghua Boutique Homestay is located in Xijingyu Village, near the border of Beijing and Tianjin, boasting a superior geographical location that makes it an ideal destination for meeting the surrounding travel demands of the Beijing-Tianjin-Hebei region. The village originally had a large number of old and vacant houses. Tuniu.com has transformed six of these courtyards: one has been converted into a restaurant offering authentic, high-quality farmhouse cuisine, while the other five courtyards have been designed in distinct styles, including Japanese, Mediterranean, and traditional Chinese dwellings, each with its own unique characteristics, setting them apart from other local homestays.

2. Highlight design features

In terms of architectural design, Tianjin Tonghua Boutique Homestay ingeniously incorporates the unique "stone" elements of Xijingyu Village, innovatively enhancing them to achieve both practicality and aesthetic appeal. The buildings retain sections of the old stone walls, with insulation materials added within the walls and glass windows installed on the exterior. Guests can appreciate the cultural charm of the "Stone Village" as if viewing a scroll painting. The renovated old walls also serve the

dual purpose of insulation and mosquito prevention, a clever idea that has inspired many other homestays in the village to follow suit.

3. Improve the quality of homestays

In terms of interior design and linen of the homestays, Tianjin Tonghua Boutique Homestay enhances the resident experience with carefully selected software and hardware facilities. Each homestay has a standalone courtyard and living room, equipped with a coffee maker with ground, branded toiletries, Dyson hair dryers, and automatic toilets, allowing guests a five-star hotel experience. Tianjin Tonghua Boutique Homestay has attracted more passenger flow volume to Xijingyu Village, effectively promoted the village to improve its overall tourism reception services, and become a benchmark in the local homestay industry and a new landmark of rural tourism.

4. Invite journalists to visit

In September 2021, Tuniu.com invited several Beijing-based mainstream media outlets and tourism industry media, including *China Tourism News*, *Beijing Youth Daily*, *The Beijing News*, Pinchain Travel, Wenlvpie, and *Beijing Business Today*, to visit Xijingyu Village for a three-day, two-night immersive experience. The media delegation thoroughly experienced Tianjin Tonghua Boutique Homestay, explored surrounding attractions, and conducted in-depth interviews with the village committee secretary, the head of the town's tourism company, homestay operators, and staff. The media team proactively published over 10 feature reports, significantly raising the project's social visibility and enhancing consumer awareness.

5. Expand online promotion

Tianjin Tonghua Boutique Homestay has actively expanded its online marketing channels, conducting regular promotions through short video platforms. The homestay managers share the picturesque scenery and unique folk culture of Xijingyu Village with fans in real-time through live broadcasts. Among these, the popular check-in spot "Xiya Overlook" has garnered over 200,000 likes, creating a strong brand effect. Through the "homestay + X" model, Tianjin Tonghua Boutique Homestay has successfully attracted diverse customer groups, including study tours, photography tours, and family trips, effectively driving the innovative development of rural tourism in Xijingyu Village.

Results

Tianjin Tonghua Boutique Homestay has brought multiple positive impacts to the local area. Firstly, it has boosted the growth of tourist flow. During its opening period, the homestay achieved an occupancy rate of over 50%, which rose to more than 95% within six months. In the first quarter of 2023, its revenue increased by 79% compared to the previous quarter, establishing it as a benchmark in the local homestay industry. Secondly, it has effectively driven local employment. Ninety percent of the homestay's managers and support staff are local villagers who have undergone professional training and acquired knowledge in hotel management and services before taking up their roles. Thirdly, it has significantly increased villagers' income. The presence of the homestay has greatly enhanced the value of local properties. In 2020, the annual rent for a courtyard in Xijingyu Village was only 20,000 yuan, but by 2023, it had risen to around 100,000 yuan per courtyard. Additionally, the homestay's management team has actively explored live-streaming sales, carefully selecting high-quality local agricultural products such as walnut oil, mushroom sauce, and Jixian honey, and selling them nationwide through online platforms. This has opened up new channels for villagers to increase their income.

Experience and Inspirations

1. Adhere to the sustainable development of rural homestays

While choosing the homestay site, full consideration is given to the rural resource endowment, tourist market, and transportation conditions, adapting to local circumstances. During the renovation process, emphasis is placed on preserving the historical appearance of the village, avoiding large-scale demolition and construction, and making reasonable use of the natural environment and cultural landscape resources through "micro-renovation", highlighting the unique culture of the "Stone Village". At the same time, attention is paid to the cultivation of local talent. Leveraging the resources and mature management experience of the self-operated Sichuan Qingcheng Mountain Tonghua Hotel professional training for homestay managers is strengthened, encouraging villagers to participate in positions related to rural homestays, and promoting the healthy and sustainable development of rural homestays.

2. Build a standardized, high-quality rural homestay brand

Committed to building up the Tonghua boutique homestay brand featuring "one homestay, one design", the team fully incorporated the natural environment, culture, history, architectural style, tourism resources and customer group profile of the destination in homestay design and operation, in an effort to create a high-standard homestay cluster. By setting industry benchmarks, promoting the high-quality development of the Xijingyu Village homestay cluster, enhancing overall tourism service standards, and increasing tourist traffic.

3. Deepen the integrated development of "homestay + X" rural industries

With the satisfaction of villagers, village committees, and tourists as the core indicators, expanding the "homestay +" characteristic products, carrying out special cultural experiences, agricultural product sales, and other activities, promoting the linkage development of resources, focusing on creating new consumption scenarios for a better life, cultivating new tourism consumption formats, providing more channels for villagers to increase income continuously, offering diversified choices and experiences for tourists, and realizing the integrated development of rural industries.

Next Steps

With the continuous implementation of favorable policies and measures, rural homestays will usher in a new stage of high-quality development. Tuniu.com has made "homestay + X" the focus of its rural revitalization work, and is actively exploring a new win-win development model based on "sustainable, long-term, and detail-oriented practices". Tuniu.com will continue to focus on rural homestays, give full play to the core advantages of internet platforms in digitalization, integrated marketing, product innovation and service improvement, and continue to introduce new rural tourism products. While working to improve the quality of homestays, it will integrate local characteristic ecology and leisure agriculture, link villages, homestays and scenic spots, open up more spaces for the sustainable development of rural industries, and effectively enhance the value of rural brands through new business forms integrating agriculture, culture and tourism, and contribute to higher-quality rural tourism.

旅游减贫案例故事（中英文双语版）
Best Practices of Poverty Alleviation through Tourism (Chinese-English Bilingual Edition)

飞猪：
数字攻略文旅服务平台助力乡村振兴

收录于《2023 世界旅游联盟：旅游助力乡村振兴案例》

摘要

　　飞猪联合阿里巴巴公益，在湖南省湘西土家族苗族自治州永顺县打造乡村振兴样板。阿里巴巴公益派驻资深员工，作为乡村特派员，在产业、人才、科技等多方面助力永顺县的乡村振兴工作。在阿里巴巴乡村特派员的支持下，飞猪依托平台，推进乡村"旅游+产业"的深度融合，构建乡村"益起寻美"数字攻略地图。通过数字攻略地图，游客实现吃、住、行、游、购、娱的全场景体验，推动农文旅产业融合，形成乡村旅游产业链，努力实现从景点旅游向全域旅游的重大转变。

挑战与问题

永顺县旅游资源丰富,但除了家喻户晓的芙蓉镇,游客对其他旅游景点了解较少。将芙蓉镇、猛洞河、老司城、不二门、塔卧、小溪国家级自然保护区等精品景区景点"串珠成链",构建独具特色、独立完整的旅游体系是永顺县文旅发展的重点。为扩大永顺县旅游知名度,带动县域发展,飞猪需要利用数字攻略地图,为游客提供个性化服务,持续丰富数字攻略的优质内容,实现精准引流。

措施

1. 打造数字定制旅游

游客使用数字攻略地图,不仅可以预订永顺县的景区门票、酒店、美食和农产品,还能在线导览实景建模的景区。此外,系统将在火车站对乘坐高铁到达永顺县的游客进行数字攻略的精准推送,依托大数据分析游客的需求和喜好,为他们量身定制乡村旅游行程,包括农耕体验、文化体验、美食品尝等,全面提升游客的乡村旅游体验。

2. 打造区域公共品牌

飞猪联合阿里巴巴"寻找远方的美好"团队,以"传奇永顺县 魅力芙蓉镇"为主题,综合永顺县的文化、历史、产业等元素,为永顺县设计区域公共品牌,永顺的农副产品、景区、城市美化等都计划启用区域公共品牌标识。

3. 打造线上线下融合新体验

为了提升景区的旅游体验,满足年轻人对拍照打卡的需求,飞猪联合阿里巴巴公益和阿里巴巴技术官,推出了"云游永顺"Vlog智能短视频和"凌云镜"景区慢直播系统。直播系统立足永顺县丰富的自然风光和历史人文,通过物联网、人工智能和大数据的技术能力,建立运营触点,形成游前吸引点和游中体验点,并通过"云游永顺"Vlog短视频,自动剪辑生成个人精美短视频,形成游后传播点,为游客带来线上线下融合的新体验。

4. 打造农特产品销售新渠道

永顺县人民政府联合阿里巴巴公益举办"云游芙蓉 食在永顺"专场直播活动,网红主播通过淘宝直播平台宣传推介永顺县老司城、芙蓉镇等人文景观,通过直播带货销售永顺猕猴桃、莓茶、油茶、腊肉等系列农特产品。

成效

数字攻略地图已成为永顺县的第二官网，不仅塑造了永顺文旅的形象，提升了其品牌价值，还为永顺县搭建展示区域形象和更多业务内容的平台。根据飞猪平台数据，2023年4月1日至5月3日，永顺县门票、线路、酒店在线成交额同比2022年增长470%，高于行业平均水平。"云游芙蓉食在永顺"阿里公益县域专场直播带货共销售5000多件农产品，销售额达16万元左右。

经验与启示

1. 做好永顺文旅顶层设计

永顺县应深度挖掘优势旅游资源，加快补齐短板弱项，以数字攻略地图为契机，全力打通县域景区景点"内循环"。围绕全域旅游总体布局，通过数字攻略地图进行全盘规划，系统性做优旅游业发展顶层设计，并不断完善。

2. 做好数字化旅游体验

在数字化时代，游客越来越多地寻求通过互联网以及其他数字媒体平台上的信息来丰富旅游体验。因此，景区需要构建数字媒体平台，丰富旅游场景，并充分利用网站、移动应用程序、社交媒体、在线广告等满足不同渠道的游客。同时，对于游客在平台上的各种反馈和评论，应进行及时的回应和解决，有助于建立游客对景区的信赖度和忠诚度。

下一步计划

为有力推动旅游产业可持续发展，在阿里巴巴乡村特派员的持续助力下，飞猪与阿里巴巴公益将继续利用自身优势持续推动"线上文化产品+线下旅游场景"协同发展，丰富飞猪"益起寻美"数字攻略地图。利用阿里巴巴平台资源加强全域宣传，利用大数据分析用户喜好，针对性发布资讯，提升永顺文旅的知名度；及时更新数字攻略地图中的景区介绍、门票预订、线上预约等功能，完善供应链；开展线上摄影大赛等多样化、趣味性的互动活动，增强用户黏度；创新旅游产品，包括VR/AR体验、虚拟游览等，提供更加丰富的旅游体验，充分带动游客消费。

Fliggy:
Digital Strategy Cultural Tourism Service Platform Boosts Rural Revitalization

Included in *WTA Best Practices of Rural Revitalization through Tourism 2023*

Abstract

Fliggy and Alibaba Philanthropy have partnered up to make Yongshun County, Xiangxi Tujia and Miao Autonomous Prefecture, Hunan Province, a model for rural revitalization. Alibaba Philanthropy dispatched senior employees there as rural commissioners to assist with Yongshun's rural revitalization in industrial development, talent cultivation, science and technology, and other aspects. Supported by rural commissioners of Alibaba, Fliggy promotes the deep integration of rural tourism and other industries on its platform and has launched a digital travel guide map called "Yiqi Xunmei". The map guides tourists through all the scenarios of catering, accommodation, transportation, sightseeing, shopping and entertainment, promotes the integration of agricultural, cultural and tourist industries, and helps form the rural tourism industry chain, and shifts the focus from scenic spot-based tourism to all-area-advancing tourism.

Challenges and Problems

Yongshun County is rich in tourism resources, but apart from the well-known Furong Town, its tourist attractions were mostly lesser known to the outside world. For Yongshun, the priority of tourism development is to "string beads into a chain", that is, stringing boutique attractions such as Furong Town, Mengdong River, the Site of Laosicheng Tusi Domain, Buermen National Forest Park, Tawo the former CPC revolutionary base, and Xiaoxi National Wilderness Area, and forming a unique, standalone and complete tourism resource system. In order to increase the popularity of Yongshun County as a destination and drive the development of the county, Fliggy needs to use the digital travel guide map to provide personalized services for tourists, continue to generate high-quality content of digital travel guides and divert traffic in an accurate way.

Measures

1. Creat digital customized tourism

Tourists using digital guide maps can not only book tickets for attractions, hotels, cuisine, and agricultural products in Yongshun County but also enjoy online guided tours of realistically modeled scenic areas. Additionally, the system will provide precise digital guide recommendations to tourists arriving in Yongshun County by high-speed rail at the train station. Leveraging big data to analyze tourists' needs and preferences, it will tailor rural tourism itineraries for them, including farming experiences, cultural activities, and culinary delights, significantly enhancing their rural tourism experience.

2. Build a regional public brand

Fliggy, in collaboration with Alibaba's "Discovering Distant Beauty" team, has themed "Legendary Yongshun County, Charming Furong Town" to design a regional public brand for Yongshun County. This brand integrates elements of Yongshun's culture, history, and industry. Plans are in place to apply this regional public brand logo to Yongshun's agricultural products, tourist attractions, and urban beautification projects.

3. Create a new experience that integrates online and offline

In order to enhance the tourist experience at scenic spots and meet the youngsters' needs to take selfies and post them on social media, Fliggy, Alibaba Philanthropy and Alibaba Technology Officer jointly launched the "Yunyou Yongshun" Vlog app and the "Lingyunjing" Scenic Spot Slow Live-Streaming System. Based on the rich natural scenery and historical and cultural legacy of Yongshun County, the live-streaming system establishes contact points with consumers with the help of the Internet of Things, artificial intelligence and big data, and displays attractions to lure tourists. The "Yunyou Yongshun" Vlog app can automatically produce personal short videos for post-tour communication, bringing a new tourist experience that blends online and offline.

4. Create new sales channels to sell agricultural products

The People's Government of Yongshun County and Alibaba Philanthropy jointly hosted a special live-streaming event titled "Cloud Tour of Furong, Taste of Yongshun". During the event, popular influencers promoted the cultural landmarks of Yongshun County, such as the Site of Laosicheng Tusi Domain and Furong Town through Taobao Live. They also showcased and sold a variety of local agricultural products, including kiwifruit, berry tea, tea seed oil, and cured meat, via live-streaming sales.

Results

The digital travel guide map has become the alternative official website of Yongshun County, not only enhanceing the image and brand value of Yongshun County as a tourist destination, but also building a platform for Yongshun County to present itself and more business content. According to Fliggy's statistics, from April 1 to May 3, 2023, the online turnover of tickets, tours and hotels in Yongshun County increased by 470% compared with 2022, higher than the industry average. The Alibaba Philanthropy county-specific live-streaming event, "Cloud Tour of Furong, Taste of Yongshun", sold over 5,000 agricultural products, generating sales revenue of approximately 160,000 yuan.

Experience and Inspirations

1. Make solid top-level designs for Yongshun's tourism industry

Yongshun County deeply taps its advantageous tourism resources, accelerates to make up for its shortcomings, and makes use of the digital travel guide map to connect all the tourist attractions in the county. Focusing on the master plan for all-area-advancing tourism, Yongshun County has formulated an overall plan based on the digital travel guide map, and systematically and continuously improved the top-level design of tourism development.

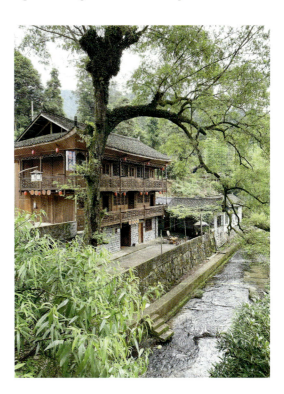

2. Deliver a sound digital tourist experience

In the digital age, tourists are increasingly looking to enrich their experience with information available on the Internet and other digital media platforms. Therefore, scenic spots need to build digital media platforms to enrich tourism scenarios, and make full use of websites, mobile applications, social media, and online advertising to meet the needs of tourists from different channels. At the same time, they must timely respond to and solve tourists' comments and concerns on the platforms, which will help win tourists' trust and loyalty.

Next Steps

In order to effectively promote the sustainable development of the tourism industry, with the continuous help of Alibaba's rural commissioners, Fliggy and Alibaba Philanthropy will continue to use their own advantages and promote the coordinated development of "online cultural products + offline tourism scenarios", and enrich the contents of Fliggy's "Yiqi Xunmei" digital travel guide map. They will use Alibaba's platform resources to promote all-area-advancing tourism, use big data to identify user preferences, release targeted information, and enhance the popularity of Yongshun County as a destination. They will timely update the scenic spot profiles, ticket booking, online reservation and other functions in the digital travel guide map, and improve the supply chain. Colorful and interesting interactive activities such as online photo contests will be hosted to enhance user stickiness, and innovative tourism products, including VR/AR experiences, virtual tours, etc., will be launched to enrich the tourist experience and stimulate tourist consumption.

抖音集团：
"山里 DOU 是好风光"，以数字能力助力乡村文旅高质量发展

收录于《2018 世界旅游联盟：旅游减贫案例》

摘要

抖音公益和抖音生活服务联合发起"山里 DOU 是好风光"公益项目，基于抖音平台内容生态、技术能力和产品能力，面向全国乡村地区，通过乡村文旅的宣传互动、人才培育、营销推广等举措，助力乡村文旅资源推广和产业发展，吸引更多游客走进乡村，带动农民就业增收。

2023 年，"山里 DOU 是好风光"项目抖音相关话题播放量累计超 120 亿次，抖音创作者发布相关短视频 52 万篇，覆盖全国 31 个省级行政区 1138 个区县，超 2 万个乡村文旅经营主体积极参与。

挑战与问题

抖音集团一直以来秉持"Inspire Creativity, Enrich Life"（激发创造，丰富生活）的使命，目前旗下拥有今日头条、抖音、西瓜视频等产品，在互联网科技领域，不断推动着技术创新。

抖音集团认为乡村文旅要实现高质量可持续发展、实现从"有没有"到"好不好"的转变，主要面临以下四个问题。

1. 产业发展主体数字化运营能力弱

乡村文旅商家规模小、资源少、抗风险能力差、信息化水平较低，这给乡村文旅商家的数字化运营带

#知秋向山行
18.7亿次播放

☆ 收藏

在乡村旅游数字提升行动和消费帮扶金秋行动工作框架下，文化和旅游部资源开发司、国家发展改革委地区振兴司指导抖音公益、抖音生活服务，发起"知秋向山行"2023年秋季乡村旅游推广活动。面向景区景点、酒店民宿、休闲观光、文化体验等全国乡村文旅经营主体，通过流量扶持、千场直播、激励计划、宣传推介等举措，"游购"乡村新消费、"激发"乡村内生力，促进消费持续恢复，推动乡村旅游目的地"出圈成名"。

▲收起

综合　　最新　　最热　　相似话题

来巨大挑战。

2. 乡村文旅创新产品不丰富

各地开发的文旅项目和产品雷同，存在盲目跟风的情况，丰富度不足，没有展现出地域特色，缺乏核心竞争力，忽视了对乡村文化、民俗、表演等内容的开发。

3. 缺乏合理有效的规划

目前，乡村旅游开发和经营普遍呈现各自为政的现象，各类资源无法形成合力，存在规模小、品牌弱、服务差等问题，忽视了乡村旅游建设的整体性，乡村文旅发展缺乏合理有效的规划。

4. 数字新媒体专业人才匮乏

乡村数字新媒体人才流失多、来源少，农村不同程度存在"空心化""老龄化"现象，导致乡村文旅发展的中坚力量严重缺乏，普遍存在从业人员文化程度较低、经营管理能力较弱的问题。

基于以上问题，抖音集团立足平台内容生态、技术能力和产品能力，发起"山里DOU是好风光"项目，挖掘"人、文、旅"三要素，打造乡村文旅推广新亮点，帮助乡村文旅经营主体掌握抖音运营技能，打通线上经营路径，发挥文旅产业的综合带动作用，吸引更多游客走进乡村，带动农民就业增收，更好地服务经济社会发展。

措施

1. "看见"乡村好风光——宣传乡村文旅资源

以"宣传推介"为目标，抖音挖掘放大特色乡村文旅资源，助力提升乡村知名度美誉度。在抖音平台，以短视频话题挑战赛、直播等玩法和极具感染力和现场感的形式，呈现民俗文化、美食、民宿等乡村特色元素，让更多人看见乡村好风光。《抖音2024乡村文旅数据报告》显示，2023年3月28日至2024年3月28日，抖音平台新增乡村内容数10.9亿个，播

放量近 2.8 万亿次；乡村内容获得超 555 亿次点赞、91 亿条评论、30 亿次分享。

2. "激发"乡村内生力——培育经营主体数字能力

以"能力提升"为目标，抖音开展乡村文旅长期扶持计划，助力乡村文旅经营主体提升数字化运营能力。精确定位刚启动线上经营的乡村文旅经营主体，通过能力培训、任务清单、公益流量激励、社群运营四大举措，解决其数字应用能力弱、缺少流量扶持等问题，增加更多就业创业机会，充分发挥乡村旅游的综合带动作用。云南黑荞母村小人国主题公园的经营主体通过乡村文旅扶持专项，持续学习专业的新媒体运营知识，改变了 2020 年只有 2 个游客的惨淡经营状况，客流量持续递增，其中七成游客来自抖音"种草"，2024 年春节期间，客流量超过了 3 万人，利润上涨 285%。

3. "游购"乡村新消费——促进乡村文旅消费

以"交易转化"为目标，抖音开启了"千场直播助力消费帮扶"活动，通过提供流量支持和消费补贴，鼓励各行业经营主体以"短视频 + 直播 + 交易"的方式进行线上营销推广，宣传景区、民宿、休闲体验等特色乡村旅游产品和精品旅游线路。2024 年 7 月，结合凉山火把节，"山里 DOU 是好风光"落地凉山州，并举办了抖音足球嘉年华赛事。活动联动百余位达人在凉山打卡拍摄，记录凉山彝族文化、当地美景美食和足球赛事，"凉山 DOU 是好风光"话题短视频播放量超 3.5 亿次。凉山州文旅局数据显示，2024 年 7 月 28 日至 8 月 4 日的火把节期间，凉山全州共接待游客 502.84 万人次，同比增长 45.02%，旅游收入 47.06 亿元，同比增长 57.5%。抖音生活服务数据显示，凉山乡村商家订单量 7 月环比上涨 39%，销售额环比增长 66%。

成效

抖音"山里 DOU 是好风光"项目通过"点""面"双结合、"内""外"同发力，在全国范围内持续开展系列活动，探索"乡村旅游 + 数字经济"新路径。在"点"上，开展陕西、甘肃、湖南等省份的区域专项活动，深挖重点省份乡村旅游潜力；在"面"上，实施春季和秋季全国乡村旅游推广活动，拓展文旅助农项目覆盖面。向"内"修，启动乡村文旅长期扶持计划，培育乡村文旅内生力；往"外"促，落地系列数字营销活动和宣传推广活动，促进乡村文旅消费力。

项目成功打造了"江南秘境 仙境丽水"浙江古村探秘精品旅游线路和串联福建山、海、村的"闽山闽水"精品旅游线路，培育了福建省霞浦县东壁村、陕西省留坝县营盘村、甘肃省甘南藏族自治州扎尔那村、湖南省吉首市德夯村、广东省南雄市帽子峰镇等乡村旅游目的地，助力贵州"村超"、篁岭"晒秋"、潮汕英歌舞等地方特色文化名片在抖音"火出圈"，并创新设计了"花开青蓝"龙泉青瓷、"山海"福建大漆、"DOU 来跃龙门"广东鱼灯系列文创产品。乡村文旅长期扶持计划覆盖云南、甘肃、广西、河北、贵州、江西等地的各类乡村文旅经营主体，挖掘了云南普者黑景区、广西防城港九龙潭景区等优秀案例。

经验与启示

1. 以抖音为代表的数字平台不仅能够助力地方文旅出火爆出圈，还可以将"网络热度"转化为"在地效益"

2023 年以来，"淄博烧烤""榕江村超""潮

汕英歌""天水麻辣烫"竞相出圈,旅游的火爆对于本地拉动内需、促进就业、活跃市场、提振信心都起到了非常重要的作用。以榕江县为例,抖音超130亿次的话题播放量,助力"村超"成为全社会关注的大事件,激发本地形成了一系列围绕"村超"的旅游体验产品和服务,游客带动本地文旅综合收入近60亿元,同时零工市场、夜市摊位等业态直接创造了8000多个就业岗位。

2. 各类文旅经营主体能够通过数字化经营提升效率和竞争力,让服务找人更精准,人找服务更便捷

抖音通过生活服务功能,在短视频和直播中挂载旅游产品链接,帮助消费者即时实现景区、酒店、线路等旅游产品的预订,大大提升"获客"效率。以普陀山的导游小庄为例,线下服务10万游客需要13年,而在抖音上仅用了3年。

3. 线上创新的消费场景加线下优质的服务能力,可以挖掘乡村文旅潜能,实现可持续的乡村文旅消费带动作用

数字平台的用户基数大、话题性强、传播迅速,活动载体丰富、销售形式多样,不仅能够带动乡村地区文旅消费增长,还可以优化游客结构,推动乡村文旅消费"网红"变"长红","淡季"变"旺季"。抖音"湖南DOU是好风光"打造湖南省吉首市德夯村旅游目的地,德夯村矮寨奇观景区在11月旅游淡季的销售额同比增长10余倍,德夯村在抖音的热度环比提升385%,成功实现"淡季不淡"。

下一步计划

抖音集团将继续发挥平台内容生态、技术能力和产品能力,从培育经营主体数字能力、丰富乡村旅游产品供给、促进乡村文旅消费、宣传乡村文旅资源、推广文旅助农工作经验方面着手,通过流量扶持、达人助力、千场直播、激励计划、免费培训、宣传推介等举措,培育乡村经营主体发展内生动力,挖掘乡村旅游消费潜力,传播乡村美景好物,展示乡村文化风貌。

Douyin Group:
"Visit Great Scenery in Mountains on Douyin" Project: Leveraging Digital Capabilities for High-Quality Development in Rural Culture and Tourism

Included in *WTA Best Practices in Poverty Alleviation through Tourism 2018*

Abstract

The Douyin Public Welfare and Douyin Local Services have come together to launch the "Visit Great Scenery in Mountains on Douyin" public welfare project. This initiative draws upon Douyin's rich content ecosystem, advanced technological capabilities, and robust product offerings, targeting rural regions across the country. It aims to enhance the promotion and development of rural cultural and tourism resources through engaging promotional activities, talent development, and marketing strategies. The ultimate goal is to draw more tourists to rural areas, thereby boosting employment and increasing income for local farmers.

In 2023, the "Visit Great Scenery in Mountains on Douyin" achieved significant milestones, with related topics on Douyin amassing over 12 billion views. Douyin creators published 520k relevant short videos, reaching 31 provincial-level administrative regions and 1,138 counties nationwide, and engaging over 20k rural cultural and tourism business entities.

Challenges and Problems

The Douyin Group has consistently pursued its mission of "Inspire Creativity, Enrich Life", owning a portfolio of products including Toutiao, Douyin, and Xigua Video. In the Internet technology sector, it is at the forefront of driving innovation.

The Douyin Group identifies four key challenges in achieving sustainable, high-quality development in rural culture and tourism, transitioning from merely existing to excelling.

1. Weak digital operation capabilities among industry players

In the rural culture and tourism sectors, businesses and organizations are usually small, with limited resources, a low capacity to handle risks, and minimal digital integration. These challenges greatly affect their ability to conduct effective digital operations.

2. Lack of diverse innovative products in rural culture and tourism

Many regions develop similar projects and products, resulting in a lack of uniqueness and diversity. This not only fails to highlight local characteristics but also undermines their competitive advantage. Moreover, it overlooks the potential of leveraging rural culture, folklore, and performances.

3. Lack of effective planning

At present, rural tourism development and business operations often suffer from a lack of coordination. This results in fragmented efforts, weak branding, and subpar services due to the failure to leverage the synergy between resources effectively. There is also neglect in considering the holistic nature of developing rural tourism, with insufficient planning for the integrated development of rural culture and tourism.

4. There is a shortage of professionals in digital new media

Rural regions are seeing a considerable drain of talent in this field, with hardly any new influx to compensate. This talent drain is causing villages to suffer from different levels of "hollowing out" and "aging", which in turn results in a stark shortage of key drivers for the development of rural culture and tourism. Additionally, there is a common problem of low educational attainment and poor management and operational skills across these areas.

Based on the issues mentioned above, the Douyin Group, leveraging its platform content ecosystem, technological capabilities, and product strengths, has launched the "Visit Great Scenery in Mountains on Douyin" project. This initiative aims to explore the three key elements of "people, culture, and travel" to create new highlights for rural cultural and tourism promotion. It equips rural cultural and tourism entities with the necessary skills to navigate operating on Douyin, enabling them to operate their businesses online. By doing so, the project aims to give full play to the comprehensive driving role of the cultural and tourism industry, drawing more tourists to rural areas, enhancing employment opportunities and income for farmers, and contributing more

effectively to the broader economic and social development.

Measures

1. Discovering the beautiful scenery of the countryside — Promoting rural cultural and tourism resources

Douyin aims to "share and promote" the unique rural cultural and tourism offerings, helping to boost its fame and appeal. Through the Douyin platform, engaging activities like short video challenges and live streams vividly bring rural life closer to people, featuring its rich folk culture, food, and homestays. This initiative helps more individuals explore and appreciate the beauty of rural areas. The *Douyin 2024 Rural Culture and Tourism Data Report* reveals that from March 28, 2023, to March 28, 2024, Douyin saw an increase of 1.09 billion posts related to rural areas, attracting nearly 2.8 trillion views. Countryside-related content received over 55.5 billion likes, 9.1 billion comments, and 3 billion shares.

2. Igniting the intrinsic power of the countryside — Enhancing the digital capabilities of business entities

Douyin has launched a long-term support program aiming at "capability enhancement", strengthening the digital capabilities of businesses in the rural culture and tourism sector. Focusing on entities that are newly entering online operations, the program provides training, actionable tasks, traffic incentives for CSR-related engagement, and community operations. This approach addresses challenges such as limited digital knowledge and insufficient traffic support, thereby promoting job creation and entrepreneurial endeavors. This highlights rural tourism as a powerful driving force for overall development. A remarkable success story is the Yunnan Heiqiaomu Village Miniature Country Theme Park. Benefiting from the support program, it has significantly increased its visitor numbers from only 2 in 2020 through continuous learning and adopting advanced new media strategies. Notably, 70% of its visitors were influenced by Douyin's promotional efforts. During the Spring Festival of 2024, the park witnessed its tourist count surge to over 30,000, and profits increased by 285%.

3. Creating new rural consumption through traveling and shopping—Boosting rural cultural and tourism consumption

With the goal of "enhancing transaction rates", Douyin has launched the "Thousand Live Streams to Support Consumption" campaign, offering traffic support and consumption subsidies. This initiative encourages businesses across various sectors to engage in online marketing and promotion through a combination of short videos, live streams, and transactions. It focuses on advertising and promoting unique rural tourism products and premium travel routes, including scenic areas, guesthouses, and leisure activities. In July 2024, in conjunction with the Liangshan Torch Festival, the campaign "Visit Great Scenery in Mountains on Douyin" was implemented in Liangshan Prefecture, accompanied by the Douyin

Football Carnival event. The event connected over a hundred Douyin creators, inviting them to Liangshan for a series of check-ins and filming sessions. These creators captured Liangshan's Yi nationality culture, its breathtaking landscapes, delicious local cuisine, and exciting football matches. The topic of "Visit Great Scenery in Mountains on Douyin-Liangshan" short videos garnered over 350 million video views. Data from the Liangshan Yi Autonomous Prefecture's Administration of Culture and Tourism reveals that, during the Torch Festival from July 28 to August 4, Liangshan hosted approximately 5.0284 million tourists, marking a 45.02% increase from the previous year. Tourism revenue soared to 4.706 billion yuan, up 57.5% year on year. According to Douyin Life Service data, the order volume for rural merchants in Liangshan increased by 39% month-on-month in July, while sales revenue rose by 66% compared to the previous month.

Results

"Visit Great Scenery in Mountains on Douyin" project combines both provincial and national strategies, as well as internal and external efforts, to carry out a series of nationwide campaigns, exploring new paths to create synergy between rural tourism and the digital economy. At the provincial level, the project team organizes special regional campaigns in provinces such as Shaanxi, Gansu, and Hunan, to tap into the rural tourism potential. On the national level, the team carries out nationwide rural tourism promotion campaigns in spring and autumn, expanding the coverage of cultural tourism and agricultural assistance projects. The project team initiates long-term support plans for rural culture and tourism and helps create internal growth drivers. The team also implements a series of digital marketing and promotional campaigns to boost consumption for rural culture and tourism.

The "Jiangnan Secret Realm and Fairyland Lishui" boutique tourism route exploring ancient villages in Zhejiang and the "Fujian Mountains and Fujian Waters" boutique tourism route connecting local mountains, seas, and villages in Fujian province has created rural tourism attractions such as Dongbi village in Xiapu county, Fujian province, Yingpan village in Liuba county, Shaanxi province, Zhagana in Gannan Tibetan autonomous prefecture, Gansu province, Dehang village in Jishou city, Hunan province, and Maozifeng town in Nanxiong city, Guangdong province. These efforts have helped iconic local cultural events such as the Guizhou Village Super League, Huangling's "Autumn Harvest" (hanging and drying crops), and the Chaozhou Yingge dance to go viral on Douyin. Innovative designs for cultural and creative products such as "Huakaiqinglan" Longquan celadon, "Shanhai" Fujian Lacquerware, and "DOU Lai Yue Long Men" Guangdong Fish Lantern series have been developed.

The long-term support plan for rural culture and tourism covers various rural culture and tourism business entities in provinces such as Yunnan, Gansu, Guangxi, Hebei, Guizhou, and Jiangxi. The plan has uncovered excellent growth stories such as the Puzhehei scenic area in Yunnan and the Jiulongtan scenic area in Fangchenggang, Guangxi.

Experience and Inspirations

1. Digital platforms such as Douyin not only help local culture and tourism go viral but also turn online sensations into local benefits

Since 2023, Zibo Barbecue, Rongjiang Village Super League, Chaozhou Yingge Dance, and Tianshui Spicy Hot Pot have all gone viral. The tourism boom has played a crucial role in boosting local demand, promoting employment, invigorating the market, and uplifting confidence. Taking Rongjiang County as an example, with over 13 billion topic-related video views on Douyin, the Village Super League became a major event that caught society's attention. It sparked a series of tourism experience products and services centered around the soccer league, driving nearly 6 billion yuan in local revenue from culture and tourism, giving birth to a gig economy and night markets, and directly creating over 8,000 local jobs.

2. Culture and tourism entities can boost their operational efficiency and market competitiveness by embracing digital strategies, helping services reach more targeted customers, and making it more convenient for consumers to access services

Through its life service feature, Douyin enables the attachment of travel product links in short videos and live streams, allowing consumers to instantly book scenic spots, hotels, travel routes, and other tourism products. This significantly enhances customer acquisition efficiency. Take Xiao Zhuang, a tour guide for Mount Putuo, as an example: servicing 100,000 tourists would normally require 13 years through traditional offline methods, yet with Douyin, this milestone was achieved in just 3 years.

3. Combining innovative online consumption scenarios with premium offline services can unlock the potential of rural culture and tourism, consistently driving the consumption of rural culture and tourism

Thanks to their large user scale, digital platforms' reliance on trending topics for growth, and rapid content distribution, along with various activities and multiple ways to sell, can boost cultural and tourism consumption in rural areas and improve the mix of tourists. This change helps rural culture and tourism transform rural cultural and tourism consumption from "internet-famous" to "long-lasting" and turning "off-seasons" into "peak seasons". The "Visit Great Scenery in Mountains on Douyin—Hunan Province" campaign has transformed Dehang village in Jishou City, Hunan Province, into a sought-after travel spot. In November, typically an off-season for tourism, the Aizhai Wonder scenic area in Dehang village experienced a sales surge, with figures climbing over ten times compared to the previous year. Dehang Village's popularity in Douyin soared by 385%, turning its traditional off-season into a bustling period.

Next Steps

The Douyin Group will keep leveraging its content ecosystem, technological capabilities, and product strengths to enhance the digital capabilities of businesses, enriching the supply of rural tourism products, promoting rural culture and tourism consumption and resources, and spreading best practices to assist agricultural growth. Through measures such as traffic support, creator collaborations, thousands of live streams, incentive programs, free training, and promotional campaigns, it plans to help grow rural businesses from within, unlock the hidden value of rural tourism consumption, share rural beauty and products, and display rural culture appeal.

穷游网：
甘肃省甘南藏族自治州夏河县非遗节日"香浪节"助力乡村振兴

收录于《2022世界旅游联盟：旅游助力乡村振兴案例》

摘要

夏河县地处甘肃省甘南藏族自治州，2020年，穷游网携手夏河县文体广电和旅游局，以甘南传统文化节日——香浪节为旅游抓手，以草原文旅为核心，策划"草原旷野计划——香浪节"活动，将香浪节打造为区域IP。通过对夏河县旅游资源的重新挖掘，全媒体推广夏河县目的地，树立了非遗节日示范性旅游品牌标杆。

挑战与问题

夏河县文化和旅游产业资源丰富，拥有7大景区51处景点，以及多个民俗文化活动。近年来，当地打造了一系列旅游专业村、示范村，并在一定程度上提升了旅游相关基础设施水平，夏河文旅正逐步走向高质量发展阶段。但夏河县旅游资源和周边区域相似度高，存在替代性空间竞争关系，易引起周边各大景区对客源市场的争夺与分割。夏河县欲借助甘南传统文化节日——香浪节，带动夏河旅游的知名度，吸引更多游客前往。香浪节过往只是当地居民的节日，如何将这一节日变为覆盖全国知名节庆活动，提高夏河县旅游综合收入，需要更为有效的渠道及手段。

下旅行的新兴潮流。崇尚自然、疗愈身心、回归野性、释放天性逐渐成为用户旅行新需求。穷游网携手夏河县文体广电和旅游局，以草原文化旅游为核心，策划夏河香浪节嘉年华活动。

3. 多元体验提质香浪节

基于草原文旅，穷游网打造500亩帐篷营地，策划多元线下体验活动。香浪节以营地为核心，打造了年轻化、创意十足的线下活动，将传统与新潮结合。通过活动招商，打造了小型的线下市集，涵盖衣食住行等方面，为游客带来全新的沉浸式体验。

4. 全媒体推广夏河县

穷游网借助香浪节，对夏河县旅游资源进行重新梳理，突出其独特优势，并通过专业内容和深度内容进行全方位包装。在专业内容方面，穷游网上线了"夏河穷游锦囊"，完整全面地整合了夏河的目的地信息及经典、小众路线等。在深度内容方面，穷游网邀请平台多位旅游达人全程体验香浪节活动，挖掘夏河旅游新玩法，产出深度游玩攻略。此外，穷游网还利用自身平台流量、新媒体矩阵、主流媒体、线下户外大屏广告宣传夏河旅游资源，以强曝光度、强冲击力、强公信力吸引了大量周边游客前往夏河参加香浪节活动。

措施

1. 市场化运作香浪节

穷游网利用多年来目的地营销经验，将甘南传统文化节日——香浪节与传统舞蹈——"则柔"进行品牌化包装，并集合藏族音乐、唐卡等藏族文化，将香浪节打造为集非遗、文旅体于一体的复合型IP，再次将当地民族文化推上新高度，赋能夏河更多自然与人文属性，将夏河文旅推向全新起点。

2. 户外旅游热点赋能香浪节

穷游网用户调研显示，露营、徒步等户外旅行方式连续2年热度上涨超过30%，户外旅行已成为当

成效

穷游网携手夏河县文体广电和旅游局打造的"草原旷野计划——香浪节"活动，全网总曝光超1.4亿人次。活动邀请了多家媒体前往体验和报道，包括新华网、人民网、央广网、环球网、中国日报、新京报、网易、新浪、搜狐、环球旅讯、劲旅网等门户类、旅游垂直类及地方媒体，总计500家参与宣传报道。香浪节活动吸引了超过17万人参与，其中当地群众6万人，全国各地游客11万人，活动直接带动夏河县旅游业综合收入约1656.5万元。穷游网联手夏河县文体广电和旅游局将传统节日与文旅体结合，成功打包输出夏河旅游品牌，树立了非遗节日示范性旅游品

牌标杆，提升了夏河的旅游影响力，通过旅游提升乡村经济的发展，助力乡村振兴。

经验与启示

1. 聚合当地特色文化

乡土文化是中华优秀传统文化的重要组成部分，各地都有自己的特色节日。然而，单一节日对游客的吸引力有限。通过将更多当地文化元素，如传统舞蹈、手工艺、服饰等进行整合，并借助节日庆典活动打包展示，能够有效激发游客的旅行兴趣和参与热情。

2. 打造高品质线下体验

穷游网和夏河县文体广电和旅游局抓住人们对绿色空间的向往，从户外旅游切入，打造500亩帐篷营地，在营地内以丰富的线下体验设施、互动体验活动，为游客带来高品质的旅行。不只是户外旅游，近年来，城市内深度游、文化潮流艺术欣赏、生态体验等旅游形式热度高涨，乡村旅游可以此为灵感，吸引更多游客前来探索和体验。

3. IP驱动多元营销

乡村旅游要紧扣IP思维，将旅游活动打造为具有广泛认知度和记忆点的IP，从而在营销推广中事半功倍。在本项目中，穷游网以香浪节为IP，线上线下同步推进传播。线上以多维度的专业深度内容推广夏河的旅游资源，成功实现目的地"种草"；线下打造"草原旷野计划"活动，邀请政府、媒体、达人、大众等现场感受并自发传播，迅速引爆夏河旅游热度。

下一步计划

未来，穷游网将继续携手夏河县文体广电和旅游局展开更全面的深度合作。一方面，双方将共同推出草原文旅升级2.0计划，在形式及内容方面创新，吸引更多年轻群体前往夏河旅行。另一方面，双方将共同探索甘南文旅复兴的更多可能，打造全时、全季的旅游吸引力，全方位带动乡村振兴。同时，穷游网将以香浪节为范本，与各目的地一起共创更多元的乡村旅游形式，为乡村振兴贡献力量。

旅游减贫案例故事（中英文双语版）
Best Practices of Poverty Alleviation through Tourism (Chinese–English Bilingual Edition)

Qyer.com:
Boosting rural revitalization by hosting the Xianglang Festival in Xiahe County, Gannan Tibetan Autonomous Prefecture, Gansu province

Included in *WTA Best Practices of Rural Revitalization through Tourism 2022*

Abstract

　　Xiahe County is located in Gannan Tibetan Autonomous Prefecture, Gansu Province. In 2020, the Culture, Sports, Media, and Tourism Bureau of Xiahe County joined hands with Qyer.com, and turned the Xianglang Festival, a traditional festival in Gannan, into a regional tourism brand, planned and organized the festival activities with grassland culture tourism at the core. They also combed through the tourist resources of Xiahe County, promoted Xiahe County as a destination in all media, and built a benchmark for exemplary tourism brands centered around intangible cultural heritage festivals.

Challenges and Problems

Xiahe County is rich in cultural and tourism resources, with 51 scenic spots in seven major tourist attractions and a number of folk cultural activities. In recent years, a number of specialized and demonstration tourism villages have emerged in the county, and the tourist infrastructure has been improved to a certain extent. The cultural and tourism industry in Xiahe County is entering the stage of high-quality development. But its tourism resources were similar to those in surrounding areas, and could be easily replaced by other destinations. Thus the local competition for tourists was fierce. To attract more tourists, Xiahe County hoped that the Xianglang Festival, a traditional cultural festival in Gannan, would boost its visibility as a destination. But to turn the local Xianglang Festival into a national famous festival and increase the comprehensive tourism income, the county needed more effective channels and means.

Measures

1. Launch the Xianglang Festival in a market-oriented way

With years of experience in destination marketing, Qyer.com branded the Xianglang Festival and traditional folk dance Zerou, and incorporated Tibetan music, Thangka and other intangible cultural heritage, tourism and sport elements into the Xianglang Festival. In this way, the local Tibetan culture has been pushed to a new height, Xiahe is empowered both ecologically and culturally, and the local cultural and tourism industry has entered a new stage of development.

2. Combine outdoor tourism with the Xianglang Festival

According to a user survey conducted by Qyer.com, the search for camping, hiking and other outdoor travel has risen by more than 30% for two consecutive years, and outdoor travel has been all the rage. More and more users want to embrace nature, heal the body and mind, and totally be themselves in the wilderness of Nature in travels. Therefore Qyer.com partnered up with the Culture, Sports, Media, and Tourism Bureau of Xiahe County to launch the Xianglang Festival carnival with grassland culture tourism at the core.

3. Introduce a diverse visitor experience to the Xianglang Festival

Based on grassland culture tourism, Qyer.com has built a 500-*mu* tent camping site and planned diversified offline experiential activities. The camping site has been equipped with trendy, creative offline activities to add a touch of fashion to this traditional festival. Through investment attraction, it also opened a small bazaar selling clothes, food, accommodation and transportation services, creating a brand new immersive experience for tourists.

4. Market on diverse media

While launching the Xianglang Festival, Qyer.

com sorted Xiahe's tourism resources, highlighted its unique advantages, and promoted it as a destination for knowledge and experiencing sharing. In terms of knowledge sharing, Qyer.com published "Xiahe Poor Travel Tips", including basic facts of the place and the most popular and niche routes. In terms of experience sharing, it invited a number of travel bloggers to participate in the Xianglang Festival, explore more beautiful sides of Xiahe County, and write detailed travel guides accordingly. On top of that, Qyer.com marketed Xiahe's tourism resources on its own website, new-media matrix, mainstream media and outdoor big screens. Such intense exposure, strong visual effects and Qyer.com's high credibility combined to lure a large number of tourists from surrounding areas to the Xianglang Festival.

Results

The "Wild Grassland – Xianglang Festival" jointly launched by Qyer.com and the Culture, Sports, Media, and Tourism Bureau of Xiahe County, generated over 140 million impressions online. Many media organizations were invited to participate in and report on the event. It was covered by more than 500 portal websites, tourism websites and local media, including news.cn, people.cn, cnr.cn, huanqiu.com, *China Daily*, *Beijing News*, NetEase, Sina, *Travel Daily*, and btiii.com. The Xianglang Festival attracted more than 170,000 participants, including 60,000 locals and 110,000 tourists from all over the country, and directly generated a comprehensive income of 16.565 million yuan in Xiahe County. In partnership with the Culture, Sports, Media, and Tourism Bureau of Xiahe County, Qyer.com combined the traditional festival with culture, tourism and sports, successfully built up Xiahe's brand as a tourist destination, and set up a demonstration tourism brand based on the intangible cultural heritage festival, enhancing Xiahe's tourism influence. It has promoted

the development of the rural economy and rural revitalization through tourism.

Experience and Inspirations

1. Gather unique elements of local culture

Folk culture is an important component of excellent traditional Chinese culture, and each place has its own special festivals. But local festivals alone have only limited appeal to tourists. By integrating more local cultural elements, such as traditional dance, handicrafts, and costumes, and showcasing them through festival celebrations, it can effectively spark tourists' interest in travel and boost their enthusiasm for participation.

2. Create a high-quality offline tourist experience

Qyer.com and the Culture, Sports, Media, and Tourism Bureau of Xiahe County capitalized on the people's longing for green space, promoted outdoor tourism, and built a 500-*mu* tent camping site and equipped it with abundant offline experiential installations and interactive activities, to create a high-quality tourist experience. Beyond outdoor tourism, the rising popularity of urban in-depth tours, cultural and trendy art appreciation, and ecological experiences in recent years can serve as inspiration for rural tourism to attract more tourists to explore and engage.

3. IP-driven marketing via diverse channels

Rural tourism should develop its own IPs, and well-recognized IPs will yield twice the result with half the effort in marketing. In this project, Xianglang Festival is the IP which Qyer.com promoted simultaneously online and offline. Online it promoted Xiahe's tourism resources from multiple dimensions, to rally users' interest in the place. Offline, it launched the "Wild Grassland" event and invited participants from different circles such as government agencies, media, travel bloggers and ordinary people. Through the word-of-mouth of these participants, Xiahe instantly became a popular tourist destination on the Internet.

Next Steps

In the future, Qyer.com will continue to work with the Culture, Sports, Media, and Tourism Bureau of Xiahe County in more areas and at a deeper level.

Firstly, they will jointly develop the 2.0 version of grassland culture tourism, introduce new forms and contents, and attract more young visitors to Xiahe County.

Secondly, they will jointly explore more possibilities for the rejuvenation of tourism in Gannan, attract tourists to it throughout the year, and promote rural revitalization in all respects.

Thirdly, based on the success of the Xianglang Festival, Qyer.com will work with other destinations to create more diverse forms of rural tourism and contribute to rural revitalization.